International Social Policy

Also by Pete Alcock

SOCIAL POLICY IN BRITAIN, 3rd edn

UNDERSTANDING POVERTY, 3rd edn

POVERTY AND STATE SUPPORT

THE STUDENT'S COMPANION TO SOCIAL POLICY, 3rd edn (*with M. May and K. Rowlingson*)

THE BLACKWELL DICTIONARY OF SOCIAL POLICY (*with A. Erskine and M. May*)

WELFARE AND WELLBEING: Richard Titmuss's Contribution to Social Policy (*with H. Glennerster, A. Oakley and A. Sinfield*)

Also by Gary Craig

COMMUNITY EMPOWERMENT (*with M. Mayo*)

COMMUNITY WORK AND THE STATE (*with N. Derricourt and M. Loney*)

JOBS AND COMMUNITY ACTION (*with M. Mayo and N. Sharman*)

SOCIAL JUSTICE AND PUBLIC POLICY (*with T. Burchardt and D. Gordon*)

COMMUNITY WORK IN THEORY AND PRACTICE (*with K. Popple and M. Shaw*)

International Social Policy

Welfare Regimes in the Developed World

Second Edition

edited by

Pete Alcock

Professor of Social Policy and Administration and Director of Third Sector Research Centre, University of Birmingham

and

Gary Craig

Professor of Social Justice and Head of the Centre for Research in Social Inclusion and Social Justice, University of Hull

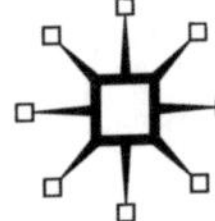

Selection, editorial matter, Introduction and Chapter 1 © Pete Alcock and Gary Craig 2001, 2009

Other chapters in this edition (in order) © John Clarke and Frances Fox Piven; Ernie S. Lightman and Graham Riches; Lois Bryson and Fiona Verity; Judith Davey and Sandra Grey; Pete Alcock; Tapio Salonen; Lutz Leisering; Valeria Fargion; the estate of Nadia Davidova and Nick Manning; Takafumi Ken Uzuhashi; Huck-ju Kwon; Ka Lin; Francie Lund 2009

All rights reserved. No reproduction, copy or transmission of this publication may be made without written permission.

No portion of this publication may be reproduced, copied or transmitted save with written permission or in accordance with the provisions of the Copyright, Designs and Patents Act 1988, or under the terms of any licence permitting limited copying issued by the Copyright Licensing Agency, Saffron House, 6–10 Kirby Street, London EC1N 8TS.

Any person who does any unauthorized act in relation to this publication may be liable to criminal prosecution and civil claims for damages.

The authors have asserted their rights to be identified as the authors of this work in accordance with the Copyright, Designs and Patents Act 1988.

First edition 2001
Second edition 2009

Published by
PALGRAVE MACMILLAN

Palgrave Macmillan in the UK is an imprint of Macmillan Publishers Limited, registered in England, company number 785998, of Houndmills, Basingstoke, Hampshire RG21 6XS.

Palgrave Macmillan in the US is a division of St Martin's Press LLC, 175 Fifth Avenue, New York, NY 10010.

Palgrave Macmillan is the global academic imprint of the above companies and has companies and representatives throughout the world.

Palgrave® and Macmillan® are registered trademarks in the United States, the United Kingdom, Europe and other countries

ISBN-13: 978–0–230–57319–2 hardback
ISBN-10: 0–230–57319–3 hardback
ISBN-13: 978–0–230–57320–8 paperback
ISBN-10: 0–230–57320–7 paperback

This book is printed on paper suitable for recycling and made from fully managed and sustained forest sources. Logging, pulping and manufacturing processes are expected to conform to the environmental regulations of the country of origin.

A catalogue record for this book is available from the British Library.

A catalog record for this book is available from the Library of Congress.

10 9 8 7 6 5 4 3 2 1
18 17 16 15 14 13 12 11 10 09

Printed in China

This book is dedicated to the memory of
Nadia Davidova

Contents

List of Tables and Figures

Tables

Figures

Notes on the Contributors

Pete Alcock is Professor of Social Policy and Administration at the University of Birmingham, UK. He has been teaching and researching in social policy for over 25 years. He is author and editor of a number of books on social policy including *Social Policy in Britain* (3rd edn), *Understanding Poverty* (3rd edn), *The Student's Companion to Social Policy* (3rd edn), *The Blackwell Dictionary of Social Policy* and *Welfare and Wellbeing*. His research is in the fields of poverty and anti-poverty policy, social security and the role of the voluntary sector and he has written widely on these and related topics.

Lois Bryson is Emeritus Professor of Sociology (University of Newcastle, Australia) and Adjunct Professor (School of Global Studies, Social Science and Planning, RMIT University, Melbourne) and Fellow of the Academy of the Social Sciences in Australia. Her books *An Australian Newtown* (1972, with Faith Thompson), and *Social Change, Suburban Lives* (1999, with Ian Winter) represent Australia's first study and restudy of an urban community. Others books include *Welfare and the State: Who Benefits?* and *Women and Survival*, an edited collection of women's stories of surviving violence.Lois has also written many papers dealing with the welfare state, public policy, gender and inequality.

John Clarke is Professor of Social Policy at the Open University, UK, where he has worked for more than 25 years. His research and teaching interests have ranged from the impact of managerialism and consumerism on social policy and practice, through to wider questions of globalization, neo-liberalism and the reworking of alignments between nations, states and welfare. Some of these are explored in *Changing Welfare, Changing States.* He recently co-authored *Creating Citizen-Consumers: Changing Public and Changing Public Services.*

Gary Craig is Professor of Social Justice and Associate Director of the Wilberforce Institute for the study of Slavery and Emancipation at the University of Hull, UK. He is President of the International Association for Community Development, a Fellow of the Royal Society of Arts and Academician of the Academy of Social Sciences. His most recent (co-edited) book is *Social Justice and Public Policy.* He specializes in research on aspects of 'race', ethnicity and welfare, migration, poverty, local governance and community development.

Judith Davey was Director of New Zealand Institute for Research on Ageing from 2002 to early 2007 and is now a Senior Associate and Associate Professor of the Institute of Policy Studies at Victoria University. From 1991 to 2001 she lectured in Social Policy and previously was the Deputy Director of the New Zealand Planning Council and a consultant on social policy and social research. Judith is a graduate of London University and did her PhD at Durham University. Before coming to New Zealand, she was also a post-doctoral researcher at the University of Cambridge.

Nadia Davidova died as this book was being completed. She was Reader in Social Policy in the Higher School of Economics, Moscow, and Senior Research Fellow, Institute of Sociology, Russian Academy of Sciences. She worked on such social problems as poverty, social exclusion, regional inequalities and social differentiation in Russia during the 1990s. Her recent interests were social stratification, socio-economic position and the behaviour of different social groups, inequality, poverty and social policy. She was a key member of the team working on the three INTAS-funded projects focusing on employment and household survival in Russia (1995–8), poverty and social exclusion (1999–2002) and health, health care and the poor (2004–7).

Valeria Fargion is Jean Monnet Chair in the Politics of European Integration at the University of Florence. Her research interests include the Italian welfare state in a comparative perspective, Europeanization, territorial politics and, more recently, global social policy. She has published on *WEP*, *Politiques et Management Public*, *Polis*, *RISP*, *South European Society and Politics*, *European Societies* and *Revue Française des Affaires Sociales*. Until 2007 she was on the Espanet Board and is still on the ISA RC19 Executive Board. She is currently editing a special issue of the *Italian Journal of Social Policy* with a selection of papers from the conference that she organized in 2007 on Social Policy in a Globalizing World.

Sandra Grey is a Lecturer in Social Policy at Victoria University of Wellington. Recent work has examined the representation of women in parliament and through women's movements in Australasia. Publications include: *Women's Movements: Flourishing or in Abeyance?*, edited with Marian Sawer; *Numbers and Beyond: The Relevance of Critical Mass in Gender Research*; and *The 'New World'? Women and Political Representation in New Zealand*. She is currently working on a comparative project examining activism by the New Zealand women's, union and anti-poverty movements.

Huck-ju Kwon is Associate Professor at the Graduate School of Public Administration, Seoul National University. He was previously Director of the BK21 Governance Programme, Sung Kyun Kwan University, Korea (2006–7), and Research Coordinator at UN Research Institute for Social Development (2002–5). He serves as Regional Editor of *Global Social Policy* for East Asia. He is also the co-editor of the Palgrave series on Social Policy in a Development Context. His book, *Transforming the Developmental Welfare State in East Asia* is one of the books in the series.

Ka Lin is Professor in the Department of Sociology, Nanjing University, and the Director of the Social Policy Research Centre of Nanjing University, People's Republic of China. He holds doctorships in the University of Tampere and University of Turku, Finland, and once worked as a Senior Research Fellow in the Department of Social Policy, University of Turku. He has published widely, including books and articles in a number of English and Chinese journals. Areas of expertise include welfare theory, comparative social policy, gender, family and welfare services.

Lutz Leisering is Professor of Social Policy at the Department of Sociology, Bielefeld University, Germany, and founding member of the Institute for World Society Studies. He undertook his PhD at the London School of Economics (1989). His research interests include comparative social policy, old-age security, poverty and social exclusion and global social policy. Publications include *Time and Poverty in Western Welfare States* (with S. Leibfried), 'Government and the Life Course', *Old-Age Pensions for Rural China?* (with S. Gong and A. Hussain). He is a national and international policy adviser.

Ernie S. Lightman studied at the University of Toronto and the University of California, Berkeley. He taught at the London School of Economics and is now Professor of Social Policy at the University of Toronto. He has published widely in both popular and academic outlets with a particular interest in the interplay between economics and social policy. He completed a study on the equity for families in Canada's tax system and has written also on social advocacy for vulnerable adults.

Francie Lund is Associate Professor at the School of Development Studies, University of KwaZulu-Natal, Durban, and is Research Director for Social Protection in the global research network WIEGO (Women in Informal Employment: Globalizing and Organizing). Her research interests in South Africa are in social policy and the impact of social spending, and she recently authored *Changing Social Policy: the Child Support Grant in South Africa*, which tells the story of this policy intervention in post-apartheid Africa. Globally her research interests span unpaid work and the position of women informal workers.

Nick Manning is Professor of Social Policy and Sociology, University of Nottingham. He has worked on Russian social policy for nearly 30 years. He has directed studies of environmental and housing movements in Russia, Estonia and Hungary (1991–4), employment and household survival in Russia (1995–8), women and social policy in Central and Eastern Europe (1998–9), poverty, ethnicity and political protest in Northern Ossetia (1999–2002), and is just writing up a project on Russian health and health care (INTAS, 2004–7). Since 2006 he has been director of the Institute of Mental Health, University of Nottingham.

Frances Fox Piven is Distinguished Professor of Political Science and Sociology at the Graduate Center of the City University of New York. She is the author or co-author of *Regulating the Poor, Poor People's Movements, Why Americans Still Don't Vote*, and most recently, *Challenging Authority: How Ordinary People Change America*. She is the immediate past President of the American Sociological Association.

Graham Riches is Professor and Director of the School of Social Work and Family Studies at the University of British Columbia, Vancouver. He has held previous academic appointments in Australia, Hong Kong and Canada, where he was for some years the Director of the Social Administration Research Unit at the University of Regina. His research has focused on poverty and welfare systems, unemployment, food security, social security and human rights. His books include *Food Banks and the Welfare Crisis* and *First World Hunger*. He was Lead Consultant of the *Right to Food Case Study: Canada*.

Tapio Salonen is Professor in Social Work and Research Leader for a multidisciplinary research group (Citizen Participation and Social Inclusion) at Växjö University, Sweden. His main research interests include poverty, marginality, participatory strategies and social policy. He has led a number of externally funded research projects at both national and international level and has been appointed as expert in public inquiries, commissions and government committees.

Takafumi Ken Uzuhashi is Professor of Social Policy in the Department of Social Welfare at Doshisha University, Kyoto, Japan. He is currently Overseas Editorial Adviser of the *Journal of Social Policy* and was a Visiting Fellow at the University of York from 1993 to 1994, being involved in comparative projects as a National Informant. His current research interests span comparative study of welfare states, income maintenance for vulnerable groups and welfare-to-work schemes. His recent publications include *Welfare States in Comparative Perspective* and *Workfare: from Exclusion to Inclusion?*

Fiona Verity is Senior Lecturer at Flinders University, where she teaches, researches and publishes in the areas of social policy and community work.

List of Abbreviations

These abbreviations are those most commonly found in this book or that might require further elaboration.

ANC	African National Congress (black-led political party taking power at ending of apartheid in South Africa)
ATSI	Aboriginal and Torres Straits Islanders (Australia)
CEO	Chief Executive Officer (usually of private companies)
CIS	Commonwealth of Independent States (federation of former USSR territories outside East and Central Europe)
CRC	(United Nations) Convention on the Rights of the Child (1990)
EU	European Union (formerly EEC, European Economic Community)
Eurostat	European Union Statistical Organization
FRG	Federal Republic of Germany (former West Germany)
GDP	Gross Domestic Product
GDR	(also DDR) German Democratic Republic (former East Germany)
GNP	Gross National Product
GP	General Practitioner (doctor offering general primary care services)
HDI	Human Development Index
HIV/AIDS	Human Immuno-deficiency Virus/Acquired Immune Deficiency Syndrome (AIDS results from HIV)
HPI	Human Poverty Index
ICESCR	International Covenant on Economic, Social and Cultural Rights (1966)
ILO	International Labour Organization
IMF	International Monetary Fund
LIS	Luxembourg Income Study
NAFTA	North American Free Trade Agreement
NGO	Non-Governmental Organization (also Third Sector/Voluntary Sector)
NHI	National Health Insurance
NHS	National Health Service (typically, of the UK)
NI	National Insurance

NPP	National Pension Programme
OECD	Organisation for Economic Co-operation and Development
SADC	Southern African Development Community (loose economic federation of 13 southern African countries)
UN	United Nations
UNICEF	United Nations Children's Educational Fund
WTO	World Trade Organization
WWI, WWII	First World War, Second World War

Introduction and Acknowledgements

This is the second edition of this book, updating and enlarging on the first edition published in 2001. As we noted in that edition, the book is intended to contribute to our understanding of the comparative study of welfare provision within the 'developed' world. The book has been edited in the UK but produced by experts resident in and/or knowledgeable about the shape of welfare provision in the 13 countries represented in this book.

We do not propose to rehearse the arguments here about the nature and importance of comparative social policy. These are set out both in the original volume and in the chapter on the comparative context which follows this introduction. Each chapter stands alone as a review – within a common structure which we set the individual authors – of the development and organization of policy within that chapter. Each author, remarkably, including everyone who contributed to the first edition of the book, was also asked to rewrite their chapters taking into account significant changes and trends which had occurred in the seven years since the first edition was completed. That each author was able to do so, and to stay broadly within the constrained timetable and word length given them, is a tribute to their scholarly abilities and we would like to thank them for their hard and skilful work in doing so, in some cases in difficult circumstances.

The first chapter on the comparative context discusses the various analyses of the national organization of welfare provision which have emerged in the past years, notably, but certainly not solely, the seminal welfare regime theory developed by Esping-Andersen, against which most more recent theories continue to be tested. The changing nature of the world, notably the rapid industrialization of some former largely rural economies, the impact of globalization, demographic change and large-scale internal and external migration, have impacted on provision in individual countries and challenged the neatness of Esping-Andersen's and other comparative analyses. This second edition reflects some of these changes both in terms of the developing analysis in each country chapter and through the inclusion of two new chapters, on China and (South) Korea, each of which can lay claim to having a recognizable and organized welfare regime. In the case of China, we felt it appropriate – particularly given pressures on space – to replace the chapter on Hong Kong (the sovereignty of which, at the time of the first edition had only just been handed back to mainland China) by a chapter on China itself.

Doubtless in the future other countries, too, such as India and Brazil, might press their case for inclusion. As we argue in the first chapter, therefore, the increasing number of countries with developed welfare systems itself presents an argument for revisiting and perhaps adapting the established current typologies of welfare provision. Over all, however, we continue to believe that the countries included here are representative of the different kinds of welfare regime to be found across the world, although it is also the case that global forces have created pressure to move most of these regimes in a common direction, towards a more neo-liberal, marketized, approach.

As with the first edition, space has been very limited for individual authors and depth of analysis has had to be sacrificed to width of coverage. This means that important detail has sometimes been glossed over, including the way in which such key social divisions such as gender, 'race' and disability are addressed, or the nature of political struggle in each individual country. We hope that the references provided with each chapter will enable readers to pursue these questions elsewhere. In some countries, the quality and availability of data remain problematic.

Since the first edition appeared, other volumes have been published contributing to the debates about comparative social policy. This book does not set out to be a comparative text but to provide the widest possible range of evidence contributing to the project of developing a robust comparative analysis of social policy and welfare provision which can stay abreast of global changes. It offers readers the opportunity to build comparative analyses between two or more countries, and our hope remains that it will be an important contribution to steadily widening debates on comparative social policy.

As this edition was completed, we received the sad news of the premature death of Nadia Davidova, joint author of the Russia chapter in each of the first and second editions. Her work in uncovering data and providing an analysis of trends within Russia was substantial and we dedicate this book to her, and to others like her who work in the most difficult of circumstances to improve our understanding of welfare and promote the interests of the most disadvantaged. We also recall with thanks the life of Jo Campling, who supported us during the early days of the first edition, and who also sadly died recently. We are grateful, as ever, for the support of Catherine Gray at Palgrave Macmillan who has remained a committed and enthusiastic commissioning editor.

PETE ALCOCK
GARY CRAIG

The editors and publishers are grateful to the following for permission to reproduce copyright material: Howard Glennerster and Basil Blackwell for permission to reproduce figure 10.1, Welfare Spending 1900–2004, from Glennerster (2007), *British Social Policy: 1945 to the Present* (3rd edn), p. 227, as Figure 6.2. Every effort has been made to contact all the copyright-holders, but if any have been inadvertently omitted the publishers will be pleased to make the necessary arrangement at the earliest opportunity.

Chapter 1

The International Context

Pete Alcock and Gary Craig

Welfare and the State

The focus of this book is on the provision of welfare in a selected number of countries across the developed world. As the Introduction notes, our aim has been to provide a resource for the comparative study of social policy or welfare. However, this undertaking raises a number of important theoretical and definitional problems. What do we mean by 'developed' countries? What do we mean by social policy or welfare provision? More specifically, to what extent are these concepts uniformly understood in each country represented in the book? And, finally, what is the most useful framework within which to pursue comparisons between countries with differing social, political and economic histories?

These are major theoretical and empirical questions and they now form the basis of a wide-ranging literature and research agenda in comparative social policy analysis. We cannot hope to summarize all this debate in this short introductory chapter; and it has not been the aim of this book to engage in such an analysis of the comparative development of welfare provision. We will try to guide readers to some of the key areas of current debate, however, and suggest what may be useful areas for further exploration. However, what many comparative theorists do increasingly agree on is the need for some contextual understanding of the political and economic development of welfare policies in individual countries, so that generic comparative data and analysis can be set alongside the specific histories and trajectories of individual nations; and it is this national context that this book aims to provide – for those countries that we have included within it (including two, China and South Korea, not included in the first edition of this book).

The countries included in this book are all taken from what has come to be called the developed world. That is, countries who have experienced, and continue to experience, industrialized economic growth and who have developed extensive state structures to manage and support that growth and to provide (to some extent) for the consequential welfare needs of their citizens. For these reasons most such countries are members of the OECD, which provides them with mutual support and information – and also now is the source of considerable important comparative data about them, as we mention below.

However, recent comparative work by Gough *et al.* (2004) has pointed out that the formal security provided by these 'welfare states' contrasts starkly with the very different economic and social development to be found in most other nations across the world. From their research on some of these other nations they argue that such welfare states are only one form of meta-welfare regime to be found in the world, and they contrast this with two other meta-welfare regimes (and see Gough, 2001, and Wood and Gough, 2006):

- *Informal security regimes* where community and family relationships are the major source of welfare support, often on hierarchical or patronage basis with resistance to any formalization of public responsibility through the state.
- *Insecurity regimes* where powerful external players can prevent any effective structures of internal support, often in cases of conflict and destabilization with no effective established political authority.

Clearly the provision of welfare within such regimes is a rather different enterprise than it is in the state-based meta-welfare regimes of the developed world; and comparative analysis of welfare provision has only recently begun to come to terms with this broader global context of policy analysis and development. In this book therefore we have concentrated only on 'the state welfare' of Gough *et al.*'s formal security regimes. Despite the many economic, social and political differences that are revealed in the chapters that follow, it is nevertheless the case that each country discussed here accepts some measure of public responsibility for meeting many of the common welfare needs, and the development of appropriate welfare provision has accompanied the growth of its industrial economy. It is perhaps one of the most striking aspects of state welfare that, however inadequately, every industrialized nation state has come to accept that it has a role in providing welfare alongside taking some role in the management of the provision of private welfare provision.

This is not to suggest, however, that the development of this welfare provision is an inevitable product of the growth of industrial economies – that social policy always accompanies economic policy. This has sometimes been referred to as the *industrialization*, or *convergence*, thesis (see Wilensky, 1975), and is distinct from the Marxist tradition which links the development of welfare directly to the class struggle within industrialized nations (see Gough, 1979). Its implication is that all industrialized countries can be located on a similar development track, converging towards common social and economic futures, though Gough, and others, would argue in response that local political struggle has been critical in shaping at least some of the differences between welfare states.

This shared social and economic development thesis was discussed more recently in a wide-ranging review of public policy development in 21 OECD nations by Castles (1999). Castles concluded then that, in the second half of the twentieth century, all underwent major changes in economic growth and policy planning although he pointed out that there was much variation between countries due (again) to different political circumstances and differing degrees of economic and social development. Despite similarities therefore, there was no sustainable evidence of the growth of welfare as a linear process, which is the natural consequence of industrialization. Even if similar trends could be identified, sharp differences of scale and direction were also observable.

Since then Castles, and others, have continued with this broad-based analysis of welfare development, drawing primarily on the data provided on trends in public expenditure and other similar data provided by the OECD. This data has itself become more extensive and sophisticated in the new century, although it is always inevitably several years out of date by the time it is available for public analysis; and it permits more detailed comparison to be made, for instance between the gross and net expenditure levels, in the latter case controlling for the effects of tax and social security contributions and tax credits and exemptions.

As Castles and Obinger (2007) point out, gross expenditure and net expenditure figures can provide different patterns of convergence and diversity among OECD nations. In particular, however, as Castles (2004) argued, more systematic analysis of this evidence does not provide any support for the dismal view that, after half a century of growth in the latter part of the twentieth century, spending patterns in all OECD nations were now following a 'race to the bottom' to reduce state welfare commitments in the light of the global economic pressures which we discuss below.

As with welfare expansion, retrenchment and contraction are not universal characteristics, and indeed rather different responses can be found in different countries to what are perceived to be the international pressures that they are facing (Castles, 2007). Hall and Soskice (2001) have discussed the different responses of nations to economic pressures as reflecting the 'varieties of capitalism' that can be found in the developed world, in particular contrasting the liberal market economy approach of the USA to the coordinated market approach of Germany and other countries in western continental Europe. Castles (2004) adopts a broader range of models of 'families of nations', contrasting four different models within Europe: English-speaking nations, Scandinavian, western continental Europe and Southern Europe. These are similar to some extent to the welfare regimes identified by the Scandinavian academic Esping-Andersen (1990), whom we shall return to discuss below. A number of these countries are included in this book, however, and, as the more detailed analysis provided by our authors reveals, in practice the patterns of development and change within these countries is even more complex than these broad regimes models might suggest.

Underlying some of the contrasting conclusions apparently reached in such broad-based comparative analysis of welfare trends is what is sometimes referred to as the 'dependent variable problem' (Clasen, 2007). Much comparative analysis utilizes public expenditure figures for different countries as the dependent variable to compare different trends in welfare policy, assuming therefore that the social and economic needs that underpin these changes are a more or less constant independent variable. Of course, this is unlikely to be the case; for instance, demographic changes such as ageing populations and declining fertility rates will be likely to lead to changed demands for welfare, as recognized by Castles (2007); and indeed other changes in labour markets or private pension markets will also influence expenditure differentially. Changes in public expenditure cannot therefore simply be read off as evidence of changes in political support for state welfare provision. Indeed, as Kuhner (2007), points out these different pressures on expenditure need to be subject to disaggregated analysis within nations and across different social policy domains to be able to establish on any firm basis to what extent they reflect political, social, organizational or other forces for change.

Clasen (2005) has sought to undertake such more detailed comparative analysis of changes across just two countries, Germany and the UK, identifying differences between the policy domains of pension and employment on the one hand and family policies on the other. These are both countries covered in this book, and Clasen's work provides a useful further analysis of the differences identified by our authors here. He has also collected together a wider range of contributions covering a number of policy domains and countries to explore in more detail the limitations that flow from the dependent variable problem (Clasen, 2007). P. Pierson's (2001) edited collection also provides extensive evidence of the divergent responses of different nations to pressures for retrenchment, and the importance of national politics in determining welfare outcomes.

What many commentators conclude, therefore, is that the broad-based comparisons between countries, drawing on the large international datasets provided by the OECD and other similar bodies such as the EU, have inevitable limitations to what they can tell us about the development and change of welfare regimes, even within the developed world. Although some similar trends and pressures can be identified, there has been no consistent convergence towards a single model of state welfare support, and no subsequent 'race to the bottom' to reduce commitments in the face of recent pressures of global economic change. Different countries have developed different 'mixes' of welfare provision, and these have been adapted or preserved differently in the light of internal political partisanship and pre-existing commitments as well as external economic pressures.

Welfare policies are to a significant extent the result of the 'path dependencies' established within different nations; and it is for this reason that we have sought to explore these paths in some detail in the national vignettes provided in the different chapters of this book – at least for those countries included within it. It remains is for the readers of the book to make the comparisons between countries or to draw out contrasts. However, the analyses of our authors have been informed by the broader developments of comparative analysis over the last two decades or more, and by the broad trends that have been identified within this.

Comparative Social Policy

Much social policy investigation – both in the UK and elsewhere – has understandably been based upon theoretical or empirical analysis of the operation or development of welfare provision within specific national contexts. For the large part welfare provision and social policy debate have been developed within national contexts, dominated by the policies and practices of national governments. However, this has been changing rapidly in the last decade or so. Comparative study of the welfare provisions and policy debates of different countries is now increasingly central to social policy research and teaching; and *international* forces are increasingly shaping the policy agendas of *national* governments, so that welfare provision is less and less the product solely of national policy debates or political considerations. In this respect as in many others, the world is becoming metaphorically a smaller place; and social policy scholars are increasingly seeking to analyze this international context of welfare development, in particular Pierson (2006), and see also Ellison (2006).

International pressures on national policy-making are in part a direct and indirect consequence of the growing competitiveness of the international capitalist economy and the power of major corporations within this – a process sometimes referred to as globalization, which we shall return to shortly. However, it is not just international markets which influence national policies; international agencies are now also seeking to control or influence the social policies of individual countries.

This is most obviously true in Western Europe of the role played by the European Union (EU) which, with the support of its now 27 member nations, is pursuing measures to harmonize social policies within the EU and developing cross-cutting supra-national policy initiatives (Geyer, 2000; Hantrais, 2007). Other supra-national agencies seeking to influence the social policy agendas of individual nations, extending beyond Western Europe include, in particular, the World Bank and the International Monetary Fund (IMF). These are the financial agencies of international capital that, through their economic relations with nations needing their support, can use powerful financial levers to press for social policy changes (Deacon, 2007; Yeates, 2008). This is a strategy that has been employed quite widely by these agencies in recent years, influencing the policy agendas of both well-developed welfare states, such as the UK since the mid-1970s

(CDPIIU, 1976), and newly developing ones, such as the post-communist countries of Eastern Europe (Deacon, Hulse and Stubbs, 1997) and even the economies of developing countries in Gough's other meta-welfare regimes (Craig and Mayo, 1995).

International influences on national policy development are not only enforced, however. They may also be welcomed and even sought out by nations. Since the late twentieth century the role of policy transfer has become an important influence on the political agenda of many nations (Dolowitz and Marsh, 1996; Dolowitz *et al.*, 2000). Policy initiatives developed in one country may well be of relevance to others who wish to address comparable welfare needs within similar social and economic circumstances. Even if ideas from one country are not directly replicable in another, they may form the basis of similar initiatives shaped by success (or failure) elsewhere. This has long been the case of the social insurance ideas promoted initially by Bismarck in Germany in the late nineteenth century; a more recent case is that of the tax credit measures used to supplement low wages in the USA (Jordan, 1998; Deacon, 2000; 2002).

These international pressures on social policy agendas have resulted in a growing body of research and writing on comparative social policy analysis, and an expanding literature with a range of different approaches and methods within comparative analysis.

- *Guides to comparative study* – intended to give an overview and introduction to comparative methods and the strengths and weaknesses of comparative analysis. Clasen (1999) is an early example of this. Kennett (2004) is now the leading collection here, but there is also a range of contributions in Part VIII of the *Student's Companion to Social Policy* (Alcock, May and Rowlingson, 2008).
- *Theoretical studies* – these attempt to explore, and to explain, variations between the welfare systems of different countries and to assess the extent to which they are the result of internal policy-making or external dynamics. Relatively early examples of this are Wilensky's (1975) US study of the development of welfare states and Titmuss's (1974) discussion of three models of welfare provision. More recently there have been broad-based international studies such as Gough (1979), Castles (1982; 1999; 2004), Pierson (2001), Pierson (2006), Offe (1984), Mishra (1990; 1999), Pfaller, Gough and Therborn (1991), Goodin *et al.* (1999), Bonoli, George and Taylor-Gooby (2000), Kennett (2001), George and Wilding (2002), Taylor-Gooby (2004), Jordan (2008) and Ellison (2006). There are also more specific attempts to develop a classification of welfare systems through comparative analysis, most notably in the seminal work of Esping-Andersen (1990), and studies of international agencies by Deacon (2007) and Yeates (2008).
- *Sectors and issues* – further texts have developed international comparison across different sectors of welfare provision, for instance, Hill (2006)

and Clasen (1999), or by focusing on one particular policy domain such as pensions (Bonoli, 2000; Bonoli and Palier, 2007), labour markets (Sarfati and Bonoli, 2002; Clasen *et al.*, 2006), social activation (Lodemel and Trickey, 2001), or social exclusion (Barnes *et al.*, 2002).

- *Policy evaluation* – research projects based on international studies have aimed to evaluate the effectiveness of specific policy interventions across a range of countries. Examples of this can be found in the work of Bradshaw *et al.* on child support (1993; Bradshaw, 2006) and Ditch *et al.* (1997) on social assistance.

Despite this burgeoning literature, however, there remain significant problems involved in the comparative study of social policy. For a start there are inevitable limitations to the scope and explanatory power of overarching theoretical accounts of international social policy development or classification. As we discussed above, such accounts attempt to explain what are in practice complex and varied social processes across differing social and political contexts. In this process the danger of over-generalization is ever-present. Even Esping-Andersen's empirically based classification of welfare regimes has been criticized for focusing upon a limited range of types of welfare provision, primarily employment and pensions, and ignoring important comparative factors, such as family policies, which might have led to very different classifications from those arrived at in his early analysis.

In addition to the risk of theoretical over-generalization there is also the problem of empirical comparability. Much comparative analysis relies upon data about the nature of social issues or the impact of social policies across a number of countries under review. There is no guarantee that such data has been gathered and published on a similar basis in each country – and indeed a significant risk that it has not. Thus, whether one is comparing levels of poverty and inequality or levels of expenditure on health services, we may not always be comparing like with like.

However, the collection and analysis of data across countries by major international agencies has become more sophisticated and extensive in the new century. Of particular importance is the data on economic development and public spending collected by the OECD, and utilized by international researchers such as Castles (2004; 2007). Eurostat, the EU's statistical service, also collects extensive data on a more or less consistent basis across its member nations and has been used by researchers to compare trends within the EU (Adelantado and Calderon Cuevas, 2006). And there are policy-specific resources such as the Luxembourg Income Study (LIS), which contains data about the income distribution of many different countries, which can be explored and analyzed by researchers worldwide using on-line computer access (Smeeding, O'Higgins and Rainwater, 1990). These international databases make comparative analysis simpler, and more robust; but they cannot overcome the diversity and path dependency of individual countries discussed above. The more detailed analysis of individual countries,

LIVERPOOL JOHN MOORES UNIVERSITY
LEARNING SERVICES

which this book provides, remains an important supplement to the generic trends identified by comparative scholars.

A Common International Context

Economics

We mentioned above that one of the defining characteristics of developed countries is the process of industrialization which changed their economic and social structures. It also created the social conditions and political conflicts that could give rise to the development of modern welfare provision. In simple terms, labour market needs and the conflicts reflecting struggles between labour and capital gave rise to pressure for the introduction of welfare measures. This impact of industrialization as an example of an international influence on social policy was explored to some extent by Wilensky (1975) in an early comparative study of welfare states; and Gough's (1979) path-breaking work emphasized the significance of organized labour in the creation of welfare provision.

The impact of industrialization on societies creates economic conditions in which the need for public welfare provision takes on a particular form. At the same time industrialization also creates a climate in which political forces pressing for welfare support, the organizations of the working class, are likely to become more influential. The development of public welfare provision is therefore to some extent a response to the needs and demands of the working classes. At the same time, such welfare provision also helps to support the continued growth of the industrial economy, for instance through improving the health and education of the population. Within an industrial economy, therefore, the development of public welfare provision can be seen as something of a compromise between the needs of both labour and capital.

The expectation that such a compromise could also result in positive economic growth, and in political consensus over the desirability of public welfare provision seemed to many to become reality towards the middle of the twentieth century. At this time in most Western nations, in particular, welfare reform was introduced at the same time as state intervention to support economic growth had become a common feature of national economic planning (Castles, 1999). In the UK this was known as the period of Keynesianism, after the economist Keynes (1936) who developed the theory of state intervention. It was also the time when most of the major state welfare institutions were introduced, giving rise to the notion of the creation of a welfare state.

As we can see from the later chapters of this book, this notion of a Keynesian 'golden age' in the development of welfare was a pattern shared by some, particularly 'Western', nations; but it was certainly not one followed by all. In Asia-Pacific nations, such as Japan and South Korea, for instance, the links between economic growth and welfare support have taken on a rather different form from that in the West; and this relationship is even more distinctive in China. Even in the West, however, the Keynesian golden age was a short-lived affair. In the last quarter of the twentieth century most of the capitalist economies of the developed world experienced periods of severe economic recession, fuelled in part by the oil price rises of the 1970s (Bonoli, George and Taylor-Gooby, 2000).

In the last quarter of the century it became clear that national economies must operate within an ever-more competitive international economy, in which some large multi-national corporations, such as General Motors or Coca-Cola, have greater economic power than do many individual nations. This process has been referred to by many as *globalization* (Waters, 1995; Mishra, 1999; Ellison, 2006) – the requirement of all governments to take account of global economic forces in their national economic and social policy planning (Gray, 1998). The impact of globalization on national policy planning is a complex, and much debated, phenomenon (Held *et al.*, 1999; Sykes, Palier and Prior, 2001). Not all countries have responded to the pressures of global forces in the same way; but, as Mishra (1999) argues, all have had to respond to them.

What is more the process of globalization has meant that economic changes within some countries have inevitably taken on a broader common international character. In particular this is true of what the economists have called *post-Fordism* (Gilbert, Burrows and Pollert, 1992). This is the move away from economic production being dominated by large-scale manufacturing industry to a situation in which a wider range of more flexible producers operate to meet more demanding and more rapidly changing consumer markets. In such a manufacturing climate the production process becomes more automated and employment shifts instead to specialized production and to work in service industries, serving both producers (insurance and banking) and consumers (catering and leisure); and labour markets become more 'flexible', with workers having to be more prepared to accept less formal terms and conditions of employment, often accompanied by downward pressures on wages. In the Western world in particular this process has been exacerbated by the relocation of the remaining labour-intensive production processes to less-developed countries with lower individual wage levels and reduced social and welfare costs. The result of these processes is that, in some of the countries examined in this book, levels of unemployment (especially long-term unemployment) have grown and much waged work has become more flexible (temporary, part time and often low paid).

The flexible, post-Fordist, international economy has thrown into greater relief the trade-off at the heart of all social and economic policy planning in advanced economies, as Esping-Andersen (1996) discusses. This trade-off is that between the provision of extensive and redistributive welfare services (equity) and investment in competitive economic growth (efficiency). It poses choices for governments in responding to the pressures of economic change, although as Hall and Soskice (2001) and others have argued, different 'varieties of capitalism' are likely to respond differently to these pressures. The choice can perhaps be characterized as that between two contrasting models for social and economic planning:

- The first – the low wage/low welfare model – involves the pursuit of growth through the reduction of welfare commitments. This implies acceptance of low wages and insecure work as the price for higher levels of employment with greater inequalities as a result, and the reduction of collective welfare costs through low taxation and social insurance payments. As a result welfare support is targeted only at the poor and welfare services are reduced to a residual role. In such a society protection and participation are provided largely through the labour market, and public welfare is only available to the casualties who cannot fend for themselves. The USA has increasingly become the paradigm example for this model, but the UK has been moving steadily in that direction.
- The second – the high wage/high welfare model – is the pursuit of growth through the maintenance of public support and the promotion of social integration and solidarity. This requires political commitment to developing a high skill/high reward labour market through generous social insurance payments and extensive collective provision for education, training and health. In such a society inequalities are reduced, in part through high levels of taxation and insurance contributions, and access to welfare services is generally provided on a universal basis. Here Sweden remains the best example.

The former approach is that championed by neo-liberal economists, who have argued that greater free market competition is the only effective response to globalization – a point discussed in more detail by Mishra (1999) and Ellison (2006). Capital investors can now move resources rapidly from country to country depending upon their judgements about economic prospects, and the major international corporations are likely to seek to operate where both the direct (wage) and indirect (tax and insurance) costs of welfare are lowest. This movement of capital could lead to what some commentators have called the 'race to the bottom' in terms of public welfare provision – what the EU describes as 'social dumping', the concentration of investment in countries where levels of wages and welfare are lowest. Not surprisingly the EU, and especially the high wage/high welfare countries which exert most power within it, are concerned about social dumping and are using the supra-national powers of the Union to counteract such pressures, for instance by seeking to impose EU-wide rights and standards (Kleineman, 2002).

In practice it is far from clear that a uniform march to the bottom has taken place across the international social policy arena, as Castles' (2004, 2007) more recent analysis of public expenditure trends reveals. Economic growth and levels of employment have been high in countries such as the USA, where low wages and low welfare costs predominate. But the high wage/high welfare countries of Europe, such as Germany and Sweden, have also been able both to maintain economic growth and to expand export markets (Goodin *et al.*,1999; Huber and Stephens, 2001; Palier and Martin, 2007). High growth has also been associated with very different mixes of work, wages and welfare in other countries such as Japan. All countries must respond to global pressures; but, as Esping-Andersen (1996, p. 258) argues, responses to wage competition have not been unidimensional. The more egalitarian and integrative welfare models of some countries have been able to sustain stable economic growth as well as avoiding some of the worst anti-welfare outcomes of the more residual welfare model.

In part, of course, the relative success of the high wage/high welfare model of capitalism is a result of the higher levels of social integration and political support that were instrumental in the establishment of such regimes and thus sustained within them. High wage/high welfare strategies can attract political support within democratic countries, even if they also extract a high price in terms of international competitiveness. Political calculations can influence economic policy-making, and ultimately can influence economic trends. This is an important element in the analysis developed by Esping-Andersen, Mishra, C. Pierson and others; and it reminds us that, while economic pressures may be important, they cannot obliterate other local factors.

Politics

It is quite clear from the different chapters in this book that the varying political contexts of different countries have led to different responses to the need for welfare services and to the pressures of economic competitiveness. The welfare state model discussed above is particularly associated with the social democratic or liberal democratic politics of Western Europe. Such political frameworks are based upon a compromise between the representatives of capital and labour over the development of public welfare provision within a predominantly market economy – the Bismarck and Beveridge models, a compromise which has taken differing forms in different countries, at different times. This has been taken up in particular in the work of Esping-Andersen (1990) and his identification of three broad welfare regimes that characterize and classify these differences, based on empirical analysis of Western welfare states.

However, social and liberal democracies have not been the only political ideologies to influence social policy and the development of welfare provision. Both socialist or Marxist politics and new right or neo-liberal politics challenge the notion of class compromise as a viable basis for the development of welfare policy and both have been influential at times in a number of countries. Socialist politics were of major importance in determining welfare services provided in Russia and Eastern Europe during the communist era, and much of that legacy still remains in some of these countries. The different socialist policies of China have provided their own distinct legacy, as discussed in Chapter 13. Socialist politics have been influential within democratic countries too, in particular as a form of left-wing pressure upon social democratic governments to abandon the politics of compromise and pursue instead a public monopoly of welfare services and a nationalization of the market economy (Deacon 1983). Such pressure has remained outside of the political mainstream, although occasionally having significant impacts in countries such as Italy and France. Neo-liberal politics have also exerted pressure upon democratic governments, in particular in the latter decades of the twentieth century. In the UK, for instance, the Thatcher governments of the 1980s were strongly influenced by the neo-liberal politics of some of their New Right members. This was also the case during the Reagan era in the US and more recently in the George W. Bush administrations of the new century.

Clearly, therefore, the power of partisan political forces has had a variable impact in different countries. Thus, where working-class organizations have been strong, state welfare services have been extensive, for instance in Sweden; and, where these organizations have been weak, welfare provision has adopted more of a residual model, for instance in the USA (Goodin *et al.*, 1999). However, it is not just the political ideologies associated with class forces that have been influential in shaping welfare. Other social forces have also had political influence, such as those organized around issues of gender, race (or racism), disability or ecology. They are discussed in more detail in Lewis, Gewitz and Clarke (2000) – and sometimes referred to as the 'new social movements'.

Feminist politics has had a significant influence on welfare policies in a number of countries in recent years, both in terms of shaping the nature of public provision (for instance, improved childcare support in Scandinavian countries and support for carers of adults in the UK) and of leading to the development of alternative forms of service (for instance, women's health self-help groups). Race and disability politics have also taken on a higher profile in many places. And environmental politics has even entered mainstream government, with Green Party representatives in Germany securing ministerial status for a time after the 1998 election, as well as, currently, two MEPs.

Politics is not just a matter of representation and campaigning, however. Within democracies in particular the political process itself has an important influence upon the determination of policy. For instance, within an electoral democracy public support for welfare is likely to be reflected in the votes cast by citizens. This has led some commentators, such as Therborn and Roebroek (1986) to argue that, once established, welfare states are irreversible by political means, because of the democratic support that the services that they provide will inevitably attract. On a more critical note such ballot-box politics has led other critics to argue that such pressures will lead to potentially damaging upward pressure on welfare growth as politicians seek to outbid each other with promises of improved services in order to secure popular support. This is the argument of the 'public choice' theorists in the USA who are concerned that such pressures will unbalance the equity/efficiency trade-off and prevent economic growth (Tullock, 1976).

Both politicians and public service bureaucrats are likely to seek to defend the public services with which they are associated, which may influence the political climate in a pro-welfare direction, despite the pressures of international economic forces. Overall therefore there is considerable evidence to underline the point that political forces and political processes can influence welfare policies, independently of the economic context within which they are operating. Politics is constructed within a social context too, however, and the social structure of advanced industrial societies has also been undergoing significant change in recent decades.

Demography

Welfare services are constructed to meet the needs of populations. They are therefore determined to some extent by the shape and structure of these populations; and inevitably these shapes and structures are subject to demographic change, as Castles (2004) discusses in his more recent comparative work. Demographic change is a complex phenomenon. It is the product of many different factors, of which birth rates, death rates, longevity and, increasingly, the impact of migration are only the most obvious features. It is also a phenomenon that impacts gradually over time as different cohorts of individuals move through the life cycle. We can identify some of the more significant factors here.

According to most commentators the most pressing contemporary aspect of demographic change, from the point of view of welfare policy, is the growing proportion of older people within most advanced industrial countries – both at the end of the twentieth century, and going into the twenty-first. It is itself a product of a number of factors including greater average longevity (a product of improved health care) and a declining birth rate in the latter decades of the twentieth century, resulting in an increasingly declining relative number of people of working age. This pattern varies significantly between countries, with the proportion of older people growing much more rapidly in Japan, for instance, than in the UK or more notably South Africa. The UN Population Division estimates, for example, that the population of the current EU members will fall by about 15 per cent to 628 million over the next 50 years leaving a labour deficit in many areas of the labour market, a deficit which, ironically, could only be met by an increase in planned migration, at a time when many such countries are imposing harsher immigration regimes (Craig, 2002).

Given these variations, and the long-term nature of demographic change, the panic reaction to the 'growing burden' of the elderly, which seems to have gripped policy-makers in some countries, may in practice be somewhat exaggerated, although the contradictions between national and international migration, social, economic and overseas development policies remain to be resolved. Pension payments and social care services will have to be provided for a larger number of people in the future; but, of course, these demands can be planned for within economic and political calculations made now (Bonoli, 2000). A growing proportion of older people within the population is not, therefore, in itself necessarily a problem.

The same is true of a declining birth rate. Reduced fertility has been experienced in a number of developed countries in the last half of the twentieth century, most notably, within the countries covered here, in Italy. At times, such reductions have been perceived to be an issue for social policy, for instance, generous child support provision in France has usually been associated with concerns to encourage families to produce more children. Conversely, relatively high birth rates may present a problem for policy-makers as large numbers of children give rise to additional demands for care and education. This is the case to some extent with the 'baby booms' that followed the end of the Second World War in countries such as the UK. Continuing concerns over high birth rates in China led to policy measures being introduced to encourage families to have only one child.

In addition to changes in the balance between the generations there have also been changes in family patterns experienced in many countries. In many Western nations, for instance, divorce levels have been rising and the numbers of lone-parent families have been increasing both relatively and absolutely. The assumption on which some social policies have been based therefore, that children will be cared for by both their natural parents in a stable 'nuclear' family structure, cannot be sustained. This has led to the need to support families in different ways, recognizing the diversity of patterns of care for children, including acknowledgement of the growth of gay and lesbian parenting patterns.

Even where significant changes are not taking place in levels of fertility and longevity, however, demographic issues influence the policy planning agenda. The welfare needs of all citizens change over the course of their lives. This is true at an individual level, but it is also true of whole cohorts within the population. And different cohorts born, and growing older, at different points in time will carry with them the expectations, and the welfare support, which they have experienced throughout their lives. Thus, for instance, in many countries the pensioner population of the mid- to late twentieth century did not have the benefit of being able to contribute to generous private or public pensions during their working lives in the earlier part of the century. Their pension needs and pension rights and expectations are thus very different from those of the cohorts reaching pension age at the end of the century, whose work incomes contributed towards their future pension needs.

These are differences to which social policies must, and in different ways do, respond. They are also, of course, to a large extent predictable developments that can be built into political debate and policy planning – although the extent to which different countries have done this effectively varies in practice, as later chapters in this book demonstrate. This is especially the case because the long-term planning, which is dictated by such demographic issues, inevitably comes into conflict with the short-term calculations characterizing economic pressures and political expediencies of national governments with terms of four or five years at most. This is revealed most sharply by the difficulties experienced by many nations in the 1990s in planning changes in pension policies but is illustrated by other short-term and unexpected events such as the relatively huge levels of migration from Eastern European states into the UK, following their accession to the EU, with consequent demands on welfare provision.

Ideology

Whatever the importance of economic, political and social pressures on welfare policy, the development of policies in practice depends also upon how the notions of welfare and need that underpin them are defined and understood. This is because different definitions are generated by different ideologies of welfare, and ideologies of welfare differ across countries and, perhaps more importantly, within them. All of us operate with ideological perceptions of welfare and need, and indeed all other social phenomena. However, most ideological differences can be located within the major broad ideological frameworks, which dominate much theoretical debate about social policy. George and Wilding (1994) provide an accessible guide to these, and their links to political debate and policy activity, and some more recent developments, are discussed in Powell and Hewitt (2002) and Fitzpatrick (2001 and 2005).

In the context of comparative study, however, it is important to bear in mind that ideological differences in what might be understood as welfare issues or social needs do lead to differences in the development and operation of welfare provision across different countries. For instance, provision of employment rights and regulation of family patterns are more commonly included within conceptualization of social policy goals in continental Europe than in the UK and other English-speaking countries. Ideological perspectives not only influence how welfare needs are defined, they also influence how they are met. For instance, in Scandinavia, the common expectation is that the needs of all will be met on a universal basis through the state, whereas in countries such as the USA, the predominant expectation is that public welfare should only be available to the poor and needy. Such differences between universal and selective approaches to the principles underlying welfare policy also influence policy debates within most developed nations, as do ideological differences about the roles accorded to public and private welfare provision. These differences are also represented in the ideological frameworks which underpin different the political traditions of neo-liberals, social democrats and others.

Ideological expectations do not just differ across countries, however; they also change over time. The understanding and measurement of welfare needs, such as poverty levels, have altered considerably throughout the twentieth century, for instance, with broader and more relative definitions replacing narrower and more subsistence-based measures (Townsend and Gordon, 2002). It is also argued by some that pressures on welfare services increased in the latter decades of the 20th century as result of higher expectations among citizens of needs that should be met by public services. For instance, many more people now continue into higher education than used to be the case in most developed countries, and more people expect health care provisions such as minor operations to be available on demand. Such ideological pressures can create counter-tendencies to the economic pressures to reduce welfare services, which must be resolved within the political processes discussed above.

Culture

The cultural heritages of different countries are in part a product of ideological perspectives and political debates; but they go beyond these, and themselves can shape or change the political climate within which social policy decisions are taken. There are a number of examples of the importance of cultural influences contained within the countries examined in the later chapters of this book:

- The entrepreneurialism and longstanding multi-culturalism of the USA has militated against the development of a strong central state welfare politics.
- The work-based, male-breadwinner family model of German social structure has mitigated against the development of broad universal welfare provision.
- The Confucian culture of East Asian societies such as Japan has supported a strong individual and family role in the provision of welfare.

Cultural differences do not just exist between countries, however. They also exist within them. Most nations now contain within their boundaries a range of different cultural traditions, resulting in large part from patterns of (mainly) postwar immigration and emigration between countries. The USA, the UK and Australia, for example, all contain a wide range of diverse ethnic cultures, with very different expectations about the structure and extent of welfare provision appropriate within these. For instance, Muslim groups have particular views about the importance of family structure and gender roles; some Catholic groups have strong views about family planning; and African-Caribbean groups in the UK and USA carry with them experiences of their subjection to slavery and the lower status that this has accorded them in the eyes of some members of the white majority population. In all of these cases, a culture of racism has influenced the way welfare policies are developed and experienced within societies. Not all cultural heritages have positive welfare manifestations therefore. Additionally, some ethnic groups are prone to particular ailments, which often are not reflected in higher demand for health services, such as the greater incidence of sickle cell anaemia among African-Caribbean populations.

Welfare Regimes

Welfare states, or welfare systems, have experienced common external pressures, yet they also have varying internal dynamics and social structures. These contrasting influences lead on the one hand to a convergence among countries towards similar patterns of welfare provision, and on the other hand to diversity reflecting differing local circumstances. These contrasting pressures have been recognized by comparative social policy analysts, such as Esping-Andersen (1996), and most attempts to compare and contrast welfare systems have endeavoured to develop analytical tools to explain and account for both similarities and differences, and predict ways in which future pressures will be responded to within different countries. This has commonly taken the form of attempts to categorize or classify welfare systems according to identifiable similarities and differences.

An early example of this was Titmuss's (1974) three-fold categorization of welfare states:

- Residual welfare systems – provision was available on a 'casualty' basis only to those who could not be expected to provide for themselves.
- Individual achievement systems – needs were met through involvement in the labour market and through work-related welfare measures.
- Institutional redistributive systems – with universal services provided for all.

A similar kind of classification was produced much later in one of the seminal empirical studies of comparative social policy by Esping-Andersen (1990) covering most of the major welfare systems of the developed Western world. He used national data on public expenditure on employment sickness and pensions and also examined the social development and political history of welfare provision. From this he extracted evidence about two key features of welfare states: the extent of *decommodification* (that is the extent to which welfare protection was available independently of market forces) and the levels of *stratification* (the extent to which access to welfare was structured by social class). The countries he analyzed were thus classified according to these two criteria and, he argued, fell into three broad clusters, representing different *welfare regimes.*

Within each cluster the countries all exhibited similar features in terms of welfare provision, and social and political circumstances; yet between the clusters there were significant key differences. He also identified three countries that provided near ideal types of the three different regimes – Sweden, Germany and the USA (see Table 1.1).

Table 1.1 Characteristics of welfare regime ideal types

	Sweden	*Germany*	*USA*
Regime	Social Democratic	Corporatist	Liberal
Political base	Broad-based compromise	Employer/worker coalition	Free market
Service type	Universal	Occupational	Residual
Public expenditure	High level	High level	Low level
Labour market	High employment/ high wage	Low employment/ high wage	High employment/ low wage

Esping-Andersen's analysis was based upon *post hoc* examination of the history and structure of these different welfare states. But he also argued that the classification could be used to predict how different regimes would respond to new economic and political challenges – an approach which he took further in later work (Esping-Andersen, 1996). According to him, therefore, all welfare systems within developed countries could be subsumed within these three broad regimes, a similar conclusion to that of Titmuss.

More recent analysts, however, have questioned the comprehensiveness and representative basis of Esping-Andersen's three regime types. The limited nature of the database for analysis, just one year's data from the early 1980s focusing on employment and pensions, has been criticized by Scruggs and Allan (2006), who went on to replicate his analysis using more extensive and up-to-date information from the OECD. This revealed some discrepancies in the location of some countries, such as Canada, Japan and Italy, within Esping Andersen's regime clusters; and discovered greater variation across the clusters for data on particular policy domains in some countries. However, overall their extension of his analysis confirmed the broad differences in ranking and the clustering of regime types.

Others have argued that, building on the three regimes identified by Esping-Andersen, further comparative analysis can reveal the existence of other welfare regimes within the developed world – leaving aside Gough *et al.*'s (2004) identification of other meta-regimes outside this. Castles and Mitchell (1991) argued that from within the countries that Esping-Andersen studied a distinct fourth regime type could be found, exemplified by Australia and New Zealand, where there was a different role for means-tested welfare provision. Leibfried (1993) and Ferrara (1996) also argued for a fourth type, this time based upon the 'Latin Rim' nations of Southern Europe, which Esping-Andersen did not examine. Since then others have gone further in expanding the range of welfare regimes to include other models of welfare provision, such as the former communist countries of Eastern Europe (Deacon *et al.*, 1992), or the new welfare systems of the Pacific Rim 'tiger economies' (Jones, 1993).

These attempts to identify new regime types are as much developments of Esping-Andersen's analysis as criticisms of it; and, as virtually all of the contributors to this book reveal, Esping-Andersen's regime analysis still provides a benchmark against which analysis of the characteristics and developments of different welfare states can be compared and contrasted. What the different chapters here also reveal are the different ways in which these regimes have responded to the international trends summarized above.

Responding to Welfare Challenges

What the detailed analysis of the country chapters in this book reveals is that a range of factors have impacted on welfare provision, although the extent to which each factor has been more significant, and the balance between the various factors, is different in each case. The key factors include:

- The impacts of an ageing population, leading to increased demands for health and social care, forms of rationing and enhanced dependence on familial or informal care.
- Increasing downward economic pressures, prompting increased tendencies towards privatization, outsourcing and reliance on non-state providers – the welfare mix thus reflects greater roles for private and NGO sectors.
- A growing crisis in land availability and consequent housing affordability, with knock-on impacts on both housing markets and on individual disposable incomes.
- The contradictory impacts of migration, both internal (with rural populations moving to urban areas) and cross-national in forms. Most developed countries now depend more heavily on migrant workers to fill the least skilled jobs in welfare provision (cleaners, night-shift workers, porters, etc.). At the same time, racism has increasingly informed political demands to reduce immigration.
- Pressures on NGO/Third Sector organizations to engage more widely as direct providers of welfare services, perhaps therefore limiting their critical political role.
- Increasing use of disciplinary measures against the poor, including workfare policies and an emphasis on who is deserving.

The picture presented in these chapters, as a result of these pressures, is of a clear, if uneven shift towards public welfare becoming more oriented towards a residual from of provision, a tendency in short towards the model most closely associated with the USA and one in which the claims of social justice are increasingly being crowded out (Craig *et al.*, 2008). The combined impacts of demography, migration and global economic pressures have therefore produced pressures for a new form of welfare convergence towards the political right.

In many countries, it has become increasingly difficult to distinguish in practice the welfare policies of social democratic parties from those of the liberal right, with spokespeople for both types of party increasingly complaining that 'their' policies are being stolen by the 'other' parties. Both ends of the political spectrum in the more developed countries now emphasize the importance of quality and choice, although, for most, this tends to translate into questions of ability to buy into the growing private welfare market, in some cases a market that extends to provision which can be purchased in other countries.

Again, in most of the countries represented here, the increased dependence on market solutions to the provision of welfare (and income) has led to increasing levels of inequality, especially in the less industrialized nations between rural and urban populations. Although some countries have attempted to address the question of growing inequality of income and wealth (Kenworthy and Pontusson, 2005) by targeting resources on the poorest, these programmes have generally barely slowed the process of enlarging income differentials and have had only a marginal effect set against the impacts of wider market forces. This may lead in due course to renewed political protest. In countries that are still industrializing, and particularly those that have emerged from state socialist regimes, welfare had always been seen as a tool to promote economic development: hence the notion of the developmental welfare state as illustrated in the case of South Korea. The option of a welfare state in these countries has therefore never really been on the table.

Whether the drift continues towards the political right and towards increased market solutions to the provision of welfare, with continuing high levels of poverty and inequality, depends in the final analysis on political struggle both within and across countries, and on the balance between different political tendencies. In the past few years left-wing political parties have been electorally unsuccessful and in some political disarray, and the trades union movement has had a decreasing impact on debates about welfare. Neo-liberalism has thus assumed a more dominant role within international discourse. The high wage/high welfare/high employment model of welfare, still associated with Sweden, is therefore an increasingly more remote response to international pressures, even within Sweden itself.

Nevertheless, as the different chapters in this book demonstrate so clearly, politics does still matter; and converging international pressures do not produce uniform national outcomes. What is more, the balance of political forces does vary across different countries, with centre-right and centre-left coalitions in control in different places at different times in recent years in most of the countries discussed here, leading to important shifts in the aim and practice of welfare policies. The value of comparative analysis thus remains of critical importance to our understanding of the diversity of the development of welfare provision both nationally and internationally. This will help both to contextualize national change and development, and to provide a more sophisticated basis for understanding how to make appropriate comparisons between differing national welfare provision.

References

Adelantado, J. and Calderon Cuevas, E. (2006) 'Globalization and the Welfare State: The Same Strategies for Similar Problems?', *Journal of European Social Policy*, 16(4).

Alcock, P., May, M. and Rowlingson, K. (eds) (2008) *Student's Companion to Social Policy*, 3rd edn, Blackwell.

Barnes, M., Heady, C., Middleton, S., Millar, J., Papadopoulos, F., Room, G. and Tsakloglou, P. (2002) *Poverty and Social Exclusion in Europe*, Edward Elgar.

Bonoli, G. 2000, *The Politics of Pension Reform: Institutions and Policy Change in Western Europe*, Cambridge University Press.

Bonoli, G., George, V. and Taylor-Gooby, P. 2000, *European Welfare Futures: Towards a Theory of Retrenchment*, Polity Press.

Bonoli, G. and Palier, B. (2007) 'When Past Reforms Open New Opportunities: Comparing Old-age Insurance Reforms in Bismarckian Welfare Systems', *Social Policy and Administration*, 41(6).

Bradshaw, J. (2006) 'Child Benefit Packages in Fifteen Countries', in J. Lewis (ed.), *Children, Changing Families and Welfare States*, Edward Elgar.

Bradshaw, J., Ditch, J., Holmes, H. and Whiteford, P. (1993) *Support for Children: A Comparison of Arrangements in Fifteen Countries*, HMSO, DSS Research Report 21.

Castles, F. (ed.) (1982) *The Impact of Parties, Politics and Policies in Democratic Capitalist States*, Sage.

Castles, F. (1999) *Comparative Public Policy: Patterns of Post-war Transformation*, Edward Elgar.

Castles, F. (2004) *The Future of the Welfare State*, Oxford University Press.

Castles, F. (ed.) (2007) *The Disappearing State? Retrenchment Realities in an Age of Globalisation*, Edward Elgar.

Castles, F. and Mitchell, D. (1991) *Three Worlds of Welfare Capitalism or Four?*, Australian National University Discussion Paper 21.

Castles, F. and Obinger, H. (2007) 'Social Expenditure and the Politics of Redistribtion', *Journal of European Social Policy*, 17(3).

CDPIIU (1976) *Cutting the Welfare State*, Community Development Project Inter-Project Editorial Team/Counter-Information Services.

Clasen, J. (ed.) (1999) *New Perspectives on the Welfare State in Europe*, Routledge.

Clasen, J. (2005) *Reforming European Welfare States: Germany and the United Kingdom Compared*, Oxford University Press.

Clasen, J. (ed.) (2007) *Investigating Welfare State Change: the 'Dependent Variable Problem' in Comparative Analysis*, Edward Elgar.

Clasen, J., Davidson, J., Ganssmann, H. and Mauer, A. (2006) 'Non-employment and the Welfare State: The UK and Germany Compared', *Journal of European Social Policy*, 16(2).

Craig, G. (2002) 'Ethnicity, Racism and the Labour Market: A European Perspective', in J.-G. Andersen and P. Jensen (eds), *Citizenship, Welfare and the Labour Market*, Policy Press.

Craig, G. and Mayo, M. (eds) (1995) *Community Empowerment*, Zed Books.

Craig, G., Burchardt, T. and Gordon, D. (eds) (2008) *Social Justice and Public Policy*, Policy Press.

Deacon, A. (2000) 'Learning from the USA? The Influence of American Ideas on New Labour Thinking on Welfare Reform', *Policy and Politics*, 20(1).

Deacon, A. (2002) *Perspectives on Welfare: Ideas, Ideologies and Policy Debates*, Open University Press.

Deacon, B. (1983) *Social Policy and Socialism: The Struggle for Socialist Relations of Welfare*, Pluto.

Deacon, B. (2007) *Global Social Policy and Governance*, Sage.

Deacon, B., Castle-Kanerova, M., Manning, N., Millard, F., Orosz, E. and Szalai J. (1992) *The New Eastern Europe: Social Policy Past, Present and Future*, Sage.

Deacon, B., Hulse, M. and Stubbs, P., (1997) *Global Social Policy: International Organisations and the Future of Welfare*, Sage.

Ditch, J., Bradshaw, J., Clasen, J., Huby, M. and Moodie, N. (1997) *Comparative Social Assistance: Localisation and Discretion*, Avebury.

Dolowitz, D. with Hulme, R., Nellis, M. and O'Neill, F. (2000) *Policy Transfer and British Social Policy: Learning from the USA*, Open University Press.

Dolowitz, D. and Marsh, D. (1996) 'Who Learns What from Whom? A Review of the Policy Transfer Literature', *Political Studies*, 44.

Ellison, N. (2006) *The Transformation of Welfare States?*, Routledge.

Esping-Andersen, G. (1985) *Politics Against Markets: The Social Democratic Road to Power*, University of Harvard Press.

Esping-Andersen, G. (1990) *The Three Worlds of Welfare Capitalism*, Polity Press.

Esping-Andersen, G. (ed.) (1996) *Welfare States in Transition: National Adaptations in Global Economies*, Sage.

Ferrara, M. (1996) 'The "Southern Model" of Welfare in Social Europe', *Journal of European Social Policy*, 6(1).

Fitzpatrick, T. (2001) *Welfare Theory: An Introduction*, Palgrave.

Fitzpatrick, T. (2005) *New Theories of Welfare*, Palgrave.

George, V. and Taylor-Gooby, P. (eds) (1996) *European Welfare Policy: Squaring the Circle*, Macmillan.

George, V. and Wilding, P. (1994) *Welfare and Ideology*, Harvester Wheatsheaf.

George, V. and Wilding, P. (2002), *Globalisation and Human Welfare*, Palgrave.

Geyer, R. (2000) *Exploring European Social Policy*, Polity Press.

Gilbert, N., Burrows, R. and Pollert, A. (eds) (1992) *Fordism and Flexibility: Divisions and Change*, Macmillan.

Goodin, R., Headey, B., Muffels, R. and Dirven, H. (1999) *The Real Worlds of Welfare Capitalism*, Cambridge University Press.

Gough, I. (1979) *The Political Economy of the Welfare State*, Macmillan.

Gough, I. (2001) 'Globalization and Regional Welfare Regimes: The East Asian Case', *Global Social Policy*, 1(2).

Gough, I. and Wood, G., with Barrientos, A., Bevan, P., Davis, P. and Room, G. (2004) *Insecurity and Welfare Regimes in Asia, Africa and Latin America: Social Policy in Development Context*, Cambridge University Press.

Gray, J. (1998) *False Dawn: The Delusions of Global Capitalism*, Granta.

Hall, P. and Soskice D. (eds) (2001) *Varieties of Capitalism: The Institutional Foundations of Comparative Advantage*, Oxford University Press.

Hantrais, L. (2007) *Social Policy in the European Community 3rd edn*, Palgrave.

Held, D., McGrew, A., Goldblatt, D. and Perraton, J. (1999) *Global Transformations: Politics, Economics and Culture*, Policy Press.

Hill, M. (1996) *Social Policy: A Comparative Analysis*, Prentice-Hall.

Hill, M. (2006) *Social Policy in the Modern World: A Comparative Text*, Blackwell.

Huber, E. and Stephens, J. (2001) *Development and Crisis of the Welfare State*, Chicago: University of Chicago Press.

Jones, C. (ed.) (1993) *New Perspectives on the Welfare State in Europe*, Routledge.

Jordan, B. (1998) *The Politics of Welfare*, Sage.

Jordan, B. (2008) *Social Policy for the Twenty-First Century*, Polity Press.

Kennett, P. (2001) *Comparative Social Policy*, Open University Press.

Kennett, P. (2004) *A Handbook of Comparative Social Policy*, Edward Elgar.

Kenworthy, L. and Pontusson, J. (2005), 'Rising Inequality and the Politics of Redistribution in Affluent Countries', *Perspectives on Politics*, 3(3).

Keynes, J. M. (1936) *The General Theory of Employment, Interest and Money*, Macmillan.

Kleinman, M. (2002) *A European Welfare State? European Union Social Policy in Context*, Palgrave.

Kuhner, S. (2007) 'Country-level Comparisons of Welfare State Change Measures: Another Facet of the Dependent Variable Problem within the Comparative Analysis of the Welfare State?', *Journal of European Social Policy*, 17(1).

Leibfried, S. (1993) 'Towards a European Welfare State?', in C. Jones (ed.), *New Perspectives on the Welfare State in Europe*, Routledge.

Lewis, G., Gewitz, S. and Clarke, J. (eds) (2000) *Rethinking Social Policy*, Sage.

Lodemel, I. and Trickey, H. (eds) (2001) *'An Offer you can't Refuse': Workfare in International Perspective*, Policy Press.

Mishra, R. (1990) *The Welfare State in Capitalist Society*, Harvester Wheatsheaf.

Mishra, R. (1999) *Globalisation and the Welfare State*, Edward Elgar.

Offe, C. (1984) *The Contradictions of the Welfare State*, Hutchinson.

Palier, B. and Martin, C. (2007) 'From "a Frozen Landscape" to Structural Reforms: the Sequential Transformation of Bismarckian Welfare Systems', *Social Policy and Administration*, 41(6).

Pfaller, A., Gough, I. and Therborn, G. (1991) *Can the Welfare State Compete? A Comparative Study of Advanced Capitalist Countries*, Macmillan.

Pierson, C. (2006) *Beyond the Welfare State: the New Political Economy of Welfare, 3rd edn*, Polity Press.

Pierson, C. and Castles, F. (eds) (2006) *The Welfare State Reader, 2nd edn*, Polity Press.

Pierson, P. (ed.) (2001) *The New Politics of the Welfare State*, Oxford University Press.

Powell, M. and Hewitt, M. (2002) *Welfare State and Welfare Change*, Open University Press.

Sarfati, H. and Bonoli, G. (eds) (2002) *Labour Market and Social Protection Reforms in International Persepctive: Parallel or Converging Tracks?*, Ashgate.

Scruggs, L. and Allan, J. (2006) 'Welfare-state Decommodification in 18 OECD Countries: A Replication and Revision', *Journal of European Social Policy*, 16(1).

Smeeding, T., O'Higgins, M. and Rainwater, L. (1990) *Poverty, Inequality and Income Distribution in Comparative Perspective: The Luxembourg Income Study* (LIS), Harvester Wheatsheaf.

Sykes, R., Palier, B. and Prior, P. (eds) (2001) *Globalisation and European Welfare States: Challenges and Change*, Palgrave.

Taylor-Gooby, P. (2004) *New Risk, New Welfare*, Oxford University Press.

Therborn, G. and Roebroek, J. (1986), 'The Irreversible Welfare State', *International Journal of the Health Sciences*, 16(3).

Titmuss, R. (1974) *Social Policy*, Allen and Unwin.

Townsend, P. and Gordon, D. (eds) (2002) *World Poverty: New Policies to Defeat an Old Enemy*, Policy Press.

Tullock, G. (1976) *The Vote Motive: An Essay in the Economics of Politics, with Application to the British Economy*, Princeton University Press.

Waters, A. (1995) *Globalisation*, Routledge.

Wilensky, H. (1975) *The Welfare State and Equality: Structural and Ideological Roots of Public Expenditure*, University of California Press.

Wood, G. and Gough, I. (2006) 'A Comparative Welfare Regime Approach to global Social Policy', *World Development*, 34(10).

Yeates, N. (ed.) (2008) *Understanding Global Social Policy*, Policy Press.

CHAPTER 2

An American Welfare State?

JOHN CLARKE (WITH FRANCES FOX PIVEN)

Varieties of Liberalism: The American Welfare State

The organization of USA social welfare has always posed distinctive problems for comparative studies of social policy. The absence of a strong, centralized welfare state providing a wide range of more or less universal benefits and services has led commentators to question whether the term 'welfare state' could meaningfully be used in this context. In contrast to European welfare models, the USA has featured more complex relationships between federal and state governments, and a mixture of corporate, philanthropic and public sources of welfare provision, exemplified in the organization of US health care, developed without a national universal health insurance system. Peters (2005) argues that the dominance of private over public provision meant that the US should be viewed as a 'corporate welfare system' since corporations provide both welfare and a route to welfare for employees.

A range of explanations has been offered for the different development of welfare in the USA (Pierson, 1990). One recurrent theme has been the relationship between the development of welfare and the role of political parties. In the case of the USA, this argument links the underdevelopment of state welfare with the underdevelopment of an organized labour movement. This type of analysis highlights the absence of socialist or social-democratic political parties associated elsewhere with the development and expansion of state welfare (Castles, 1989; Esping-Andersen, 1990). A second approach stresses the USA's distinctive racial formation, deriving from its settler and slave society origins, producing distinctive social and political divisions around welfare (Omi and Winant, 1986; Quadagno, 1994 Neubeck and Casenave, 2001).

This chapter focuses on three periods of major welfare reform and innovation, beginning with the 1930s and the 1960s, two periods that feature as formative in most accounts of US welfare, where major structural changes in welfare organization and provision took place. These two periods acquired politicized significance in later controversies about US welfare. The distinction between the 'New Deal' and the 'Great Society' welfare programmes emerged as a central feature of the politics of welfare in the 1980s. We then examine the transition from the twentieth to the twenty-first century, a period in which the USA became the leading edge of the movement from welfare to workfare states (Peck, 2001). Across these periods, we can see shifts in the 'liberal' character of US welfare, moving from economic liberalism to an expansive or social liberalism and finally to the dominance of neo-liberalism (albeit in alliance with neo-conservative social and moral ideologies).

From New Deal to Great Society: The Elements of US Welfare

Before the 1930s, social welfare in the USA was organized and delivered at local level, through states and cities, voluntary and philanthropic agencies, with the exception of Civil War Veterans' pensions (Skocpol, 1992). The 1930s economic depression exposed the limitations of this highly differentiated welfare patchwork. The scale of unemployment and resulting poverty rapidly outran the capacity of philanthropy and local state arrangements to cope. This failure provoked substantial social movements among the poor and unemployed, demanding public intervention to remedy unemployment and relieve poverty.

Roosevelt's 'New Deal' combined measures to remedy unemployment through public works schemes supported by federal funds with longer-term programmes establishing more systematic and rigorously administered welfare benefits. Amenta (1998) described this as the creation of a 'work and relief state' rather than a 'welfare state', as a way of emphasizing the central role of employment-creation measures. The creation of the Public Works Administration in 1933 was followed by the Social Security Act of 1935, providing the foundation for the subsequent structure of welfare benefits by creating a social insurance system offering benefits for old age and federal support for state schemes for unemployment insurance. It was later extended to widows and their dependants, and to cover sickness and disability. The scheme's central principle was the accumulation of insurance contributions records through employment. Many occupations, including many in which black people and female workers were concentrated, such as agriculture and domestic work, were excluded. Others involved pay too low to qualify for insurance payments and benefits, again disproportionately affecting both white women and black workers (Quadagno 1994).

Socialized, rather than individual, insurance had been established earlier as a core principle of welfare provision in Europe. Its introduction into the USA was consistently resisted by politicians and employers' organisations as undermining both the workings of the market and the incentives to individuals to make provision for their own needs (Skocpol and Ikenberry, 1983).

The scale of social dislocation created by the Depression led to wider acceptance of the need to supplement local public and philanthropic assistance with a more integrated social insurance system (Piven and Cloward, 1993). The insurance model adopted sought to maintain proper incentives to work and embodied three core principles:

1. Social insurance should not be directed at the elimination of all hardship, but only be concerned with a limited range of specified risks (unemployment, ill-health, old age and widowhood) which were not voluntary conditions.
2. Workers should see the connection between their income, their insurance payments and the benefits that they received, avoiding expectations of high benefit levels and maintaining work incentives.
3. The scheme should be clearly distinguished from public assistance, such that benefits were 'earned' as a right through a contribution record rather than being a stigmatizing and means-tested relief from the public purse or private charity. (Katz, 1986, pp. 236–7)

The Committee on Economic Security, overseeing the development of social security, was concerned that the development of new welfare measures should not blur the line between insurance-based provision and 'public assistance' (locally provided, means-tested support for the poor). Only two New Deal initiatives threatened this principle. The first was the decision to pay old-age pensions immediately to those who had no contribution record – but a temporary arrangement, to last only until the scheme was fully established. Subsequently, a means-test for those not insured was reintroduced.

The second was the creation of ADC (Aid to Dependent Children) in the 1935 Act, allowing the federal government to contribute to the costs of states' programmes for benefits to be paid to families in poverty for the maintenance of children. ADC itself was based on the 'mothers' pensions' programmes which a number of states had developed in the 1920s to provide assistance to widowed or 'deserted' mothers with young children. ADC's federal funding moved public assistance part-way to being a national scheme, although the schemes' administration remained at local level (Koven and Michel, 1993; Gordon, 1994; Bussiere, 1997).

ADC provides a paradigm of the interrelationship between welfare, 'race', class and gender in the USA. Where social insurance was earnings-related, ADC was available if the candidate family passed a series of 'tests', the means-test being one. The legislation also included a 'suitable home' provision, which allowed benefits not to be paid if investigation showed that children were being brought up in an unsuitable environment. This provision effectively became a 'morals test' applied to mothers seeking assistance, drawing on well-established assumptions about 'moral fitness' developed in the mothers' pensions schemes:

> The New Deal was a small and limited revolution – producing what Katz (1986) called a 'semi-welfare state'. Although it maintained the formal separation between federal and state or city administration of different aspects of welfare, it nevertheless created some national schemes and used federal funding more extensively to support the delivery of locally based welfare. It laid the foundation for a nationally co-ordinated system of social insurance, with benefits and entitlements for limited categories of the population. The creation of an insurance system aligned the US with other Western societies in the decommodification of limited welfare rights relating to unemployment, old age, disability and ill-health. Such decommodification was restricted to those with contributions' records earned through employment. For those inside the insurance system, the New Deal represented a considerable step forward. But the combination of social insurance with the preservation of local public assistance created a 'two-tier' welfare state in which those outside the insurance system had to prove both need and moral worth to receive assistance. This categorisation reflected wider structures of inequality. (Mink, 1991, p. 113)

These reforms established the pattern for US welfare until the 1960s, in particular, establishing the distinction between insurance-based benefits and public assistance that overshadowed the later politics of welfare.

The Great Society: A War against Poverty?

The 'great society' programmes of welfare reform associated with the 1960s Kennedy and Johnson presidencies need to be understood in the context of the social movements generating the impetus for reform. Katz (1986, p. 251–2) summarizes the pressures to welfare reform, indicating how traditional concerns about welfare intersected with changing social conditions, political circumstances and social movements:

> Racial conflict, urban riots, militant welfare clients and increased out-of-wedlock births among black women impelled a search for new ways to preserve social order and discipline. Unemployment induced by technology, functional illiteracy, or inadequate education; fear of Soviet competition; new manpower theories; and the realisation that welfare regulations discouraged work, all encouraged the use of welfare policy to shape and regulate labor markets.

Of particular significance were Civil Rights challenges to existing patterns of welfare (Piven and Cloward, 1993). Activists combined with anti-poverty workers in attacking the 'suitable home' provisions of the ADC scheme, used by many states as a racially exclusionary mechanism (Bell, 1965). Such alliances were significant in focusing political attention on the urgency of welfare reform and in shaping policies that increased the resources of the poorest through food stamp, nutritional and health programmes (West, 1981).

Poverty was primarily understood as the inadvertent effect of historically created barriers 'blocking' people from taking advantage of opportunities that the USA presented. Theories of 'cultural deficit' or 'cultural deprivation' among the poor therefore played a leading role in shaping policy responses (Katz, 1989). Conceptions of poverty as the effect of structural economic inequality were marginalized. Initiatives such as the Office of Economic Opportunity (OEO) (employment) and Operation Headstart (education) were thus designed to overcome barriers to participation in American opportunity structures by enhancing the skills and capacities of the poor.

Specific programmes targeted particular aspects of social life in poor communities, such as juvenile delinquency, civil rights, job training and education. Briefly, one of the most salient features of these initiatives was the role given to community action, which stressed the need for the 'maximum feasible participation' of the residents (Title II of the Economic Opportunity Act). This stress on programmes being carried out *by* the community rather than *for* the community identified state and city politicians and welfare agencies as part of the problem to be overcome (Marris and Rein, 1967). In reality, the attempt to make funding bypass existing power structures was quickly curtailed, with political resistance leading to restrictions on the OEO's ability directly to fund community groups. The programme ended in 1974 when the Nixon administration closed the OEO, transferring its responsibilities to other government departments.

Such projects were part of a wider 'war on poverty', conceived in the Kennedy administration, carried through by Johnson and continued in the Republican Nixon administration. From the Public Welfare Amendments of 1962 to the Social Security Amendments of 1974, a major restructuring and expansion of US welfare occurred. Between 1965 and 1972, federal welfare spending rose from US$75 billion to US$185 billion, from 7.7 per cent of America's 1960 Gross National Product to 16 per cent by 1974. This expansion had three main features:

1. increasing numbers of those eligible for welfare services and benefits;
2. a changing balance between services and benefits; and
3. a new relationship between social security and public assistance.

The reforms expanded the numbers of people eligible for welfare services and benefits in two main respects. The most visible was the reduction in racially discriminatory welfare programmes, particularly in the shift from ADC to AFDC (Aid to Families with Dependent Children). The less visible, but numerically more significant, change was the withdrawal or reduction of means-testing across a range of welfare services, turning them from conditional entitlements into unconditional rights. This change in access criteria had some effect in destigmatizing public services, moving them from a focus on assessing, investigating and supervising the poor towards seeing services as means of promoting greater social integration and participation.

Second, the reforms placed a greater emphasis on the provision of services (for example health care, housing and access to legal services) rather than on direct cash payments. Between 1964 and 1974, federal spending on 'in-kind' programmes increased from 3 per cent to 20 per cent of social welfare costs (Katz, 1986, p. 265). The most significant of these developments related to public housing, nutritional programmes (particularly the provision of food stamps) and health services. Health care became a particular focus of attention. The costs of obtaining health care (either directly for services or indirectly through private insurance) had effectively excluded many Americans. At the same time, however, proposals to socialize health care were forcefully resisted by health and insurance industry lobby groups. What emerged instead was a package of measures to subsidize health costs among those in need. Medicare and Medicaid programmes provided public funding for health costs among eligible groups, but the two schemes reproduced the different logics of social security and public assistance:

> Though adopted together, Medicare and Medicaid reflected sharply different traditions. Medicare was buoyed by popular approval and the acknowledged dignity of Social Security; Medicaid was burdened by the stigma of public assistance. While Medicare had uniform national standards for eligibility and benefits, Medicaid left states to decide how extensive their programs would be. Medicare allowed the physician to charge above what the programme would pay; Medicaid did not and participation among physicians was far more limited. (Starr, 1982, p. 370)

This split in funding health care reproduced the distinction between social security and public assistance in US welfare. The two programmes remained the core of US welfare policy and spending and played a major role in its expansion during the 1960s and early 1970s. In relation to public assistance, AFDC played the leading role with the numbers covered by the scheme increasing from 3.1 million in 1960, 4.3 million in 1965 and 6.1 million in 1969 to 10.8 million in 1974 (Patterson, 1981, p. 171). Popular challenges to entitlement restrictions underpinned federal and state relaxations of conditions that increased both numbers of eligible families and take-up rates.

Despite the dramatic increase in AFDC assistance, it was social security that grew most in the period, partly through demographic trends affecting the numbers eligible for insured benefits, and especially the elderly. But, as Katz argues, its demography was less significant than its social and political composition:

> Social security cut across class lines. Like public education, it offered at least as much to the middle classes as to the poor. Its constituency, therefore, was broad, articulate, effective and, above all, respectable. In 1970, social security payments to the elderly, $30.3 billion, were about ten times higher than federal payments for AFDC, $2.5 billion. By 1975, the gap had widened: social security cost $64.7 billion and AFDC $5.1 billion. Throughout the late 1970s and early 1980s the disparities increased even more. (1986, p. 267)

Social security emerged as the dominant feature of US welfare, combining income benefits for the elderly, disabled people and the unemployed, with insurance of health costs for eligible groups. The value of social security benefits was enhanced by changes throughout the late 1960s and 1970s that increased benefits beyond the cost of inflation and extended welfare to the 'non-poor'. Attempts by Presidents Nixon and Carter to reform welfare further towards a closer integration of insurance- and assistance-based schemes (through proposals for a guaranteed family income) failed because, Katz argues, they threatened the underlying distinction between the deserving and undeserving poor, embodied in the split between insurance and assistance (1986, p. 269). This distinction between the programmes emerged as the central focus for the politics of welfare in the 1980s.

The Welfare Backlash: The New Right in the 1980s

> The Soviet Union is the immediate danger perceived by Americans. Yet it is not the real threat to our national security. The real threat is the welfare state. (Friedman and Friedman, 1984, p. 73)

Welfare played a central role in the New Right's agenda for the reconstruction of the USA in the 1980s, reflecting its ability to incorporate a variety of themes about the economy, the state, the family, 'race' and gender that were essential to its diagnosis of America's fall from grace and its prescriptions for a return to greatness. Just as the period of welfare expansion is one that the US shared with other Western societies, so, too, the period of welfare backlash and retrenchment is one that links the USA to other societies. Where the long postwar boom underpinned welfare expansion, so the onset of world recession from the mid-1970s provided a starting point for challenges to the costs of welfare. In part, this appeared as a simple question of economics: 'can we afford welfare?' But it was also caught up in how economic and political crises are represented, and the ideological practices through which their causes are explained and remedies defined. The simple question about the cost of welfare was itself part of the changing ideological framework, which now defined welfare as an 'unproductive' cost to national economies, making them less competitive. In the 1960s, at least in part, welfare had been construed as expenditure necessary to modernize society and make it more competitive, as well as more harmonious and socially just.

While the USA shared social and economic changes in common with other societies, the particular response to them was the product of domestic political forces and alliances. The reshaping of the right in American politics proved to be a decisive process. A new alliance, composed of different social and ideological groupings, including neo-liberals, neo-conservatives and the radical right, came to dominate the Republican Party and supported the Reagan presidencies (Saloma, 1984). Neo-liberalism provided an economic rationale for change, identifying an over-regulatory, over-interfering and over-taxing state as a major cause of America's declining competitiveness. Individual and corporate 'enterprise' needed to be liberated from the state. Neo-conservatism provided a political and moral rationale for change, arguing that the 'elite liberalism' of the 1960s and 1970s had gone too far, producing an over-extended state and a collapse of national leadership. The radical right (itself an uneasy confederation of moral majoritarians, anti-communists and white supremacist groupings) provided a moral rationale for change, arguing that the 1960s liberalism had undermined fundamental American values, denied bedrock American freedoms (for example, through enforced desegregation of schooling) and created a moral vacuum (Clarke, 1991).

The Problem of Dependency

For the New Right, the major mistake of welfare expansion in the 1960s and 1970s was clear in its effects on the poor. Where social security programmes, for the main part, could be seen as promoting independence by virtue of earning the benefits one received, public assistance (AFDC, in particular) had the effect of undermining independence and creating a culture of 'demoralization'. The basic components of this view stretch back to nineteenth-century beliefs embodied in the Poor Law and public relief programmes. Giving people welfare stops them trying to help themselves, makes them dependent on the benefits they receive and undermines the will to self-improvement. The more particular version of this theme in relation to AFDC pointed to the growth of lone-parent families, arguing that its existence meant that men could father children without financial responsibility, and that women were freed from the responsibility of keeping men in the household and in employment. The existence of the benefit, it was argued, created 'perverse incentives' and rewarded inappropriate behaviour.

This critique was exemplified in Charles Murray's *Losing Ground* (1984), a huge and apparently well-documented survey of the impact of welfare on employment, family life and achievement amongst US black people. It was influential far beyond America in its critique of welfare and in the way it linked welfare to the emergence of an 'underclass'. Murray used four key indicators to demonstrate the demoralizing effects of poverty programmes:

1. labour force participation (very low for young black males);
2. illegitimate births (very high for young black females);
3. the number of lone-parent families (very high among black people); and
4. the number of homicide victims (very high among young black males).

Together, these indices mapped a section of the population that, he suggested, had become demoralized and dependent. Murray used statistical comparison about the fortunes of black and white people in the USA as the basis for arguments about poverty, despite the fact that twice as many white people as black were living in poverty. Claiming that there was no usable data about the poor, he insisted that black people provide a satisfactory 'proxy' for poor people. The effect of this device was to construct an elision between the categories of 'poor' and 'black' and to tell the story of black America only from the standpoint of welfare. Such constructions were endemic to the New Right's attack on welfare to the extent that many commentators argued that 'welfare' became simply a synonym for 'race' in US politics during the 1980s.

The complex mixture of the metaphors of a 'dependency culture' and the 'underclass' in the New Right's demonology of welfare underpinned the 1980s retreat from welfare spending: the toughening up of welfare eligibility and conditions and a greater concern with the use of welfare as a way of controlling the poor. This strategy concentrated on public assistance rather than social security, reflecting their different political constituencies. The exception was benefits paid to disabled people under the Social Security Act. Congress amended the Act in 1980 to require a periodic review of all cases, which the Reagan Administration accelerated. Katz notes that, between March 1981 and April 1982, 400,000 cases were reviewed of which half were ruled ineligible (1986, p. 286). The major assault, however, was on public assistance and social service programmes:

> by 1983, under complex, new regulations, 408,000 people had lost their eligibility for AFDC and 299,000 had lost their benefits . . . Through these reductions federal and state governments saved $1.1 billion in fiscal 1983. Other regulations restricted eligibility for food stamps and sliced $2 billion out of the program's $12 billion budget . . . Spending on Medicaid dropped 3 per cent in fiscal year 1982 . . . The social services block grant to the states was chopped by 20 per cent in 1981. (Katz, 1986, p. 287)

The cumulative effect of these and other changes are shown in reductions in spending as a result of government action on a number of programmes between 1982 and 1985:

AFDC:	12.7 per cent
Food stamps:	12.6 per cent
Child nutrition:	27.7 per cent
Housing assistance:	4.4 per cent
Low income energy assistance:	8.3 per cent

(*Source*: Katz, 1986, p. 288)

These changes set the tone for welfare policy and politics in the 1980s. Although the Reagan administrations did not 'abolish the welfare state', as some New Right ideologists would have wished, its programmes, staffing and resourcing were significantly diminished – albeit selectively – by 1990. The brunt of the 'war on welfare' was borne by the poorest – those dependent on public assistance programmes rather than social insurance.

The Failure of Health-Care Reform

President Clinton's election (1992) reopened a public discussion about the organization, coverage and cost of US health-care provision. A complex and costly system had historically excluded many Americans or, at best, provided them with minimal coverage and services. Economic uncertainty in the 1980s and 1990s led to many more American citizens becoming anxious about the security of their health-care arrangements. Many of these citizens were covered by health insurance schemes arranged by employers, and widespread job losses (particularly in white-collar and middle-class occupations) threatened both insurance arrangements and workers' sense of health security.

The other key issue on health care was the problem of rising costs, a challenge shared by other Western health-care systems. All have faced rising costs in the context of rising demand, changing demographies (with increasingly elderly populations) and the rising costs of medical services. What distinguished the USA was the organizational setting of these problems, with direct public provision forming only a small part of health care. Most provision had been arranged through private (for-profit and not-for-profit) organizations, with payment for services financed though a variety of routes. The balance of funding had shifted from the 1930s pattern of direct payments by users, supplemented by public assistance for the poor through non-profit mutual insurance schemes organized by hospitals, such as Blue Shield, to one dominated by employment-based health insurance plans. By 1983, 58 per cent of Americans were covered by employment-based schemes, 12 per cent were covered by Medicare and 8 per cent were covered by Medicaid; 15 per cent of Americans had no health coverage (Staples, 1989). Health insurance followed familiar patterns of employment stratification, reproducing labour market disadvantages in terms of 'race', gender and class.

Two particular changes affected the mix of provision. One was the growth of Health Maintenance Organizations (HMOs), which offered health-care packages on the basis of an annual fee (which employers might pay or contribute towards). The HMOs then either provided direct services themselves or contracted with other service providers. By the late 1980s, HMOs covered about 12 per cent of the population (Ginsburg, 1991, p. 129). The second major development was the growth of 'for-profit' hospitals and health provision. Wohl (1984) coined the phrase 'the medical–industrial complex' to describe this trend towards the corporate domination of health-care provision. It was a trend seemingly likely to create a tripartite division of health care, with the corporate sector 'creaming off' the most profitable patients, a second layer of not-for-profit or smaller for-profit hospitals taking all but the uninsured, and the bulk of Medicaid patients remaining in an increasingly residualized public hospital system (Ginsburg, 1991, p. 129).

This system posed major problems for those worried about cost containment. For the most part, it was driven by the power of the medical profession, which had resisted attempts to socialize the costs of health care through national health insurance since the 1940s. One result of the system's complexity was that no alternative concentrations of power existed to check the power of the medical profession, given that payment for health care was distributed between state and federal governments, insurance schemes, employers (paying workers' health insurance) and private individuals. The 1980s saw changes that challenged the institutional dominance of the medical profession, including federal attempts to impose bureaucratic means of limiting medical costs (Bjorkman, 1989). These moves were paralleled by pressure from insurance companies and employers for greater cost control. The growth of corporate health-care provision suggests a third source of financial pressure: the corporations' desire to rationalize costs and increase profits. Wohl (1984) and Starr (1982) both argued that this corporate pressure, and the ability of the corporations to exercise greater control over doctors who are employees and not independent professionals, may be the most significant long-term development in cost containment.

Clinton took up the issue of health-care reform in 1993, establishing a task force headed by his wife Hillary. Although health-care reform was a popular issue, the task force's proposals were abandoned in 1994. Many reasons have been advanced for their failure, including problematic political tactics, a widespread public mistrust of government, and the powerful and effective lobbying campaigns of medical, insurance and employer interest groups likely to be adversely affected by the reforms. Skocpol's (1997, p. 178) analysis highlighted other political issues, arguing that the reform proposals were vilified by the Republican Right as an extension of 'big government', creating more 'bureaucracy' and 'government interference', limiting 'individual freedom' and threatening the quality of the 'best health care in the world'.

Skocpol links these challenges to the Clinton plan to a wider view of political dynamics in the post-Reagan period, exploring the paradoxes of a Democratic politics framed by neo-conservative and neo-liberal ideologies. 'Reagan's revenge' (Brinkley, 1994) is a combination of anti-government politics, tax cut promises (at least in personal and corporate taxation) and a large budget deficit (requiring 'fiscal conservatism' in government to control or reduce it). Skocpol suggests that Clinton's health-care reforms were trapped in these conflicting legacies. The political and ideological paradoxes surrounding the role of government in promoting forms of social welfare created an impact that went beyond the failure of the health-care reform proposals. In particular, other areas of social welfare became the ground on which the new Democratic conservatism of the Clinton

Presidency encountered the revival of the Republican Right, an encounter that resulted in a competition between a Democratic President and a Republican Congress to bring about 'the end of welfare' (Piven, 1998).

Ending 'Welfare As We Know It'

The distinction between 'entitlements' (social security) and 'welfare' (AFDC) continued to play a central role in conflicts over social policy in the 1990s (Gordon, 1994; Clarke, 2004). Welfare remained a primary target for neo-conservative and neo-liberal attacks (Tanner, 1996). The most dramatic policy change, however, was President Clinton's commitment in 1992, showing his credentials as a 'new Democrat', to 'end welfare as we know it' by bringing about reforms that would 'time-limit' welfare and get people 'off welfare and off to work' (Piven, 1998, p. 21). This commitment was fulfilled in 1996 when the President signed a bill effectively terminating AFDC, changing federal funding, instituting a two-year maximum for welfare benefits, and enabling states to operate tighter time limits as well as 'behavioural conditions' in respect of mothers and their children.

The Personal Responsibility and Work Opportunity Reconciliation Act (PRWORA) of 1996 dramatically transformed the character of welfare and the status of welfare recipients (Goode and Maskovsky, 2001). The Act's preamble redefined the purposes of welfare to:

1. provide assistance to needy families so that children may be cared for in their own homes or in the homes of relatives;
2. end the dependence of needy parents on government benefits by promoting job preparation, work and marriage;
3. prevent and reduce the incidence of out-of-wedlock pregnancies and establish annual numerical goals for preventing and reducing the incidence of these pregnancies; and
4. encourage the formation and maintenance of two-parent families.

(Quoted in Mink 1998, p. 66)

The 1996 Act had three significant features. First, it placed a premium on the idea of work rather than welfare as the basis of personal and familial independence. Neither the federal government nor individual states were obliged to find or provide employment for claimants. 'Personal responsibility' had a strict interpretation in the Act: a maximum of two years' welfare benefit could be claimed before the state withdrew any support.

Policy analysts have argued that 'welfare mothers' have been subjected to oscillating interpretations of their role and responsibilities (Gordon, 1994; Handler, 1995; Mink, 1998). In the early twentieth century, 'maternalist' policies, such as mothers' pensions and ADC, had been introduced to support poor women in the task of raising children. Other policies subsequently emphasized the mothers' responsibility to go out to work to provide for their children. The PRWORA announced that the primary obligation of poor mothers was to find employment (a requirement that distinguishes them from non-poor mothers).

The second significant feature of the PRWORA was its explicit commitment to the 'formation and maintenance' of two-parent families. Marriage was put forward as the only legitimate alternative to employment for poor mothers, and the patriarchal norms of conventional family formation were to be both encouraged and enforced by the states through welfare conditions (Mink, 1998). For example, under the Act, states can refuse additional benefit for any child born to a mother already receiving welfare. The Act marked a significant moment in the conflict over 'family values' in the USA, embodying the backlash against household diversity in general, lone parents specifically, and against aspects of greater female economic independence. The triumph of 'family values' meant that one form of household formation (the 'conventional' family) became the only 'valued family' through its embodiment as a governmental objective in legislation (Stacey, 1998). The PRWORA created a combination of incentives, demands and powers to engage the states in policing the morality of their poorest citizens.

There was a third significant element of the 'end of welfare'. The PRWORA redefined relationships between the federal government, states and citizens. It broke the link between the federal government and citizens in need of welfare by shifting funding for AFDC to block grants to the states, thus undoing the welfare relationship established in the New Deal. The cash-limited central subsidy to the states provided them with an incentive to cut benefit levels and numbers of recipients – which most took advantage of. At the same time, the Act gave states greater 'flexibility' in the implementation of welfare reform.

The Clinton administration continued the practice inaugurated under presidents Reagan and Bush of granting waivers of the Social Security Act (to 43 states in all) to permit the states to 'experiment' by imposing time limits on the receipt of AFDC benefits and various sanctions against disapproved benefit recipient behaviours. Disgruntled at the Democratic effort to capture 'their' issue, the new Republican Congressional majority elected in 1994 replaced AFDC entirely by Temporary Assistance to Needy Families (TANF), a programme imposing strict federal time limits and work requirements on lone mothers receiving cash assistance and giving the administration of the scheme to the states.

The effect of these changes was to create substantial geographical unevenness in the conditions for, and administration of, welfare across the USA (Peck, 2001). The PRWORA did indeed mark 'the end of welfare as we know it'. It represented the culmination of neo-conservative and neo-liberal attacks on 'welfare' that had been developing since the late 1970s. The ideological segregation and demonization of 'welfare mothers' as a cause of America's social and economic problems thus resulted in their disentitlement, stigmatization and subjection to new forms of moral surveillance and economic discipline. Even this outcome, however, failed to satisfy the 'reforming' zeal of neo-conservatives and neo-liberals. For neo-liberals, the fact that government remained in the 'business' of welfare at all was a problem. They would rather have seen the 'needy' and the 'philanthropists' settle matters within civil society without government interference (Tanner, 1996).

The labour market consequences of these welfare changes were predictable. As hundreds of thousands of women lost welfare benefits, whether because of time limits or sanctions or of the bureaucratic obstacles inevitable when conditions for eligibility become complex and discretionary, they streamed into the labour market to compete with other women, and men, for less-skilled and low-paying jobs. Many of them actually failed to find steady work, even in a booming economy with low overall unemployment levels (although not necessarily low unemployment levels among the less skilled, especially in the older central city ghettos). State estimates varied, but between 40 and 70 per cent of those dropped from the welfare rolls appear to have been unemployed, and few of those who were employed were earning wages sufficient to bring them above the poverty line. Whether they found work or not, wages in these sectors of the labour market where they were competing for jobs were likely to be driven down, by about 12 per cent according to early estimates – and falling more in states where proportionally more people had been on welfare. One estimate suggested a wage reduction of 26 per cent in the exposed sectors of the labour market in New York City, the displacement of 58,000 workers, or some combination of the two.

Welfare cutbacks were only the most publicised of the changes in decommodifying programmes. Under the Reagan administration, the federal formula measuring state unemployment levels, which triggered the availability of long-term unemployment benefits in a state, was revised to reduce their availability, with the little-noticed but nevertheless dramatic consequence of reducing the proportion of the unemployed who received these benefits, from 75 per cent in the 1970s, to a mere one-third in the 1980s (Meerpool, 1997). Other obscure changes were made in social security, the main old-age pension programme, where the age of eligibility was raised, although so gradually as to attract little comment, from 65 to 67 years, while adjustments to the cost of living formula cut pension benefit levels, and new rules encouraged the pensioned to continue to work. This was an opening shot in a continuing campaign to undermine public confidence in social security and build support for the privatization and retrenchment of old-age pensions.

New restrictions on social support for immigrants were also incorporated in the PRWORA. With some exceptions, legal immigrants were no longer entitled to Medicaid, food stamps, or cash assistance. In reality, the idea that benefit cut-offs would deter immigration has hardly been confirmed by data or experience (Massey, 1998) and the exclusions simply ensured that immigrants who did enter the USA remained without any public protection to tide them over periods of unemployment or low wages. This may indeed be just what was intended, since the congressional bloc that led the fight to cut benefits for immigrants simultaneously opposed tighter controls on immigration (Stern, 1998). During 1996, the year that cutbacks on aid to legal immigrants were made law, almost a million legal immigrants were admitted to the USA, the largest number since 1914 (Schuck, 1998).

Making a Workfare State: Cutback or Commodification?

However, these much-publicized cutbacks did not tell the whole story. The pattern of change in the income maintenance programmes was uneven, and complicated. While families on welfare fared badly, some of the much-heralded cuts of the early 1980s were rather quickly reversed and spending on some programmes actually increased. Overall federal expenditures on major means-tested programmes steadily increased, from US$88 billion in 1980 to US$205 billion in 1995 (OMB, 1996). The widely held view that the USA has simply retrenched its spending on the poor does not fit these facts (Melnick, 1998).

First, not all the attempted cuts succeeded. An early Reagan proposal to do away with a legal minimum payment in social security pensions was quickly defeated by an overwhelming vote of the Congress. The huge reductions in the disability rolls of the early 1980s were largely restored by the courts by the end of the first Reagan term. Expenditures on the Supplemental Security Income (SSI) programme, which included payments to the impoverished aged and disabled, then slowly rose during the remainder of the 1980s, and accelerated upward by 20 per cent per year in the 1990s, largely as a result of the expansion of the disabled rolls (Melnick, 1998). Federal spending on health care for the poor under Medicaid also rose rapidly, from US$26.3 billion in 1980, to US$89.1 billion in 1995 (measured in 1995 dollars). The food and nutrition programmes had been sharply cut in the early 1980s, but subsequent steady increases pushed spending – and the number of beneficiaries – up to levels higher than prior to the cuts. In 1996, under the aegis of the Republican Congress intent on welfare reform, the food stamp programme was targeted for further cuts, but a number of these cuts were rescinded the following year. Meanwhile, and despite vigorous political argument discrediting public housing programmes, federal expenditures on housing assistance for low-income people increased steadily throughout the period (Jencks, 1998).

These twists and turns require a complex explanation. One possibility is simply that industrial-era theories which posited the durability of the welfare state because of the economic, social and political 'functions' it served in a democratic and capitalist society should not be so quickly dismissed. Another possibility is suggested by the fact that different programmes fared quite differently, which suggests that the influence of provider groups with an interest in some of the programmes might account for their durability; the continued expansion of the health-care programmes is a case in point. A further possible explanation is offered by Hartmann (2005), who argues that although neo-liberal rhetoric talks about shrinking government, in practice neo-liberal efforts to reorganize economic and social relationships turned out contradictorily to depend heavily on using governmental power and policies to create the 'new order'.

However, there is no doubt that a major shift occurred, away from spending on less work-conditioned, or less commodified programmes, to spending on programmes that shore up labour-market participation, or commodify labour. Spending continued to rise essentially because even commodified programmes cost money. Indeed, this is just what relief reformers discovered in the past when they succeeded in replacing direct relief with 'houses of industry'. The most dramatic commodification occurred in TANF, where federal requirements stipulated that states should show that a rising proportion, year-on-year, of the mothers receiving aid were working. The arrangements varied: in many states, recipients were assigned to private employers who paid them the minimum wage and received the welfare cheque (and handsome tax write-offs) as subsidies. Alternatively, recipients might simply work for their welfare cheque, either for private employers, or for local government. The most important of the new labour market-related programmes was the Earned Income Tax Credit, which operated like a negative income tax with earnings below US$24,000 per year, but only if the family head was working. The programme originated as a little-noticed tax provision in 1975, and with the support of presidents Reagan and Bush, and later Clinton, was expanded from the late 1980s. It was further extended during the presidencies of George W. Bush between 2000 and 2008 alongside a radical programme of tax cuts in personal income and corporate taxation (Aberbach, 2006).

The impact of changing social policies on labour markets is, however, not only the result of the interplay between the material incentives of wage work and income maintenance programmes, characteristic of the policy shifts in many Western countries. The commodification of welfare in the USA has also been affected by cultural sanctions. The programmes and the discourse surrounding them also help to define the identities of those who participate in the labour market and those who don't. The campaign to reform welfare was itself a powerful intervention in American culture that proclaimed the worthlessness of poor women raising children on the dole. And the new punitive practices ushered in by the legislation – sometimes called 'tough love' – reinforced those derogatory meanings at the same time as reinforcing the importance of work regardless of declining real wages and increasing hours. Indeed, at first glance, these welfare reforms seemed to be entirely about questions of the personal morality of the women who subsist on the dole and not about labour markets. The problem was, the argument went, that a too-generous welfare system was leading women to spurn wage work for lives of idleness and 'dependency' (Fraser and Gordon, 1994), thereby undermining sexual and family morality among the poor.

Intensifying Social Divisions in a Workfare State

In this period, the question of workfare has been intimately entwined with moral and cultural denigration of the poor – and in particular of those social groups who are taken to represent the poor (Goode and Maskovsky, 2001; Neubeck and Casenave, 2001). The chorus of criticism focused relentlessly on personal morality, always tapping into the deep antipathies in American culture towards the poor, towards black and Latina minorities, who were widely understood to be the main beneficiaries of welfare, and drawing on the energy and excitement evoked by public debate about women and sex and sin. In reality, though, it had a good deal to do with labour markets, for it created a national drama that heaped insult on women who were poor if they were presumed not to work (Harris, 1993). The politics of the 1960s had reduced the stigma of being on the dole, and as a consequence, more people in need applied for welfare and the welfare rolls rose; the politics of the 1990s increased stigma, and contributed to the rapid fall in the rolls. This aspect of the reconstruction of American programmes also inevitably reverberated upward, underlining for the working poor and less-than-poor the imperative of waged work and the degradation of falling out of work (Abdela and Withorn, 2002).

Over the past 30 years, income inequalities in the USA have risen spectacularly, while wages have stagnated or declined. Even on official indicators, poverty has increased substantially – and its unequal distribution among particular social groups has intensified. Peele (2005) notes for example that even in terms of the official and unsatisfactory definition of poverty in the USA, the numbers of those adults and children in poverty and the poverty rate had increased over the years, and that poverty had a strongly racialized dimension with blacks, Hispanics, Asians and indigenous people more prone to being in poverty.

The large-scale dynamics of the relationship between the new 'workfare' and social divisions of class, gender and race are mirrored in micro-dynamics of the welfare-to-work schemes put in place after the 'end of welfare'. Korteweg (2006) shows how such schemes reinforce and reproduce gendered assumptions about the relationship between work, family and care in ways that intensify the burden on poor women. Davis (2004, p. 285) explores how racialized and gendered dynamics combine to direct poor black women into forms of service work, reinventing 'the black mammy' through workfare and its allocation of jobs and training through racialized codes.

Welfare reform, as we noted earlier, was never just about the labour market and work. Rather, it has reorganized and reinforced deep divisions within American society, driven by both neo-liberal and neo-conservative ideas of how that society should be organized, ordered and disciplined. Political discourses of 'putting people to work', or the preference for 'a hand up, not a hand out' disguise how welfare reform has, in fact, set out to reform poor people – with the aim of making them fit to take their place in the world. Whether the overall strategy of welfare reform is considered a success depends rather a lot on the standpoint from which success if defined and measured (Schram and Soss, 2002). The number of people receiving public welfare has certainly fallen, but the numbers seeking help or assistance from voluntary or philanthropic agencies has increased enormously (Kilty and Segal, 2003). The use of corporate subsidies and low-income tax credit has contributed to the expansion of employment, but mostly in the form of poor, contingent and vulnerable jobs. Meanwhile, the private sector – the main route to corporate welfare and the underpinning for George W. Bush's dream of 'privatizing' pensions (enabling individuals to use part of their social security savings to invest in the stock market) – has also proved to be more fragile than expected. In particular, the raids that corporations mounted on company pension schemes to sustain share value threatened the assumption of what Peters (2005) calls the US 'corporate welfare' model. The new 'workfare state' may prove to be as contradictory and crisis-prone as its predecessors.

References

Abdela, R. and Withorn, A. (eds) (2002) *Lost Ground*, South End Press.

Aberbach, J. (2005) 'The Political Significance of the George W. Bush Administration', *Social Policy & Administration*, 39(2), pp. 130–49.

Amenta, E. (1998) *Bold Relief: Institutional Politics and the Origins of Modern American Social Policy*, Princeton University Press.

Bell, W. (1965) *Aid to Dependent Children*, Columbia University Press.

Bjorkman, J. W. (1989), 'Politicizing Medicine and Medicalizing Politics: Physician Power in the US', in G. Freddi and J. W. Bjorkman (eds), *Controlling Medical Professionals*, Sage.

Brinkley, A. (1994) 'Reagan's Revenge: As Invented by Howard Jarvis', *New York Times Magazine*, 19 June, pp. 36–7.

Bussiere, E. (1997) *(Dis)Entitling the Poor: the Warren Court, Welfare Rights and the American Political Tradition*, Pennsylvania University Press.

Castles, F. G. (ed.) (1989) *The Comparative History of Public Policy*, Polity Press.

Clarke, J. (1991) *New Times and Old Enemies: Essays on Cultural Studies and America*, Harper Collins.

Clarke, J. (2004) *Changing Welfare, Changing States: New Directions in Social Policy*, Sage.

Davis, D. A. (2004) 'Manufacturing Mammies: The Burdens of Service Work and Welfare Reform among Battered Black Women', *Anthropologica*, 46, pp. 273–88.

Esping-Andersen, G. (1990), *The Three Worlds of Welfare Capitalism*, Polity Press.

Fraser, N. and Gordon, L. (1994) 'A Genealogy of Dependency: Tracing a Keyword of the Welfare State', in P. Jones (ed.), *Critical Politics: From the Personal to the Global*, Arena Publications, pp. 77–109.

Friedman, M. and Friedman, R. (1984) *The Tyranny of the Status Quo*, Harcourt Brace Jovanovich.

Gans, H. J. (1995) *The War Against The Poor*, Basic Books.

Ginsburg, N. (1991) *Divisions of Welfare*, Sage.

Goldwater, B. (1960) 'Wanted: A More Conservative GOP', *Human Events*, 18, February, Section II, pp. 1–2.

Goode, J. and Maskovsky, J. (eds) (2001), *The New Poverty Studies: The Ethnography of Power, Politics and Impoverished People in the United States*, New Poverty Studies.

Gordon, L. (1994) *Pitied But Not Entitled: Single Mothers and the History of Welfare, 1890–1935*, The Free Press.

Handler, J. (1995) *The Poverty of Welfare Reform*, Yale University Press.

Harris, K. M. (1993) 'Work and Welfare among Single Mothers in Poverty', *American Journal of Sociology*, 99(2), September.

Hartmann, Y. (2005) 'In Bed with the Enemy: Some Ideas on the Connections between Neoliberalism and the Welfare State', *Current Sociology*, 53(1), pp. 57–73.

Jencks, C. (1998) *The Homeless*, Harvard University Press, pp. 97–8.

Katz, J. (1986) *In the Shadow of the Poorhouse: A Social History of Welfare in America*, Basic Books.

Katz, J. (1989), *The Undeserving Poor*, Pantheon.

Kilty, K. and Segal, E. (eds) (2003) *Rediscovering the Other America: The Continuing Crisis of Poverty and Inequality in the United States*, Haworth Press.

Korteweg, A. (2006) 'The Construction of Gendered Citizenship at the Welfare Office: An Ethnographic Comparison of Welfare-to-Work Workshops in the United States and the Netherlands', *Social Politics*, 13(3), pp. 313–40.

Koven, S. and Michel, S. (eds) (1993) *Mothers of a New World: Maternalist Politics and the Origins of Welfare States*, Routledge.

Marris, P. and Rein, M. (1967) *Dilemmas of Social Reform: Poverty and Community Action in the United States*, Routledge & Kegan Paul.

Massey, D. (1998) 'March of Folly: U.S. Immigration Policy After NAFTA', *The American Prospect*, March/April, pp. 22–3.

Meerpol, M. (1997) 'A Comment on the Wood-Magdoff vs. Cloward-Piven Debate', unpublished manuscript, Western New England College.

Melnick, R. S. (1998) 'The Unexpected Resilience of Means-Tested Programs', paper prepared for delivery at the 1998 Annual Meeting of the American Political Science Association, 3–6 September.

Mink, G. (1991) 'The Lady and the Tramp: Gender and Race in the Formation of American Welfare', in L. Gordon (ed.), *op. cit.*

Mink, G. (1998) *Welfare's End*, Cornell University Press.

Murray, C. (1984) *Losing Ground: American Social Policy, 1950–80*, Basic Books.

Neubeck, K. and Casenave, N. (2001) *Welfare Racism: Playing the Race Card against America's Poor*, Routledge.

OMB (1996) *Economic Report of the President*, Office of Management and Budget, US Government Office, p. 367.

Omi, M. and Winant, H. (1986), *Racial Formation in the United States*, Routledge.
Patterson, J. T. (1981) *America's Struggle Against Poverty*, Harvard University Press.
Peck, J. (2001) *Workfare States*, Guilford Press.
Peele, G. (2005) 'Electoral Politics, Ideology and American Social Policy', *Social Policy and Administration*, 39(2), pp. 150–65.
Peters, B. G. (2005) 'I'm OK, You're (not) OK: the Private Welfare State in the USA', *Social Policy and Administration*, 39(2), pp. 166–80.
Phillips, K. (1993) *Boiling Point*, Random House.
Pierson, C. (1990) 'The Exceptional United States: First New Nation or Last Welfare State?', *Social Policy and Administration*, 24(3), pp. 168–98.
Piven, F. F., (1998) 'Welfare and Electoral Politics', in C. Y. H. Lo and M. Schwartz (eds), *Social Policy and the Conservative Agenda*, Blackwell.
Piven, F. F. and Cloward, R. (1993) *Regulating the Poor: The Functions of Public Welfare*, 2nd edn, Vintage Books.
Pollin, R. (1998) 'Living Wage, Live Action', *The Nation*, 23 November.
Quadagno, J. (1994) *The Color of Welfare: How Racism Undermined the War on Poverty*, Oxford University Press.
Saloma, J. S. (1984) *Ominous Politics: the New Conservative Labyrinth*, Hill & Wang.
Schram, S. and Soss, J. (2002) 'Success Stories: Welfare Reform, Policy Discourse and the Politics of Research', in S. Schram, *Praxis for the Poor*, New York University Press.
Schuck, P. H. (1998), 'The Open Society', *New Republic*, 13 April.
Skocpol, T. (1992) *Protecting Soldiers and Mothers: The Political Origins of Social Security in the United States*, The Belknap Press of Harvard University Press.
Skocpol, T. (1997) *Boomerang: Health Care Reform and the Turn Against Government*, 2nd edn, W. W. Norton and Company.
Skocpol, T. and Ikenberry, J. (1983) 'The Political Formation of the Welfare State. An Historical and Comparative Perspective', in R. F. Tomasson (ed.), *Comparative Social Research*, 6, Jai Press.
Solow, R. (1998) *New Yorker Review*, 5 November.
Stacey, J. (1998) 'The Right Family Values', in C. Y. H. Lo and M. Schwartz (eds), *op. cit.*
Staples, C. (1989) 'The Politics of Employment-based Insurance in the United States', *International Journal of Health Services*, 19(3).
Starr, P. (1982) *The Social Transformation of American Medicine*, Basic Books.
Stern, M. (1998) 'A Semi-Tough Policy on Illegal Workers', *The Washington Post National Weekly Edition*, 13 July.
Tanner, M. (1996) *The End of Welfare: Fighting Poverty in the Civil Society*, The Cato Institute.
West, G. (1981) *The National Welfare Rights Movement: The Social Protest of Poor Women*, Praeger.
Wohl, S. (1984) *The Medical-Industrial Complex*, Harmony Books.

CHAPTER 3

Canada: One Step Forward, Two Steps Back?

ERNIE S. LIGHTMAN AND GRAHAM RICHES

Introduction

In the early 1900s, Wilfrid Laurier, the Prime Minister of Canada stated that 'the twentieth century belongs to Canada'. Few would have challenged him, for Canada had seemingly infinite natural resources in great demand in the USA, Europe and (in later years) the countries of the Pacific Rim; there was an endless supply of hard-working, white immigrants mainly from Central and Northern Europe, bringing with them traditions of self-help and social solidarity; railways had been laid to link the vast reaches of the country from one side of the continent to the other; and Canada was at peace with its only land-based neighbour, a relationship certain to grow closer with the passing years.

The century, as it evolved, did not prove Laurier entirely correct. Though the natural resources generated massive wealth for some, at the beginning of the twenty-first century much of this wealth is draining abroad as Canada's natural resources are now largely foreign-owned: world economies have substantially shifted from a resource base to an information and technology base, areas in which Canada has no particular comparative advantage; immigration through the century shifted to include many new arrivals from the Third World, resulting in racial problems previously unanticipated; aboriginal peoples (both First Nations and Inuit) neither assimilated into the mainstream nor died off, but instead remained in poverty and squalor, with average life expectancies of about 35 years, glaring testimonies to the worst excesses of capitalist exploitation; intimacy with the USA proved a mixed blessing, at best, as resources and jobs flowed south and cultural/political/military domination came north.

Social solidarity in Canada was increasingly replaced by a Darwinian individualism and belief in the unconstrained market. Since the early 1980s, charitable food banks have become the main response to growing hunger, particularly among children; women's rights have been seriously eroded through cuts to childcare and equity programmes; and in 2007 homelessness in major cities such as Toronto and Vancouver, to say nothing of the housing blight in First Nations and northern Inuit communities, remains a national disgrace.

The twentieth century produced considerable aggregate economic well-being for Canada, but the equity – the distribution of the spoils of this growth – proved far less acceptable. A recent United Nations Report (UNDP, 2006, p. 283) ranked Canada sixth among 21 developed countries in terms of its Human Development Index (HDI) for 2004, a decline from first place in 1995. Canada also placed sixth on the Human Poverty Index (HPI) for OECD countries, Central and Eastern Europe and the CIS (UNDP, 2006, p. 295). In other words, Canada was a great place to live, but not for the poor or marginalized. Despite a decade of massive federal budget surpluses (projected at C$10.8 billion for 2007–8, *Economic and Fiscal Update*, Canada 2006), the disparities between the haves and have-nots have clearly been widening in the face of radically neo-conservative governments in several provinces, and the election of a minority conservative Federal government in 2006.

In the past, the most serious threat to Canada, however, did not emerge from the growing economic disparities between rich and poor. Rather, Canada's very existence as a country came under fundamental challenge because of the separatist movement in the largely French-speaking province of Quebec. The most recent referendum on separation in Quebec voted against secession from Canada by the narrowest of margins (50.4 per cent to stay: and among the French-speaking population there was a clear majority in favour of separation). Though the threat of separation by Quebec has been present at least since the first election of a separatist provincial government in 1976, and though separatism seems relatively dormant today, the broader issue of conflict between the federal government and the provinces has been pervasive throughout Canada's history. To understand Canada, and the past and future of Canadian social welfare in particular, it is essential to plunge into the muddy waters of federalism, of federal-provincial agreements and conflicts, of shared and joint and exclusive responsibility for the delivery of various social programmes and of restricted and unlimited access to the tax base.

Overview

In framing the *British North America Act* (1867), the Fathers of Confederation in Canada, unlike the architects of the US constitution a century earlier, opted for a highly centralized federal state. High on their agenda was the economic development of the vast country, and to attain this goal efficiently most powers would be lodged at the central level. Thus the federal government was given unlimited powers of taxation, while the provinces were restricted to certain enumerated categories of 'direct' taxes;

service-delivery responsibilities of the federal government were substantial (within the context of what a government was expected to do in 1867), while the provinces had much more limited tasks to perform. Just as the passage of time, reinforced by court interpretations, reversed the original intentions for the American federal system, so too a series of early Canadian Supreme Court decisions headed it in the direction of a highly decentralized federal state. This resulted in provinces having exclusive jurisdiction (formally at least) over the social policy arena which barely existed in the early years of the century and which has shown exponential growth over the years.

However, there are significant differences between the provinces. Oil-rich Alberta, heavily influenced by immigration from the USA, manifests residual and market-based approaches to social welfare. Conversely, the neighbouring province of Saskatchewan, settled by European immigrants, has reflected social democratic ideals; Quebec's social policy prior to the 1960s was dominated by the Church, while today the state is a significant force in health, income security and social services. Today Quebec has a very exciting programme of universal day care at a cost of C$7.00 a day, while Ottawa has ended funding for publicly and non-profit childcare in favour of for-profit services. In more recent years, the need to placate separatist tendencies in Quebec (by showing how national and cultural aspirations of the French-speaking population could be satisfied while remaining in Canada) has led to what some today would suggest is the world's most decentralized but still functioning federal state.

Thus, there emerged over time the central, recurring and fundamental dilemma of social policy in Canada: the imbalance between fiscal capacity and responsibility for the delivery of services in a federal state. Today, social policy, including health and post-secondary education comprises the largest share of governmental fiscal responsibility in Canada: but the provinces lack the necessary tax base to pay the bills. The result has been a series of creative, often acrimonious, frustrating and seemingly permanent federal–provincial negotiations, leading to tax-sharing arrangements, shared-cost programmes and even constitutional amendments. The most recent of these ritual dances – labelled the 'Social Union' talks – was met with massive public indifference in 1999, as the federal and provincial governments attempted to disentangle their respective areas of in terms of both service delivery and fiscal capacity. While a full historical understanding of Canadian social welfare state would require a review of provincial, municipal and First Nations social programme developments, we focus principally on federal social policy, primarily concerned with developments in the field of income security (see Box 3.1) and health care (Box 3.2).

Esping-Andersen has located Canada within the cluster of liberal welfare state regimes, along with the USA and Australia, in contrast to the corporatist cluster comprising Austria, France, Germany and Italy, and the social democratic grouping of the Scandinavian countries (1990). This 'liberal' categorization of Canada is in many ways correct. Yet, it is important to note that post-Second World War, at least until 1988 when the North American Free Trade Agreement (NAFTA) began to bind Canada and the USA more closely together, Canada's more collectivist social policies (such as family allowances, old-age security, medicare) set it apart from its more individualist and residual neighbour to the south. Indeed Lightman (1991) documents identifiable differences in attitudes to the welfare state between Canada and the USA, though he expresses apprehension about whether these differences would be sustainable over time in a context of free trade between the two countries, concerns that have been well-founded.

The Early Years to 1945

In the years after Confederation, there was little role for government except to promote the economic development of the vast frontier. Social needs, when they were acknowledged, would be met by voluntary and charitable, often church-based, local organizations. Customs and excise duties were the main source of government revenue, and it was not until the First World War that the first personal income tax was introduced, a 'temporary, emergency measure', which was never removed. The first system of workers' compensation was introduced (1914 in Ontario) as an employer-funded and -operated programme; employees were denied the common law right to sue for job-related injuries; instead, payments were allocated administratively.

The Great Depression hit Canada hard, as foreign markets for the natural resources (wheat, fish, minerals, wood and paper) largely disappeared. By the end of the 1930s, unemployment was so severe that a national unemployment insurance scheme became necessary. Only the federal

Box 3.1 Income Security

(All federal schemes unless noted otherwise)

Early Development

Income maintenance developed with an employer-funded workers' compensation scheme in 1914 covering most of the paid labour force. In

(*continued*)

(*Box 3.1 continued*)

the 1940s, following the UK Beveridge model, insurance-based schemes were introduced, including:

- Unemployment insurance, funded jointly by employers and employees – frequent eligibility changes; replaced by Employment Insurance (see below);
- Family allowances (non-contributory) for all children, funded from general taxation;
- Old-age security pensions, also funded from general taxation.

High Tide (1960s)

Further developments included:

- Canada Pension Plan (1965), contributory premiums for all earners; pay-as-you-go replaced by fuller funding in 1998);
- Canada Assistance Plan (1966), basic public assistance, based on determination of need, funded by taxation jointly from federal and provincial governments;
- Guaranteed Income Supplement (1967), means-tested benefit for poor elderly, funded from general taxation.

A Period of Increasing Selectivity and Steady Cuts (1970s onwards)

- Child Tax Credit (1978) and Canada Child Tax Benefit (1998), for children in low-income families, funded from general taxation and delivered through tax system; CCTB for working poor only; and the Universal Child Care Benefit (2006) which replaced the former Liberal government's proposed national and universal childcare programme;
- Registered Retirement Savings Plans, for those with taxable income: pensions for higher earners, highly regressive;
- Employment Insurance, limited scheme, funded 60:40 between employers and employees;
- Canada Health and Social Transfer (1996) provides block funding to provinces, resulting in sharp cutbacks in provincial social assistance programmes.

Box 3.2 Health and Social Services

- These areas are constitutionally the responsibility of the provincial governments, though there is usually a federal role in funding and, at times, in setting Canada-wide standards for service delivery.
- Service delivery is a provincial responsibility though this can be devolved to municipalities, voluntary agencies or NGOs, and/or to the commercial (for-profit) sector.
- Variations across provinces in the sharing among government, voluntary and commercial sectors are substantial and cannot be readily summarized, except to note that the neo-conservative provinces (mainly Alberta) tend to rely most on the commercial sector; others use a mix; while in Quebec the state has traditionally assumed an active role, viewed as an agent of nation-building.

Education – a provincial responsibility with major federal financial support for post-secondary education and manpower training. Federal support was cut with the introduction of the Canada Health and Social Transfer (CHST) in 1996.

Health: Hospital Insurance – since 1954, this covers all (non-physician) insured health services in hospitals. Financing varies across provinces, usually based on general taxation revenues with some element of premiums in certain provinces.

Health: Physician Services – since 1966, all insured health services, including doctors, are covered in a universal health-care programme for all residents, with no user fees or other charges at the point of use. Coverage is portable (from province to province) and administered by a public non-profit agency in each province. The definition of 'insured services' varies across provinces and there are differences in financing including premiums, payroll taxes and (primarily) general revenues.

Royal Commission on the Future of Health Care in Canada (2002) – This report proposed sweeping changes to ensure the long-term sustainability of Canada's health-care system including a *Canada Health Covenant*, updating of the *Canada Health Act* (1984), an established funding base and targeted funding (rural and remote access, diagnostic services, primary health care, home care and catastrophic drugs) and proposals regarding the integration of priority home-care services, waiting list management and a national personal electronic health record system. The overall intention of the Commission's recommendations, otherwise

(*continued*)

(*Box 3.2 continued*)

known as the Romanow Report after the commissioner and former premier of Saskatchewan, was to preserve the universality and integrity of Canada's health-care system.

Personal Social Services (family services; childcare; youth services; home care) – also a provincial responsibility with federal financial support, often on a project or area basis. Substantial devolution to municipalities, NGOs, voluntary agencies and the commercial sector, which varies across provinces depending on factors such as ideology and local fiscal capacity. No summary data are available.

Housing – until the 1990s there was always a major federal role, primarily in the financing area. In the last few years, Ottawa (home of the federal government) has ceded this area to the provinces. The result has been a dramatic increase in homelessness, Canada-wide, and in many provinces a complete end to the construction of co-op, non-profit and low-income housing. Recent bilateral agreements with the majority of provinces suggest a more active federal funding role in support of affordable housing.

Immigration – this is an area of shared federal–provincial responsibility, though only Quebec has chosen to assume an active role as it seeks to ensure a large French-speaking population in that province. Other provinces rely largely on federal decision-making.

First Nation Peoples – Inuit and status Indians hold a sovereign status and attempt to negotiate with the federal government as equals, as sovereign peoples with Aboriginal rights and treaties. They formally refuse to deal with provincial governments, though there is some involvement with the delivery of personal social services. Metis (mixed French-Aboriginal) peoples also claim Aboriginal rights by virtue of their share in Indian Title.

government had the capacity (and the interest) to develop such a programme, but employment was deemed to be within provincial jurisdiction: the solution was to enact a formal constitutional amendment (which, at the time, had to be formally passed as a statute by the British Parliament), so that today unemployment insurance remains the only significant social programme exclusively within federal jurisdiction. The first Canadian unemployment insurance programme became law in 1940. This period reflected a limited role for the state and a primary reliance on the church and voluntary sector.

Postwar: The Influence of Keynes and Beveridge

As elsewhere, the Great Depression did not simply 'burn out', ending on its own. The onset of the Second World War gave policy-makers everywhere a clear example of how government spending could draw a country (or a world!) out of recession. The ideas of Keynes seemingly worked in practice, as unemployment disappeared almost overnight. As the war began to wind down and Germany's defeat appeared inevitable, policy-makers in Canada began to fear for the postwar period. There was a concern that with the end of government spending on war-related matters, aggregate demand would decline and the country would slip back into recession. In 1943, the Report on Social Security in Canada (known as the Marsh Report after its author who was both a colleague of Beveridge and a disciple of Keynes) was released. It represented, in modified form, Canada's own version of the Beveridge Report (Canada, 1943). While it was not as comprehensive as its British counterpart, it nevertheless firmly placed Canada in the Keynes–Beveridge tradition.

In part to ensure the adequacy of consumer demand in the postwar period, 1945 saw the introduction of Canada's Family Allowance (FA) programme, a universal non-taxable monthly payment to the mother for every child (to age 16). This was followed in 1952 by Old Age Security (OAS), a universal, non-taxable monthly payment to every senior over the age of 65 who met a residence (but not a citizenship) requirement. These two federal programmes, together with the Unemployment Insurance scheme and the National Housing Act of 1944, formed the foundation of Canada's welfare state.

Family Allowances

The family allowance programme was of limited importance operationally, as monthly payments were small to begin with and were not increased regularly thereafter. The major importance of the programme was perhaps symbolic, in that it spoke to universality, social solidarity and the legitimacy of claims upon the state to assist in the costs of rearing children. In 1984, when Brian Mulroney led the Conservative Party in the federal election, he ran on a mildly anti-welfare platform, making great rhetorical statements about the waste involved when his personal banker received a government cheque each month. Women's groups, in particular, pointed out that the cheque was payable to the banker's wife, rather than the banker, and thus helped, in a modest way, to redress income and power imbalances within families. A later book, entitled *The Wealthy Banker's Wife* (McQuaig, 1993), documented in some detail the extent of financial benefits delivered to upper income groups in Canada through the tax system. It made the simple point that relatively few dollars every month directed to children were trivial alongside the other substantial advantages that a regressive tax system provided to the rich. When the Family Allowance programme was terminated by Mulroney in 1992, replaced by a means-tested child benefit, the maximum monthly payment per child was hardly enough to make a significant impact upon a family's living standard.

Old Age Security

In contrast to FA, OAS was built on the assumption that many seniors had no personal savings or other sources of income, and that they would be completely financially dependent upon the monthly government cheque. The amounts were more substantial than the Family Allowances and provided an income that was almost sufficient to live on. There has always been considerable political support for this programme: though its net benefit was reduced in later years by making payments taxable, a major government initiative fundamentally to revamp the programme was suddenly abandoned in 1998 when it was clear that public support was not there. The proposals were badly designed in that the targeting to the poor came at the expense of the middle class and the benefits were to be based on family, rather than individual, incomes, thereby reinforcing woman's traditional financial dependence upon the male earner. But, arguably, the OAS programme was also seen as important in its own right, with many seniors arguing the case for social rights and entitlements. The postwar years witnessed an increasing role for the state, with heavy reliance on the voluntary sector.

1965–73: High Points of Welfare State Development

Canada reached the high point in its welfare state development during the 1960s. Three important pieces of legislation, within a two-year period, formed the reference point against which all subsequent retrenchments may be assessed. Except only for an expansion of the unemployment insurance scheme in 1971, virtually all social policy activity since 1973 has consisted of cutting benefits, restricting entitlements and narrowing the boundaries of the public sector.

Canada Pension Plan

The Canada Pension Plan (CPP, 1965), the Canada Assistance Plan (CAP, 1966) and Medicare (1966) were the three landmark programmes of the federal government. CPP, whose introduction was strenuously opposed by private insurance lobbies, was a contributory (employer and employee equally) earnings-related, occupationally based pension scheme for those in the paid workforce. The ceiling for maximum contributions was reached at a relatively low level of earnings, meaning that the greatest benefit was derived by the lower middle classes. The programme included a disability pension (Canada's only system of publicly administered disability insurance), child and survivor benefits and a small death benefit.

Because the government wished the initial benefits to be available quickly, CPP was largely funded on a pay-as-you-go scheme, in which premiums are credited to general government revenues and current benefits are paid from the same source. This approach stands in contrast to building a fund, as is done with private insurance: Quebec, which chose to operate its own parallel Quebec Pension Plan, used the funded approach which today has yielded massive revenues, invested for public social purposes.

It should be noted that, in 1967, the Guaranteed Income Supplement (GIS) was introduced as an add-on to OAS for those seniors who had not paid into the CPP scheme and lacked private resources. The GIS was means-tested and based on family rather than individual income; this typically disadvantaged women as their independent access to financial support was replaced with a dependence on the income of the male wage-earner in the household. Though the importance of the ideological shift in moving from the universal entitlements of the OAS to the Poor Law tradition embedded in the GIS should not be underestimated, the two programmes together have largely served their intended purpose. Today, serious poverty among seniors is relatively rare in Canada, compared to most countries.

However, during the 1990s a crisis emerged with respect to anticipated future payments out of CPP, resulting from a major demographic bulge as the postwar 'baby boomers' approached retirement. The numbers expected to claim CPP in the early years of the next century would place a massive financial burden on a decreasing labour force, which would have to pay for the benefits out of current taxation. The year 1999 saw a major increase in CPP premiums, and further options now being considered include raising more money (for example through further increases in premiums or raising the ceiling on covered earnings) or decreasing future payouts (by decreasing payments or by delaying the age of retirement, both of which are probably politically unacceptable). While some have even called for the abolition of CPP and its replacement by compulsory, tax-supported private savings schemes in which people would have greater control over the investment possibilities for their 'own' contributions, the CPP does now appear to be in a more secure position.

According to Denison, CEO of the Canada Pension Plan Investment Board, its assets today are worth more than C$110 billion with its investment programme producing investment income of more than C$41 billion for the CPP fund. In the past four years its annualized real rate of return was

11.5 per cent, which according to Canada's Chief Actuary is comfortably above a long-term 4.2 per cent real rate of return (AARP International, 2007).

Canada Assistance Plan

The second Act, the Canada Assistance Plan (CAP) stands as one of the most progressive pieces of social legislation in Canadian history, a prime example of cooperative federalism. CAP constituted the basic public assistance programme, the final and ultimate safety net, and also provided federal funding to support the development of provincial personal social services, including child welfare. Ottawa, wishing to act in this area, offered to cost-share with the provinces provided they met certain basic conditions (set by Ottawa). The federal government would pay 50 per cent of all eligible provincial expenditures on public relief, without absolute limit. These national standards (as they are known) included eligibility for assistance based solely upon a determination of need; the right to income in any province without a minimum residence requirement; and the right to appeal. The provinces were given considerable latitude in assessing whether an individual was, in fact, 'in need', but once this condition was satisfied no further barriers could be imposed upon the receipt of benefits. This meant, in practice, that receipt of public assistance could not be conditional upon the performance of any task (such as workfare or enrolment in a training programme).

The right to benefit was absolute and unconditional. In practice, however, provinces used their discretion to determine whether an individual was 'in need' as a way of separating the deserving from the undeserving claimants and the adequacy of provincial welfare benefits have remained a contentious issue. They have always fallen well below Statistics Canada's low income cutoffs ('poverty lines').

Almost immediately upon enactment, CAP became a source of controversy. Critics on the right attacked its allegedly generous eligibility terms, arguing for a tougher and more punitive American-style welfare programme. Far more significant, however, was the opposition to CAP from within the federal bureaucracy. Senior Department of Finance officials did not like the open-ended federal financial obligation: for planning purposes, it was difficult to prepare the annual federal budget without knowing the final total obligation for CAP until after the end of the fiscal year when the provincial bills were submitted for reimbursement. (Federal scrutiny of eligible provincial expenditure was also weak, or perhaps non-existent, from an auditing perspective.) Thus, virtually from day one, the Finance Department began its quest to eliminate CAP, a task made more difficult by the belief that though CAP was a piece of federal legislation, most believed it could only be altered with the unanimous consent of all provinces. While CAP was under constant scrutiny, it survived relatively unscathed until 1991 when, as part of a federal expenditure control programme and at a time of high unemployment resulting in great demands on CAP, Ottawa unilaterally imposed an absolute ceiling on the dollars it would contribute in the three wealthier provinces of Ontario, British Columbia and Alberta. In these three settings, the federal contribution dropped well below the 50 per cent level specified in CAP – to 32 per cent in Ontario in 1991–2 (Graham and Lightman, 1992). Court action determined that the federal government had the unilateral right to alter its own legislation and that there was no legal obligation to secure provincial approval.

In 1996, the Department of Finance finally got its way when, as a result of the Canada Health and Social Transfer (CHST), CAP was abolished and replaced by per capita, essentially unconditional, grants to the provinces as part of a major restructuring of federal–provincial fiscal relations. The end of the conditions for federal payment to CAP meant the provinces were now free to 'experiment' with American-style welfare reform and new ways to deliver public assistance. While Alberta and Saskatchewan had experimented with workfare – work as a condition of receiving assistance – by the late 1990s, such programmes became established across the country. There is no evidence that workfare actually created jobs or even improved employability on a wide scale, but rather the programme served a largely symbolic purpose, a punitive and inefficient exercise carried out on the backs of the poor (Shragge, 1997).

Currently, there is important advocacy led by the Canadian Council on Social Development, to introduce a Canada Social Transfer with earmarked funds and conditions for social programmes including welfare. If enacted, such social spending would not be lost by the provinces as they respond to the more politically driven health and post-secondary education demands of the wider public. However, in the current political climate it is difficult to see the introduction of such a measure.

Medicare

The real jewel in the social policy crown of the 1960s was Medicare, involving a uniquely Canadian approach towards ensuring universal health care. Though many Canadian social programmes were built upon early British experiences, the NHS model was deemed unacceptable for Canada, in part because of the even greater political power of the Canadian medical profession and its linkages with more extreme US medical lobbies. The Canadian story began in 1954 when hospital health care was provided without user charge. Because virtually all hospitals were publicly owned and operated on a not-for-profit basis, there was little organized opposition to the early moves – particularly as physicians continued to be paid on a fee-for-service basis and their perks were not touched. By the 1960s, however, it was clear that free (at the point of use) health care in hospitals induced people to use that high-cost mode of service provision compared to less costly alternatives in the community (such as visiting a doctor's office).

In 1962, in the face of a doctors' strike, Saskatchewan introduced Canada's, indeed North America's, first medical insurance scheme. The scheme proved successful and the Royal Commission on Health Services Report (Canada 1964) led to the introduction in 1966 of Medicare across the country. For jurisdictional reasons, Ottawa's role was limited to sharing costs with the provinces, though in this case there were five key principles to be honoured in order to secure federal monies: universal access; public administration; no user fees; portability; and comprehensive coverage. While Medicare since its inception has enjoyed considerable public support, there have been continuing pressures favouring privatization. In 1984 the Canada Health Act was introduced with the intent of safeguarding Medicare from the threat of user fees/extra-billing. More recently, since 1995, Medicare has again come under serious attack largely because of federal and provincial underfunding. However, Ottawa has consistently used its cost-sharing powers to withhold payments from provinces that were not in compliance with Medicare's five principles. In the end, the provinces inevitably fall into line.

The release in 2002 of the report of the Royal Commission on the Future of Health Care in Canada (see Box 3.2) was a response to continuing public uncertainty about the future of universal health care in Canada. While the Romanow report rejected the privatization of the health-care system, there remains a strong lobby led by the President of the Canadian Medical Association to introduce privatized medicine. Indeed, in 2005, the Supreme Court of Canada in a split 4:3 decision ruled that the Quebec government could not disallow people from using private insurance to pay for health-care procedures under Medicare. The debate about public versus market models of health care remains very much alive.

Unemployment Insurance Expansion

By 1970, it was clear that many Canadians still fell through gaps in the income security net, but that substantial expansion of CAP was neither feasible nor desirable. As a result, the Minister responsible for Unemployment Insurance (UI) developed a major expansion of that programme: generous maternity benefits were introduced and, perhaps more importantly, seasonal benefits were introduced: many industries in Canada have very short seasonal work periods through the year. Fishing in the Atlantic region, for example, can occur for as few as 10 or 12 weeks (due to the hostile climate), and there are few alternative sources of regional employment for the rest of the year. Logging is often subject to similar seasonal limitations. The 1971 UI amendments drastically reduced the number of weeks of work required to qualify to as few as 12, depending on the regional unemployment rate. The result was a famous 12/40 scheme, in which some people contributed to UI for 12 weeks and drew benefits for the remaining 40. In effect, whatever actuarial or insurance base UI may originally have had was replaced with an income redistribution focus in which the wealthier provinces transferred funds (through UI premiums) to poorer provinces (where benefits dramatically exceeded contributions). The 1965–73 period proved to be that of maximum state involvement, with a more limited role for the voluntary and private sectors, especially in health care.

Cutting Back: The Arab Oil Embargo and After

Canada's welfare state was at its most fully developed during that period to 1973. Since then, it has been a story of continuing cutbacks and a slow decline from institutional to residual arrangements. Though Canada was at least self-sufficient in oil, on a net basis, prices were those of the world markets, set by the multinational companies. Thus Canada was fully affected by the huge increases in world oil prices. Many social benefits and other government spending were indexed to the rate of inflation, and thus overall nominal public sector spending rose rapidly. Revenues, however, did not increase commensurately, as this was the era in which Ottawa discovered the beauty of tax expenditure. Exemptions, deductions, credits and other measures to reduce tax liability began to proliferate through personal and corporate tax systems: through them government was able to target tax relief very specifically without the visibility associated with direct government spending. Tax revenues consequently lagged behind spending; substantial deficits began to accumulate, steadily increasing the total public debt.

A major review of the social services was begun in the early 1970s, a process that involved extensive consultation with stakeholders. However, in 1976, the election of an avowedly separatist government in Quebec threw all the planning into disarray. Federal Prime Minister Trudeau, an implacable foe of the provincial government, was determined to show Quebec that their national aspirations could be met within a decentralized Canadian federal state. As a result, the social service review was aborted and, in 1978, Established Programs Financing (EPF) was put forward as Ottawa's answer to separatism. This Act combined all federal contributions in three areas of hospital care, Medicare and post-secondary education into one lump sum block grant to each province, to be given annually with an automatic escalator provision based on factors such as population change. There were few conditions attached to the use of the funds (except continuing adherence to the principles of Medicare and a requirement that the funds be spent in the three designated areas). In this way, provinces were given considerable discretion over the allocation of federal (and provincial) monies and were thereby encouraged to determine their own priorities.

There was fear, however, within the social policy community of a possible displacement effect by the provinces, through which the EPF dollars would be spent in the designated areas, but other provincial discretionary money would be reallocated away to other areas (such as building highways): there was no federal requirement that total provincial spending in the three areas would be required to increase, or even remain constant.

A Fuller Assault: The Mid-1990s

Talk of the importance of deficit reduction continued through the Mulroney years, but it was not until the Liberals returned to power 1993 that action began in earnest. Reducing the federal deficit to zero was deemed essential to retain the confidence of the business community, domestically and abroad. This was to be achieved through a fundamental restructuring, downsizing and downloading of federal social policy responsibilities.

In 1996, CAP was terminated; with it went the conditions for federal cost-sharing and national welfare standards. Ottawa's payments to the provinces for CAP were combined with the EPF monies to produce a single lump sum annually, known as the Canada Health and Social Transfer (CHST). There were virtually no federal restrictions on the use of this money, except for continuing adherence to Medicare principles. However, in the process of combining the various payments, Ottawa also moved to reduce its total fiscal contributions, so that CHST actually entailed a very substantial decrease of C$6 billion in federal transfers to the provinces. In addition, the provinces were now free to cut back on welfare (formerly delivered through CAP and subject to a variety of conditions) and to introduce programmes such as workfare for claimants. Some of the provinces, such as wealthy Ontario, now ruled by a neo-conservative government, piggybacked their own cuts onto federal cuts to social programmes. At the time it was feared that battles for funding among the areas covered by the CHST would advantage the politically powerful (Medicare and the doctors' lobbies) at the expense of the weaker and less popular areas (assistance for the poor) (Torjman and Battle, 1995).

The federal government also terminated its extensive involvement in social housing. Ontario followed suit, also withdrawing and downloading all responsibility for social housing to the municipalities; these were clearly incapable of responding given their limited tax bases. Major changes also occurred to the unemployment insurance programme in 1997. Now renamed Employment Insurance (EI), benefit levels were cut modestly, and eligibility tightened dramatically. Whereas in the early 1990s, over 80 per cent of unemployed persons received benefits from UI, after the reforms less than one-third of the same population qualified for EI. For many years earlier, premiums had increased regularly, and the UI fund built up a surplus far in excess of what might be required in times of serious recession: each year the Finance Minister made a bookkeeping transfer of the UI surplus into general revenues, and so was able to use the money to reduce the deficit. The struggle was ultimately successful, and the last federal budget of the century was the first in many years to produce a budgetary surplus, thanks in part to the appropriation of the UI/EI surpluses over many years.

Since then, as noted previously, there has not been a federal budget without a massive surplus. Canada's failure to make a significant reduction in the 15 per cent rate of child poverty in 2005 – it ranked 19th out of 26 OECD countries studied (UNICEF 2005) – or to close the growing income gap between rich and poor has not been dictated by budget shortfalls, but rather by deliberate policy choice. Indeed as the UNICEF study states, variation in government policy appears to account for most of the differences in child poverty levels between OECD countries (Torjman and Battle, 1995).

The Long Road Back: Towards and into the New Century

Three new federal initiatives emerged in the last years of the twentieth century, all in response to the extreme cuts earlier imposed through the CHST.

Millennium Scholarship Fund

As part of a millennium effort to improve access to higher education in Canada, the Prime Minister announced substantial new funding for a federal scholarship fund. The details were consciously vague, but the scheme was presented in a context of future human capital investment. Though the provinces had been informed of the plan in advance, they were not were really consulted at this intrusion into their constitutional domain, and argued that they wanted to control the money, to direct as they saw fit within the realm of higher education. The scholarship fund was never presented as part of a comprehensive strategic government review of Canadian higher education funding, but was widely seen as simply a federal attempt to solve a problem by throwing money at it. The government soon went on to new issues, believing that it had now 'solved' a major problem of inadequate investment in Canada's human capital.

Canada Child Tax Credit (CCTC)

In 1998, a Canada Child Tax Credit (CCTC) was introduced, the first substantial new social programme in over a decade. The federal programme, developed in conjunction with the provinces, was targeted specifically at the working, rather than the welfare, poor. It was designed to replace a variety of previous federal child-focused initiatives. As with the previous RCTC, eligibility was to be determined and payments to be delivered through the income tax system. Maximum payments were to go to the very poor, with a tapered reduction as earned income increased. Although payments were to be made to all low-income households, provinces were permitted to reduce welfare payments, dollar for dollar, provided the funds would be reinvested in child-focused programmes such as expanded childcare; the working poor, by contrast, would suffer no income reductions and would be better off as a result of the programme. The payment amounts were sufficiently large that within a few years it was anticipated that most poor children in Canada would be supported through the CCTC and would be removed from the welfare rolls. The two major criticisms of the programme were that there was no benefit for families on welfare (who, arguably, needed the most help), and there were no meaningful measures to ensure appropriate provincial reinvestment of the funds clawed back from those on welfare.

Health Care

Federal discussions concerning a national pharmacare plan (Canadian prescription drug prices being among the highest in the world) and a coherent system of home care, in the face of hospital and institutional closures and an ageing population, were brought forward. The provinces wanted no part of these schemes, but instead wanted the money back that had been removed with the introduction of the CHST. Ottawa, for its part, was ready to invest in health care out of its newly discovered surplus, but did not trust the provinces – particularly extreme neo-conservative Alberta and Ontario – to spend the money 'appropriately'. There followed an extremely complex set of negotiations, which were under pressure to deliver, as inadequate access to health care was now ranked by polls as Canadians' top concern. Leading contenders for the prime ministership all felt the need to highlight social agendas.

Failing the Most Vulnerable

In the early years of the twenty-first century, the outlook for progressive social policy remains uncertain at best and bleak at worst, and especially for Canada's most vulnerable populations. On the brighter side it can be claimed that the Canada Pension Plan is now in a more secure position, which is no doubt satisfying to ageing baby boomers. Also it can perhaps be said there is growing attention to the supply of social housing and a recognition that the issues of homelessness and mental illness are inextricably linked. Yet for children the continuing lack of a national childcare plan remains an affront to women who must work outside the home to ensure bread is on the table. Disturbingly 824,000 people turned to charitable food on a monthly basis in 2005, an increase of 24 per cent since 1997 and 118 per cent since 1989 when such data was first collected. Forty one per cent of food bank users are children and young people (CAFB, 2005). In 2001 the *Canadian Community Health Survey* reported 3.7 million Canadians (15 per cent of the population) living in food-insecure households, while a more restrictive CHHS survey conducted in 2004 reported a figure of 2.1 million hungry Canadians or 6.8 per cent of the population (Tarasuk and Power, 2006). As the state has turned away, charity has moved to fill the gap but is often unable to cope (Riches, 2006).

In short, the basic human needs of food, clothing and shelter are being neglected by the state, which continues to act in violation of its obligation under international law as ratified in the ICESCR and the CRC. In May 2006 the UN Committee on Economic, Social and Cultural Rights noted 23 areas in which Canada and the provinces were in domestic non-compliance with their obligations including lack of legal redress available to individuals when governments fail to implement the Covenant; absence of an official poverty line; insufficiency of minimum wage and social assistance benefits; failure to include domestic violence as a specific offence in the criminal code; high level of food bank usage due to insufficient social assistance; and the fact that the Federal Government, in its Fifth Periodic Report to the UN Committee, provided insufficient evidence indicating that the National Homelessness initiative was achieving success. Estimates of homelessness in Canada today range from 100,000 to 250,000 people (UNESC, 2006).

Future Prospects: Government as Dilettante

It is difficult to look to the future with much optimism about the prospects for Canadian social policy. Universality is seriously wounded, if not dead, and residual welfarism rules. The rise and institutionalization of food banks are at once symptoms of the breakdown of the social safety net (in terms of the gaping holes left by the changes made to unemployment insurance and public assistance) and symbols of this new residualism and lack of regard for the citizenship rights of the poor and vulnerable, many of whom are women and children (Riches, 1997). Hunger, homelessness, child poverty, unemployment and the continuing exclusion of First Nations peoples, crowd the social policy agenda.

There is a deep irony in all of this, given the introduction of the Charter of Rights and Freedoms in 1982 and the ratification by Canada over the years of a number of United Nations human rights conventions. These include the 1976 ICESCR and the 1991CRC, which commit governments, internationally and domestically, to respect, protect and fulfil their obligations to meet basic human needs and assert the rights of their peoples. However, the fact is that over the past two decades, Canada's social policy landscape is littered with cutbacks and denials of entitlements. It has truly been a case of one step forward, two steps back.

Through the 1990s, the justification for the cuts was based on economic imperatives, the need to reduce the debt and balance the budget; by 1998 the federal budget acknowledged the end of deficits and the arrival of an era of surpluses. This then loosened the gates on more overtly ideological debates about the future of Canadian social policy, debates certain to continue well into the future. Some have argued that surpluses should be directed towards reducing the aggregate debt, a rather pointless exercise given that it is really only the carrying costs on the debt that are relevant for policy purposes (Mendelson, 1998). The more crucial debates are between the desirability of tax reductions, inevitably regressive in impact, and social reinvestment of the surpluses to rebuild the infrastructure – both human and physical capital – decimated in the last decades. But the debate may well be an uneven struggle: of the five parties currently in the House of Commons, none is prepared unambiguously to argue the case for social investment, and two parties at least are reaching for the far right end of the political continuum. Over a decade of free trade with the USA (since 1988) has not produced clear economic gains to the majority of the population, but the greater intimacy has led to increased cultural domination and hegemony: classic American values of extreme individualism and reliance upon voluntary charities combined with the unpaid labour of women in the home are now promoted as legitimate and appropriate paths to Canada's future. The early British welfare state legacy is fading fast, if it has not already disappeared. Homogeneity in the message of the media is virtually complete with quasi-monopolistic control of the newspaper industry and little to choose among the radio and television options.

The transition in Canada from a modest welfare state to a more market-oriented society occurred quickly and with little debate. The shift has largely been from government and well-funded non-government organizations directly to the for-profit world, private charity and the exploitation of women. Canada was in a fortunate position, potentially, and had the opportunity to learn from the mistakes made abroad. Britain's experience with Thatcher clearly showed that ideological purity is not enough to meet basic human needs, and that the ideology of the right is perhaps more frightening than that of the left, given that the right, in power, actually attempts to implement its ideology. The end of the Thatcher years left a Britain that was certainly wealthier overall, but it was also a Britain that was deeply unequal in access to income and wealth, starved of compassion and institutional help for the vulnerable.

While Mulroney engineered the shift to the right in Canada, it was not really until Thatcher and indeed Reagan and Bush in the USA had all left office that Canada began its plunge to the abyss of the market. So history is perhaps doomed to repeat itself, and Canada seems fated to follow the neo-conservative path, knowing full well the direction in which it leads. The Americanization of Canada's welfare state seems increasingly assured, confirming Esping-Andersen's view that Canada is firmly situated within the liberal welfare-state regime. The prospects for a middle way as typified by Blair, Jospin and Schroeder, let alone the Scandinavian examples, which perhaps offer more caring and less punitive models for Canada to follow, seem unlikely. The highly decentralized nature of the Canadian federation, and by implication its welfare state, is a complicating factor, as is the continuing threat of Quebec separation. In other words the recurring crisis of federalism makes future predictions difficult. What is clear is that if the twentieth century did not exactly belong to Canada, it seems highly improbable that twenty-first-century Canadian social welfare will provide a beacon for its citizens and the international community.

References

AARP (2007) *The Canadian Pension Plan: A Model of Reform Presentation*, David Denison to AARP International, 19 April (www.aarp.org/research/international/events/apr19_07_CPPIB.html).

Armitage, A. (1996) *Social Welfare in Canada Revisited*, 3rd edn, Oxford University Press.

Badgely, R. and Wolfe, S. (1967) *Doctors' Strike*, Atherton Press.

Battle, K. and Torjman, S. (1996) 'Desperately Seeking Substance: A Commentary on the Social Security Review', in J. Pulkingham and G. Ternowetsky (eds), *Remaking Canadian Social Policy*, Fernwood.

CAFB (2005) *Time for Action. Hunger Count 2005*, Annual Report, Canadian Association of Food Banks.

Canada (1943) *House of Commons Advisory Committee on Post-war Reconstruction*, Queen's Printer.

Canada (1964) *Royal Commission on the Health Services*, Queen's Printer.

Canada (2002) *Royal Commission on the Future of Health Care in Canada*, Government Printer.

Esping-Andersen, G. (1990) *The Three Worlds of Welfare Capitalism*, Polity Press.

Graham, B. and Lightman, E. (1992) 'The Crunch: Financing Ontario's Social Programs', in T. Hunsley (ed.), *Social Policy in the Global Economy*, Queen's University.

Guest, D. (1997) *The Emergence of Social Security in Canada*, 3rd edn, University of British Columbia Press.

Lightman, E. (1991) 'Support for Social Welfare in Canada and the United States', *Canadian Review of Social Policy*, 28, Autumn, pp. 9–27.

Lightman, E. (2003) *Social Policy in Canada*, Oxford University Press.

McQuaig, L. (1993) *The Wealthy Banker's Wife*, Penguin.

Mendelson, M. (1998) *To Pay or Not to Pay: Should the Federal Government Pay Down Its Debt?*, Caledon Institute of Social Policy.

Riches, G. (ed.) (1997) *First World Hunger: Food Security and Welfare Politics*, Macmillan.

Riches, G. (2006) 'The Right to Food: A Recipe for Action', *Canadian Issues*, McGill Institute for the Study of Canada.

Shragge, E. (1997) *Workfare: Ideology for a New Under-Class*, Garamond.

Tarasuk, V. and Power, E. (2006) *The Impact of Income on Healthy Eating in Canada*, paper presentation, Health Canada Policy Forum #60, 23 March.

Torjman, S. and Battle, K. (1995) *The Dangers of Block Funding*, Caledon Institute of Social Policy.

UNESC (2006) *Concluding Observations of the Committee on Economic, Social and Cultural Rights: Canada*, United Nations Economic and Social Council, 1–19 May.

UNICEF (2005) *Child Poverty in Rich Countries 2005*, Report Card No. 5, Innocenti Research Centre.

United Nations Development Programme (UNDP) (2006) *Human Development Report*, http://hrd.undp.org/hdr2006

Vedan, R. and Tester, F. (1998) 'Resistance and Renewal: Social Programs and Aboriginal People', in N. Pollack with R. Vedan and F. Tester, *Critical Choices, Turbulent Times*, University of British Columbia.

CHAPTER 4

Australia: From Wage-Earners to Neo-Liberal Welfare State

LOIS BRYSON AND FIONA VERITY

Introduction

In 1901, in a climate of optimism and social experimentation, six British colonies, all but one a former penal settlement, federated to become states of the Commonwealth of Australia. Much later the states were joined by two territories, which play a similar role, but lack the constitutional protection of their status, so are more subject to Commonwealth veto. This chapter is focused primarily on the development of social policy since the birth of Australia as a nation in 1901. However, its prehistory is still evident not only in the administrative boundaries between states but also in the, now somewhat modified, constitutional divisions of powers between the two tiers of government. In general the Commonwealth has increasingly gained in powers since Federation, but the history and distinctive patterns of state, and later territory, politics have ensured there remains a relative independence between these first and second tiers of government. This is well illustrated by the fact that, from 2002, Labour held political power in all states and territories while the conservative coalition government remained in power federally until 2007.

Colonial labour history is important for understanding the direction taken by Australian social policy and is the basis of a prominent academic debate about whether Australia is most appropriately classified as a liberal welfare state (Esping-Andersen, 1990) or a special variant of this (along with New Zealand), which Castles (1985; 1994) termed 'a wage-earners' welfare state'. This debate is essentially about that key issue for all social policy analysis, 'who benefits?', and in this case revolves around how much workers (though more accurately, white male workers) were beneficiaries (Bryson, 1992).

Answers to the question 'who benefits?' are inevitably neither simple nor unchanging, though Indigenous Australians have remained, since British settlement, the most disadvantaged. Women, despite many gains, have failed to achieve genuine 'equality' and this applies to other Australians, including some ethnic groups and people with disabilities. More generally, however, benefits from the total range of social policies, by the late twentieth century, were redirected more towards the better-off than had been the case earlier. By the twenty-first century, as the gap between rich and poor widened and workers' power in the negotiation of labour conditions were diminished, the claim for Australia being a 'wage-earners' welfare state' was debatable. A trend away from a social-democratic to a neo-liberal approach to policy moved Australia more into line with other liberal welfare states, through, for example, policies distinguishing between the deserving and undeserving poor similar to those in the USA, historically the least developed of the 'liberal welfare states' (Esping-Anderson, 1990). However, changes wrought by the radical neo-liberal economic turn of social policy have arguably moved Australia even beyond the scope of Esping-Anderson's tripartite model, and are better covered by the term 'neo-liberal welfare state'.

The Development of Australian Social Policy

The Prehistory Phase

Although, from 1788, settlement of Australia was as a number of penal colonies, within a few decades, permanent settlers became intent on developing these as outposts of Empire. The flip side of this commitment to their British origins was a racist attitude to 'non-whites', which resulted in the dispossession of Indigenous Australians (Reynolds, 1996; 2003) and, from Federation, the formal exclusion of non-white potential immigrants, via a 'White Australia Policy'. This policy was only officially abandoned in the 1960s. Populist racism can still readily be activated in support of anti-immigrant and refugee causes as occurred in the mid-1990s (Marr and Wilkenson, 2003; Fear, 2007).

British intellectuals contributed greatly to early political debates in Australia. These included John Stuart Mill, who was influential in the campaign for women's suffrage, achieved in 1894 in the colony of South Australia. Fabian socialists were also important, with political debate stimulated by 'a large troupe of visiting social reformers', including Beatrice Webb and Sidney Webb (Kingston, 1988, p. 173). New Zealanders too contributed, as they were concerned with similar issues, even considering joining the federation (Pember Reeves, 1969[1902]).

Castles' notion of Australia as a 'wage-earners' welfare state' highlights the prominent role played by the labour movement, which in the 1890s, after a series of unsuccessful strikes, established labour parties in each colony. The national Australian Labour Party (ALP) was formed in 1896. The commitment to a parliamentary road for labour politics bore fruit as early as 1891 in New South Wales, when labour candidates won 35 of the 141 seats in the colony's legislature. In 1899, the world's first (brief) Labour government was elected in Queensland (Buckley and Wheelwright, 1988, p. 198).

At the national level there were then two brief periods of Labour Party minority government, and between 1910–13 and 1914–16, Labour formed majority governments, which were world firsts, the next being New Zealand Labour in 1938 and Sweden's Social Democratic Party in 1940 (Castles, 1985, p. 18). Electoral success for Labour owed much to payment of parliamentarians and equal weighting for each vote (Beilharz, 1989).

A political settlement (Kelly 1994) reached at that time was effectively underpinned by a concept of a white, male 'wage-earners' welfare state' rather than aiming for universal, insurance-based, social policy measures typical of European 'social democratic welfare states' (Esping-Andersen, 1990). While workers were the major political activists, there was also considerable cross-class enthusiasm for interventionist government (Pember Reeves, 1969[1902]) and thus Australian history also reflects the 'expression of the middle class interest in servicing and mediating between capital and labour' (Beilharz, Considine and Watts, 1992, p. 73).

Developing Australia's Welfare Provisions

The foundations of Australia's national welfare system were laid soon after Federation, mirroring the general distinctive combination of occupational and social welfare typical of earlier colonial policies. Central among these were: progressive taxation, state regulation of wages and employment conditions, tariffs to protect the interest of workers and employers, reliance on public enterprise, the promotion of home ownership and 'free, secular and compulsory' education. These policies were strongly influenced by Australia's circumstances, as a white settler nation that became affluent through 'commodity production under circumstances of extreme labour scarcity and strong statism' (Castles and Shirley, 1996, p. 90). The (white male) workerist framework remained a central feature of policy until the 1970s, when increasing globalization made protected trade less viable and economic liberal economics challenged, and gradually overtook, the broadly social democratic philosophy that had underpinned Australian social policy from colonial times.

In 1908 age and invalid pensions, Australia's first national welfare provisions, were established by the Commonwealth, though three states had earlier introduced age pensions. These were non-contributory, means-tested and modest, features continuing to underpin Australia's safety-net provisions. In the 1920s and 1930s a universal insurance-based system, with contributions from workers and employers, was discussed, culminating in the passing of the National Insurance Act 1938. However, it was never implemented, ostensibly because of concern about finances that would be needed for the Second World War effort. As Kewley (1977, p. 161–2) pointed out, these financial concerns merely allowed 'latent opposition to the scheme to become manifest', because a contributory scheme was unpopular with both workers and employers. The principle of universality was more acceptable in respect of support for children and a maternity allowance was established in 1912 (abolished in 1976). This involved a payment of £5 to both married and unmarried mothers, on the birth of a live child, though Indigenous Australians and most Asians and Pacific Islanders were excluded (Kewley, 1977, pp. 103–5). This type of benefit was reinstated in 2004, as a 'maternity payment', partly in response to a fall in the birth rate.

Further major developments did not occur until the 1940s when widow's pensions and unemployment, sickness and special benefits were enacted. These, as with the earlier pensions, were means-tested and showed little of 'the broad vision of social reform, the comprehensive multi-functional planning and mass excitement . . . obvious in Britain' at the time of the Beveridge reforms (Jones, 1990, p. 39). Again though, as with the earlier maternity allowance, universality was more acceptable for child benefits and a child allowance was introduced in 1941. In this period, policies targeted to white male wage-earners' interests included a full-employment and national development strategy, facilitation of home ownership and a public housing programme (Mendelsohn, 1979). Encouragement of home ownership had a long history and ownership reached 50 per cent in 1911, whereas in the United Kingdom this level was not reached until 1971. The Australian rate peaked at 72 per cent in the 1960s and then remained around 70 per cent, but dropped to 65 per cent by 2006 (Milligan, 1983; AIHW, 2005: 11; ABS, 2007a), in part reflecting an increasing divide between rich and poor.

The next major changes to social policy were those introduced by the Whitlam 1972–5 Labour government. These were more radical and inclusive than earlier policies, putting Australia out of step with international developments, where it was becoming widely accepted that there was a 'crisis of the welfare state' (Offe, 1984). None the less the Labour government did move the welfare regime in a social-democratic direction. As Whitlam (1985, p. 360) has since reflected: 'we wanted to establish a welfare apparatus which was devoid of class discrimination and could not be stigmatised as providing charitable concessions to the "deserving poor"'.

Policies initiated at the time included: automatic adjustment of pensions in line with the consumer price index; pensions for mothers who had not been in a permanent relationship; a non-means-tested retirement pension for people over 70; the abolition of university fees; a national health service (Medibank); a regional programme to decentralize and stimulate the development of local social services; and the promotion of equality for Indigenous Australians, women and migrants. The Whitlam government period represents the only time in the history of Australian social policy that the principle of universalism was pursued in a systematic way. However, this policy agenda was short-lived and, as economic conditions declined, the Whitlam government, after just less than three years in office, was dismissed from office in 'the most dramatic political event in history of Australia's Federation' (whitlamdismissal. com). A notable legacy of this period was a wage-earners' welfare state

LIVERPOOL JOHN MOORES UNIVERSITY
LEARNING SERVICES

made more inclusive, through, for example, moves towards equal pay for women and greater recognition of and support for minorities.

Towards Neo-Liberal Economic Policies – from the 1970s

The worker-oriented egalitarianism that had been established early in Australia's history was systematically modified from the 1970s, with the first moves towards reduced levels of industry protection attempted by the Whitlam government (Kelly, 1994, p. 22). These moves met with little success, but flagged the direction of future change and made the point that the tariffs that protected local industry needed modification if the Australian economy was to thrive in a globalizing world. However, it was not until the 1980s that tariff protection was significantly changed, as neo-liberal economic theory became a major international force, reinforced by bodies such as the OECD and International Monetary Fund.

From the 1980s, neo-liberal restructuring in the cause of national economic development was championed by both the political left and right, with Labour's policies justified by 'realistic supporters of the social democratic settlement', who accepted the need to reassess priorities in social policy in the light of world change (Quiggin, 2005, p. 37). The Labour government (1983–96) pursued systematic economic deregulation, including the dismantling of tariff protections. Even though the effects were partly counter-balanced by some ingenious worker-friendly policies, the wage-earners' welfare state was effectively weakened through Labour's facilitation of freer trade. A key result of this was a reduction in union power through allowing bargaining at an enterprise, as well as at industry level where unions had most clout (Hawke and Drago, 1998). Service users were also affected, for example, when university fees were reintroduced in 1987. However, the effects of this were modified by an ingenious administrative device, the Higher Education Contribution Scheme (HECS). This allowed payment of university fees to be postponed until a graduate was in steady employment and had reached a reasonably high level of income, when quite gentle repayments were required. The HECS significantly reduced the effects of the change for poorer graduates.

While a neo-liberal direction was pursued by Labour, the neo-liberal economic project was far more attractive to conservatives and a more radical version was pursued by the Howard coalition government from its election in 1996. A basic difference in values is clear in the way the social democrats sought to enhance the State's capacity, for example, by introducing new public-sector management strategies such as the HECS, while the conservatives, viewing the state itself as 'harmful', moved to limit its interference in market activity (Quiggin, 2005, p. 37).

By the twenty-first century, neo-liberal policies had changed the face of Australian social policy and trades union power was further diminished by the Coalition's deregulation of working conditions and encouragement of individual and enterprise work contracts. Hence, for many, wages and work conditions were reduced, at the same time as massive payments for senior executives became widespread (Stilwell and Jordan, 2007) and welfare recipients were coercively required to move from welfare to work. The gap between rich and poor widened and social benefits increasingly favoured the better-off, especially private business. The welfare sector itself became increasingly privatized, as government funding was paid to businesses to provide social services, while citizens were subsidized to purchase the services offered on a for-profit basis.

The language of welfare services moved away from rights and took on a neo-liberal and punitive tone. Citizens claiming their 'rights' to social security benefits, in 1997 became 'customers' of Centrelink, the administrative organization responsible for dealing with the claims of the unemployed, homeless, single parent and Indigenous Australian 'customers'. Work-testing became more stringent and 'mutual obligation' was invoked particularly for the unemployed, but was expected too of disabled pensioners and single parent recipients of allowances. Voluntary work became a requirement if paid employment wasn't available. The Minister for Family and Community Services claimed that, 'our very successful Work for the Dole Programme has started to change the expectation among some young people that the taxpayer owes them something for nothing' (Newman, 1999, p. 3). The eligibility period for sole parent benefits was reduced, a process started by Labour, though Labour also injected a strong retraining element. Indigenous Australians too became a focus of concern about welfare dependency (Saunders, 2005) and the government and some Indigenous leaders supported welfare payments being contingent on a claimant achieving specified social welfare objectives, such as ensuring children's school attendance.

The late twentieth-century neo-liberal economic doctrine was in line with world trends, and had been directly promoted in Australia for many years, including through a visit in 1976 by leading US proponent, Milton Friedman (1962). Also a number of conservative think-tanks were established, the oldest being the Institute of Public Affairs (IPA), which was set up in 1946. These were later joined by other very active bodies, including the H. R. Nichols Society and Centre for Independent Studies (CIS) (Mendes, 2003). A significant effect of adjusting to a more individualist economic theory for a country with a folksy pride in equality and everyone getting a 'fair go' (Thompson, 1994) has been reconciling this much older ideology with the increasing number of very wealthy citizens and the growing gap between rich and poor. This gap is vividly illustrated by the rise in the remuneration of chief executive officers in relation to average weekly earnings. For 50 top companies this went from a ratio of 18:1 in 1989 to 63:1 in 2005 (Stilwell and Jordan, 2007, p. 27). Also by the twenty-first century, Australian social policies retained far fewer features aimed explicitly at benefiting workers. Esping-Anderson's 'liberal welfare state' classification thus became a more appropriate descriptor of Australia than Castles' 'wage-earners' welfare state'. Arguably, however, 'neo-liberal welfare state' is even more appropriate, despite the apparent contradiction in terms.

Australia's Indigenous 'Welfare' Regime

Were welfare provisions to be judged in terms of those who are worst off, the Australian welfare state would have to be assessed in respect of the well-being of its Aboriginal and Torres Strait Islanders (ATSI) people, making up about 2 per cent of the total population of 20 million. They have, however, been subjected to a separate, paternalistic, oppressive 'welfare', or more accurately 'illfare' regime. In the twenty-first century a high proportion remain severely impoverished and living in third world conditions (see Table 4.1).

Initially colonial governments 'veered from policies of protection to the mounting of punitive expeditions and the declaration of martial law' (Reynolds, 1996, p. 128). Later Indigenous Australians were dealt with on the basis of the misconception that they would soon 'die out'. Their treatment included forced relocation to reserves, travel from which required passes, signed by administrators, who were often racist, brutal and defrauded those under their 'protection' of their entitlements (Stevens, 1984). Even when personnel were benign, this apartheid system failed disastrously and in the 1950s was replaced by one of 'assimilation'. Indigenous Australians became eligible for pensions and benefits in 1959 unless 'nomadic or primitive', a proviso removed in 1966 (Markus, 1994, p. 177).

In the 1970s, policy changes were made by the Whitlam government, under pressure from international rights organizations and political action by Indigenous Australians themselves. This action included a landmark

Table 4.1 Characteristics of Aboriginal and Torres Strait Peoples, 2004

Aborigines and Torres Strait Islanders		*Non-Indigenous Australian Population*	
% of total population	2.4	% of total population	97.6
Median age	21	Median age	36
Life expectancy – female	65	Life expectancy – female	82
Life expectancy – male	59	Life expectancy – male	77
% school retention rates to year 12	40	% school retention rates to year 12	77
% Unemployed	20	% Unemployed	6
Mean equivalized gross household income	A$396	Mean equivalized gross household income	A$665
% Home owned/purchasing	30	% Home owned/purchasing	70
Ratio of homeless	3.5	Ratio of homeless	1.0
% in overcrowded dwellings	9.5	% in overcrowded dwelling	≤1.0
% of prison population	21	% prison population	79

Source: AIHW (2005).

Aboriginal Tent Embassy, which was outside the Commonwealth Parliament for many months, and 'freedom rides' which challenged racial segregation especially in country towns. Indigenous Australians became more involved in their own affairs, with ATSI organizations established, which have since taken a leading role in legal, health and childcare services.

During the 1970s, the issue of land rights also reached the public agenda and the Commonwealth exercised its constitutional power over Australia's territories to recognize Aboriginal land rights in the Northern Territory. South Australia, New South Wales and Queensland followed suit and a considerable amount of crown land was returned. However, the fiction that, at British settlement, Australia had been a 'terra nullius' ('empty land') was not officially overturned until a High Court of Australia decision, in the Mabo case of 1992 (Reynolds, 1996). This decision established ATSI's continuing ownership rights, where they have not been extinguished by the Crown and not conflicting with the rights of other owners or leaseholders.

A settlement with a function similar to, though more modest than, that of New Zealand's Treaty of Waitangi, was closer at this time than at any other. However the moment was lost when the Coalition was elected federally in 1996. Paternalism was again to the fore and a rift between Prime Minister Howard and Indigenous Australians emerged over what became known as the '*Stolen Generation Report*' (Wilson, 1997). This was concerned with the assimilation policies of the mid-twentieth century, which involved the forcible removal from their families of Aboriginal children who had one white parent. Thousands were raised in children's homes, usually church-sponsored, with devastating consequences for children and their families.

The inquiry exposed grave maltreatment and injustices, and sparked a popular movement to achieve formal reconciliation between Aboriginal and non-Aboriginal Australians. However, this was blocked by the Prime Minister's persistent refusal to apologize for the wrongs of the past. This in turn provided a background against which an acrimonious debate, referred to as the 'history wars' (Windshuttle, 2002; Manne, 2003), erupted among historians. This polarized opinions as those on the right rewrote the historical evidence of unjust and often brutal treatment of Indigenous Australians, while those on the left continued to provide evidence of this. Some revisionist historians were rewarded by positions on Howard government boards.

Paternalism was also vividly reasserted in a 2007 top-down child-saving intervention by the federal Coalition government, using its constitutional power over the Northern Territory. This aimed at addressing a long-recognized serious problem, the health and well-being of Aboriginal children. However, there was a radical edge to the intervention in its failure to consult with Aboriginal communities. This included a failure to provide an up-front explanation of the role of the military personnel deployed, it emerged later, to arrange the process with solely logistical and organizational intent. Others, however, have interpreted this intervention as 'coercive reconciliation' (Altman and Hinkson, 2007).

The legacy of ATSI dispossession remains unfinished business for Australian social policy; its effects are evident in poverty, poor housing, high levels of suicides, deaths in police custody, violence, ill-health, alcoholism and a life expectancy of 20 years less than non-indigenous Australians. However, among the meagre number of positive outcomes of the late twentieth century was an increasing number of university graduates, able to fill key positions in policy-making and service delivery, though the rate of Indigenous graduation only reached half that of other Australians.

Australia's Mixed Welfare Economy

Although, historically, Australia's welfare mix has depended on selective distribution, the mix was leavened, in 1976 by Medicare, the national universal health scheme, and in 1992 by a universal superannuation scheme. Additionally, government support for education had become more universal, if more inequitable, as wealthy private schools received increasing support. Thus relationships between the various segments of the welfare economy have been realigned, at the same time as the welfare economy has been expanded.

In Australia, as in virtually all welfare regimes, considerable complexity and a number of levels are features of the contemporary welfare economy. At Federation, responsibility for Australia's social policy became divided between the national and state levels, something that allowed for greater uniformity across the country, and a more equitable distribution of benefits, because the states varied considerably in size and wealth. Local councils form a third tier of government, with a history going back to the 1840s, though they have mostly had relatively restricted functions. A historically active fourth level is what Shaver (1982) has called the 'non-government state', a term that neatly encapsulates the network of not-for-profit organizations that, from early colonial days, delivered needed services. This level of the welfare economy became, however, less central as for-profit businesses took over, with government subsidies, much service delivery, including for child and age care. Although the market had always played a key role, this neoliberal change altered considerably the balance of the welfare economy. A constant factor in the social support mix though has been the informal sector, consisting mainly of family members, who provide bedrock care.

Commonwealth government: Although the welfare system remains multilayered, the Commonwealth in the twenty-first century has major responsibilities. This was not, however, the case at Federation when, as with Canada and the USA, the Commonwealth was ceded limited powers. With respect specifically to social welfare, the Constitution (Section 51: xxiii) in 1901 granted the Commonwealth only the capacity to 'make laws . . . with respect to . . . invalid and old-age pensions' though, as part of its defence powers, veterans' welfare was also covered. In respect of workers' issues, the

Commonwealth was ceded power in industrial relations only when matters crossed state borders. This, however, proved of major importance (Kelly, 1994, p. 8) in establishing a 'wage-earner's welfare state', as the federal Arbitration Court was able to waive state excise duties for companies that paid 'fair and reasonable wages' and in a landmark decision in 1907, known as the Harvester Judgement, the Court established a minimum 'family' wage, on the basis of expenses for the needs of five people 'living in a civilized community'. As well as food and energy needs, the expense list included newspapers, fares, school requisites, holidays and even intoxicating liquors and tobacco (Kelly, 1994, p. 8). However, this was a white male minimum wage only, as the level for working women was for many decades half that of men, while many Indigenous workers were not paid wages at all.

The Commonwealth markedly increased its power when, to finance the Second World War effort, it became the recipient of income taxation revenue. It has maintained responsibility for income security payment, Medicare, superannuation and a wide net of legislative, regulatory and funding functions. However, the actual delivery of most services, including health, education and social services, happens mainly at the state and territory levels.

State governments: The early colonial governments led the way in the development of social policy underpinning the wage earners' welfare state. The pre-federation days saw considerable innovation with some trades achieving an eight-hour day as early as the 1850s, this becoming the norm before the end of the century. Also all colonies had mechanisms for settling industrial disputes prior to Federation; New South Wales, Victoria and Queensland had non-contributory age pensions, later superseded by the Commonwealth pension scheme. Only Denmark and New Zealand introduced such non-contributory benefits earlier (Castles and Uhr, 2007). The colony of South Australia was also a world leader in relation to voting rights for women, first, in 1861 for local government, then (1894) the right to vote and stand for Parliament.

A legacy of early power divisions between the Commonwealth and the states/territories, and the two levels of government's at times competing political values and objectives, is an institutional maze of social policies. This legacy has not only had ramifications for policy-making and service delivery, but also for citizens attempting to navigate the puzzling and often obscure social welfare language, system entry points and the complexity of entitlements.

Local government: A third tier of government comprises about 800 local governments, a number that declined through amalgamations, as part of the 1990s economic restructuring agenda. First established in the 1840s, Australian local government has not traditionally been greatly involved in social policy, but rather has largely provided services in respect of property. The Whitlam Labour government attempted to develop a broader role for regional government; but this didn't last. There still remains, however, some scope for councils to exercise discretionary roles in the delivery of community services, such as childcare and support services for the ill or aged, though provision usually occurs only with Commonwealth or state funding.

Employers: Employers are clearly of central relevance for a wage-earners' welfare state, and they have long been involved in Australia's welfare mix. Their role has included the discretionary provision of private retirement pensions, in Titmuss's (1974) term a classic form of 'occupational welfare' among more highly paid workers. However, such pensions became far less relevant from 1992, when a national superannuation scheme created a radical break with Australia's history of selective non-contributory age pensions paid from consolidated revenue. The 1992 Superannuation Guarantee Scheme (SGS) involves a statutory role for employers in supporting employees' retirement income, as they must pay a sum equivalent to 9 per cent of an employee's salary or wages into a superannuation fund.

Originally timed by the Labour government to substitute for a union claim for higher wages, superannuation is consistent with Australian Labour's tradition of promoting occupational welfare, though its universality represents a break with the past, apart from policies of the Whitlam era. The charge applies in respect of all employees between 18 and 70 years earning more than A$450 per month. Other workers and non-workers must rely on safety net provisions. When the programme matures in 2030, retirees on average weekly earnings (with a consistent employment record) will receive far greater proportions of pre-retirement income than age pensions ever provided.

In 2007 a significant alteration to the SGS effectively shifted the balance of benefits from superannuation. The change allowed workers not only to make additional voluntary payments, but provided highly favourable tax treatment for such contributions. This extensively advantaged the better-off; superannuation also systematically favours those with long, continuous employment histories. Women therefore are particularly disadvantaged (Olsberg, 2005). At the same time this mode of retirement support extends financial inequality into older age, far less the case earlier, because the age pension was widely relied on.

Employers are also responsible for other protections, including insurance against workplace accidents, and have a statutory obligation to provide at least five sickness days and four weeks' paid recreation leave per year on full pay. Long-service leave is mandatory after ten years' service, as is maternity leave, after one year, though only unpaid leave is compulsory. Many employers, particularly government and other large employers, do provide paid maternity leave. Despite improvement of retirement income, for many workers employment conditions deteriorated as the effects of neo-liberal economic policies came into play. This occurred through a weakening of union power, which resulted in fewer protections for workers. For example the proportion of workers without leave entitlements rose from 24 per cent in 1994 to 28 per cent in 2004 (AIHW 2005, p. 33).

Voluntary organizations: A historically important layer of Australia's mixed welfare economy is made up of voluntary organizations focused on a wide spectrum of issues and services. In the pre-welfare state era, charitable organizations, mostly under religious auspices, were the major dispensers of services, often with government financial assistance (Dickey, 1980). They remain important and the sector was estimated in 1996 to include some 700,000 voluntary or non-profit organizations (Lyons and Hocking, 2000). Some organizations, however, did achieve a more prominent role after the Coalition government came to power at Commonwealth level and, in 1999–2000, granted A$4.8 billion to this sector. By 2007, allocations noticeably favoured certain non-government organizations, often church-based, including evangelical groups such as the Hillsong Church, rather than some government-run services and those run by organizations with a more explicitly political focus, such as those representing Aboriginals, women and gay constituencies. A major departure from past practices was the undermining of the Commonwealth's own Employment Service for job placement of the unemployed, in favour of contracting the function to church-based and private (including for-profit) organizations through a new national network of organizations known as the Job Network Services.

The line between market and non-market services became increasingly blurred, to the detriment of those that were strictly non-market, small and often focused on sport or other recreational activities. Such organizations felt pressure to close if they could not adjust to the new orientation, which involved, for example, dealing with risk management and insurance. This proved perplexing because of the additional and expensive expertise that was required. Hence some organizations experienced pressures to close, to the detriment of their members and supporters (Verity, 2006). At the same time as this commercialization of voluntary organizations increased, however, greater participation in voluntary work actually occurred. This rose from 24 to 34 per cent of the adult population between 1995 and 2002 (AIHW, 2005, p. 49), though largely the increase reflects the potency of the mutual obligation policy, which required those unable to find paid employment to do voluntary work.

Markets: Markets have always played a key role in Australia's welfare regime in respect of health, education, housing and community services though recent neo-liberal economic policies systematically have promoted far greater market reliance. Medical services historically have been paid for on a fee-for-service basis and the successful introduction in the 1970s of the national health scheme (Medibank) was dependent on the maintenance of doctors' market independence. This was funded by a taxation surcharge, which, because it did not cover the full costs, was topped up from consolidated revenue. A change of government in 1975 led to a diminished national health scheme, though this was revitalized after 1984 by the incoming labour government and renamed Medicare.

Doctors are reimbursed according to standard fees for various services

(Biggs, 2004), though are free to charge more, unless the patient is a pensioner with full entitlements to health-care coverage (established by means-testing). Medicare funds are also provided to a range of private allied health providers for services for certain chronic conditions. Private health insurance covers services not, or only partly, covered by the national scheme, including dental, optical and physiotherapy services, private hospital accommodation and choice of doctor in public hospitals. In 1998, around 30 per cent of Australians had private coverage (ABS, 1999), but this increased to 44 per cent by 2000, when tax concessions were offered to those who joined and a tax penalty charged to higher income earners who did not (Leeder, 1999).

Markets have also been the major source of housing for all Australians. Unlike the UK and many European countries, interest on owner-occupied house repayments has never been tax deductible nor has imputed rent on owner-occupied homes been taxable. Governments have, however, facilitated home ownership, a crucial factor in making workable Australia's low-cost welfare state, especially in relation to the aged (Castles, 1985, 1994; Kemeny, 2004). Low-interest long-term, government guaranteed loans were early made available by the then state-owned Commonwealth Bank, including for the purchase of publicly constructed housing, which between 1945 and 1970 accounted for 36 per cent of all housing built in Australia. More recently, however, and in line with general economic policy, assistance has been made available through a lump sum subsidy to first-home buyers (Burke, 1998; AIHW, 2005, p. 270). This effectively, however, favours sellers, as it fuelled increased house prices.

By the 1980s, reduced public house-building meant that little housing stock was left in government hands. What there was had largely become welfare rental housing, catering for social security recipients. This, however, accounted for only around 6 per cent of all housing, so rental subsidies were also made to the poor in respect of private housing (Paris, Williams and Stimson, 1985; ABS, 1997). The private rental market became increasingly central to the welfare regime and from 1987 rental assistance for private housing became the major form of housing assistance (AIHW, 1997. p. 156; AIHW, 2005, p. 289; SCRGSP, 2006, p. 16.7). In the wake of what Yates and Milligan (2007, p. 1) call 'a twenty-first century problem' of housing affordability, demand for rental assistance continues unabated.

Markets have also taken a more central role in the delivery of the broad raft of 'community services', which previously were provided directly by governments or through funding for voluntary agencies. Markets became contractors of goods and service delivery with cash allowances or tax concessions increasingly made to individuals to facilitate their utilization of the market, as happened with housing. The move towards profit-making services is well illustrated by the sale by the Salvation Army of its large network of nursing homes to Retirement Care Australia, part of a huge conglomerate owned by the Macquarie Bank. This organization outlined the economic logic of its entry into the aged-care market thus: 'The aged care industry provides stable, underlying revenue streams and predictable cash flows, primarily from government funding and subsidies' (dela Rama, 2007, p. 2). Two other commercial organizations, among the many involved in aged care, were ANZ Capital (associated with Australian National Bank) and AMP (Australian Mutual Provident). Private provision now accounts for 26 per cent of all aged-care residential beds across Australia (AIHW, 2007, p. 9).

The trend to privatization is also illustrated by childcare services. From 1991, parents received payment in respect of children, rather than having access to state-funded services (AIHW, 1997, p. 106). By 2004, however, the main recipients of government funds in respect of long-day childcare were private providers (AIHW, 2005, p. 88). Other services were also privatized including the detention of illegal immigrants and convicted criminals. Roth (2004, p. 4) has noted that 'Australia has the highest proportion of inmates in private prisons of any nation, at around 17 percent.'

Informal care: A crucial layer of support on which all welfare rests is informal care, mostly from families and households. From 1996, some more traditional aspects of this informal care received greater recognition by the Coalition government, propelled partly by the intention to reduce the size of government. Greater recognition of informal care was accompanied by increased home care and personal support for carers, including the provision of a carer's pension and respite care programmes. As well, there was improved statistical recognition of the household sector's extensive contribution to the provision of care. In 1995–6 this voluntary contribution was estimated to be of the value of $A16.6 billion, compared with a total monetary expenditure of $A8.9 billion (AIHW, 1997, p. 10). By 2003the imputed value had risen to A$30.2 billion (AIHW, 2005, p. 363). This greater statistical recognition, while important symbolically, in no way addresses the problem of unmet need for more formal care.

Education: Education also vividly illustrates the complexity of Australia's social policy mix and the direction taken by of neo-liberal change. Universal education took shape from 1872 as the six colonial governments successively established 'free, secular and compulsory' education for children aged six to 14, though at the time, attendance was not necessarily enforced (Buckley and Wheelwright, 1988). A vision of creating a brave new world led governments to act as both 'financial and administrative controller' of public education before the state adopted a similar role in Britain (Branson and Miller, 1979, p. 57), though New Zealand went the same way in 1875.

While private education has had a longer history in Australia, it was not until the 1970s that the Whitlam Labour government controversially provided state aid to non-government schools. This reflected its support for universalism and was aimed mainly at assisting Catholic schools which, though severely under-resourced, enrolled a large proportion of the students of non-government schools. Subsequent governments, particularly the 1996 Howard Coalition government, gradually diverted an increasing proportion of education funding to the most affluent non-government schools, which were modelled on British 'public' schools and educate Australia's elites. State schools thus started to receive a comparatively reduced proportion of the education budget at the same time as retention rates to the final year of secondary schooling (age 17–18 years) increased from around 40 per cent in the early 1980s to over 76 per cent (81 per cent for females) in 2004 (AIHW, 2005, p. 104).

With government schools under pressure, private schools (both independent and Catholic) attracted more students, and the proportion of enrolment steadily rose from 22 per cent in 1974 to 29 per cent in 1995 and 33 per cent in 2005 (ABS, 1997, p. 69; ABS, 2007b). In 1995, the government system catered for 71 per cent of all primary and secondary students, a figure that had dropped to 67 per cent by 2005. Also in 1995 the government system accounted for 74 per cent of all schools, but only 72 per cent by 2005 (ABS, 1997; ABS, 2007b). Australian education thus became increasingly unequal because of the retrenchment of the state system.

While primary and secondary education have been free, secular and compulsory, tertiary education is secular and voluntary and, for most of its history, fee-paying, with a few talented poor students provided access through scholarships. The Whitlam government's bold move to make tertiary education free in 1975 lasted only until 1987. However, when fees were reintroduced by Labour in 1987 they were quite low, managed through the Higher Education Charge Scheme. This requires repayments only after graduation and in annual amounts proportional to income, though only after steady employment has been achieved and a threshold income reached (Chapman, 2006). Although the HECS remained in place after Labour's term, the 1996 Coalition government gradually encouraged universities to offer non-HECS, full fee-paying places. This effectively set up a dual system, which provides another example of a neo-liberal transformation of Australian social policy. A commercial market emphasis developed, particularly in relation to overseas students, and inadequate government funding resulted in fees becoming increasingly relied on by individual universities.

The overall distribution of responsibilities is illustrated in Box 4.1 below.

Box 4.1 Welfare in Australia: division of responsibilities

Housing

- Owner-Occupied (2006 – 65 per cent households)
  Housing purchased with mortgages from commercial institutions. Commonwealth provides First Home-Buyer's Grant (A$7,000). Tax concessions apply for owner-occupied houses.

(*continued*)

(*Box 4.1 continued*)

- Private Renting (2006 – 27 per cent households)
  Commonwealth Rent Assistance for low-earner private renters. Provision of rental housing encouraged by favourable tax treatment for landlords.
- Public Housing (2006 – 4.0 per cent households)
  States/territories control public housing, with matched Commonwealth funds (from 1945). Access is means-tested. State/territory allocations are made for Indigenous and community housing. Rent is charged at 25 per cent of household income.

Education

Education is compulsory from 6–15 years (in two states 6–16).

- State education (2005 – 72 per cent of schools): States and territories fund, determine curriculum and administer education with Commonwealth contribution. State education is free. Students with disabilities attend both special needs and mainstream schools. School-based apprenticeships and traineeships available from 15 years.
- Non-government schools (most are church sponsored) are independently owned and managed, supported by funds from Commonwealth/states/territories.
- Higher education – optional, with entry requirements. A dual university system: full fees are charged for some undergraduate and most post-graduate courses. Commonwealth supports majority of students through deferred fees (Higher Education Charge Scheme). Repayments, proportional to income, are required after a reasonable income is achieved.
- Government-funded vocational education and training offered through government colleges or approved providers.

Income Support

Commonwealth government

- Income- and asset-tested payments: Age Pension, Mature Age Allowance (for those unemployed and near retirement), Veterans' Affairs Service Pension, carers payments, Disability Support Pension (permanent condition), Sickness Allowance (medium term), Newstart Allowance (unemployment), Child Care Benefit (for childcare fees), Parenting Payment (until child six years).

(*continued*)

(*Box 4.1 continued*)

- Welfare to Work programme – for recipients of unemployment benefit, disability pensions (if deemed work-capable), parenting payments (work required when youngest six years). Mutual obligation, involving voluntary or work for the dole programmes and regular assessments, with penalties of up to eight weeks for 'serious failures'.
- Income-tested tax reductions include: Family Tax Benefits, Child Care Tax Rebate. Concessions for low earners to assist with medicine costs.
- Universal payments include: Baby Bonus (payment on birth of child), Maternity Immunization Allowance and Carer's Allowance (care for adult with disability).

Superannuation (administered by Australian Taxation Office)

- Employer provides tax-deductible contribution – 9 per cent of employee earnings.
- Employees may make voluntary payments (with tax benefits).
- Commonwealth provided co-contributions for low-income earners (up to A$1,500 pa).

State/territory and local government

- Concessions to low earners on payments for: electricity, public transport, council rates, water and sewerage.

Health Provisions

National Medicare covers or provides subsidized rebates for medical and some allied services. Users pay for charges above standard rates. Doctors may choose to accept standard fee and bill Commonwealth direct.

- States/territories are mostly responsible for tertiary, secondary and primary health-care services.
- Except for some public hospitals, most services are privately owned and managed.
- Private health insurance (43 per cent covered in 2006) involves Commonwealth tax rebate for those covered and a tax penalty applies to the uninsured.

Social Welfare Services

- Child welfare and protection services are provided by state/territory governments. Foster care may be a government responsibility, but

(*continued*)

(*Box 4.1 continued*)

increasingly is contracted. Family support programmes are delivered through state/territory governments and NGOs.

- State/territory government and non-government services cover: youth, women, disability, mental health, crisis support, refugees, family violence and other services.
- Network of aged services includes: personal care, health and community care, respite and residential care. Programmes are delivered by government, non-government, local government and increasingly private providers.

The Twenty-First Century: Where to for Australian Social Policy?

The fragmentary available evidence suggests that early in its history, though only for its non-indigenous population, Australia achieved less poverty and a narrower social hierarchy than was found in most other societies at the time. This was achieved particularly through the power of the labour movement to influence policy, particularly employment conditions (Encel, 1970; Mendelsohn, 1979). Means-tested age and invalid pensions that were achieved were relatively generous for the time and were taken up by over 30 per cent of the age cohort. Thus, considerable redistribution was achieved. Until the 1940s, probably provisions in only Germany and Denmark were more generous (Jones, 1990, p. 24; Castles, 1994). An OECD survey published in 1976 considered pre- and post-tax income inequality in 12 countries and concluded that 'Australia and Japan, in that order, rank as the least unequal countries on most measures' (Mendelsohn 1979, p. 67). However, such commentaries were very much focused on the 'white male' wage-earning population, with the fate of Indigenous Australians, women and many others largely ignored. By the twenty-first century, though Japan maintained its top position, Australia had clearly slipped in the equality stakes, with United Nations figures showing it behind not only Japan, but also all the Scandinavian countries, Germany, France and Canada (Stilwell and Jordan, 2007, p. 41).

Amongst OECD countries, until recently, Australia was consistently ranked as a low welfare spender (Castles and Uhr, 2007), but this historically was partly compensated for by high rates of home ownership. This expenditure rating, however, changed from the early 1990s, notably because of the introduction of the Superannuation Guarantee Scheme, but also through increases in government health spending (AIHW, 2005, p. 300). However, much of the latter increase was spent on tax subsidies in respect of private health insurance (Castles and Uhr, 2007), something that very much favoured the better-off. Funding provision for child, family and aged care (AIHW, 2005, p. 369) also increased and Australia's overall position moved up the international ladder in what Wilson, Meagher and Breusch (2005, p. 102) contend was 'an expansion unrivalled among the English speaking nations'. Expenditure for services required of individuals, however, also rose over the period, through, for example, increased out-of-pocket health-care costs as entitlements failed to cover the total charge. By 2001, Australia's ranking among OECD countries for social expenditure, while improved, remained relatively low at 17th, when superannuation was taken into account and 25th when it was not.

Increased private profit from the provision of welfare service represents a particularly dramatic change in the structure of Australia's welfare services. For instance ABC Learning Centres Limited, operators of 20 per cent of Australia's long-day childcare centres, reported significant growth in profits and business expansion, with annual revenue for 2005–6 of A$632 million, which grew in the subsequent year by 115 per cent (ABC, 2006, p. 1; 2007, p. 3). Expanding profit was also evident in the health sector with a company such as the Symbion Health Group, a large private health company providing GP services, pharmacies, pathology and hospital services, recording an increase of 10 per cent in net profit after tax for the overall group for the 2006/7 financial year (Symbion, 2007, p. 3).

These revenue and profit figures vividly illustrate a new face of Australia's evolving neo-liberal social policy regime. Meagher (2004) refers to this as 'privatisation of the Australian welfare state', while Castles and Uhr (2007, p. 117) point out that the 'institutions that gave the Australian system of protection an egalitarian and distinctive cast . . . [were] substantially undermined . . . producing a victory for the conservative variant of the old politics'. Markets became lodged at the very heart of the welfare state with enormous private profits accruing. Australian policies thus became geared to a neo-liberal free enterprise model. While this had some benefits in terms of increasing the quality of some services, access to these was far more available to the rich than the poor.

In the twentieth-first century, 100 years after the establishment of Australia's first national social policy regime, a climate of social experimentation was again evident in Australian policy, arguably as radical as when the Australia's wage-earners' welfare state was formed. The philosophy of social rights and solidarity that underpinned that development has been largely replaced by doctrines of profit-making and charity. Supporting policies that aimed at promoting greater equality have been replaced with policies that discipline powerless citizens by stipulating the manner and measure of their individual self-reliance. In Shaver's words, this represents a move 'from citizenship to supervision' (2002, p. 331). At the same time, taxation and a number of other policies have blatantly advantaged the better-off. Ironically, there has been encouragement of commercial investment and profit-taking through the delivery of social services oiled by government subsidies.

Australia's worsening position in the international equality stakes vividly reflects the outcome of this radical social policy direction. It also makes clear that, without a dramatic turnabout of policy, inequality in Australia, which the wage earners' welfare state, despite its racist, sexist and other limitations, did keep in check, is likely to continue to increase.

References

ABC Learning Centres Limited (2006) Annual Report 2006, http://www.childcare.com.au/index.php, accessed 25 September 2007.

ABC Learning Centres Limited (2007) 2007 Financial Results, http://www.childcare.com.au/index.php, accessed 25 September 2007.

Australian Bureau of Statistics, ABS (1997) *Australian Social Trends 1997*, Catalogue, No. 4102.0, Australian Bureau of Statistics.

ABS (1999) *Australian Social Trends 1999*, Catalogue No. 4102.0, Australian Bureau of Statistics.

ABS (2007a) Census QuickStats, http://www.censusdata.abs.gov.au, accessed 21 September 2007.

ABS (2007b) *Year Book Australia*, Catalogue No. 1301.0, Australian Bureau of Statistics.

AIHW (1997) *Australia's Welfare, 1997*, Australian Institute of Health and Welfare.

AIHW (2005) *Australia's Welfare, 2005*, Australian Institute of Health and Welfare.

AIHW (2007*) Residential Aged Care in Australia, 2005–2006: A Statistical Overview*, Australian Institute of Health and Welfare.

Altman, J, and Hinkson, J. (eds) (2007) *Coercive Reconciliation: Stabilise, Normalise, Exit Aboriginal Australia*, Arena Publications.

Biggs, A. (2004) *Medicare-Background Brief*, Parliament of Australia, http://www.aph.gov.au/library/intguide/SP/medicare.htm, accessed 21 September 2007.

Beilharz, P. (1989) 'The Labourist Tradition and the Reforming Imagination', in R. Kennedy (ed.) *Australian Welfare History*, Macmillan.

Beilharz, P., Considine, M. and Watts, R. (1992) *Arguing about the Welfare State: The Australian Experience*, Allen and Unwin.

Branson, J. and Miller, D. (1979) *Class, Sex and Education in Capitalist Society*, Sorrett Publishing.

Bryson, L. (1992) *Welfare and the State: Who Benefits?* Macmillan.

Buckley, K. and Wheelwright, T. (1988) *No Paradise for Workers: Capitalism and the Common People in Australia 1788–1914*, Oxford University Press.

Burke, T. (1998) 'Housing and Poverty', in R. Fincher and J. Nieuwenhuysen (eds), *Australian Poverty Then and Now*, Melbourne University Press.

Castles, F. G. (1985) *The Working Class and Welfare: Reflections on the Political Development of the Welfare State in Australia and New Zealand, 1890–1980*, Allen and Unwin.

Castles, F. G. (1994) 'The Wage-Earners' Welfare State Revisited: Refurbishing the Established Model of Australian Social Protection, 1983–93', *Australian Journal of Social Issues*, 29(2), pp. 120–45.

Castles, F. and Shirley, I. F. (1996) 'Labour and Social Policy: Gravediggers or Refurbishers of the Welfare State', in F. G. Castles, R. Gerritsen and J. Vowels (eds), *The Great Experiment: Labour Parties and Public Policy Transformation in Australia and New Zealand*, Allen and Unwin.

Castles, F. G. and Uhr, J. (2007) 'The Australian Welfare State: Has Federation made a Difference?', *Australian Journal of Politics and History*, 53(1), pp. 96–117.

Chapman, B. (2006) *Income Contingent Loans as Public Policy*, Occasional Paper 2/2006, Policy Paper # 5, Academy of the Social Sciences in Australia.

dela Rama, M. (2007) 'Private Equity and the Australian Care Sector', *Perspective*, ABC, Radio National.www.abc.net.au/rn

Dickey, B. (1980) *No Charity There*, Nelson.

Encel, S. (1970) *Equality and Authority*, London.

Esping-Andersen, G. (1990) *The Three Worlds of Welfare Capitalism*, Polity Press.

Fear, J. (2007) 'Under the Radar: Dog-whistle Politics in Australia', Discussion Paper, 96, Australia Institute.

Friedman, M. (1962) *Capitalism and Freedom*, University of Chicago Press.

Hawke, A. and Drago, R. (1998) *The Spread of Enterprise Bargaining Under Labor*, Discussion Paper Series, National Institute of Labour Studies, Flinders University.

Jones, M. A. (1990) *The Australian Welfare State*, 3rd edn, Allen and Unwin.

Kelly, P. (1994) *The End of Certainty*, Allen and Unwin.

Kemeny, J. (2005) '"The Really Big Tradeoff" between Home and Welfare: Castles' Evaluation of the 1980 Thesis, and a Reformulation 25 Years on', *Housing, Theory and Society*, 22(2), pp. 59–75.

Kewley, T. H. (1977) *Social Security in Australia*, Sydney University Press.

Kingston, B. (1988) *The Oxford History of Australia, vol. 3: 1860–1900*, Oxford University Press.

Leeder, S. R. (1999) *Healthy Medicine*, Allen and Unwin.

Lyons, M. and Hocking, S. (2000) *Dimensions of Australia's Third Sector*, Centre for Australian Community Organisations and Management, Universisty of Technology.

Manne, R. (2003) (ed.) *Whitewash: On Keith Windshuttle's Fabrication of Aboriginal History*, Black Inc.

Markus, A. (1994) *Australian Race Relations*, Allen and Unwin.

Marr, D. and Wilkenson, M. (2003) *Dark Victory*, Allen and Unwin.

Meagher, G. (2004) 'Do Australians Want a Private Welfare State? Are they Getting One Anyway?', *The Drawing Board: An Australian Review of Public Affairs*, Digest, May, http://www.econ.usyd.edu.au/drawingboard/digest/0405/meagher.html

Mendelsohn, R. (1979) *The Condition of the People*, Allen and Unwin.

Mendes, P. (2003), 'Australian Neo-liberal Thinks Tanks and the Backlash Against the Welfare State', *Australian Political Economy*, 51, pp. 29–56.

Milligan, V. (1983) 'The State and Housing: Questions of Social Policy and Social Change', in A. Graycar (ed.), *Retreat from the Welfare State*, Allen and Unwin.

Newman, J. (1999) 'The Future of Welfare in the 21st Century', address to National Press Club, Canberra, 29 September.

Offe, C. (1984) *Contradictions of the Welfare State*, Hutchinson.

Olsberg, D. (2005) 'Women, Superannuation and Retirement: Grim Prospects Despite Policy Changes', *Just Policy*, 35, pp. 31–8.

Paris, C., Williams, P. and Stimson, R. (1985) 'From Public Housing to Welfare Housing', *Australian Journal of Social Issues*, 20(2), pp. 105–17.

Pember Reeves, W. (1969 [1902]) *State Experiments in Australia and New Zealand*, Macmillan.

Quiggin, J. (2005) 'Economic Liberalism: Fall, Revival and Resistance', in P. Saunders and J. Walter (eds), *Ideas and Influence*, University of New South Wales Press.

Reynolds, H. (1996) 'Segregation, Assimilation, Self-determination', in J. Wilson. J. Thomson and A. McMahon (eds), *The Australian Welfare State: Key Documents and Themes*, Macmillan.

Reynolds, H. (2003) 'The Nullius Ideal: On Terra Nullius Reborn', in R. Manne (ed.) *op. cit.*

Roe, J. (1976) *Social Policy in Australia*, Cassell.

Roth, L. (2004) *Privatisation of Prisons*, Background Paper No 3/04, NSW Parliamentary Library Research Service.

Saunders, P. (CIS) (2005) *Australia's Welfare Habit and How to Kick It*, Duffy and Snellgrove.

SCRGSP (Steering Committee for the Review of Government Service Provision) (2006) *Report on Government Services 2006*, Productivity Commission.

Shaver, S. (1982) 'The Non-Government State: The Voluntary Welfare Sector', Paper delivered to Conference, *Social Policy in the 1980s*, Canberra, 28–30 May.

Shaver, S. (2002) 'Australian Welfare Reform: From Citizenship to Supervision', *Social Policy and Administration*, 36(4), pp. 331–45.

Stevens, F. (1984) *Black Australia*, Aura Press.

Stilwell, F. and Jordan K. (2007) *Who Gets What? Analysing Economic Inequality in Australia*, Cambridge University Press.

Symbion Health (2007) *Preliminary Final Report*, http://www.symbionhealth.com/127.asp

Titmuss, R. (1974) 'The Social Division of Welfare: Some Reflections on the Search for Equity', in *Essays on 'The Welfare State'*, Allen and Unwin.

Thompson, E. (1994) *Fair Enough: Egalitarianism in Australia*, University of New South Wales Press.

Verity, F. (2006) 'It's Line Dancing . . . Not Lion Dancing!', *Volunteering Australia Journal*, 11(1), pp. 50–8.

Whitlam, G. (1985) *The Whitlam Government 1972–1975*, Penguin.

Wilson, R. (1997) *Bringing them Home: Report of the National Inquiry into the Separation of Aboriginal and Torres Strait Islander Children from their Families*, Commonwealth of Australia.

Wilson, S., Meagher, G. and Breusch, T. (2005) 'Where to for the Welfare State?', in *Australian Social Attitudes: The First Report*, University of New South Wales Press.

Windschuttle, K. (2002) *The Fabrication of Aboriginal History*, Macleay Press.

Yates, J. and Milligan, V. (2007) *Housing Affordability: A 21st Century Problem*, Australian Housing and Urban Research Institute.

LIVERPOOL
JOHN MOORES UNIVERSITY
I.M. MARSH LRC
Tel: 0151 231 5216

CHAPTER 5

New Zealand: From Early Innovation to Humanizing the Market

JUDITH DAVEY AND SANDRA GREY

Overview

Internationally Aotearoa/New Zealand is often seen as a place of 'experimentation' in social policy, beginning with the introduction of universal suffrage and old-age pensions in the late nineteenth century. Social innovation continued in the mid-twentieth century when economic prosperity and an egalitarian outlook contributed to development of a comprehensive welfare state. More recently, the country took welfare reforms based on free-market principles and economic rationalism further than most developed nations. Well within the space of a lifetime there was a shift to a minimalist approach to welfare, with extensive targeting and 'user-pays' policies. However, since the late 1990s coalition governments have provided a brake on further marketization. Given this background, New Zealand provides interesting examples of social policy change and the influences behind it.

The Treaty of Waitangi and Maori Sovereignty

The early development of politics and policy in New Zealand was a product of the impact of British colonization, and its concern with individual rights, on traditional Maori culture, with its base in collective organization. This was captured in the Treaty of Waitangi between the Crown and some Maori tribal chiefs in 1840. The Treaty promised a balance between colonization and indigenous rights, which, as pressures for European settlement grew, it was unable to deliver (Orange, 1987). Wars, disease and growing immigration meant that Maori were a minority in their own country by 1880 and 'British' culture came to dominate the nation. Even though ignored for decades by the Pakeha (European) majority, since the 1980s there has been growing recognition that the Treaty of Waitangi is indeed the founding document of New Zealand as a bicultural state. While understandings of the Treaty are highly contested, government policy gives priority to recognizing the three articles of its English version. The first is seen to cede governance to the British Crown; the second assured Maori of continuing possession of and authority over their lands and property; and the third gave Maori the 'rights and privileges of British subjects'. For Maori, the principle of *tino rangatiratanga* (chieftainship or sovereignty) is seen as an essential part of the founding compact (Kawharu, 2005; Maloney, 2007, p. 37).

Early State Intervention

Oliver (1988) saw nineteenth-century social policy as synonymous with European settlement and whatever was required to facilitate it. This included the transfer of land into settler ownership; bringing Maori into the 'civilizing influences' of the cash economy; the construction of road and rail infrastructure; and assisted immigration. Much of this required governments to borrow heavily from international sources.

Traditional sectors of social policy involved a 'colonial Poor Law'. The provinces were responsible for the indigent and Charitable Aid Boards were established. Those who could not afford to pay privately for health care depended on a patchwork of hospitals lightly supervised by a state department and financed by charities and government contributions (Oliver, 1988). The hospital system provided not only medical treatment but also custodial care for the old, chronically ill and feeble-minded. The particular characteristics of the settler population – predominantly male, highly mobile and with dispersed families – meant that care of old people became a problem and led to the introduction of an old age pension in 1898, a decade before this happened in Britain (Cheyne, O'Brien and Belgrave, 2004). This was, however, subject to tests for moral fitness, residence and financial need; many applications were rejected.

Until the 1850s, New Zealand schools were privately run and funded. The present system of free, secular and compulsory education came in with the Education Act of 1877 (Department of Statistics, 1990, pp. 262–3). This covered all European children aged seven to 13 (currently all children from six to 16). Maori children were compelled to attend school from 1903. Other early policy innovations included female suffrage in 1893, the first in the world at national level. A Department of Labour was created to oversee working conditions and in 1894 the Industrial Conciliation and Arbitration Act was passed. This strengthened the bargaining position of trades unions and set up an Arbitration Court which exercised a dominant influence on wages and conditions of work for 75 years.

State benefits were gradually extended at the start of the twentieth century. Pensions were granted to widows in 1911, miners in 1915 and the blind in 1924. Concern about housing led to several pieces of legislation, including the Housing Act of 1919. Considerable emphasis was placed on home ownership, and as early as 1919 53 per cent of homes in New Zealand were owner-occupied, when the equivalent figure in Britain was 10 per cent (Ferguson, 1994). The government and local authorities built houses for subsidized rental.

Progress was made in child welfare with the establishment of the Royal New Zealand Society for the Health of Women and Children (Plunket) Society in 1907 – a partnership of women volunteers and professional nurses – to improve maternity and child health services through clinics and home visits (Department of Statistics, 1990, p. 157). The expansion of the health sector followed the serious influenza epidemic of 1918. School medical and dental services were developed in the 1920s. The 1925 Child Welfare Act set up children's courts and child welfare services and the 1926 Family Allowances Act introduced a means-tested benefit for third and subsequent children. Government intervention in the economic and labour markets continued in the early twentieth century. The 'wage-earner welfare state' (Castles, 1985) was institutionalized in 1936 when the Arbitration Court set in place a 'family wage'. Working men were to receive wages adequate to support themselves, their wives and children. This seriously disadvantaged women workers until the passing of the Equal Pay Act in 1972.

The Flowering of the Welfare State

The modern welfare state in New Zealand is usually dated from the incumbency of the Labour government of 1935–49, following a disastrous economic recession. In 1938 it passed the Social Security Act, to provide income support and free health care (Cheyne, O'Brien and Belgrave, 2004, p. 33). While welfare benefit coverage was more extensive than before, the provisions were still residual with all benefits means-tested, except for a small universal superannuation. Medical benefits, financed through taxation, were progressively extended, but this met with opposition from the medical profession. Doctors responsible for primary care gained the right to charge patients above the government subsidy and the cost of medical services steadily increased in the following decades. Hospital care (including specialist care) was completely free. Health standards were high. New Zealand prided itself on having the lowest infant mortality rates in the world and conducted regular surveys of the height and weight of school children, which showed regular improvement in both (Department of Statistics, 1990, pp. 240–1). High fertility levels and immigration led to population growth of nearly 70 per cent between 1945 and 1971 (from 1.7 to 2.9 million).

As well as the Arbitration Court ruling, cementing the male wage-earner welfare state, a number of state-funded measures aimed at ensuring greater social equality for families. In 1946 Family Benefit was made universal and from 1958 it could be capitalized to provide housing finance. Housing assistance was delivered through the State Advances Corporation, which began a rental housing construction programme as well as continuing to provide low-interest mortgage finance (Wilkes and Shirley, 1984, p. 219).

The Labour government welfare provisions remained substantially in place for more than 40 years, 'often questioned, sometimes examined, but only marginally altered' (Oliver, 1988, p. 25). In the 1950s and 1960s, New Zealanders enjoyed the flowering of the welfare state and economic prosperity underpinned some of the highest living standards in the world. The state controlled exchange transactions, domestic credit, interest rates, incomes and prices, import licences and tariffs (Oliver, 1988, p. 33). Nevertheless, as Goldfinch and Malpass (2007) have noted, New Zealand was no more interventionist during this period than similar developed nations.

Challenges to the Welfare State

In 1972 the Royal Commission on Social Security concluded:

> we have not been persuaded that our social security system should be radically changed at this time . . . no alternative which we examined is likely to do better. (Royal Commission of Inquiry, 1972, p. 32)

But things *were* beginning to change. Social, economic and demographic changes dented confidence in the state's ability to smooth the boom and bust cycles of capitalism. After many years during which markets for primary produce – butter, meat, wool – seemed inexhaustible, Britain's intention to join the EEC was a threat; and a recession occurred following the oil price rise of the early 1970s (Dalziel and Lattimore, 2004, p. 9–10). The New Zealand government initially sought to maintain domestic economic activity at the expense of an increase in overseas debt, but was forced to change this policy in the 1976/77 financial year and another sharp economic contraction followed.

Full employment – the key to New Zealand's prosperity – began to falter. In 1977 the registered unemployment rate rose towards 1 per cent for the first time since the Second World War (Dalziel and Lattimore, 2004, p. 22) and grew to 7 per cent by 1986 (Economic Monitoring Group, 1989, p. 12). Means-tested benefits fell behind wage increases and the cost of living. Annual inflation grew from well under 5 per cent in the 1950s and 1960s to peak at over 15 per cent in the later 1970s (Economic Monitoring Group, 1989, p. 11). The provision of hospital beds and resources for education fell behind the rapid population growth of the 'baby boom' years.

At the same time cultural 'consensus' in New Zealand was being eroded (Cheyne, O'Brien and Belgrave, 2004, p. 35). Television was introduced in 1960, and by 1966 half a million licences were held (Department of Statistics, 1990, p. 340). Air travel promoted more rapid communication and international mobility. The Maori population became urbanized. In 1945 three-quarters lived in rural areas, but by 1981 four-fifths were in towns and cities (Department of Statistics, 1990, p. 157). This led to social dislocation, but by the 1970s a cultural renaissance began, pointing out the relative disadvantage of Maori, and calling for the Treaty of Waitangi to be honoured. This was epitomized by a land march to Parliament in 1975. Calls for ethnic self-determination and the redress of grievances had much in common with the reassertion of indigenous rights elsewhere in the world and found a sympathetic ear in the 1973 labour government, which set up a tribunal to consider claims relating to the Treaty principles. The resolution of such claims has become a goal of successive governments. By 2004 over NZ$600 million of assets – including land, fisheries, forests and geothermal resources – had been transferred, and the process was estimated to be about halfway to completion. In 2006 legislation was enacted to set a closing date of 1 September 2008 for lodging all historical claims, with settlements to be dealt with by 2020.

While this period may have questioned the 'Keynesian' consensus, the state continued its highly interventionist economic management. Natural gas and oil discoveries (driven on by the 'oil shocks' of the early 1970s) provided the basis for government-promoted 'Think Big' industrial projects, which did not ultimately prove to be good investments. There were also new social policy programmes. In 1973 the Domestic Purposes Benefit (DPB) was introduced for lone parents, who previously had received only emergency benefits. In 1972 the Accident Compensation (ACC) scheme came in to provide medical benefits and income replacement for accident victims. A contributory retirement income scheme was introduced by a Labour government in 1974 but this was replaced by a tax-funded universal scheme when the National Party was elected in 1975.

A Step to the Right

The 1984 General Election was a landmark in the history of New Zealand social policy. The new Labour government inherited serious economic problems, including a currency crisis and a large fiscal deficit (Dalziel, 1994). The response was neo-liberal economic reforms similar to Thatcherism in Britain and Reaganomics in the USA (Cheyne, O'Brien and Belgrave, 2004, p. 38). Deregulation of the financial sector was rapid, exchange controls were lifted, agricultural subsidies withdrawn and trade liberalized. There was a shift to indirect taxation, with a flat-rate Goods and Services Tax (GST), introduced in 1986 at 10 per cent and increased to 12.5 per cent in 1989. The state sector was restructured (Boston *et al.*, 1996, p. 99) and many departments with commercial operations were turned into state-owned enterprises (Le Heron and Pawson, 1996, p. 214). This led to job losses, particularly affecting small towns. Following global trends of privatization, the government announced the sales of Air New Zealand and Postbank in 1988, followed later by the Bank of New Zealand, State Insurance, Telecom, state forests and New Zealand Steel (Le Heron and Pawson, 1996, p. 220). These measures, along with tax changes, helped to improve the government's economic position despite a share market crash in 1987.

State restructuring led to programmes of devolution and deinstitutionalization. An inquiry into education administration led to greater autonomy for parent-run school Boards of Trustees. The health sector was restructured through the 1989 Area Health Boards Act. This created 14 regionally based, largely elected bodies, subject to new public sector accountability rules (Le Heron and Pawson, 1996, p. 221). Devolution also helped to shape Labour's Maori policy. A Ministry of Maori Affairs was formed to represent Maori interests and give policy advice, while operational programmes were progressively devolved to tribal authorities, which developed their own social and economic programmes. These included several important educational initiatives. *Te Kohanga Reo* (language nests) are early childhood education centres, using Maori language and promoting cultural revitalization and parent education. *Kura Kaupapa* Maori (total immersion Maori schools) were also established and bilingual classes became much more common. These education initiatives were bolstered when Maori became an official language in 1987. Maori initiatives in the health services include cultural support in hospitals, education of the health workforce in cultural sensitivity, and the encouragement of Maori nurses, health and medical personnel (through reserved training places and scholarships). Health clinics have been established on *marae* (Maori community centres) and special preventive programmes targeted at Maori such as smoking cessation and diet improvement. Some of these, along with remedial services, are now provided by tribal organizations and urban Maori institutions through state-funded contracts.

While economically neo-liberal, the Labour government was socially liberal. Changes included the Homosexual Law Reform Act and the establishment of the Ministry of Women's Affairs, both in 1986. And the government retained enough of its traditional Labour ideology to flinch from serious deregulation in labour relations and dismemberment of core social policy provisions put in place by its predecessors. A manifesto commitment of the 1984 Labour Government led to a Royal Commission on Social Policy in 1986 whose emphasis on universalism and state responsibility was obviously out of tune with the times. The commission submitted a weighty five-volume report, a gold mine for social policy students, but with little influence on policy.

The National government had no qualms in tackling labour market deregulation and core social policy provisions when they won the 1990 election. In short order it announced cuts to welfare benefits and brought in sweeping changes to health, housing, education and income support in the direction of much greater targeting, 'user pays' and exhortations to self-reliance. It passed the Employment Contracts Act, sweeping away the century-old wage-setting system, replacing it with contractual arrangements between employers and employees – an approach that stripped the unions of their traditional powers and status. In part these were a response to internal and external economic shocks. A serious drought in several parts of the country affected agricultural production, while there was a fall in demand for New Zealand exports following the 'Asian economic crisis' (Dalziel and Lattimore, 2004, p. 9–10).

The principles forming the basis for social policy reform under National were fairness, self-reliance, efficiency and greater personal choice (Boston and Dalziel, 1992, p. 7). 'Fairness' was seen as strict targeting determined by genuine need; 'self reliance' suggested that individuals be encouraged to take care of themselves and their families; 'efficiency' was (re-)defined as value for money; and 'choice' the encouragement of alternative providers of health, education and welfare services (Shipley, 1991). Stricter eligibility criteria for welfare benefits were introduced, such as age limits and stand-down periods. Major changes to retirement income were announced, including income-testing. However, after an electoral outcry (and financial recalculations) some changes were reversed and a tax surcharge was reintroduced, at a higher level. Lifting of the age of eligibility for superannuation, from 60 to 65, was retained, completed in stages by 2001.

Health care policy was overhauled again, with the aim of setting up –quasi-markets to improve efficiency and choice (Upton, 1991). Health boards were replaced by four Regional Health Authorities that purchased services from public, private, voluntary and Maori health providers. This separated funding and provision, and left the Ministry of Health with mainly policy-advice functions. Health-care subsidies were delivered by means of a Community Services Card, issued on an income-tested basis to all age groups.

Marketization was also evident in the provision of state assistance for housing. The 1991 Budget brought in market rentals for state housing, replacing all forms of housing assistance with a single targeted cash payment – the Accommodation Supplement (Shipley, 1991, p. 55). This was available to renters in both public and private housing, to boarders and mortgagors (thus meeting the 'choice' objective).

During the term of the National government, education policy changes centred on tertiary institutions (Shipley, 1991, p. 69). Tertiary students' allowances became more tightly targeted, with eligibility depending on parental income (both parents) up to the age of 25. The state changed tertiary education funding, setting its support at 95 per cent of course costs for those under 22 and 85 per cent for others. Tertiary institutions were allowed to set their own fees and interest-bearing student loans were introduced to cover fees, course and living expenses. Student debt had grown to NZ $8 billion by 2007.

Compared to the 1984–90 period, National's tenure saw a move away from universal provision of public services such as health and tertiary education, towards targeted provision in which higher-income individuals were expected to pay for a greater share in direct part-charges, rather than indirectly through taxation (Dalziel and Lattimore, 2004, p. 120). The objective of ensuring that all citizens are 'able to feel a sense of participation in and belonging to the community', articulated by the Royal Commission on Social Security in 1972, was replaced by a 'modest safety net' for those unable to meet their own needs (Boston and Dalziel, 1992, p. 1). The quid pro quo was personal income tax cuts in 1996 and 1998.

Humanizing Market Reforms?

Since 1996 there has been some modification of the neo-liberal policy approach. 'By the time of the general election in October 1996 . . . there were concerns that the reforms had not achieved their principal objectives of increasing living standards for all New Zealanders' (Dalziel and Lattimore, 2004, p. 30). In 1993 New Zealanders voted to change the electoral system from first-past-the-post to Mixed Member Proportional representation (MMP). The 1995 general election resulted in a coalition government dominated by the National Party, but with the centrist New Zealand First Party as a powerful junior partner. This saw some retreat from the targeted and minimalist stand on social policy. Health services for children under age six were made free. The tax surcharge for superannuitants was abolished. However, rifts in the coalition soon became apparent, and the partnership was dissolved in mid-1998.

The 1999 election brought continued readjustments to social policy under Labour-led coalition governments. These included the reinstatement of income-related rents for state housing and a mortgage insurance scheme to help low-income families purchase property. The system of privatized workers' compensation put in place by National lasted only 12 months and ACC was renationalized. From 2004 the government began to roll out a package of 'in-work' payments (administered through the tax system) to low- and middle-income families under the title 'Working for Families'. Interest on tertiary education loans was abolished for residents. More recently the KiwiSaver retirement savings scheme has been established, with contributions from employees, employers, and the state (although membership is voluntary). This policy was prompted by economic reasons as much as individual financial security, as low household savings mean that New Zealanders rely rather heavily on foreign savers to support their lifestyles (Duncan, 2007, p. 237). The health system has undergone more changes with the establishment of Primary Health Organizations, to deliver and coordinate primary health services and increased primary health-care funding, and the establishment of 21 majority-elected District Health Boards to oversee the provision of secondary care.

Labour-led governments, often tempered by left-wing coalition partners, have also sought to soften market approaches to labour force policy. In 2000, the Employment Relations Act reinstated a more central role for unions in wage bargaining, even though by 2005 union coverage was only 22 per cent. Legislated minimum wage rates have been increased and holiday provisions extended from three to four weeks annually. State-funded Paid Parental Leave was introduced in 2002, and by 2004 was extended to meet the ILO minimum standard of 14 weeks. Social liberalization has also continued under Labour-led coalitions. In 2004 the Civil Union Act was passed providing for legal unions for both same-sex and heterosexual couples. The repeal of Section 59 of the 2007 Crimes Act removed a defence of justifiable force for parents or guardians arrested for beating their children.

The changes since 1999 have been heralded by Labour as a return to 'social democracy' – a 'third way' (picking up on international rhetoric). However, it is a very different style of social democracy than that instituted by earlier governments. The 'third way' favours pragmatic, middle-of-the-road changes in order to preserve broad political support (Duncan, 2007, p. 232). There has been little explicit discussion by Labour of the ideological framework surrounding its policies (Eichbaum, 2007, p. 57). Many of the economic policies of the neo-liberal era remain in place. Even in labour market policy there is no indication of a return to former levels of regulation (Barrett, 2007, p. 589). A recent survey concerning 'ease of doing business' sponsored by the World Bank (2006), rates New Zealand fourth in the world (just behind China) for its flexibility of labour regulations, including issues associated with hiring and firing employees and rigidity of hours of work. Overall, the New Zealand labour market remains lightly regulated and certainly not union-friendly (Duncan, 2007, p. 235).

Rather than seeking the objective of full employment, current social policy aims to improve individual employability through training and education, and by making welfare entitlements more strictly dependent on compliance with job-seeking activities. 'The state's role is no longer to guarantee a basic level of social security, as a right, for all citizens, but instead to manage the social and fiscal risks posed by those citizens who 'fail' to be competitive or whose behaviour is dysfunctional' (Duncan, 2007, p. 246). Another indication of deviation from the usual 'social democratic' tendencies, pointed out by Eichbaum (2007, p. 55), has been the 2007 reduction in the company tax rate, from 33 per cent to 30 per cent. Several commentators suggest that, in total, changes since 1999 do not challenge the fundamental reforms introduced between 1984 and the late 1990s (Kelsey, 2002; Duncan, 2007). As Aimer (2007, p. 356) notes, the economic middle ground has moved well towards the liberal end of the socialism–liberalism scale.

Basic Themes of New Zealand Social Policy

A wide range of factors have impacted upon on the shape of New Zealand social policy. The colonial heritage that affected the nature and timing of early welfare innovations continues to have resonance. Demographic changes, including population ageing and greater diversity in family structures, have led to welfare policies being revisited and challenged. Institutional, constitutional and political arrangements have also had their influence.

The Impact of Geography and Political Institutions

The development of social policy in New Zealand has been, and continues to be, strongly influenced by the country's history and geography. Immigration policy has played an important part in population change and composition. Early migration to New Zealand was relatively homogeneous, dominated by British settlers in the nineteenth century, and large intakes from the Pacific Islands in periods of labour shortage in the twentieth century. However, over the past two decades there has been greater variety in sources of immigrants. Immigration policy now emphasizes the potential economic contribution of applicants for permanent settlement – their work skills and asset-holding – rather than their racial or geographical origins.

The Maori people did not die out or become assimilated as was expected in the late nineteenth century. They never forgot the Treaty of Waitangi and continued to petition for recognition and redress. From being a colony and subsequently a 'British farm', New Zealand has developed an identity incorporating expressions of its bicultural heritage. The country is nevertheless a small society of just over 4 million people; a small economy, distant from markets and centres of power, one of the world's most isolated countries (Pio, 2007, p. 71). One advantage is that New Zealand has been protected from the consequences of over-population, has developed a 'clean, green' image (despite lapses more evident from within the country), and in the post-9/11 environment is seen as relatively safe from external security threats. On the negative side, the country is comparatively helpless in the face of international economic influences. History highlights how major policy changes have often been prompted by international economic 'crises' such as the 1930s depression, the 1970s oil shocks and Britain's move into the EEC, and the 1990s Asian economic crisis.

New Zealand is not the only nation, however, with such experiences, so what explains the speed and intensity of reforms over the last 100 years? The answers may lie in constitutional and political factors (Tennant, 2004, p. 26). The first-past-the-post electoral system prior to 1996, combined with abolition of the Upper House in 1950, allowed for cabinet domination of parliament and, as a result, rapid legislative change. A brake on rapid reform came with the introduction of MMP in 1995. The need to form coalition governments has allowed minor parties to bring influence to bear on social and economic policy (Cheyne, O'Brien and Belgrave, 2004, p. 41).

Outside parliament, changing power dynamics have also impacted upon social policy. 'Both Labour and National governments prior to 1984 were happy to govern a pluralistic society in which the major corporate sectors of the economy were recognised and involved in decision-making at the national level' (Gustafson, 2007, p. 7). From 1984, powerful unions, bolstered by compulsory unionism and arbitration, were dethroned. Business influence during neo-liberal reforms played a key role in the historic shift in policy-making (Roper, 2006, p. 179).

The Myth of Egalitarianism

New Zealand's image as an egalitarian society originates in its colonial heritage, where 'Jack is as good as his master'. Many early immigrants left Britain to escape class discrimination. The pioneering lifestyle was one of opportunity, but also of hardship and struggle. Governments promoted an egalitarian society through an industrial relations system founded on strong occupation-based trade unions and a system of general wage orders. The government also made health, education and social welfare universally available, funded by general taxation. Regulations were used to control the price of many basic goods and services, such as bread, milk, telephone services and electricity (Dalziel and Lattimore, 2004, p. 16).

Cheyne, O'Brien and Belgrave (2004) challenge the myth of egalitarianism and social consensus on several grounds. Underlying the veneer of unity they see sexism, racism and an agenda of controlling the poor. The systems in place in the 1950s to 1970s led to stratification. The golden weather shone rather more brightly on the 'typical' family headed by an able-bodied, unionized, award-covered, working male, than it did on those who did not fit this profile. The welfare regime fostered stratification by creating inequalities between workers in different occupations, between owner-occupiers and state house tenants, and between males and females (Rudd, 1997, p. 244). The image of exemplary race relations, which New Zealand cultivated, masked the outcomes for Maori, which have been far from egalitarian. Maori represent 14 per cent of the population but well over 14 per cent of people living on benefits or low incomes, in prison or dying prematurely. Maori education and health standards lag well behind those of the total population. Standardized, even universal, provision did not deliver the equality promised by Article 3 of the Treaty of Waitangi.

Inequalities in New Zealand have increased since the implementation of

Given reliance on employment as a route out of poverty and dependency, it is significant that unemployment has fallen from a peak of 11 per cent in late 1991, to just under 4 per cent in 2007, being relatively stable since falling below 4 per cent in the second half of 2004 (Department of Labour, 2006). Ethnic inequalities persist, however. In the year to September 2006, the unemployment rate for Maori fell to 8 per cent (the lowest rate since the Household Labour Force Statistics began in 1986). The rate for Pacific people declined to 6 per cent, while the average unemployment rate for Europeans remained just below 3 per cent (Department of Labour, 2006).

Future Prospects and Challenges

The key goals of the current New Zealand government are threefold. In 2007 Prime Minister Helen Clark argued that,

> our challenge is to . . . build a *sustainable economy* based on innovation and quality in a world where high volume, low quality goods and services will always undercut us on price . . . sustain *family and community* living standards in our open, competitive economy . . . sustain our unique culture, values, and *national identity* in a world of globalised media and culture. (Clarke, 2007, p. 2, emphasis added)

Each of these goals poses a number of challenges.

An important constraint on long-term growth prospects is the country's continuing dependence on commodities, most of them agriculture- or forestry-related. The state's response has been to create a distinct national brand. 'Efforts to reinvent New Zealand's national identity have emerged not as a form of resistance or opposition to the power of global capital, but instead as a way to capture the attention of powerful investors, talented people, foreign tourists and consumers' (True, 2007, p. 80).

Sustainability also requires attention to demographic change. The government has a 'window of opportunity' before baby boomers reach retirement age (PRG, 1997). During this time it must consolidate a system of retirement income support which is sustainable and equitable (both intergenerationally and in terms of current society). While the government has recently responded with the launch of the KiwiSaver scheme, it is too early to tell how the citizenry will react to this. New Zealanders in the past have rejected compulsory superannuation savings, and favour the continuation of the tax-funded universal scheme.

Another demographic challenge is increased ethnic and cultural diversity. While the Pakeha population is expected to retain its dominance in coming decades, the Maori and Pacific shares will increase (Statistics New Zealand, 2006). There have been significant recent increases in the population of

Asian origin, which now has a percentage share equal to Pacific people. This diversity has emerged against a background dominated by the politics and ethics of the Treaty of Waitangi. There have been calls for the adoption of binationalism, to recognize the partnership between the Maori and non-Maori populations. But this approach may conflict with multi-cultural approaches and raises the complex problem of power-sharing within society (Smits, 2007). While the 'third way' model supposedly promotes partnerships between the state and society at all levels, there is little indication that governments are prepared to relinquish power and foster true partnerships (Cheyne, O'Brien and Belgrave, 2004, p. 235).

Sustainable standards of living for families and communities may be challenged by patterns of power and resource sharing. New Zealanders have in the past met their needs through a variety of systems (RCSP, 1988, vol. 2, pp. 773–92) and welfare pluralism continues in the twenty-first century. Families and communities (both spatial and generic) provide the majority of personal care, often on a reciprocal basis. The private sector, sometimes with government subsidies, is playing a growing part, for example in health care and in the new system of retirement savings. New Zealand has always had a strong voluntary sector, ranging from multi-million dollar enterprises with well-developed bureaucracies – IHC (dealing with intellectual disability), Barnardos and Presbyterian Support – to informal support and self-help groups. A special feature is service delivery through Maori organizations. The important issue is how to ensure that 'third way' and networked modes of governance ensure a vibrant community sector, without overburdening families and communities.

The emphasis on paid work, which underpins the current welfare mix in New Zealand, challenges the capacity of citizens to provide unpaid informal care. Yet the family and informal sectors may increasingly be called upon in the context of an ageing population and moves to reduce institutional care for older people (Boston and Davey, 2006). New Zealand must resolve the question of how responsibility for care, especially of older, frail and dependent adults, should be shared between public, private, voluntary and informal sectors.

Finally, the goal of nationhood is challenged by the increasing polarization of society. The social exclusion of beneficiary families, as well as the inequalities suffered by Maori and Pacific people, is a core challenge for New Zealand social and economic policy. A work-focused model does not necessarily provide a way out of poverty and may merely shift people from benefits to low paid and casualized work. In a deregulated labour market, low-paid workers often lack the resources to improve their conditions of employment. The challenge is for the New Zealand state and society to examine how the 'work-focused' model will allow the development of a genuine sense of participation and belonging to the community.

The Key Features of Welfare Provision

Income Support

*Main Income Replacement Benefits**

	Number of recipients	*Expenditure NZ$000*	*Purpose, coverage and eligibility*
(a) Main benefits			
	265,747	6,637,761 (Projected 2007/8 expenditure)	Main benefits are Unemployment Benefit, Independent Youth Benefit, Domestic Purposes Benefit, Sickness Benefit, Invalids Benefit, Transitional Retirement Benefit, Widow's Benefit and Emergency Benefit. Moves are underway to combine all of these into a 'Single Core Benefit'.
(b) Other social security payments			
New Zealand Superannuation	505,900	6,817,735	Payable to persons who are 65 years of age and over, and meet a residential qualification.
Student allowances	45,100	387,979	A means-tested payment for students enrolled full time in recognized tertiary programmes. Means-tested against joint parental income for students up to the age of 25.

Health Services

Primary Care Services	*Access*
General practice	All GP visits for those enrolled in Public Health Organizations (PHOs) are subsidized by the state and the average subsidized GP charge is NZ$20–50. Extra subsidies are available for Community Services Card (CSC) and 'high use' card holders.
GP care for children under 6	Subsidies are intended to cover all GP consultation fees and prescription costs (but may not always do so).

Education Services

Service	*Description*
Early childhood care and education services	Age range 0–4. Most children are in childcare centres, kindergartens, Playcentres, Te Kohanga Reo (Maori pre-schools), home-based childcare, Pacific Island pre-schools. Various funding regimes and establishment grants.
Primary and intermediate schools	The age of compulsory schooling is 6–16 but most children attend at age 5. Most children (primary and secondary levels) attend state-funded schools that adhere to a national curriculum.
Secondary schools	Age range 13–16 (compulsory) and beyond (post-compulsory).
Maori immersion schooling – primary, intermediate and secondary levels	In 2001, 14 per cent of Maori students were enrolled in Maori medium schools – where 31 per cent of teaching is in the Maori language. 3.5 per cent of Maori attend Kura Kaupapa Maori schools, in which all instruction is in Maori language.
Correspondence school	Primary and secondary education for students unable to attend a school for reasons of: isolation, living overseas, special education needs and medical conditions. Also available for subjects not available at a student's normal school. Free apart from adult students.
Special education	Special schools and classes are established for students with special needs, e.g. sensory disabilities, severe learning or behavioural problems. Schools receive extra funding for special needs students.
Tertiary education – universities, polytechnics, colleges of education, wananga (Maori tertiary institutions)	The Tertiary Education Commission (TEC) oversees all tertiary training. Costs are predominantly covered by state funding; however, students pay around 25 per cent of course costs. Fee and course cost maxima are set by TEC. Interest-free student loans are available to residents to cover fees, course costs and living expenses. Admission based on school performance for young students with open entry from age 25. Government funds institutions predominantly on a student-number basis, but also through the Performance-Based Research Fund.

Housing

Tenure	*Percentage of private dwellings*	*Comment*
Owned by usual residents with mortgage	28	Obtained from the private sector, especially banks. A government-backed mortgage insurance scheme is aimed at helping low-income families into private ownership.
Owned by usual resident without mortgage	21	High rates of mortgage-free ownership among older people.
Family trust-owned property with mortgage	5	
Family trust-owned property without mortgage	6	
Total ownership	60	Home ownership rates have been declining in the last decade.
Rented in private sector	21	The vast majority rent from private individuals, small landlords owning fewer than 10 properties.
Rented in public sector	5	4 per cent Housing NZ or other central government agency; 1 per cent local authorities.
Occupied rent free	4	Housing attached to workplaces, farm cottages.
Total rented	29	
Not elsewhere included, or arrangements not defined	11	

Source: 2006 Census, QuickStats About Housing, Table 6.

Social Services and Other

	Description
Ministry of Social Development	The Ministry provides strategic social policy advice to the government and provides social services to more than 1 million New Zealanders. Included are programmes through: Work and Income NZ (social security); Child, Youth and Families (child protection); Office for the Voluntary and Community Sector; Office for the Disability Sector; Office of Senior Citizens; and Ministry of Youth Affairs.

(*continued*)

	Description
NZ Disability Strategy	The Public Health and Disability Act 2000 provided the base for setting up an office for the disability sector which is responsible for developing a disability strategy aimed at the full social and economic involvement of people with disabilities.
Children and Young Persons Service (CYPS)	The Children, Young Persons and their Families Act, 1989, established a system of Family Group Conferences to deal with care and protection cases. The service also provides information and referral services, family support services and custodial and guardianship services for children and young people. The Youth Justice service operates under the same act and manages the process of dealing with offenders up to and including age 16. An adoption service deals with inter-country adoption and activities under the Adult Adoption Information Act 1985.
Child Support	Operates under the Child Support Act of 1991. The Child Support Agency, part of the Inland Revenue Department, accepts applications, assesses amount of support, collects payments through the PAYE system and pays them out. It also collects and pays spousal maintenance. Payments are passed on to the government if the recipient is receiving a welfare benefit and to the custodial parent if they are not receiving a benefit.

References

Aimer, P. (2007) 'Labour Party', in R. Miller (ed.), *New Zealand Government and Politics*, 4th edn, Oxford University Press, pp. 354–65.

Alfred, M. V. and Martin, L. G. (2007) 'The Development of Economic Self-Sufficiency Among Former Welfare Recipients: Lessons Learned from Wisconsin's Welfare to Work Program', *International Journal of Training and Development*, 11(1), pp. 2–20.

Barrett, P. (2007) 'Social Policy', in R. Miller, *op. cit.*, pp. 583–93

Benson Pope, D. (2006) (Minister for Social Development) 'Working for Families Package – Outcome', New Zealand Parliamentary Debates, 29 March.

Boston, J. and Dalziel, P. (eds) (1992) *The Decent Society? Essays in Response to National's Economic and Social Policies*, Oxford University Press.

Boston, J. and Davey, J. (2006) *Implications of Population Ageing: Opportunities and Risks*, Institute of Policy Studies, Victoria University.

Boston, J., Martin. J., Pallot, J. and Walsh, P. (1996) *Public Management: The New Zealand Model*, Oxford University Press.

Castles, F. G. (1985) *The Working Class and Welfare: Reflections on the Political Development of the Welfare State in Australia and New Zealand, 1890–1980*, Allen and Unwin.

Cheyne, C., O'Brien, M. and Belgrave, M. (2004) *Social Policy in Aotearoa/New Zealand: A Critical Introduction*, 3rd edn, Oxford University Press.
Clark, H. (2007) 'Prime Minister's Statement to Parliament', New Zealand Parliamentary Debates, 13 February.
Commission of Inquiry (1971) *Housing In New Zealand; Report of the Commission of Inquiry*, Government Printer.
Dalziel, P. (1994) 'A Decade of Radical Economic Reform in New Zealand', *British Review of New Zealand Studies*, 7, pp. 49–72.
Dalziel, P. (1996) *Poor Policy: A Report for the New Zealand Council of Christian Social Services on the 1991 Benefit Cuts and the 1996 Tax Cuts*, Council of Christian Social Services.
Dalziel, P. and Lattimore, R. (2004) *The New Zealand Macroeconomy: Striving for Sustainable Growth with Equity*, 5th edn, Oxford University Press.
Deeks, J. and Boxall, P. (1989) *Labour Relations in New Zealand*, Longman Paul.
Department of Labour (2006) 'Employment and Unemployment – September 2006', at http://www.workinsight.govt.nz/publications/lmr/archive/hlfs-sep06/lmr-HLFS.asp
Department of Social Welfare (1996) *Strategic Directions: Post-election Briefing Paper*, Department of Social Welfare.
Duncan, G. (2007) *Society and Politics: New Zealand Social Policy*, 2nd edn, Pearson Education-SprintPrint Prentice Hall.
Economic Monitoring Group (1989) *The Economy in Transition: Restructuring to 1989*, New Zealand Planning Council.
Eichbaum, C. (2007) 'The Third Way', in R. Miller *op. cit.*, pp. 47–61.
Ferguson, G. (1994) *Building the New Zealand Dream*, Palmerston North: Dunmore Press Ltd.
Goldfinch, S. and Malpass, D. (2007) 'The Polish shipyard: myth, economic history and economic policy reform in New Zealand', *Australian Journal of Politics and History*, 53(1): 118–137.
Gustafson, B. (2007) 'New Zealand since the War', in R. Miller, *op. cit.*, pp. 3–13.
Health Benefits Review (1986) *Choices for Health Care*, Report of the Health Benefits Review.
Kawharu, M. (2005) 'Rangatiratanga and Social Policy', in M. Belgrave, M. Kawharu and D. Williams (eds) *Waitangi Revisited: Perspectives on the Treaty of Waitangi*, Oxford University Press, pp. 105–22.
Kelsey, J. (2002) *At the Crossroads – Three Essays*, Bridget Williams.
Le Heron, R. and Pawson, E. (eds) (1996) Changing Places: New Zealand in the Nineties, Longman Paul.
Maloney, P. (2007) 'New Zealand's Ideological Tradition', in R. Miller, *op. cit.*, pp. 36–46.
Ministry of Social Development (2006) *Social Report*, http://www.socialreport.msd.govt.nz/economic-standard-living/income-inequality.html
Ministry of Social Development (2006) *New Zealand Living Standards 2004*, MSD Centre for Social Research and Evaluation.
Oliver, W. H. (1988) 'Social Policy in New Zealand: An Historical Overview,' *The April Report*, 1, pp. 3–45.
Oliver, P. (2004) 'Treaty Settlements Half Way Through', *New Zealand Herald*, 20 February.
Orange, C. (1987) *The Treaty of Waitangi*, Allen and Unwin/Port Nicholson Press.

Pio, E. (2007) 'International Briefing 17: Training and Development in New Zealand', *International Journal of Training and Development*, 11(1), pp. 71–83.

PRG (1997) *1997 Retirement Income Report: A Review of the Current Framework*, Interim Report, Periodic Report Group.

RCSP (1987) *The Treaty of Waitangi and Social Policy*, Discussion Booklet No.1, The Royal Commission on Social Policy.

RCSP (1988) *The April Report: Report of the Royal Commission on Social Policy*, Government Printer.

Roper, B. (2006) 'Business political activity in New Zealand from 1990 to 2005', *Kotuitui: New Zealand Journal of Social Sciences Online*, 1, pp. 161–83.

Royal Commission of Inquiry (1972) *Social Security in New Zealand*, Government Printer.

Rudd, C. (1997) 'The Welfare State', in C. Rudd and B. Roper (ed.), *The Political Economy of New Zealand*, Oxford University Press, pp. 237–55.

Shipley, J. (1991) *Social Assistance: Welfare that Works*, GP Print.

Smits, K. (2007) 'Multicultural Identity in a Bicultural Context', in R. Miller, *op. cit.*, pp. 25–35.

Statistics New Zealand (2006) 'New Zealand in Profile', http://www.stats.govt.nz/products-And-Services/new-Zealand-In-Profile-2006/default.htm

Stephens, R. , Waldegrave, C. and Frater, P. (1995) 'Measuring Poverty in New Zealand', *Social Policy Journal of New Zealand*, 5, pp. 88–112.

Tennant, M. (2004) 'History and Social Policy: Perspectives from the Past', in B. Dalley and M. Tennant (eds), *Past Judgement: Social Policy in New Zealand History*, University of Otago Press, pp. 9–22.

The Treasury (1990) *Briefing for the Incoming Government*, The Treasury.

True, J. (2007) 'Globalisation and Identity', in R. Miller, *op. cit.*, pp. 73–84.

Upton, S. (1991) *Your Health and the Public Health*, GP Print.

Wilkes, C. and Shirley, I. (eds) (1984) *In the Public Interest: Health, Work and Housing in New Zealand*, Benton Ross.

CHAPTER 6

The United Kingdom: Constructing a Third Way?

PETE ALCOCK

Overview

Welfare policy in Britain in the twenty-first century can be traced back to the early years of the nineteenth century, and indeed beyond that to the onset of industrialization and capitalist economic relations in the seventeenth century. However, we cannot explore such a distant history here (see Digby, 1989; Fraser, 2003; Harris, 2004); and it is sufficient to gain an understanding of current, and prospective, welfare policies to see the ways in which these emerged from the key political, economic and ideological developments within the twentieth century. This historical context can be divided loosely into six broad stages of development:

- *Early Reform* – during the first two decades of the last century a new role for the state in providing welfare services for a wider range of citizens was introduced in a number of key areas. These included: social security through state insurance for pensions, unemployment and sickness; primary education (up to 12 years of age) in local state schools; the establishment of a Ministry of Health; and the beginning of building of public sector houses to rent.
- *Responding to Recession* – between the two world wars Britain, in common with most other Western industrial nations, experienced severe economic recession. Although there was piecemeal growth in welfare services during this period the pressure of social need meant that in many areas limited public provision could not meet expected public demand, leading to some cuts (for instance, in social security benefits in 1930) and much suffering.
- *The Postwar Welfare State* – in the late 1940s, following the end of the Second World War, the newly elected Labour government engaged in the most significant and rapid period of welfare reform in the century. During this period, as we shall discuss below, public services providing near universal coverage for most welfare needs were introduced with

widespread popular and political support. The period is often regarded as leading to the establishment of the British 'welfare state'.

- *Incremental Growth* – throughout the 1950s and 1960s, a political consensus over the desirability of state welfare was allied to a long period of economic boom, resulting in gradual growth in welfare provision and welfare expenditure within the services established by the postwar reforms. Between 1951 and 1976 welfare spending on education, health and social security grew as a proportion of gross domestic product (GDP) from 11 to 22 per cent.
- *Containment and Retrenchment* – In the mid-1970s the long postwar boom came to an end and economic and political priorities altered sharply in Britain. In the 1980s, Conservative governments openly hostile to the collective values of state welfare provision were in power, the proportionate rise in welfare spending was halted and significant reforms were introduced to privatize and marketize welfare provision.
- *The New Welfare Mix* – at the beginning of the twenty-first century, state provision of welfare remains significant and widespread, and public expenditure on this is again rising in both absolute and relative terms. At the same time, however, other private, voluntary and informal forms of welfare provision are now openly encouraged and promoted as alternative forms of provision within a new 'welfare mix'. This new welfare mix is part of a broader attempt by the Labour governments in power since 1997 to 'modernize' welfare provision, which has sometimes been championed as a 'third way' between state monopoly welfare and private market provision.

The changes outlined here are discussed in more detail in, in particular Timmins (2001), Lowe (2005) and Glennerster (2007). Despite the shifts in both policy and ideology, however, there are significant continuities within British welfare policy, especially when compared with policy developments in other countries throughout the developed world. Britain provides an interesting case of the Anglo-Saxon welfare model, sometimes also referred to as the 'Beveridgean Welfare State', which contrasts starkly with the more residual approaches found in the USA, Canada and Australia, and the 'social state' model adopted in Germany and other continental European countries.

From this perspective British welfare provision is associated most closely with the major national reforms of the late 1940s and the establishment of universal, redistributive, national welfare services. The clearest exposition of the rationale behind these reforms was provided by the 1942 Beveridge Report. Here, Beveridge outlined a plan for a peculiarly British social insurance scheme for social security, based on all-inclusive flat-rate benefits; but he also talked about the need for comprehensive health and education services and for state support for full employment (for men). His ideas were largely taken up by the postwar Labour government. Despite the reforms which have been made since then, the basic structure of much of the Beveridge vision remains in place.

The British Welfare State

Beveridge and Keynes

The 1940s British welfare reforms were based upon both policy and political alliances. In policy terms, the creation of the welfare state involved significant changes to both economic and social planning. Beveridge's report on social insurance envisaged a commitment to social policy provision through the state in order to guarantee that key welfare needs were met for all citizens. He characterized this graphically as the combating of five great social 'evils' – want, disease, ignorance, squalor and idleness. These were to be removed from postwar society through new policy initiatives – comprehensive social security protection, free state education, a national health service, public housing for all who wanted it and employment for working-age men (Timmins, 2001).

The social policy changes needed to deliver on these promises, and more, were introduced by the postwar Labour government. However, the latter promise, in particular, involved a change also in economic policy, to utilize state involvement and state investment to boost economic activity and ensure full employment. This broad strategy of 'demand management' had been advocated by Beveridge's contemporary, the economist Keynes. The marrying of such strategies for economic growth with the public provision of social welfare was referred to by some as the Keynes/Beveridge approach (Cutler, Williams and Williams,1986). Of course, welfare reform also supported and was supported by economic growth, for instance, providing a healthier and better-educated workforce for the growing manufacturing industries. It was a virtuous circle, which seemed over the next two decades to have produced the success of well-being for all within the broader capitalist economy; and, although it was not without its critics, even socialist commentators have pointed to the ways in which welfare policy coexisted with capitalist economic growth (Gough, 1979).

It is perhaps not surprising that this joint policy approach attracted ideological and practical support across a wide spectrum of political opinion. In particular the Keynes/Beveridge approach was supported by both the major parties of government – indeed, it even attracted a pseudonym, *Butskellism*, based on an amalgam of the names of the Labour Chancellor of the Exchequer, Gaitskell, and his Conservative successor in 1951, Butler. Butskellism within the political sphere meant that, despite changes in government, social policy development would continue along similar lines to cement welfare policy within the British social order in the latter half of the twentieth century – although it came under strong challenge in the last quarter.

National or Local Welfare?

One of the major themes of the postwar welfare reforms in Britain was the establishment of national services with guaranteed minimum standards for all – symbolized in the titles of the National Health Service (NHS) and National Insurance (NI) scheme. However, much of the development of public welfare provision in the country in the earlier part of the century had been pioneered not by national, but by local or municipal government. Public provision for education, health, housing, social security and personal social services all had their roots in local government initiatives. What is more, despite the radical character of much of the postwar welfare reforms, the practical policy aim was to base the delivery of the new national welfare services on the infrastructure of existing, local, welfare provision. Beveridge himself was clear that reformed public services would draw on the principles and the practices of previous welfare provisions. Decisions therefore had to be taken about how far the 1940s British welfare state should be based upon a 'nationalization' of past local activity.

In some measure this is what happened – especially in the cases of the NHS (which took local hospitals into national control and marginalized the role of local government) and the NI scheme (which replaced all existing private and public social insurance cover with a compulsory scheme run by central government). But in practice this process of nationalization was not as far-reaching as contemporary political rhetoric might have suggested.

The other three major public welfare services remained (or were placed) in local government hands. State education up to age 15 (later 16) was to be provided for all children; but was to be managed, as before, by municipal government through local education authorities (LEAs). The building of public housing for rent had been pioneered by local authorities early in the twentieth century and remained under their control, although now subject to national standards and supported by new central government subsidies. Social services, or social work, provision for vulnerable adults and children was placed on a new statutory footing in the 1940s as a state-funded public service, administered by local government.

In practice therefore the organizational basis of the postwar welfare state in Britain was a combination of central control and local administration. National standards were set and national funding provided for all services; but management, and political control, of some remained at local government level. Although this involved some reduction in the range of local government responsibility, it remained responsible for a growing proportion of public expenditure. As demand for improved services for education, housing and social care grew, so too did expenditure on these – both absolutely and as a proportion of public spending.

Therefore, in the 1980s and 1990s attempts to control the expansion of public welfare expenditure led to conflicts between central and local government over these local services; and following this even greater control was taken by central government. As a result, in the twenty-first century, there is less delegation of policy-making over social policy to the local level in the UK than in many other OECD nations. Delivery remains locally based in many cases, however; and recently, government has initiated debate about the extent to which such local delivery can be made more responsive to service users' needs by a 'double devolution' to neighbourhood-based policy fora.

There has been another significant change in the national structure of policy planning in the UK at the beginning of the twenty-first century as a result of the formal devolution of some policy-making powers to the separate administrations established in Scotland, Wales and Northern Ireland. In practice this is a complex change, with different political structures established in each of these 'subnations'; and with only certain policy areas devolved to them – education, health and housing have been devolved, but employment and social security have not (Adams and Schmueker, 2005). Nevertheless the consequence has been some increased policy diversity within the country with, for example, free home care for older people in Scotland and free NHS prescriptions in Scotland and Wales.

Universalism and Selectivity

One of the defining characteristics of the Beveridge welfare state was its formal commitment to the universal provision of welfare services. This can be found most obviously in health, education and social services where access to the main features of public provision is free for all citizens, irrespective of means, social status or contributions paid. In practice, however, there are charges for some aspects of these services (such as provision of medicines on prescription, first introduced in 1950), and there is strong evidence that social barriers of gender, race or disability have prevented all citizens from pursuing their rights to all services (Williams, 1989; Craig, 2007). Nevertheless the principle of universalism had remained strong in the UK since the middle of the previous century, associated most significantly with the National Health Service (NHS).

Social security provision following the war was also couched in universal terms, with the NI scheme expected by Beveridge to provide comprehensive protection for all outside the labour market. NI benefits were paid at a flat rate to all claimants. However, entitlement to them was based upon the condition that certain contributions had been made towards the scheme and, as with social insurance schemes in other countries, this meant that in practice some were not protected by this.

Beveridge was aware of the danger of exclusion from the NI scheme and for this he proposed the retention of a means-tested assistance scheme (National Assistance). This meant that some element of selectivity was included as a key feature of the British welfare state, with assistance benefits being targeted at poor citizens who had to undergo a formal test of means to establish that they had no other sources of support. The expectation of Beveridge and others was that such selectivity would play a minor, and declining, role within British welfare provision; in practice this has proved to be far from the case.

Dependence upon means-tested benefits has grown significantly in the UK in recent times. A large proportion of social security claimants now rely on means-tested benefits for at least part of their income. Under New Labour governments from 1997 selectivity in income maintenance has also been extended to those in low pay and to families with children through the introduction of tax credits for workers and child carers, paid to those falling below income thresholds. Such expanded selectivity is a core feature of twenty-first-century policy planning, with universal provision increasingly used to establish basic standards on which either private protection or selective support can be built.

A Mixed Economy of Welfare

The postwar welfare reforms had the primary aim of establishing comprehensive state welfare services in Britain. However, in practice this comprehensive approach did not imply the creation of a monopoly over service provision. The retention of an alternative of privately purchased health care or education was a key element in the political compromise over these services, and *private market* provision has remained a significant, and now expanding, feature of welfare for the better-off, backed-up in some areas by personal insurance protection.

State health and education services interact with private markets in other ways:

- through the purchase of equipment (drugs and books) from private manufacturers; and
- through the use, especially since the 1980s, of private contractors to supply catering and other services.

Private market provision has also grown in importance in social security and social care:

- private and occupational pensions to supplement basic state support;
- support from employers for sickness and maternity support; and
- residential provision for vulnerable adults in private nursing homes.

In housing, either private ownership or private renting has been the dominant form of provision within the country, with owner-occupation in particular growing dramatically from 26 per cent in 1945 to 69 per cent at the beginning of the new century, while private renting has declined to around 10 per cent. Public rented housing, initially available on a universal basis, declined from around 30 per cent of provision in the 1970s to 15 per cent in the early years of the new century. This has been fuelled mainly by the transfer of houses from public ownership to private owner-occupation or to new private or independent landlords; and it has had the consequence of leaving remaining public sector provision as a residual sector for the less well-off.

However, welfare is not only a mixture of state and market. There are also important elements of voluntary and informal provision. Voluntary and community organizations have played a key role in providing some welfare services operating between both state and market. These range from major national bodies such as the National Society for the Prevention of Cruelty to Children (NSPCC) to local community centres and playgroups; altogether they have an annual income of over £26 billion and employ over 600,000 workers, around 2.2 per cent of the UK workforce (Wilding *et al.*, 2006).

Informal welfare is more difficult to quantify and define, and yet in volume terms it is probably more important. Informal care and supervision in the family and community provides the major means of support for most children and up to 6 million vulnerable adults. Community care at family or neighbourhood level is now championed by government as an alternative to public residential provision for many sick and disabled people, although in practice this generally means unpaid care at home by close family members, which often places a hidden burden on those who provide such care. State support exists to assist with home-based care, through the provision of day centre, respite care and domestic support, although increasingly control over access to these services is being passed to users who can be given 'direct payments' to put together packages of care support (Alcock, 2008, esp. chs 8, 11).

Redistribution

For many of the Fabian and social democratic reformers who had supported the development of state welfare in Britain, a major goal of public social policy was the redistribution of resources from rich to poor – what Tawney called a 'strategy of equality'. Redistribution can be achieved by state welfare policy both through the direct transfer of cash by taxation and social security, and through the indirect transfer of benefits in kind through the differential use of welfare services.

In practice there is evidence that the postwar welfare reforms achieved redistribution of both kinds, especially in the early decades after the war. Of course, measuring the distribution of resources over time is a notoriously difficult activity, given the relative lack of comparable statistical information; but Goodman and Shepherd (2002) have traced changes in the Gini coefficient in the UK over four decades, comparing it both before and after the calculation of housing costs (which for many are a fixed expenditure) (see Figure 6.1).

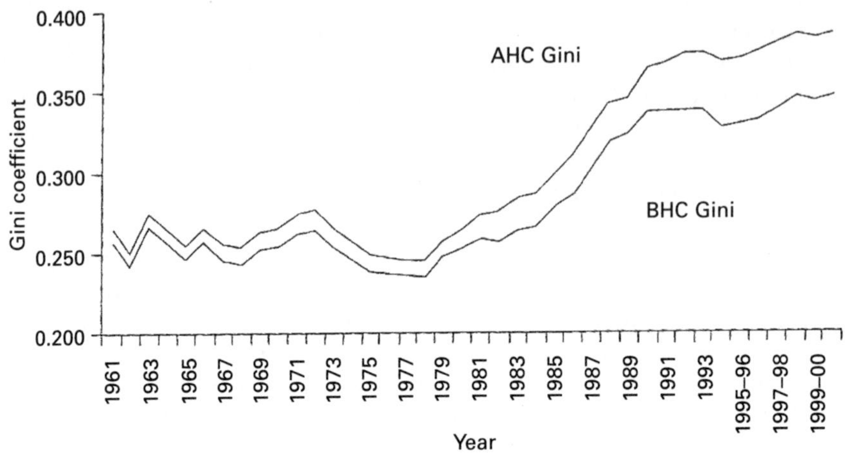

Figure 6.1 Changes in the Gini coefficient measure of inequality in the UK
Source: Goodman and Shepherd (2002), Figure 5.

This reveals evidence of a gradual decline in inequality up to 1980 but then a stark rise in inequality in the 1980s and 1990s.

Inequality in incomes can be offset to some extent by differential benefit from welfare services, however, and there is some evidence that poorer citizens do benefit more from welfare services – sometimes referred to in Britain as the 'social wage'. Hills (2008) has also analyzed the distributive impact of these and found that those at the bottom of the overall income distribution do benefit disproportionately from health, education and housing as well as cash-based services.

Redistribution through welfare also operates in other ways. In addition to this *vertical* redistribution there is also the *horizontal* affect of redistribution across the life cycle. This has always been both a direct and indirect goal of state intervention, as exemplified through the provision of child and family benefits and pensions, and through the differential use of services such as education (young) and health (old). As Hills (2008) argues therefore, redistribution within the welfare state includes both this 'savings bank' transfer of resources across the life cycle, as well as the 'Robin Hood' transfers from rich to poor.

Containment and Retrenchment

Economic Crisis

Steady growth in welfare provision and social expenditure in the decades following the British postwar reforms were accompanied, as in all developed countries, by a period of sustained economic boom. In a growing economy, meeting increased demands for welfare from expanding public services was a relatively painless process; and, as we can see in Figure 6.2 below, expenditure grew dramatically in the early postwar years as a proportion of GDP.

In the mid-1970s, however, the long boom came to an end, precipitated in part by the 1973 oil price rise. This had significant consequences for social policy throughout the world, as other chapters reveal. In Britain, however, its consequences were particularly far-reaching, especially as they were accompanied at the end of the 1970s by the election to power of a right-wing Conservative government, which, rejecting the Butskellite welfare consensus, argued that the crisis required a significant change in direction for social policy. The rise in social expenditure slowed down therefore, rising much more gradually over the next two decades as policies of containment and retrenchment took over from expansion in welfare policy.

These policies of containment and retrenchment were informed by a neo-liberal critique of state welfare which has had a similar impact on welfare regimes across the world (Ellison, 2006). In the 1980s the UK government were, in principle at least, strong proponents of the neo-liberal model; and as a result social policy development in the country experienced a broader assault on state welfare which made the British experience of reform and retrenchment more dramatic than that experienced elsewhere. Welfare reform in the 1980s went beyond the mere curtailment of costs.

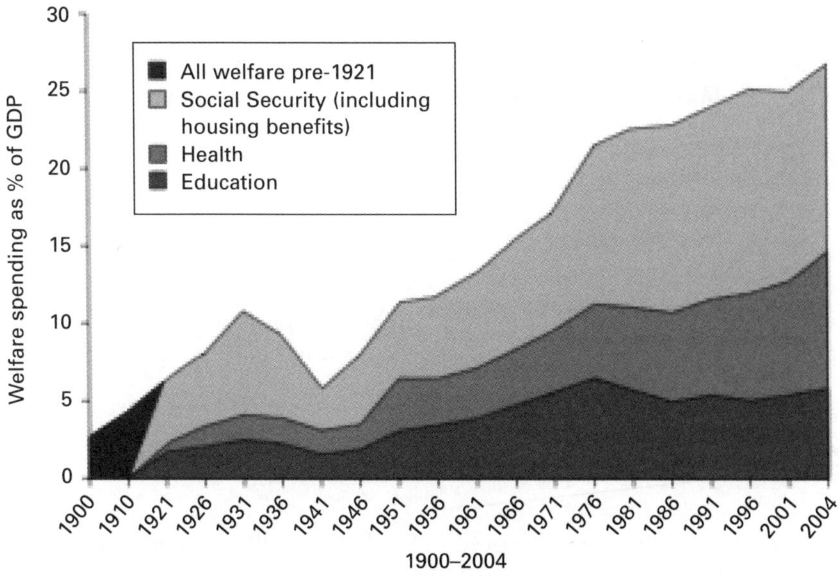

Figure 6.2 Welfare Spending 1900–2004
Source: Glennerster, 2007, Figure 10.1, p. 227.

However, the impact of this neo-liberal political rhetoric should not be over-played. In practice significant reductions in the costs of welfare were impossible to achieve and overall spending continued to grow, as revealed in Figure 6.2. What is more, the reforms that were made led for the most part to changes in the structure and operation of state welfare services rather than the wholesale abandonment of them.

Targeting

One area in which the 1980s UK governments sought to achieve change in welfare policy was in the distribution of resources through the state. In particular they were critical of some of the universal features of the postwar welfare state and argued instead for the need for selectivity – or, as they put it, the targeting of (limited) resources at those in need.

Increased selectivity was pursued most vigorously in social security provision, where NI benefits were cut back and means-tested provision expanded. The result of this was a doubling (from 4 to 8 million) of the numbers of people dependent upon the major social assistance benefit, Income Support, and an increase in overall dependency upon means-testing to affect around a third of the population. However, increased selectivity was experienced in other areas. In public housing there was a shift towards more targeted expenditure both by design (by shifting public subsidies from overall building costs to means-tested support for rent payments – Housing Benefit) and by default (because the sale of public houses to tenants meant that those remaining in the state sector were disproportionately from the poorest groups). In the 1980s the cost of Housing Benefit rose from almost £3 billion to almost £7 billion; and by 1994 76 per cent of public tenants were in the bottom 40 per cent (by income) of the population (Glennerster and Hills, 1998, pp. 153, 183).

Privatization

The pursuit of initiatives to privatize state welfare provision in the UK in the 1980s was a product both of economic and social policy priorities to:

- reduce commitments to spending; and
- encourage people to provide for themselves and to promote market-based choice.

In fact, however, both goals proved to be elusive. Public expenditure did not decline in real terms, as can be seen from Figure 6.2, although expenditure on education, and to a lesser extent health, did slow significantly. Choice, as discussed later, remains a controversial goal of welfare policy. But in any event the increasing choice provided by most of the 1980s privatizations was that which only a small minority of the better-off were able, or willing, to take up.

In housing, there was one of the earliest, and most high-profile, moves to privatization with the introduction in 1980 of the right for public tenants to buy, at significant discounts, their rented dwelling. This resulted in the transfer of around 2 million dwellings from public renting to individual private ownership. It was followed in 1988 by the transfer of whole estates into private ownership, although most of these in practice moved to independent social landlords, created to manage the tenancies in the place of the previous local authority landlords. In both cases choice was a rather one-way process with tenants individually or collectively choosing to move away from public renting, with the result that tenancies remaining in public hands became an increasingly residualized sector for those unable to afford to buy (Lowe, 2004, ch. 8).

In education and health, encouragement was given to the small private markets that had survived the postwar welfare state reforms, for private hospital care and for places in private (or independent) schools. There was some growth here, in particular through the expansion of private medical insurance, which grew from covering 3.6 per cent of the population in 1970 to 10.6 per cent in 1995 (Glennerster and Hills, 1998, p. 98). Private education remained as a smaller proportion of provision at around 7 per cent, although this varied significantly in different parts of the country. In all cases though, it was only those with higher incomes who were able to afford to purchase these alternatives to universal state provision.

Privatization in health policy also took the form of contracting out the provision of certain non-medical services, such as cleaning and catering, to commercial companies, although in many cases contracts for these were in practice retained by original public sector providers. In social services there was significant growth in private provision in residential care for vulnerable people, although this too was indirectly supported by public expenditure in the form of means-tested support for the cost of charges in private nursing homes, and was later reduced by moves to base more care in the community.

It was in social security where the pursuit of privatization was perhaps most controversial. Some significant changes were made here, although not necessarily leading to any real increase in consumer choice. Occupational welfare was expanded through the transfer of responsibility for support for sickness and maternity protection from the state to employers, but this was a compulsory measure for all. Individual private provision for pensions was openly encouraged as an alternative to the earnings-related element of state pension protection. Over the 1980s the number of people covered by private pension schemes grew from around 1.5 to around 14 million, although these figures included some small policies into which no current contributions may have been being made (Glennerster and Hills, 1998, p. 284); and in the early years of the new century new pension reforms have been introduced to regularize this provision and to provide for a clearer partnership between state and private protection.

Marketization

The commitment to the role of markets in providing for choice in welfare provision was also extended into the public sector itself in the 1980s, in particular after the 1987 election. This was achieved through the development in a number of areas of provision of what came to be called *quasi-markets* (Bartlett, 1993; Bartlett, Roberts and Le Grand, 1998). Quasi-markets were most widely used within those state services – education, health and social services – which themselves remained very largely in public hands despite the reforms introduced elsewhere after 1980. In all three areas, the overall aim was to give the consumer of public services 'choice' over access to these by creating a semi-artificial competition between different public sector providers.

This can be seen most simply in the area of education. Following legislation in 1998 parents could choose to send their children to any state school that would accept them, rather than being allocated places by the local authority. In making this choice, they had access to information about examination performance, which the schools were now required to provide. Schools were thus encouraged to compete with each other for pupils, with schools with the better reputations attracting more pupils, and hence more state resources. Of course for many parents – and their children – these choices were largely hypothetical. Most schools had a full quota of pupils in any event and would only take those from the local area, as had been the case before. But for those with the commitment, and resources, to shop around (including the Labour Party leader and later Prime Minister, Tony Blair) there was the chance now to get your children educated in the state sector at the school of your choice, a privilege previously only available to those paying fees in the private sector.

In education, quasi-markets did at least place the principle of choice in the hands of public service users. In health and social services, however, the introduction of quasi-markets took on a more complicated form. Here the 'choice' for service users was to be exercised on their behalf by professionals employed by the state, such as doctors and social workers. In the new quasi-market structure, however, these professionals became *purchasers* who use a budget allocated to them on behalf of their clients to purchase the services that they require from other public service *providers*, such as hospitals or residential care homes. In health therefore the move to quasi-markets led to a separation between purchasers and providers in the public sector, with the latter being encouraged to compete for business from the former. In social services provider roles, such as residential or day care support for vulnerable adults, could be played by voluntary or private sector agencies, so that an element of mixed economy provision was promoted.

Modernization and the New Welfare Mix

The Third Way

The election of the (New) Labour government in the UK in 1997 led to ten years of power for Labour under Prime Minister, Tony Blair, succeeded by Gordon Brown in 2007. Blair was determined that Labour governments of the early twenty-first century would be different from the earlier administrations of the previous 50 years, captured in the description of the government as 'New Labour'. In part this meant recognizing the changes that had been introduced by the Conservatives in the 1980s and 1990s, but without accepting some of the more extreme pro-market aspects of these. In part it also meant supporting and expanding the public delivery of services, but without a return to the monopolistic and bureaucratic agencies of the welfare state.

These New Labour governments wanted to promote a new approach to policy development 'between the state and the market', in practice encompassing both. This was referred to by Blair himself, and by one of his key policy advisors, Giddens, as the development of a 'Third Way' for welfare reform (Blair, 1998; Giddens, 1998). In fact there has been much debate within the UK policy community about the extent to which the Third Way is in any sense a new approach to policy development, or the extent to which the policies that have been pursued by the government have been significantly different to the state or market-based policies of the past (Powell, 1999, 2002; Driver and Martell, 2006). Many have argued that in practice the Third Way has been little more than a pragmatic attempt to make policy development depend primarily upon a judgement of who can offer the best service, rather than any preconceived idea of what form of provision might be desirable; and in the later 2000s the Third Way title seems largely to have been dropped.

Indeed, the notion that pragmatism, rather than principle, should determine policy development has been the feature of policy planning that has been most openly embraced by New Labour. There has been widespread commitment to attempts to ground policy provision upon evidence of which providers are able to offer the best service. In part this is based upon attempts to use empirical research on service provision to drive policy change, referred to as the implementation of evidence-based practice. In part it is based upon the use of contracting for services, with potential providers required to bid for service provision against clear specifications for delivery. In keeping with the aim of the government to use simple phrases to describe their policy goals, this is referred to as a 'what works' approach.

Modernization

When Labour first came to power in 1997 it committed the government to remaining within the spending limits set by the previous Conservative administration for the first two years of its office. This was linked to other measures to control overall inflation and was in large part to ensure the broader financial and economic stability in which they wanted to base future social and economic policy development. This proved relatively successful, resulting in the UK experiencing a decade of stable economic growth and improved levels of employment. This was a considerable contrast to high unemployment and 'boom and bust' fluctuations of the previous 20 years and also meant that the economic situation compared favourably with a number of the UK's major economic competitors.

One consequence was that the government was able to increase social expenditure in the UK. After 1999 the government introduced a three-year planning frame for public spending, called the Comprehensive Spending Review. After 2000 this led to significant increases in welfare spending, in particular on health and education, including both infrastructural investment in hospitals and schools and improvements in the numbers and the salaries of professionals working in these services. Overall social expenditure began to grow again in the early 2000s therefore, although still only up to around 25 per cent of GDP, below other similar EU countries, although above most other non-European comparators (Hills, 2004, pp. 128–39).

The New Labour governments, particularly of 2001 and 2005 have restored investment in public social services therefore; but they have also been concerned to ensure that these additional resources are delivering increased value, and increased responsiveness to the consumers of services. The inefficient, unresponsive and bureaucratic nature of many public services was one of the reasons for the 1980s and 1990s privatization and marketization reforms. These governments have also been concerned to ensure that public services in the twenty-first century can no longer be accused of failing to deliver value or of not responding to the needs and preferences of users.

These concerns have led to significant increases in the use of mechanisms to ensure efficiency and accountability in the delivery of public services. These include financial accountability to monitoring bodies such as the Audit Commission and the National Audit Office, public inspection of service delivery by independent agencies such as the Office for Standards in Education (OFSTED), and public reporting of performance in delivery as measured by national indicators of service level performance. They have also led to reforms in public service delivery to make services more responsive to consumer preference. These include, as noted, allowing parents to apply to send their children to the state school of their choice, giving general practitioners and other primary care providers the power to choose which acute services to refer patients to, and even providing cash (called 'direct payments') to some service users in the social-care sector to purchase services from the providers that they choose. It is planned that the range of users able to do this will increase substantially, including not only people with disabilities but also many older people.

Here, too, simple jargon has been used to describe the policy framework being pursued by government. The reforms are referred to as concerned with providing for *choice* and *standards*. Choice means that all services should be delivered in a way that is responsive to consumer preferences, achieved by ensuring that there are alternative providers within public services and across other sectors of provision. This has meant a continuation of many of the privatization and marketization reforms of the 1980s and 1990s. Standards means ensuring that all services meet at least minimum levels of adequacy and efficiency, achieved in turn by the setting of performance targets and the monitoring and inspection of all providers to ensure they are met.

In practice, of course, there are significant problems in meeting these modernization targets. The choice available in many service areas is often a spurious one. For instance, in education, most popular state schools are full and so not all parents who want to can send their children there; and in health most acute service providers (in practice large hospitals) have a virtual monopoly over local service provision and control most of the public resources for health care. Minimum standards may also not always be easy to achieve, with some evidence from the OECD suggesting that improvements in literacy and numeracy in schools declined after early success; and, perhaps most pointedly, the government failed to meet its own target of reducing child poverty in the UK by a quarter by 2004/5 (as part of a longer commitment to eradicating it altogether by 2020: Walker, 1999). There are also problems and contradictions at the heart of the use of performance targets to measure public service delivery, in particular the tendencies to set easy targets and to lose sight of broader policy goals (Boyle, 2001; Alcock, 2004).

A New Welfare Mix

One of the ways in which choice is provided for within UK welfare services is through government increasingly embracing the mixed economy of welfare provision. Although the establishment of the postwar welfare state led to the replacement of many earlier private and voluntary welfare services with comprehensive public provision, private and voluntary sector welfare providers have never disappeared from the UK welfare scene. In the 1980s the anti-state encouragement of private welfare provision led to an increase in non-state provision as a (more desirable) alternative to state provision, notably, for instance, in areas such as residential social care and earnings-related pensions. At the beginning of the twenty-first century, therefore, private and voluntary sector providers exist alongside public provision of welfare, and indeed have been growing in prominence.

Informed in part by the 'what works' philosophy, the UK government have welcomed and promoted such a mixed economy as a means of ensuring that choice can be provided to welfare users and that service standards can be delivered by those best able to offer value for money. This means planning for a mixed economy of providers and ensuring that appropriate administrative and regulatory frameworks are in place to maintain service standards. Partnership in policy planning and delivery is thus increasingly built into policy implementation. This is the case at the level of broad principle, for instance, pension planning in the UK now assumes that most future pensioners will invest in private or occupational protection to supplement their basic state pensions. But it is also a feature of practical organization, for instance, through the requirement on both children's and adult social care services to be subject to local planning in partnership with provider agencies from the public, private and voluntary sectors (Alcock, 2008, Ch. 6). Partnership working, however, has been criticized as favouring those with power and resources; and smaller organizations drawn into partnership working sometimes feel they are used as political cover for developments that they would not necessarily support (Powell, Glendinning and Rummery, 2002).

Support for the mixed economy of welfare also extends to public investment in support for non-state providers of welfare services. This applies particularly to the voluntary/Third Sector. In the early years of the new century there has been a major programme of investment in measures to improve the capacity of Third Sector agencies to contract for and deliver welfare services, including the establishment of a new Office of the Third Sector at Cabinet Office level, the development of a 'compact' to govern relations between government and agencies in the sector, and the introduction of programmes of temporary public support to improve the efficiency and accountability of agencies involved in service provision, such as Futurebuilders and ChangeUp (Alcock and Scott, 2007). Government support for the new welfare mix includes active intervention to promote and develop alternatives to state welfare therefore, and places the mixed economy at the centre of policy development (Powell, 2007). The emphasis on encouraging Third Sector organizations to bid for public service delivery has been criticized within and outside the sector as favouring only larger organizations and compromising the autonomy and critical edge of voluntary organizations, while the 'compact' has too often been overruled by powerful partners when financial pressures make themselves felt (Craig and Taylor, 2006).

Future Prospects

There seems little doubt that the modernized mixed economy approach to the UK welfare state will dominate political debate and policy development for the early part of the new century. This is because it builds on changes to the postwar welfare state, which have been cumulatively introduced over the last two decades of the twentieth century, and because all the major political parties in the country have expressed their support for the broad features of the model. Even if Labour were to lose the next general election therefore, it is unlikely that a replacement Conservative government would pursue a significantly different approach.

Where difference may become more prevalent, however, is within the devolved political structure of the UK in the twenty-first century. The decision to devolve significant political and policy autonomy to the Scottish Parliament and Welsh and Northern Irish Assemblies may lead to increasing divergence in these nations from the policy model developed at the UK Parliament in Westminster, although at present, despite some significant differences in particular policy areas, the evidence is ambiguous as to the extent to which this is happening (Schmueker, 2008). Significant departures in policy include free NHS prescriptions in Scotland and Wales, free long-term social care and now university fees in Scotland, and selection in secondary education in Northern Ireland (although this is a long-standing difference). It is possible that further policy difference will emerge in the future, especially as different political parties secure power in the devolved administrations; and this is leading to a renewed debate about the extent to which English policy should also be separately developed. At present policy for England is decided by the UK Parliament, which includes members from Scotland, Wales and Northern Ireland; there may be pressure for one or more separate English political fora to be created.

The other major factor likely to drive policy change in the UK in the early twenty-first century is demographic change, and in particular the growing proportion of the elderly within the population. Between 2001 and 2031 the proportion of the population aged 65–74 will rise from 13.4 to 17.6 per cent, and the proportion over 75 from 7.8 to 11.6 per cent (Alcock, 2008, table 16.2). This has already led to significant changes in pensions policy, with state pension provision in the future providing only a basic minimum protection and citizens being expected to take out additional private and occupational protection to supplement this. There are also plans to raise the state pension age over the next two decades to reduce the numbers depending on this.

As Figure 6.1 reveals, however, at the beginning of the new century the UK remained a profoundly unequal society. Although the numbers below half of average incomes have stabilized since the late 1990s, there has been no return to the much lower levels of the postwar decades. What is more, research shows that, while there has been some redistribution since then from the higher paid to the lower paid across the middle of the income range, the incomes of those at the bottom have been declining and those at the top have been rising – especially the top 1 or 2 per cent who have experienced rises much higher than any other group (Brewer *et al.*, 2007). This growing inequality at the margins of UK society is likely to threaten the more general trends towards social inclusion which the government claims to be pursuing, with the super-rich able to buy their way out of public services and those in poverty likely to struggle to secure access to even the basic service standards.

The next few years may be critical for welfare provision in the UK if some of these profound contradictions surface more prominently. Despite considerable investment, the government target of abolishing child poverty is far from realized, with the third of children lifted out of poverty being those closest to the poverty line. The UK now has the most flexible labour market in the OECD, which means, in reality, that millions of people, including hundreds of thousands of migrants recently arriving, together with large numbers of refugees (working legally) and asylum-seekers (working illegally), work in effectively unregulated and exploitative conditions. There is also evidence that disadvantage continues to be disproportionately associated with certain characteristics, notably ethnic origin (Craig, 2007). Future governments therefore may find it difficult even to sustain the modest gains made in the past few years, especially if the period of sustained economic growth of the last decade comes an end.

Key Features of Welfare Provision

Social Security

Social Insurance

- NI contributions from employees and self-employed where paid between lower and upper earnings limited, supplemented by employers and general taxation.
- NI benefits:
  - Retirement Pensions – basic flat-rate state pension, with limited second state pension for low wage-earners.
  - Incapacity Benefit – for long-term sick and disabled, with increasing restrictions on entitlement
  - Job Seekers' Allowance – for 6 months' unemployment

Social Assistance

- Income Support – means-tested benefit for economically inactive
- Job Seekers' Allowance – means-tested benefit for unemployed after 6 months
- Working Tax Credit and Child Tax Credit – means-tested supplements to wages for low wage-earners and families
- Housing Benefit – means-tested supplement to rent payments

Universal Benefits

- Child Benefit – to carers of all children
- Disabled Living Allowance – to meet limited costs of care and mobility for severely disabled

Private Market Benefits

Personal and Occupational pensions – widespread coverage to supplement state provision
Mortgage protection for private house owners – limited coverage

National Health Service

Public Health Care – free access

- Purchasers – local Primary Care Trusts, representing general practitioners
- Providers – Acute Trusts – hospitals, ambulance services, etc. Some with independent 'foundation' status

Health Promotion – state funded

- Led by Primary Care Trusts in partnership with local government

Private Health Care – private medical insurance

- Private consultants, private hospital beds

Education

State Education

- 5–16 – compulsory primary (5–11) and secondary (11–16) education in locally controlled or direct-grant schools – national curriculum and generic examinations
- 16–18 – Optional further education in schools or further education (FE) colleges for generic or vocational qualifications, plans to extend compulsory attendance to 18
- 18 + – optional further education in FE colleges – no financial support
- 18 + – optional higher education in universities, subject to entry requirements – financial support through grants and loans, contribution to fee through repayable loans (though not in Scotland)
- 18 + – part-time or occupational education in FE colleges

Private Education

- 5–18 – fee-paying access to exclusive primary and secondary schools, privately funded and controlled

Social Services

Children's Services

- Statutory – children's trusts, local partnerships between education and social services – responsible for monitoring childcare and abuse – power to remove vulnerable children to foster parents or residential homes
- Voluntary – Third Sector agencies (Childline, NSPCC, Barnardos) offering support or residential care for vulnerable children

(*continued*)

Adult Services

- Statutory – Primary Care Trusts working in partnership with local authority social services to assess needs and procure provision for vulnerable adults. Direct payments to consumers to purchase some services. Limited hospital care for cases of acute mental illness.
- Voluntary and private – residential and day care services for vulnerable adults run by range of public, commercial and voluntary sector agencies.

Housing

Owner-Occupied 2001 – 69 per cent population

Dwelling bought for cash price on open market (or from public landlord under 'right to buy'). Most purchasers borrow a large proportion of the cost as a mortgage from a bank, repaid over 20 or 25 years.

Public Renting 2001 – 15 per cent population

Local authorities are major landlords, most property built between 1945 and 1980. This sector declining as properties are sold to tenants or transferred to social housing. Rents subsidized for low paid and unemployed.

Private Renting 2001 – 10 per cent population

Tenants pay rent to private landlord, based on market for tenancies. Rents subsidized for low paid and unemployed at fixed local level.

Social Housing 2001 – 6.5 per cent population

Housing associations/registered social landlords – Third Sector bodies with public regulation and subsidy, now replacing public landlords. Tenants pay rent based on cost of dwelling. Subsidies for low paid and unemployed.

References

Adams, J. and Schmueker, K. (eds) (2005) *Devolution in Practice 2006: Public Policy Differences within the UK*, Institute for Public Policy Research (IPPR).

Alcock, P. (2004) 'Targets, Indicators and Milestones: What is Driving Area-Based Policy Action in England?', *Public Management Review*, 6(2).

Alcock, P. (2008) *Social Policy in Britain*, 3rd edn, Palgrave.

Alcock, P. and Scott, D. (2007), 'Voluntary and Community Sector Welfare', in M. Powell (ed.), *Understanding the Mixed Economy of Welfare*, Policy Press.

Bartlett, W. (1993), 'Quasi-Markets and Educational Reforms', in J. Le Grand and W. Bartlett (eds), *Quasi-Markets and Social Policy*, Macmillan.

Bartlett, W., Roberts, J. and Le Grand, J. (1998) *A Revolution in Social Policy: Quasi-Market Reforms in the 1990s*, Policy Press.

Blair, T. (1998) *The Third Way*, Fabian Society.

Boyle, D. (2001) *The Tyranny of Numbers: Why Counting Cannot Make Us Happy*, Falmingo/HarperCollins.

Brewer, M., Goodman, A., Muriel, A. and Sibieta, L. (2007) *Poverty and Inequality in the UK: 2007*, Institute for Fiscal Studies, Briefing Note No. 73.

Craig, G. (2007) 'Cunning, Unprincipled, Loathsome: The Racist Tail Wags the Welfare Dog', *Journal of Social Policy*, 36(4).

Craig, G. and Taylor, M. (2006) *The Paradox of Compacts*, Home Office.

Cutler, T., Williams, K. and Williams J. (1986), *Keynes, Beveridge and Beyond*, Routledge & Kegan Paul.

Digby, A. (1989) *British Welfare Policy: Workhouse to Workfare*, Faber & Faber.

Driver, S. and Martell, L. (2006) *New Labour*, 2nd edn, Polity Press.

Ellison, N. (2006) *The Transformation of Welfare States?*, Routledge.

Fraser, D. (2003) *The Evolution of the British Welfare State*, 3rd edn, Palgrave.

Giddens, A. (1998) *The Third Way: The Renewal of Social Democracy*, Polity Press.

Glennerster, H. (2007) *British Social Policy:1945 to the Present*, 3rd edn, Blackwell.

Glennerster, H. and Hills, J. (eds) (1998) *The State of Welfare: The Economics of Social Spending*, 2nd edn, Oxford University Press.

Goodman, A. and Shephard, A. (2002) *Inequality and Living Standards in Great Britain: Some Facts Briefing Note No. 19*, Institute for Fiscal Studies.

Gough, I. (1979) *The Political Economy of the Welfare State*, Macmillan.

Harris, B. (2004) *The Origins of the British Welfare State: Social Welfare in England and Wales, 1800–1945*, Palgrave.

Hills, J. (2004) *Inequality and the State*, Oxford University Press.

Hills, J. (2008) 'The Distribution of Welfare', in P. Alcock, M. May and K. Rowlingson (eds), *The Student's Companion to Social Policy*, 3rd edn, Blackwell.

Lowe, R. (2005) *The Welfare State in Britain since 1945*, 3rd edn, Palgrave.

Lowe, S. (2004) *Housing Policy Analysis: British Housing in Cultural and Comparative Context*, Palgrave.

Powell, M. (ed.) (1999) *New Labour, New Welfare State? The 'Third Way' in British Social Policy*, Policy Press.

Powell, M. (ed.) (2002) *Evaluating New Labour's Welfare Reforms*, Policy Press.

Powell, M. (ed.) (2007) *Understanding the Mixed Economy of Welfare*, Policy Press.

Powell, M., Glendinning, C. and Rummery, K. (eds) (2002) *Partnerships, New Labour and the Governance of Welfare*, Policy Press.

Schmueker, K. (2008) 'Social Justice in the UK: One Route or Four?', in G. Craig, T. Burchardt and D. Gordon (eds), *Social Justice and Public Policy*, Policy Press.

Timmins, N. (2001) *The Five Giants: A Biography of the Welfare State*, new edn, HarperCollins.

Walker, R. (1999) *Ending Child Poverty: Popular Welfare for the 21st Century*, Policy Press.

Wilding, K., Clark, J., Griffith, M., Jochum, V. and Wainwright, S. (2006), *The UK Voluntary Sector Almanac 2006*, NCVO.

Williams, F. (1989) *Social Policy: A Critical Introduction*, Polity Press.

CHAPTER 7

Sweden: Between Model and Reality

TAPIO SALONEN

Swedish Society

No other country has so often served as a role model in international social policy comparisons as Sweden. In the second half of the twentieth century, in particular, it was singled out as a welfare state with distinctive characteristics. In the mid-twentieth century Sweden was presented as an attempt to find a 'middle way' between capitalism and socialism (Childs, 1947), and in later years it was considered a prototype of the institutional welfare model (Mishra, 1981). In modern literature on the emergence and characteristics of Western welfare states, Sweden has been categorized as the most developed example of a universal welfare state (Flora, 1986; Esping-Andersen, 1990, 1996; Vogel, 2004). However, underlying assumptions for yardsticks of this kind have often been a blurred mix of normative ideas and empirical data. Some scepticism about such 'Swedocentrism' (Shalev, 1983) – a tendency to use Sweden without reflection as a role model for other countries – is therefore in order. Undoubtedly, there is some justification for analyzing Sweden as a distinct country in the broad field of social policy, but it is a mistake uncritically to confuse the popular role model of Sweden with the variability seen in real life.

Although Sweden, by international standards, has undoubtedly reached relatively high levels of citizen-related social-policy benefits and rights, this does not mean that these aspirations to universalism apply in all situations or for all groups. We shall explore these nuances in an examination of the complex and rapidly changing development of the Swedish welfare state. The core of the model of Sweden as an institutional welfare state lies in the interplay between these three policy areas:

- social security
- public service
- labour market policy.

In many prominent macro-analyses of modern welfare states there has been a narrow-minded focus on social security provision between countries. This is most likely due to easier access of comparable data here. However, Sipilä (1997) convincingly demonstrated the missing story of 'the secret Scandinavian social care model'. Furthermore, a deeper understanding of the specific Swedish features must also take the influence of labour market policies into account. Esping-Andersen (1994b, p. 76) has clearly pointed out that the unique composition of the Swedish model has been its capability to combine measures to promote productivity in markets with preventive social policies. This strategy presupposes a strong interventionist state that manages at the same time to maintain a balance between, on the one hand, active labour market policies aiming at full employment and, on the other hand, universalistic welfare reforms. These three general elements of the Swedish welfare state will, therefore, serve as a guiding structure for this chapter.

Sweden shares many of its characteristic features in the development of the welfare state with its neighbouring Northern European countries. Sometimes they are jointly described as a 'Nordic' or a 'Scandinavian' model of modern welfare states (Titmuss, 1974; Eriksson *et al.*, 1987; Kautto *et al.*, 1999; Hvinden and Johansson, 2007). In terms of living conditions in everyday life, the distribution of income equality and public services, there is strong evidence that these Nordic countries form a distinct group in international comparisons (Vogel, 1997, 2004). Sweden, together with Denmark, Norway and Finland, undoubtedly demonstrate examples of higher degrees of state interventions based on relatively high taxes and public expenditures. But there are also clear variations between these neighbouring countries due to differing historical circumstances. For example, the impact of international economic trends affected the countries' abilities to uphold welfare ambitions quite differently in the last decades of the twentieth century. All Nordic countries have introduced reform changes due to recent economic pressure, but it is unclear whether they have adopted similar patterns in their efforts to renew social policies in the first decade of the twenty-first century (Kautto *et al.*, 1999; Hvinden and Johansson, 2007).

The Development of the Swedish Welfare State

In contrast to many other countries, Sweden has not witnessed dramatic change in the development of the modern welfare state. On the contrary, the Swedish road to an advanced variant of the welfare state developed gradually since the beginning of nineteenth century without involvement in wars or revolutions. To understand the birth and development of the Swedish welfare state, therefore, we must analyze it in connection with underlying political and economic driving forces.

Until the end of the nineteenth century, Sweden was a poor backward agrarian country on the outskirts of Europe. Years of famine and hardship had forced nearly 1 million Swedes to emigrate overseas from the mid-nineteenth century until the First World War. The industrialization of Sweden took place long after the boom in continental Europe, but the transformation of Swedish society in the twentieth century was exceptionally swift and with an extraordinary impact unmatched in earlier centuries. In that single century, Sweden both entered and left industrialized production-dominated society. The standard of living among the Swedish population, reckoned in narrow material terms, on average rose at least 12-fold between the beginning and end of the twentieth century.

A more thorough analysis of this exceptional phase in Swedish history has to take account of many intertwining factors in the spheres of production, economics, politics and socio-cultural behaviour. Distinct periods in the evolution of the modern welfare state in Sweden are not self-evident or indisputably identified. One often forgotten overall factor explaining the breakthrough of extended social policy reforms in Sweden has to do with its strong centralist and nationally homogeneous traditions. No matter who – kings, clergy, bourgeoisie or political parties – has been in power in Sweden, the last few centuries have reflected a prolonged tradition of compromise and coalition in a relatively homogeneous society, in terms of religion, ethnicity and language. For national and universal policy development this has been a significant advantage.

The Liberal Reform Era

The emergence of the Swedish welfare state has often been associated with the Social Democratic Party's entry into government in the 1930s. A more reasonable starting point to consider is the vigorous reform period that followed the rapid industrialization at the turn of the century. Between the 1880s and the First World War, far-reaching reform activity resulted in the first social insurance for working people. These reforms (sickness benefits, injury insurance and old-age and invalidity pensions) were shaped in a context where liberal reformers dominated the political scene in competition with a growing labour movement. This early Swedish social policy discourse had clear connections with the German Bismarckian influence, but 'was simultaneously less despotic, less etatist and less elitist' (Olsson, 1990, p. 83). One motive was to achieve a peaceful development of the evolving labour market. Many of the modern features of the welfare state were adumbrated in this early reform period but were only revived and implemented in the mid-twentieth century. Many social policy ideas, such as universal security for all people, were already recognized as guiding policy principles, and some observers therefore rightfully claim that the welfare state in fact emerged at the start of the twentieth century (Edebalk, 1996). However, this reform era came to an end due to the international recession following the First World War.

The People's Home Reform Era

The inclusive reformist strategy initiated by the Social Democratic Party, when it came to power in 1932, was first introduced by Prime Minister Hansson in a famous parliamentary speech in 1928:

> The basis of the home is community and the feeling of togetherness. The good home knows no privileged or disadvantaged individuals, no favourites and step-children. There, one does not look down upon another; there, nobody tries to gain an advantage at the cost of another, the strong one does not hold down and plunder the weak. In the good home equality, consideration, helpfulness prevail. Applied to the great people's and citizens' home, this would mean the breaking down of all social and economic barriers, which now divide citizens into privileged and disadvantaged, into rulers and dependants, into rich and poor, propertied and miserable, plunderers and plundered. (Quoted in Olsen, 1992, p. 98)

This strong vision of a society treating all individuals in an equal way was the overall political concept that informed nearly half a century of parliamentary dominance by the Social Democrats (1932–76), underpinned by integrative links promoting cooperation and coalition across Swedish society.

In the *political* arena the Social Democratic Party was concerned to promote extended solutions in cooperation with other political parties. This was true for electoral reasons in the 1930s and 1940s with the Farmers' Party, but was also promoted later as a general principle of political practice. This specific kind of consensus-based political cooperation was named 'Harpsund democracy' (after a rural estate used for government purposes). In the mid-twentieth century this strategy was broadened to gain support from growing numbers of white-collar workers. Even in the late 1970s and at the beginning of the 1990s, when Social Democrats were in opposition, major policy decisions drew on consensus planning.

In the *labour market* arena we find another crucial pillar in creating this historical compromise. Until the beginning of the 1930s the labour market had been characterized by tensions and social unrest, with a high frequency of strikes and lockouts (Korpi, 1978). After the electoral victory of the Social Democrats in 1932, industrial leaders were motivated to avoid further legislative interventions. Instead, the SAF (Swedish Employers' Federation) reached a Basic Agreement with LO (the blue-collar Trades Union Confederation) in 1938, known as the Saltsjöbaden procedure, which promoted peaceful order in the Swedish labour market. Many strategic policy decisions were shaped in a tripartite understanding between the Social Democratic government and the contestants on the labour market.

The shaping of the 'People's Home' strategy influenced reforms in all major political areas: education, housing, working life and social security. The long-term goal was to tear down barriers and eradicate conditions that shaped class-related inequalities. Within the Social Democratic Party there was initially no unified understanding as to how to achieve these aims. In fact, two conflicting reform strategies were represented in Social Democratic thinking and pragmatic decision-making; the 'cash strategy' and the 'in-kind strategy'. While the former stressed the introduction of different kinds of allowances, the latter underpinned the importance of building up a broad supply-side arsenal of services in education, health and social services. The Minister of Social Affairs until 1951, Gustav Möller, was the most outspoken advocate of the more egalitarian strategy, while Alva Myrdal was the most pugnacious representative of a more elitist implementation of 'the good life' (Rothstein, 1984; Edebalk, 1996). Möller, however, was the most influential architect behind the Swedish welfare state. In fact, he was the first to use the term 'welfare state' in a manifesto in 1928, long before it was internationally associated with Beveridge and the postwar programme for the UK. Möller's idea was that social insurance systems after the Second World War should be built on a universal minimum-standard model. This flat-rate principle was to guarantee everyone decent income security. In addition to this state-financed insurance, people could top up with supplementary insurance. Only after Möller had resigned was it possible for the Social Democratic government to accomplish an insurance package.

The Middle-Class Reform Era

This period from the 1950s to the 1970s is also called the 'golden age' of welfare states (Esping-Andersen, 1996), a period when welfare reforms were introduced in most Western industrialized countries. In Sweden this included particularly the involvement of the growing white-collar middle class in public systems. For instance, there were debates over pension reform in the 1950s, which marked a new direction for the Social Democratic reform scheme. The post-Möller era also opened up social security reform, where flat-rate principles were combined with income-related benefits. This was the case in all major benefit systems in the mid-twentieth century; and it remained more or less unchanged until the end of the century.

Far-reaching Swedish active labour market policies also took shape in the 1960s. Instead of focusing on the passive measures that predominated in most other countries (including the other Nordic countries), labour market policies in Sweden complemented a Keynesian counter-cycle policy on the macro level with a more dynamic regulation of the labour force on the micro level. In the longstanding economic boom of the 1950s and 1960s, in particular, special policies were created to promote labour-force mobility, education and occupation flexibility. This active strategy has popularly been called the 'AMS policy', after the abbreviation of Arbetsmarknadsstyrelsen (the National Labour Market Board), which has been the central actor in promoting this policy. The Swedish welfare state took an active role in subsidizing movements from the declining countryside to flourishing major cities, encouraging labour immigration.

This was the heyday of the Swedish mood of cooperation between organized labour movements and the national capitalist leaders. The growth in production permitted both high profits in markets and increasing revenues financing evolving welfare reforms; the building of 1 million apartments in a ten-year period (1965–74), for example, was one of the most ambitious political plans to be fulfilled. The material standard of living saw a general rise, promoting economic equality between different classes. The growing public sector also played an increasing role in the longstanding endeavour for full employment and equality between the sexes. Until the mid-1960s, the traditional housewife model had dominated Swedish households, but there was a subsequent rapid increase of women in the workforce. No other Western welfare state has witnessed such a rapid increase in the female employment rate, from around 50 per cent in the 1960s to 80 per cent in 1990.

The Transition to the Post-Industrial Era

In the last two decades of the twentieth century the relative homogeneity of the Swedish welfare state came under challenge from various pressures. The period has also been characterized in competing and different ways. For a start, the era could also be divided into two specific periods with the deep recession at the beginning of the 1990s as a clear watershed. Until then the expansion of the welfare state had been forceful and combined with ambitions to uphold full employment for both sexes. However, many observers argue that the crisis in the 1990s can also be understood in terms of the changed conditions in economy and politics after the oil crisis of the 1970s. This economic crisis hit the Swedish economy but did not in principle affect the long-term expansion of the welfare state. On the contrary, the public service area – especially in health care and care for children and the elderly – expanded enormously.

If Sweden really diverged significantly from the overall trends of Western welfare states, it was in the years of the late 1970s and the 1980s. Unlike most other countries, even Nordic neighbours like Denmark, employment rates stayed high for men and rose rapidly for women. Esping-Andersen (1990) discerned this employment pattern as a growing gender division between male-dominated industrial and female-dominated service sectors. In several crucial areas in Swedish society, however, the former consensus-based contract was shattered. In the political arena the Social Democrats lost electoral ground and were in opposition between 1976–82 and 1991–4. And when in government the Social Democratic Party was dependent on support from other parties. Within the labour market the former highly centralized model of agreements was replaced by more uncertain decentralized negotiations. A starting-point for the abandonment of the earlier understanding between organized labour and capital (Olsen, 1992) was the proposal to increase the power of employees over private companies by wage-earners' funds; and by the end of the twentieth century the once strong tripartite corporative system had faded away in the face of increasingly global markets.

From the mid-1980s an overall shift of priority between full employment and monetary goals (low inflation) could be noticed at the governmental level. Since the Social Democratic postwar programme in 1944, full employment had been a political top priority. Due to the globalization of the economy and neo-liberal influences, Sweden also followed the overall international trend towards deregulation of financial and business markets. In the first years of the 1990s Sweden was hit by a crisis comparable with the great Depression at the beginning of the 1930s. Unemployment went up from internationally extremely low levels, around 1.5 per cent, to rates above 10 per cent between 1990 and 1993. The job losses amounted to more than half a million, first in the industrial private sector, then in the public service sector. Huge deficits in public finances forced both Social Democratic and centre-right governments to introduce tough packages of budget cuts, and a broad range of retrenchments took place in most public areas between 1992 and 1997. When the Social Democrats came back to power in 1994 the public budget deficit was around 16 per cent of GDP. A promise to balance the budget in 1998 was fulfilled, with a combination of firm cutbacks in social transfers and services and expanding income policies. In the last few years there has been a diverse trend; on the one hand, further cutbacks in social benefits and service and, on the other, the restoration of benefits formerly affected by cutbacks and the introduction of special grants to secure quality standards in local social services, particularly in public schools, day care for children and especially the care of the elderly.

Since the mid-1990s the Swedish economy has recovered significantly, with a persistent high economic growth that is internationally recognized (OECD, 2007). In real terms the GDP boomed with a rise of over 20 per cent between 2000 and 2005, which also increased the economic standard for households overall (SCB, 2007). In spite of Sweden's strong economic performance there are remaining worrying signs of differentiation and exclusion among its population (SOU, 2001, p. 79; Fritzell, Gähler and Nermo, 2007), discussed later. In the general election of autumn 2006 a centre-right coalition formed a majority-led government with the Conservative Party as dominant actor. The political platform for this Alliance for Sweden is based on continuity, not a systemic shift away from universal ambitions within a strong welfare state. In the Swedish report to the EU for social protection and social inclusion this was marked by the following overall statement: 'A universal welfare policy and an active labour market policy are features of the Swedish social model' and an overarching objective to 'promote social cohesion with equal opportunities for all through adequate, accessible, financially sustainable, adaptable and effective social protection systems and social inclusions policies' (p. 8). In the short run there will be efforts to lower taxes and promote growth and jobs.

In conclusion, some of the reductions from the policies of austerity in social security and social services have been redressed; and, at the beginning of the twenty-first century, the preconditions of the Swedish welfare state are quite different from those at its breakthrough after the Second World War. Sweden is no longer a peripheral, small, economically isolated country. In its ambitions to form new sustainable societal contracts in a post-industrialized world there are new kinds of challenges.

Some Characteristics of the Swedish Welfare State

Preconditions

One elementary circumstance is, of course, the *economic foundation* on which to build an extensive welfare state that is able to redistribute growing wealth. As already illustrated above, the shaping of the Swedish welfare state coincided with strong long-term economic growth. The Swedish case also displays a more complicated interrelationship, the expanding welfare system itself promoting economic prosperity.

To follow Esping-Andersen (1994b, p. 10), a distinct Nordic or Swedish model first came into existence in the 1970s and 1980s, 'with the shift towards active labour market policies, social service expansion and gender equalisation'. Until the mid-1970s Sweden followed the average OECD rate of social expenditure, from which point the OECD countries as a whole have only marginally increased on this rate. As Table 7.1 shows, the Swedish figures boomed until the beginning of the 1980s. Thereafter, social expenditure has been more or less stable, at around one-third of the annual GDP. This does not mean, as we exemplify later, that social provisions came to a

Table 7.1 Social expenditures as a percentage of GDP in Sweden, 1960–2005

Year	*Social expenditure (per cent of GDP)*	*per cent change over previous 5 years*
1960	12	
1965	14	+ 2
1970	20	+ 6
1975	25	+ 5
1980	33	+ 8
1985	31	− 2
1990	36	+ 5
1995	36	0
2000	31	− 5
2005	32	+ 1

Source: Statistics Sweden.

definitive halt in Sweden from the 1980s. Instead, it illustrates a more differentiated and dynamic composition of services and security in a budget-limited framework in recent decades. In an international comparison, Sweden devoted a larger share of GDP to social expenditures in 1970s and 1980s. However, in recent decades many other countries in the EU have demonstrated similar levels of overall social expenditure.

A second precondition is the *political framework*. As described above, the formation of the Swedish welfare state can be explained by strong relationships between central actors in both politics and economics. In the literature this kind of power dimension is highly disputed. In the 'power resource theory' Sweden is frequently used as an obvious example of successful building of strong networks, bridging major conflicts in a capitalist society (Korpi, 1985; Esping-Andersen, 1985). This was at least the prevalent notion at the culmination of the industrial period. In later years there seems to have been more of a 'race to the middle' in Swedish politics, that is, ideological differences between the two major parties, Social Democrats and Conservatives, decreased. The Swedish Conservative Party (Moderaterna) has adapted the 'universal' welfare state as an irreplaceable principle, which seems highly resilient to fundamental changes in the post-industrial period (Lindbom, 2006).

A third circumstance in the Swedish case has been the strategy of an expansive public sector and large-scale policy interventions. For its success this modernistic approach has been reliant on the development of *expertise* and *professional organizations*. No other Western developed country has such a high proportion of the workforce employed in the public sector as in Sweden. A nation's *demographic* trends also play a significant role shaping specific provisions of welfare. Sweden seems to be ahead of most other Western countries in terms of its increasing elderly population, which rose from 10–17 per cent of the population between 1950 and 2000. In the same period the proportion of children has decreased, especially more recently. Swedish household composition has undergone a gradual change, with an increase in single households and in the proportion of children with separated parents.

Sweden also now has become a country of immigration, with over a million residents born outside the country (i.e. 12 per cent). The pattern of immigration has changed dramatically from work-related immigrants from nearby countries (especially Finland) in the 1960s and early 1970s, to immigrants from non-Nordic countries, often as refugees, in the last decades of the twentieth century. Sweden has thus become a multi-cultural society; this challenges many traditional values.

A fifth basic precondition for a strong interventionist welfare state is of course its *legitimacy* among the population. Repeated surveys report strong support for an expansive welfare state, including high tax-based expenditures for basic public services (Svallfors, 1995, 2004; Statistics Sweden, 1997). Universal programmes tend to gain greater popular support than targeted programmes and during the crisis years in the 1990s support for extensive welfare provisions seems to have grown among Swedish people in general.

Measures

Social security

Nearly every element of the Swedish social security system has gradually undergone a tightening of entitlement conditions and compensation levels in the 1990s. This 'insecurity shock' especially hit households with weak economic positions: low-income families, especially single parents, newly arrived immigrants and young people. These kinds of cutbacks in the crisis period have been followed by more expansive and generous provisions in the social insurance systems in later years. A remaining question is whether the Swedish security system also reveals growing differentiation between insiders and outsiders. The current centre-right government proposes a range of changes within social security which emphasize individuals' 'willingness to work, their ability to take responsibility, their inventiveness, enterprise and courage to invest in the future' (Prop., 2006/07:01, p. 3).

Social services

In the 1990s there was extensive rationalization in the *childcare system*, with a higher children-to-staff quota, and employment within the sector has decreased. At the same time the proportion of children (age one to six) attending pre-school day care has continuously increased to a level of 84 per cent (2005).

In *health care* and the *medical service sector* the most obvious changes in recent years concern the decrease of social insurance benefits and the rise of fees. In the municipal personal service system there have also been several changes, such as cuts in institutional care and continuous rises in patient fees.

The Swedish system of *care for the elderly* is probably the welfare sector in which the transformation of the welfare state has been most visible. At the municipal level, service charges have risen, and means-tests have been more frequently applied. The outcome of these changes has been that proportionately fewer elderly people have received public service and care, with care measures more and more concentrated on those demanding the most care. An overall analysis shows that financial resources for elder care have declined continuously since the beginning of 1990s in relation to the increasing number of old people (Szebehely and Trydegård, 2007). Another significant change is the new legal framework, which has facilitated a transition towards new administrative systems in local care organizations, such as purchaser–provider models, and outsourcing. Changing service patterns and the greater demands on the individual have increased the importance of the family and personal network, a trend of informalization of elderly care. When it comes to resources for *disability care* an opposite trend can be noted, that is, substantial increase of entitlements and everyday services (Szebehely and Trydegård, 2007).

Labour market policy

In the 1970s and 1980s, in periods of a well-balanced labour market and low unemployment, the active *labour market programmes* in Sweden took care of 2–4 per cent of the labour force. In the crisis years of the 1990s this rate dramatically increased to 6–7 per cent and in the mid-1990s the total expenditure for labour market policy, including unemployment compensation, accounted for 6 per cent of GDP. According to many observers, labour market programmes tend to lose efficiency when the share of the labour force increases. In Sweden, too, it is clear that labour market programmes cannot easily create new jobs without the risk of squeezing out existing ordinary jobs. Labour market policies alone, even in the most ambitious Swedish version, are incapable of eliminating mass unemployment or securing stable economic growth. Sweden has increased the reliance on work-related activation policies for clients that are in need of public benefits (i.e. social assistance) and many municipalities have implemented activation programmes for unemployed social assistance recipients (Salonen and Ulmestig, 2004; Ulmestig, 2007).

However, the picture of the Swedish labour market policies must be complemented with an intensified investment in the *education sector*. This can be noted at all levels of education. Nowadays nearly all young people complete 12-year basic schooling. Special efforts have been in operation to upgrade adults without upper secondary-level qualifications through the Adult Education Initiative. In the area of higher education a number of new regional *högskolor* have been established. These can be described as undergraduate colleges with no research facilities, but a clear concentration on technical education. The governments' intention has been both to strengthen the regional aspect of higher education and to use higher education as a variant of active labour market policy. Nowadays nearly half of every youth cohort attends undergraduate studies at a university or university college.

Outcomes

During the last decades Swedish living standards have increased significantly, and disposable income has increased by 33 per cent since 1995, measured in fixed prices by consumption unit (SCB, 2007). One important factor in this development over the last two decades has been the sharp rise of employment among women. However, growth in living standards has not benefited all parts of the population equally. Income differences have increased gradually since the beginning of 1980s and have never been greater than in the first decade of the twenty-first century. Younger adults and immigrants have been most affected by the social and economic changes in society. The development described here concerning income and income inequality reveals that the last quarter of century has in some respects meant a questioning of the 'universal' Swedish welfare model. Another indicator of growing social and economical differentiation is that poverty rates in Sweden have shown a tendency slowly to increase from their extremely low levels in the 1980s (SOU, 2001, p. 79; Social Report, 2006). Foreign-born persons, young people and single mothers tend to be over-represented in poor economical conditions. These groups tend to lag behind in living conditions even a decade after the severe mid-1990s recession (Fritzell, Gähler and Nermo, 2007).

Recent Patterns and Trends

Five issues sum up recent patterns and trends in the Swedish welfare state:

1. Degree of *universality/selectivity*. Principles of universal rights of security and service are more or less guaranteed in childhood and old age. In working age, however, the decline of employment in the 1990s has also demonstrated that the Swedish provision system is basically a performance-related system. Due to increased unemployment, the number of non-qualified persons or persons with insufficient levels in public provision has grown.
2. Patterns of *commodification*. In most public systems, both insurance and service, the labour work requisite has strengthened, which has turned the long-term trend of de-commodification to its opposite: re-commodification. In Sweden, as elsewhere, the flexibilization of working life is an increasingly common feature, supporting renewed emphasis on the importance of paid work.
3. *Activation*. In contrast to earlier decades the activation policies in the crisis period of the 1990s have more often taken the form of selective work-to-welfare programmes. Sweden seems to have followed a general workfare trend in the Western world, with tightening of eligibility for means-tested assistance.
4. *Decentralization*. Since the mid-twentieth century the Swedish welfare state has become more of a local welfare state. Growth has taken place in the traditional areas for local service provision: schools, health care, and care for children and the elderly; starting in the 1960s, responsibilities were transferred from central government to county councils and municipalities.
5. *Welfare pluralism*. The welfare mix has been frequently referred to in analyses of changing patterns in advanced welfare states. In Sweden,

welfare pluralism refers to a shift from formerly more homogeneous ways to control, finance and produce welfare services and distribute social insurance. However, the trend to privatization in public services in Sweden is still very modest – even in the 1990s the share of private alternatives only increased from 4 per cent to 8 per cent of all employed in the traditional public service sector (SOU, 1999, p. 133).

Future Challenges

Most observers of Swedish welfare policies seem to agree that this system has overcome its worst test in the deep economic recession of the 1990s (SOU, 2001, p. 79; Social Report, 2006; Fritzell, Gähler and Nermo, 2007). Despite political and economic pressure the main features of the Swedish welfare state remain more or less intact – extensive public social policies financed by public taxes and based on a solid foundation of public legitimacy. However, this overall picture doesn't mean that the Swedish welfare state will not face some further major challenges.

One threat is the growing tendency of *polarization* between insiders and outsiders in relation to labour market and public welfare systems. The official Social Report (2006) points out specifically that the majority of the population has seen welfare improvement but around 6–7 per cent of the population has experienced no improved development at all. Poverty and exclusion in Sweden is a question of being outside both the labour market and social insurance systems. The centre-right government states that 'despite good growth more than one million people are outside the labour market and social exclusion is widespread'. Compared with before the 1990s recession, there are more people of working age outside these systems in the beginning of the 2000s, despite overall favourable economic development. An indicator of growing polarization is that those groups especially hit by recession – young people, immigrants and single mothers – continue to lag behind in the 2000s (Fritzell, Gähler and Nermo, 2007). Another sign of growing polarization is that the probability of being able to exit long-term means-tested social assistance in the 2000s is lower than at the beginning of the 1990s (Bergmark and Bäckman, 2007).

The basic problem in the current Swedish welfare state is how the work-oriented strategy, underlying the system, will function in a future labour market characterized by flexibility and insecurity. Recently social rights throughout the working years have been increasingly dependent on the individual's achievement in terms of paid work, with universalistic principles eroded as a result of a diminishing labour market and a declining welfare state. In the short term, the development of the labour force and unemployment rates are major objectives in Swedish inclusion policies. In the

Table 7.2 Employment rate in Sweden among men and women aged 15–64, 1970–2005 (per cent)

Year	*Men*	*Women*
1970	87.6	58.4
1980	86.3	72.4
1990	83.6	79.4
2000	74.8	71.0
2005	74.3	70.2

Source: Statistics Sweden.

longer term, greater equality in income and paid work and the capability to combine new labour market patterns with social citizenship rights will have to be scrutinized.

In the last few years the unemployment rate has moved up again slightly, but it is still far from the high levels of the late 1980s (see Table 7.2). This reinforced 'activation principle' contains a broad spectrum of new policy measures. The official goal is to strengthen growth and jobs and make it more worthwhile to work and run a business. It may be questioned whether this welfare policy will be successful in gaining economic prosperity as well as equality in a post-industrial society. It is a great challenge for the Swedish welfare state to succeed in including marginalized groups in working life as well as the public welfare systems – especially when those at the bottom of the income and education distribution live more segregated lives in the most deprived housing areas and tend to be ethnically concentrated.

In other European countries, unemployment and social exclusion are being tackled by reducing working time. In Sweden, however, this issue has almost been non-existent. The latest Act, from 1973, stated that the total working time in one week should be 40 hours. Since then no national reductions have been made, and during the last decade the actual working time per employee has increased. The total number of overtime hours in the Swedish labour market has been much higher recently than in the 1980s.

Thus the complex nature of the advanced welfare state in Sweden is not easy to capture in simplistic terms, and some healthy scepticism is recommended. The most optimistic interpretation of the Swedish case would argue that the crisis period in the 1990s was just a 'bump' in the road towards improvement of the universal welfare model. On the other hand, a more critical view might argue that the universal model has never really existed and that many of its basic preconditions are in a state of hazardous change in the ongoing transition to a post-industrial society. The present transformation of the welfare state raises the same fundamental questions of equality, efficiency and power as in earlier stages of the emerging welfare state.

Key Features of Welfare Provision

Social Security

	Provisions
Social insurance, families and children	Parental cash benefit Maternity benefit Benefit in the event of adoption Child allowance
Health	Sickness benefit Benefits to close relatives and carriers of contagious diseases In-patient health care and general primary health care Private out-patient treatment financed by counties and municipalities Private dental treatment financed by National Social Security Office Other social measures such as ambulance service provided by counties and municipalities
Disability	Anticipatory pension as basic pension including supplements Anticipatory pension as labour market pension Care allowance Disability compensation Rehabilitation benefit Support for buying a car
Old age	Old-age basic pension Labour market supplementary pension Special supplements, including child and wife supplements Private service pensions from collective labour market insurance Partial retirement pension
Housing	Housing benefits for families with children Housing benefits to recipients of old-age pension, wife supplement Housing benefit to young people
Social assistance	Municipal means-tested social assistance Introductory compensation to refugees

(*continued*)

Services

	Provisions
Education	Compulsory schooling free of charge for all children aged 7 to 16, including transportation and free lunch. State grants for independent (private, non-profit) schools. Additional home language training. Three-year upper secondary school Municipal adult education.
Social services	Municipal childcare for children aged 1 to 6 years Municipal school-age childcare Home-help services for old age and persons with disability Special housing for old age – group homes etc. Accommodation for old age – old people's homes, nursing homes etc. Municipal expenditure on special housing for elderly, including care, treatment etc. Municipal expenditure on support to the elderly in ordinary flats Transport service for elderly and persons with disability Psychiatric service and care Legal family case-work Youth counselling Family counselling Counselling and treatment for drug abusers

Labour Market Measures

- Unemployment insurance (union-based but state funded)
- Expenditure on labour market support
- Support to start a business
- Educational supplements for labour market training
- Vocational training benefit for labour market, job-seeking and rehabilitation
- Support for youth placements
- Removal grants

References

Bergmark, Å. and Bäckman, O. (2007) 'Socialbidragstagandets dynamik – varaktighet och utträden från socialbidragstagande under 2000-talet' [The Dynamics of Means-Tested Social Assistance Take-Up – Duration and Exits from Social Assistance in the 2000s], *Socialvetenskaplig Tidskrift*, 2–3.

Childs, M. (1947) *Sweden: The Middle Way*, Yale University Press.

Edebalk, P. G. (1996) *Välfärdsstaten träder fram: Svensk socialförsäkring 1884–1955* [The Welfare State Emerges: Swedish Social Insurance 1884–1995], Arkiv.

Eriksson, R., Hansen, E. J., Ringen, S. and Uusitalo, H. (eds) (1987) *The Scandinavian Model: Welfare States and Welfare Research*, M. E. Sharpe.

Esping-Andersen, G. (1985) *Politics Against Markets*, Princeton University Press.

Esping-Andersen, G. (1990) *The Three Worlds of Welfare Capitalism*, Polity Press.

Esping-Andersen, G. (1994a) 'Jämlikhet, effektivitet och makt' [Equality, Efficiency and Power], in P. Thullberg and K. Östberg (eds), *Den svenska modellen* [The Swedish Model], Studentlitteratur.

Esping-Andersen, G. (1994b) *After the Golden Age: The Future of the Welfare State in the New Global Order*, UNRISD, Occasional Paper No. 7.

Esping-Andersen, G. (ed.) (1996) *Welfare States in Transition: National Adaptations in Global Economies*, Sage.

Esping-Andersen G. (1999) *Social Foundation of Postindustrial Economies*, Oxford University Press.

Flora, P. (ed.) (1986) *Growth to Limits: The Western European Welfare States Since World War II*, Vol. 1, de Gruyter.

Fritzell, J., Gähler, M. and Nermo, M. (2007) 'Vad hände med 1990-talets stora förlorargrupper? Välfärd och ofärd under 2000-talet' [What Happened to the Disadvantaged Groups of the 1990s? Welfare and Disadvantage during the First Years of the New Millennium], i *Socialvetenskaplig Tidskrift*, 2–3.

Ginsburg, N. (1992) *Divisions of Welfare*, Sage.

Gould, A. (1996) 'Sweden: The Last Bastion of Social Democracy', in V. Georgeand P. Taylor-Gooby (eds), *European Welfare Policy – Squaring the Welfare Circle*, Macmillan.

Hansen, H. (1998) *Elements of Social Security. A Comparison Covering: Denmark, Sweden, Finland, Germany, Great Britain, Netherlands and Canada*, The Danish National Institute of Social Research, 98, p. 4.

Hvinden, B., and Johansson, H. (2007) *Citizenship in Nordic Welfare States: Dynamics of Choice, Duties and Participation in a Changing Europe*, Routledge.

Kautto, M., Heikkilä, M., Hvinden, B., Marklund, S. and Ploug, N. (eds) (1999) *Nordic Social Policy*, Routledge.

Korpi, W. (1978) *Arbetarklassen i välfärdskapitalismen* [The Working Class in Welfare Capitalism], Prisma.

Korpi, W. (1985) 'Power Resources Approach vs. Action and Conflict: On Causal and Intentional Explanation in the Study of Power', *Sociological Theory*, 3, pp. 31–45.

Lindbom A. (2006) *The Swedish Conservative Party and the Welfare State*, Working Paper 2006: 12, Institute for Future Studies.

Mishra, R. (1981) *Society and Social Policy*, Macmillan.

NOSOSKO (1998) *Social Protection in the Nordic Countries 1996: Scope, Expenditure and Financing*, Nordic Social-Statistical Committee, 9, p. 98.

OECD (2007) *Sweden: Achieving Results for Sustained Growth*, Policy Brief, March.

Olsen, G. M. (1992) *The Struggle for Economic Democracy in Sweden*, Avebury.

Olsson, S. E. (1990) *Social Policy and the Welfare State in Sweden*, Arkiv.

Prop. 2006/07:01 *Budget Statement. Economic and Budget Policy Guidelines*, SwedishGovernment.

Rostgaard, T., Holm, T., Jensen Toftegaard, D. and Byrgesen, Graff C. (1998) *Omsorg for børn og ældre – kommunal praksis i Europa* [Care for Children and Old Age – Local Practice in Europe], Socialforskningsinstituttet, 98, p. 19.

Rothstein, B. (1984) 'Gustav Möller, välfärdsstaten och friheten' [Gustav Möller, the Welfare State and the Freedom], *Tiden*, 81.

Salonen, T. and R. Ulmestig (2004) *Nedersta trappsteget. En studie om kommunal aktivering*. [The Lowest Step. A Study of Local Activation Policy], Växjö Universtity

SCB (2007) *Inkomstfördelningsundersökningen 2005* [Income Distribution Survey 2005], HE 21 SM 0701, Statistics Sweden.

Shalev, M. (1983) 'The Social Democratic Model and Beyond: Two "Generations" of Comparative Research on the Welfare State', *Comparative Social Research*, 6, pp. 315–51.

Sipilä, J. (ed.) (1997) *Social Care Services. The Key to the Scandinavian Welfare Model*, Avebury.

Socialstyrelsen (1997) *Barnomsorgen sparar* [Savings in the Care of Children], Pressmeddelande 60, National Board of Health and Welfare.

Socialstyrelsen (1998) *Social Report 1997*, National Board of Health and Welfare.

SOU (Official State Inquiries) (1999) *Kommunkontosystemet och rättvisan – momsen, kommunerna och konkurrensen* [The System of Municipal Accounts and Justice – VAT, the Municipalities and Competition], Ministry of Finance, 133.

SOU 2001:79 *Välfärdsbokslut för 1990-talet* [Welfare in Sweden: The Balance Sheet for the 1990s], Fritzes.

Statistics Sweden (1997) *Välfärd och ojämlikhet i 20-årsperspektiv 1975–1995* [Living Conditions and Inequality in Sweden – a 20-Year Perspective 1975–1995], Report No. 91, Statistics Sweden.

Stephens, J. (1996) 'The Scandinavian Welfare States: Achievements, Crisis and Prospects', in G. Esping-Andersen (1996), *op. cit.*

Svallfors, S. (1995) *In the Eye of the Beholder – Opinions on Welfare and Justice in Comparative Perspective*, Bank of Sweden Tercentenary Foundation.

Svallfors, S. (2004). 'Class, Attitudes and the Welfare State: Sweden in Comparative Perspective', *Social Policy and Administration*, 38(2), pp. 119–38.

Szebehely, M. and Trydegård, G.-B. (2007) 'Omsorgstjänster för äldre och funktionshindrade: skillda villkor, skilda trender? [Care Services for Elderly and Disabled Persons: Different Conditions, Different Trends?], i *Socialvetenskaplig Tidskrift*, 2–3.

Titmuss, R. (1974) *Social Policy*. Allen and Unwin.

Ulmestig, R. (2007) *På gränsen till fattigvård? En studie om arbetsmarknadspolitik och socialbidrag* [Return to Poverty Relief? A Study on Labour Market Policies and Social Assistance], Lund Dissertations in Social Work No. 27, Lund University

Vogel, J. (1997) *Living Conditions and Inequality in the European Union*, Eurostat Working Documents, Population and Social Conditions, EEE/1997-3.

Vogel J. (2004) 'Towards a Typology of European Welfare Production', in J. Vogel (ed.), *Perspektiv på välfärden* [Perspectives on Welfare], Rapport 106, Statistics Sweden.

CHAPTER 8

Germany: A Centrist Welfare State at the Crossroads

LUTZ LEISERING

What is 'Germany'?

Since the late nineteenth century, Germany has undergone more drastic changes, both of political regime and territory, than most countries. During four decades after the Second World War there were two diametrically opposed regimes coexisting within Germany. Imperial Germany, the Reich (1871–1918), was followed by the Weimar Republic, the first German democracy (1919–33), and by National Socialism, the Third Reich (1933–45). After a period of occupation, a democratic and capitalist West Germany, the Federal Republic of Germany (FRG), and a totalitarian and communist East Germany, the German Democratic Republic (GDR), were founded in 1949, only reuniting in 1990. These historical periods have left their marks on social policy as on other areas of policy. Yet, despite the changes, there were considerable institutional continuities across political regimes. Unification in 1990 was a takeover of the GDR by the FRG. On one day, all FRG legal and social institutions were imposed on the eastern part, including basic institutional social policy arrangements.

Since its foundation as a national state in 1871, Germany has been a federal state consisting of (currently) 16 states (*Länder*). Federalism was abandoned only during National Socialist and communist rule. This diversity stems from pre-1871 traditions when 'Germany' was split into numerous small states and principalities. The federal structure of the German polity is laid down in the Constitution of 1949 in Article 20, which cannot be changed even by a 100 per cent majority in parliament. A major aspect of German federalism is that education almost exclusively falls within the Länder's competence. Unlike other countries, education is therefore not normally considered as part of 'social policy' and does not figure in the social budget.

The Evolution of a Welfare State Model (1880–1995)

Germany came late to industrialization, but pioneered modern state welfare. Several historical phases can be distinguished:

- *Laying the foundations* (1880–1918). In the 1880s, Chancellor Bismarck introduced social insurance systems to protect workers – and, from 1911, white-collar workers also – against the risks of sickness, industrial injury and old age. These were paternalist and authoritarian reforms with a double edge both against the economic liberals of the day and the socialist workers' movement, which were seen as a threat to the imperial regime. While Britons think of the late 1940s as the founding years of 'the welfare state', Germans think of Bismarck as the founding father of their social insurance state. Primary education had already been made compulsory in Prussia (the largest pre-1871 German state) in 1825. During the First World War, foundations were laid for modern industrial relations between trades unions and employers.
- *Democracy and economic crisis* (1918–33). The first years of mass democracy gave rise to substantial departures in social policy such as the introduction of social rights in the new Constitution, the creation of a new branch – unemployment insurance – of social insurance, and social democratic policies in the municipalities, for example, in the field of health and family services. However, massive economic and social problems and political confrontation led to societal breakdown and the emergence of National Socialism.
- *The National Socialist 'welfare state'* (1933–45). One of the original promises of the regime was to replace mass unemployment and misery by new welfare. The racist and authoritarian ideology left its mark on social policy, by orienting health, family and education policies towards eugenic aims, replacing trades unions and the labour party by a fascist organization of industrial relations, the principle of self-government of social insurance by authoritarian rule, and by expelling Jews and critics of the system from the civil and welfare services. However, much basic institutional structure of social insurance remained intact or was even extended.
- *Establishing the postwar welfare state* (1949–66). After the Allied occupation, the two Germanies were founded in 1949. In the FRG, this chapter's major focus, debates about a new, more egalitarian welfare state along the lines of Beveridge or the ideas of the German labour movement soon subsided. Instead, ingrained social policy institutions were restored by a centre/centre-right government led by the Christian Democratic Party (CDP), increasingly backed by the social democratic (SDP) opposition. Economic reconstruction, promoting house-building

and integrating millions of migrants were the main social policy tasks of the early years, followed by gradual expansion and reform of social security. The 1949 Constitution introduced the welfare state (or rather the 'social state') as an unalterable principle of the FRG. The major 1957 old-age pensions reform act became postwar welfare's legitimating cornerstone.

- *Modernizing the welfare state* (1966–75). With the Social Democrats in government, unprecedented expansion of social policy followed, provoking high hopes of social planning and active policies directed to enhancing 'the quality of life' for all groups in society, and not only for workers, as in traditional industrial social policy. Education boomed and a wide range of new or extended benefits and services was introduced, for example, housing benefit, means-tested grants for students and active labour market policies. Keynesian economic policy and neo-corporatist systems of negotiation between state, employers and employees were also introduced. It was also the formative period of social work as a semi-profession.
- *Consolidation and new expansion* (1975–c. 1995). Economic crisis and political challenges terminated the era of expansion. Fiscal constraints began to dominate policy-making, and social security systems were restructured rather than extended. Unlike Thatcher, however, Chancellor Kohl's neo-conservatism largely remained rhetorical during his 16 years of office (1982–98). Benefits were cut repeatedly but key structures remained intact. There were even new departures, especially benefits and social rights for families and mothers and, above all, the explosion of social spending triggered by the unique historical event of unification with the economically run-down East Germany in 1990. In 1996 social spending (not including education) reached a peak of 31 per cent of GDP. After unification, social expenditure reached an historic scale of about two-thirds of the (East German) regional GDP. Without this effort, mainly flowing from annual transfers of some DM150 billion from west to east, the enormous problems of mass unemployment and social upheaval could not have been handled with political safety (Ritter, 2006).
- *The socialist 'welfare state' – the GDR* (1949–90). The GDR, too, was a welfare state but counter-posed to the Western variety. It claimed to deliver more social security than West Germany. Rather than redistributing wealth produced in a market as in western states, the GDR model aimed to abolish the market altogether and establish a command economy oriented towards 'social' aims, for example, by securing jobs for everybody, by massive subsidies of basic consumer goods and by tying housing, social services and pension entitlements to the workplace. The design of social services and benefits broke with the Bismarckian tradition even more than had the National Socialists. Centralized and uniform benefit schemes prevailed. Early on, active discrimination policies against

> children from bourgeois families achieved higher equality of opportunity in higher education than in West Germany. However, social security benefits were low, social services (e.g. old people's homes) were in poor condition and there was collective as well as individual (relative) poverty. In the late 1980s, the GDR became the first welfare state to collapse beneath its social services burden.

Bismarck's initial policies have left their mark till now, basic principles and forms of organization having survived. However, the widespread notion of continuity needs qualification. In an evolutionary process of gradual change, especially in the years after the Second World War, German social policy has been substantially transformed. What started as social insurance for limited groups of workers and with low benefits, gradually grew into a comprehensive, quasi-universalist network of social services for everyone. Only after 1949 did Germany become a fully mixed society, representing a third way between economic liberalism and a residual welfare state on the one hand and a socialist or communist system of totalitarian and authoritarian provision of goods by the state on the other. When Germans prefer the term 'social state', as entwined in the postwar Constitution, to the term 'welfare state', they want to add a dividing line between social policy that respects the freedom of the individual and the market as a general principle ('social state') and a hypertrophied system of state provision and control ('welfare state').

Nevertheless the West German welfare state has expanded considerably during the postwar decades, with social spending reaching almost one-third of gross net product (see Figure 8.1)

In 1950 the FRG started with the highest level of social spending among Western countries, although in later decades some countries spent even more. At the same time the numbers of social services clients as well as of staff providing and delivering services have increased drastically. Currently, more than a third of the population derive most of their income from the welfare state, either as clients or as staff (Schmidt, 2005, pp. 153ff.). Social law has expanded equally, with more complex legal regulations than in most other welfare states.

Continuity still remains a key feature of German social policy development. It can be seen, first, in the survival of the principle of social insurance, which in Germany has the specific meaning of a 'pay-as-you-go' system financed not primarily by taxes but by contributions of employers and employees and run by semi-autonomous non-state bodies administered by those interests; second, in the deeply entrenched federal structure of government with each of the three levels – central government, Länder and municipalities – having their own domains of social policy; and, third, in the informal great welfare state coalition shaping social policy since 1948. Both big parties alternately leading the Federal Government – the CDP and the SDP – have been welfare state parties throughout, fostering the expansion of the welfare state and joining forces in all major social policy reforms in

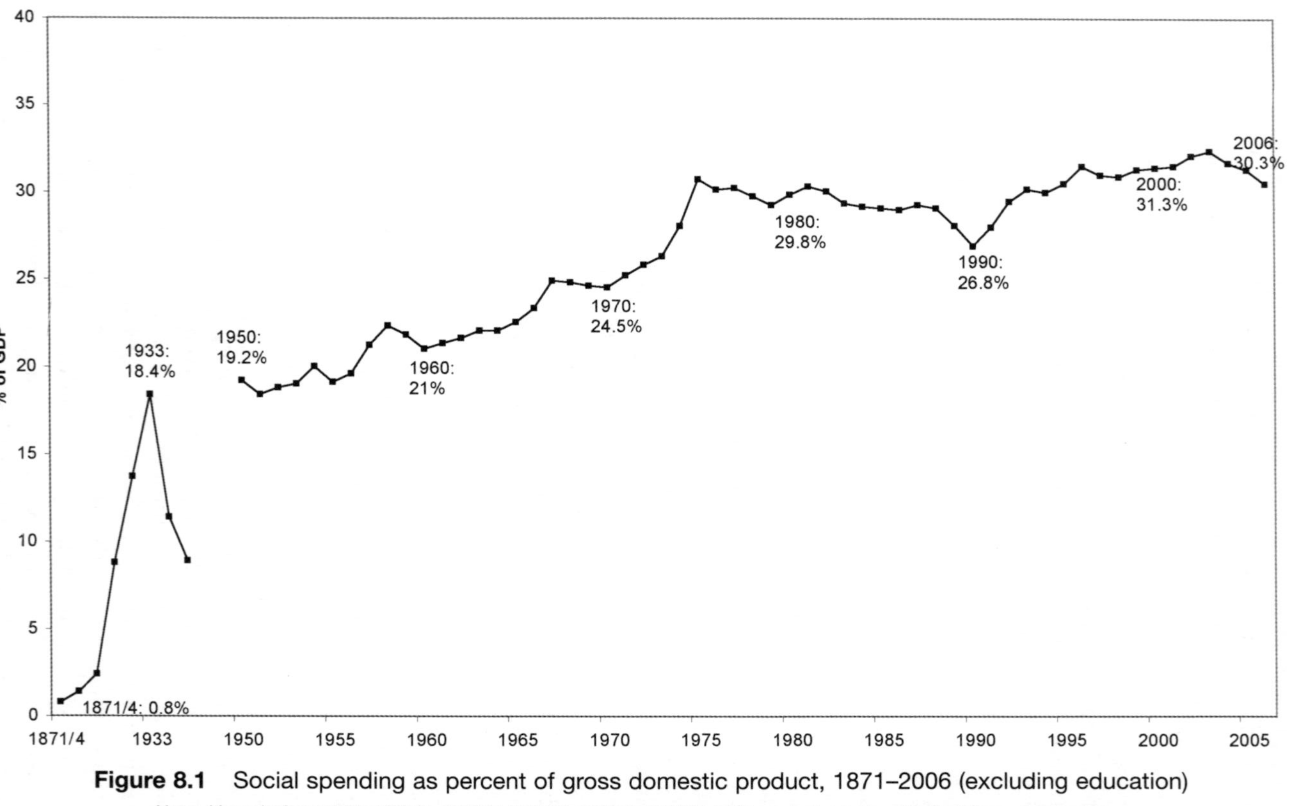

Figure 8.1 Social spending as percent of gross domestic product, 1871–2006 (excluding education)

Note: Years before 1950: 1871/4, 1885/9, 1900/4, 1925/9, 1930/2 1933 peak due to low GNP at time of depression.
Source: Computed from Lampert/Althammer (2004, p. 311), Schmidt (2005, p. 157), Federal Ministry of Labour and Social Affairs (2007, p. 6).

postwar Germany. Since the mid-1990s, some of these principles are being questioned. Are we nearing the end of a model of social policy that started almost 120 years ago?

Consensus

German political culture is oriented towards consensus and compromise. Compared to other countries there has been little confrontation either in politics or industrial relations. The expansion of state social policy could draw on relatively homogeneous pro-welfare state beliefs and values backed by all political parties. Policy-making was dominated by a centre/centre-right party (the CDP) leading the government during two-thirds of the FRG's first half-century, mostly supported in an informal socio-political coalition by the non-socialist SDP, itself open to compromise in postwar reconstruction. In this sense the FRG has been a 'centrist' welfare state (Schmidt, 1998, p. 220).

More generally, Germany is a consensus democracy (juxtaposed by Lijphart with the Anglo-Saxon majoritarian democracy). A multi-actor system with proportional representation rather than majority vote and a federal polity create pressure for cooperation, negotiations and consensus. Economic liberalism among the Christian Democrats is tempered by a pronounced conservatism with regard to family and social relationships, the social element being tangible in the strong, well-organized labour wing of the party. The Social Democrats, even while upholding the flag of socialism in the 1950s, supported legislation that restored the ingrained fabric of the welfare state. The small liberal party, the Free Democratic Party (FDP), in government for most of the postwar years alternating between coalitions with the Christian Democrats and the Social Democrats, was generally more critical of the welfare state but joined the general consensus in practical politics. The Green Party, founded in 1980 and in government coalition with the Social Democrats 1998–2005, is an innovative, less dogmatic, pro-welfare-state party. Radical liberal critics of the welfare state always had a voice in the debate, but only from the mid-1990s did their views gain weight.

The relationship between labour and capital is equally geared to social integration and consensus. Their cooperation as 'industrial partners' (*Tarifpartner*) is also based on compromise, reflected in very low levels of industrial conflict. The German model of industrial democracy, enacted in 1951 and 1976, with strong trades union representation on the executive boards of private companies (co-determination, *Mitbestimmung*), has received attention worldwide. Social insurance as the core of the German welfare state expresses a normative compromise and consensus between collective and individualist values, through compulsory membership and earnings-related benefits.

Ludwig Erhard and the 'Social Market Economy'

The term 'Social Market Economy', coined in 1946 and explicitly designed as a 'third' or middle way, has been the hallmark of postwar West German democratic welfare capitalism. The concept originated from the German school of economics called ordo-liberalism, developed in the 1930s and 1940s against both unfettered liberalism and the experience of totalitarian rule and command economy under fascism and Stalinism.

Social Market Economy, with its promise of regaining wealth and welfare in a free society, won the CDP the first (1949) election. Its main protagonist, Ludwig Erhard, Minister for Economic Affairs 1949–63, became the 'father of the economic miracle' in postwar Germany. Erhard had a narrow conception of Social Market Economy, a kind of people's capitalism (Abelshauser, 1996), geared to increases in wages, consumption and property for all strata of society, rather than substantial state-provided social services. He advocated measures like anti-inflation, currency and anti-trust policies to strengthen, not contain, the operation of the market. It was not a variety of, but an antidote to, the welfare state. Erhard saw the 'welfare state' – negatively – as a 'modern paranoia'.

The great 1957 old-age pensions reform which Chancellor Adenauer had to fight through against Erhard, was the first political defeat for Erhard's perspective and a major step towards interpreting 'social market economy' in a pro-, not anti-welfare-state way. By the early 1960s, it had become the widespread term signifying consensus and social peace in the middle ground.

Intermediate Agencies and Corporatism

Dating back to the absolutist, militarist Prussian tradition and idealistic Hegelian social philosophy, a strong belief in the 'state' – an essentialist term preferred to the more pragmatic Anglo-Saxon term 'government' – is deeply entrenched in German social thought. Still the German politico-administrative system, especially in respect of social policy, is less centralized, less 'statist' than many other welfare states. This is reflected in the social budget, the budget not of any government agency or body but a sum of elements from a variety of budgets of mainly non-governmental institutions. Most is spent in the five branches of social insurance, by para-state bodies, mainly funded and administered by its members and employers; the two largest branches, health and old-age pensions, account for half. However, social insurance, like other non-state bodies, is subject to legal regulation, to some financial support and to political control by the state. Old-Age Pensions Insurance receives an annual state subsidy of some €79 billion (in 2005).

The corporatist structure, the variegated web of semi-autonomous actors, groups and institutions, has been typical of German social policy since its inception. Social welfare is produced by a broad range of intermediate agencies, which are neither purely governmental (such as a national health service) nor entirely independent (such as occupational pensions and private insurance). These agencies have been granted privileged status as providers or coordinators of welfare services, adding up to a tightly regulated structure of society. Liberal critics claim this accounts for much of Germany's inflexibility in adapting to the new global economy.

The key elements of German corporatism are:

- The five branches of social insurance (see below).
- Social professions, above all medical doctors: they have higher socio-legal status and long had higher incomes than doctors in most countries. Since 1955, doctors who have signed in with Health Insurance have a monopoly. Treatment by private doctors is not reimbursed by Health Insurance so that they have remained marginal in the health sector. Contractual doctors are paid fixed price fees-for-service.
- 'Social partners' – associations of employers and trades unions in industrial relations.
- Systems of coordination, negotiation and bargaining between corporate actors: between the 'social partners' – their autonomy being guaranteed by the Constitution – and between sickness funds and associations of medical doctors.
- Voluntary welfare organizations, which will be described in more detail since they occupy a central position in the organization of personal social services.

Subsidiarity, a key principle of the German welfare mix, laid down in the Social Assistance Act and in the Children and Youth Welfare Act and rooted in Social Catholicism, means that small units have priority over larger units, especially over the state, whenever appropriate. Help by bureaucratic organizations is subsidiary to support relationships within the family, and state aid is second to aid by voluntary welfare associations. This principle pertains to all personal social services directed to age groups (youth and elderly), to families and to 'problem groups' (the poor, people with disabilities). Welfare associations employ 1.16 million waged employees (2000; up from 382,000 in 1970; Lampert and Althammer, 2004, p. 459) and large numbers of unpaid (voluntary) helpers.

Major umbrella organizations of voluntary welfare include Caritas (Roman Catholic) and Diakonie (Protestant), mirroring the bi-confessional structure of German Christianity; the Non-Denominational, Workers and Central Jewish Welfare Associations; and the Red Cross. These associations act as service providers in service centres, hospitals, residential homes and care for elderly and people with disabilities and sheltered employment. In addition, they are political actors – in the field of children and youth services they have a formal say in the administrative board. Besides their welfare associations, the churches also play a direct part, for example, by running social work schools.

After many years of privileged symbiosis with the state and a high degree of bureaucratization, the associations now find themselves under pressure to improve efficiency to survive in competition with commercial providers in the social services market developing under the new Care Insurance (since 1995). In social policy debates, they have subsequently moved from conformism with official policies to sustained criticism of benefit cuts and lobbying for the poor.

A Federal Welfare State – National and Local

The German political system has a three-tier structure, with each tier – central government, Länder and the municipalities – having distinct legislative, fiscal and administrative powers. Domains are demarcated in detail in the Constitution, which also gives to the municipalities the right to self-governance (Article 28). Conflicts between the three levels often cut across party lines. Since the 1980s, for example, the federal government has repeatedly cut unemployment benefits to shift burdens to Social Assistance, which is regulated by central law in a fairly standardized way but financed by the Länder and the municipalities (since 2005 federal government co-finances). Even after the growth of national social spending ended, social spending's share of municipalities' budgets still almost doubled from 12 per cent in 1980 to 23 per cent in 2005 (Bäcker *et al.*, 2008, p. 139).

Although social assistance funding and administration is less centralized than in Britain, provisions do not vary as much between regions and communes as in Italy. The emphasis of local social policy is on personal social services and social work: social planning for youth, elderly and the poor, arranging a local mix of voluntary and municipal welfare agencies, and securing quality of services. Health activities are limited because the centralized system of sickness funds and contractual doctors has tended to absorb the entire health service. In their predominant field, education, the states have not, however, lived up to the expectation to raise quality through competition and their role in financing and planning hospitals has been a major obstacle in the reform of Health Insurance.

The Welfare Mix – Public and Private

As in other countries state welfare is only one segment of the social production of welfare although the public sector is larger than in many other countries. There is a mix of public and private services, even within the 'public' welfare domain. As noted, most of the institutions of the German welfare state are not 'state' proper but 'intermediate' agencies. This is reflected in the financing of the social budget: Figure 8.2 clearly shows the three levels of government and also the massive share of social insurance contributions paid by employers and employees who also administer the scheme.

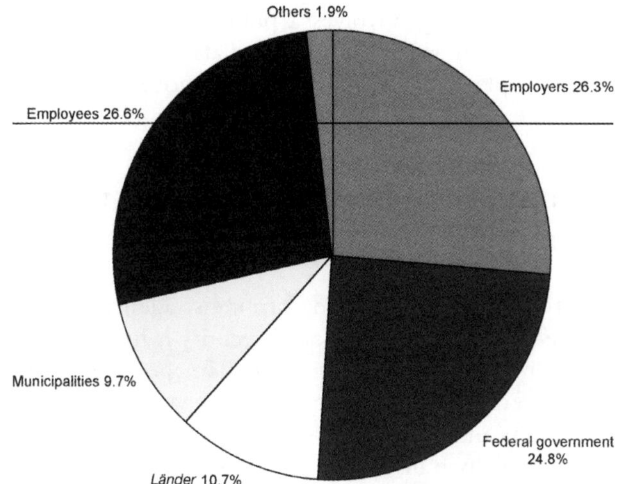

Figure 8.2 Financing the welfare state (2005; excluding education)

Note: 'Employees' includes non-waged members of social insurance such as the elderly members of Health Insurance and some self-employed persons.
Source: Federal Ministry of Labour and Social Affairs (2007, p. 31).

Thus, even in the comprehensive German welfare state, there has always been a mix of provision.

- Security in old age rests on (para-)state pensions, occupational pensions and private pensions, but the state pillar dominates. A full multi-pillar model has only been evolving since the 2001 Reform Act.
- In the field of health insurance, the longstanding 'peace boundary' between public and private insurance – the income threshold where compulsory membership of public health insurance ends – has remained undisputed until recently. Due to the high quality of public services, the publicly insured are not driven to take up a (more than supplementary) private insurance. Tenured civil servants (*Beamte*) can claim special allowances, covering half of medical bills, leaving the other half to private insurance.
- The complex institutional arrangement of health insurance includes links to semi-markets: to pharmaceutical industries and producers of medical technology, and to the doctors who are not employees of the state or of any sickness fund but business-like monopolistic providers with special privileged contractual relationships with Health Insurance. This corporatist welfare mix is regulated by government.
- The German 'Dual System' of vocational training for youth, which has long been considered a model by other countries, combines state schooling during part of the week with company-based work and practical qualification (Thelen, 2007). This has led to higher qualification levels and less youth unemployment than in many other countries.

- German 'social housing' involves a public–private partnership. Private landlords get state subsidies for building flats if they agree to let them to low-income people at modest rents fixed by government.

Social Insurance – The Road to Quasi-Universalism

Given the variety of intermediate and corporatist agencies, the picture of a highly fragmented system emerges. Social security is fragmented by occupational groups, with social insurance in all its branches serving private sector (and some public sector) employees and with separate schemes for tenured civil servants, farmers and some professional groups. However, changes since the 1950s have gradually transformed the system. The social insurance state has been increasingly integrated and extended. With regard to benefits, funding and institutional structure, this fragmented system has given way to a tightly interwoven quasi-universalism:

- *Integration*: The difference between the white-collar and the blue-collar branch of Old Age Pension Insurance established in 1889–1911 has been steadily removed. The two branches formally merged in 2005. The Health Insurance used to comprise hundreds of regional or occupational sickness funds but their number has been reduced and different sickness funds nowadays offer virtually identical services to their members. A system of financial compensation accounts for different distributions of risks among the clientele, especially between West and East German funds.
- *Extension of coverage and benefits*: Non-waged groups, for example self-employed, students, housewives and artists, were admitted to insurance. Aspects of family policy were introduced, especially in 1985 and 1997, thus acknowledging family work, that is, raising a child, as an independent source of entitlement to benefits in addition to paid work ('natural contribution'). Under the 1997 Act, raising one child equals three years of paying contributions. In Health Insurance, non-waged (house)wives and children of an employed father have always been entitled to full services without paying contributions.
- *Extension of bargaining systems* ('corporatization'): Hospitals and, to some degree, the pharmaceutical industry, have been included in corporatist bargaining and planning, originally confined to medical doctors running surgeries outside the hospital system.

The system is thus nearing universality. More than 90 per cent of the population are currently covered by social insurance for old age and health. By contrast, truly universal citizenship-based schemes are rare in the German system. The most important universal scheme is Child Benefit, repeatedly reformed since the foundation of the FRG. Since the 1990s there has been a strong pressure from all parties to raise it.

There is also a substantial range of selective benefits, particularly Social Assistance (SA), which covers every resident in need. Since 2003/5 Social Assistance has been split into separate schemes for different groups (Boeckh, Huster and Benz, 2006, p. 280) although the schemes are similar and still add up to covering everybody in need (see below). Due to the strength of social insurance schemes, the number of SA claimants is lower than in many other countries, although unemployment, growing numbers of lone mothers, and immigration have led to the number of SA claimants (excluding Special Needs Support mainly pertaining to residential care) more than quadrupling since 1970 to 4.5 per cent in 2004 (including all Social Assistance schemes), before the 2005 reforms. Non-take-up amounts at least to 50 per cent of those entitled and half the claimants leave after less than a year. The momentous reform of 2005 has increased the number of social assistance claimants to well above 10 per cent of the population (claimants of the new Unemployment Benefit II: c. 9 per cent in 2007, other social assistance schemes: 1.35 per cent in 2005).

Security First, Equality Second

Although people often associate the welfare state with egalitarian values, many welfare states, and Germany's in particular, are geared more to achieving security than equality. Security is an objective of social policy in two ways:

- Some transfers and services aim to guarantee basic or minimum incomes and minimum provisions. The 1961 Social Assistance Act introduced the right to assistance, establishing a socio-cultural (not just physical) minimum, including full coverage by health services.
- Security can also mean safeguarding a status attained earlier in life. This is mainly achieved by social insurance. Pensions, industrial injury insurance and Unemployment Benefit I are earnings-related. The bulk of the German welfare state, therefore, is not directed to the poor but to the broad middle mass. This is redistribution over the individual life course, not between rich and poor.

However, the system also has egalitarian components:

- Health insurance and (long-term) Care Insurance not only redistribute between the sick and the non-sick but also between rich and poor, since services are not earnings-related, while contributions are.

LIVERPOOL JOHN MOORES UNIVERSITY
LEARNING SERVICES

- In addition, there is massive redistribution in favour of married couples and families with children because they pay the same contributions as singles unless the spouse is in full-time employment.
- Survivors' pensions for old age create entitlements for people who have not paid contributions, thereby enhancing equality.
- There was a strong commitment to equality between age groups prior to the Reform Acts of 1997 and 2001.
- Health insurance does not ration services for the elderly.
- Higher education was free until the early 2000s.

Social security policies have largely been effective. The rate of income poverty (60 per cent threshold) is European average (16 per cent in 2003) but lower than in most large countries. Numbers of Social Assistance claimants in East Germany are surprisingly low, reaching the West German level only in 2004. One reason is the enormous amount of money paid for labour market measures such as job creation schemes. Another reason is the extension of the West German system of old-age pensions to the East, which turned East German elderly into unification 'winners'. Moreover, the stigma of Social Assistance is higher in the East.

The German welfare state and German society at large are more gender-biased than other countries. The insurance system is geared to the male breadwinner based on contributions paid out of wages. The welfare state sets incentives for women to stay in the family and stay out of the labour market. Labour market participation among women, especially among married women, is rising but still low. One of the reasons, besides the conservative ideology of the CDP, is the scarcity of social services allowing women to delegate housework and childcare and, at the same time, creating job opportunities for women. Only from 1996 was there a (formal) guarantee of a place in a nursery school for each child from the age of three. Germany thus generally lags behind in the move towards a service society. There are relatively few service jobs and few part-time jobs. The influence of the EU on German social policy has been particularly pronounced with regard to gender equality, for example, through judgements on German labour law by the European Court of Justice.

Key Features of Welfare Provision

Social Insurance: five branches

- Financed equally by contributions from employers and employees, administered by both (accident insurance: only employers), supplemented from general taxation (mainly in old-age insurance)
- Compulsory for most employees except tenured civil servants

(*continued*)

(*continued*)

Old-Age Pensions Insurance (34 per cent of social budget, 2006 – pay-as-you-go funding plus state subsidy c. 1/3)

- Retirement pensions – earnings-related, no minimum pension; from age 65 or earlier
- Incapacity pension – for permanently incapacitated
- Survivors' pensions – for widow(er)s and orphans
- Rehabilitation – medical treatment, regeneration, retraining
- Pension entitlements on grounds of child raising or caring

Health Insurance (21 per cent of social budget, 2006)

- Prevention – treatment – rehabilitation
- Free access for non-waged dependents
- Corporatist administration by sickness funds, doctors' associations and the state
- Contractual private providers – doctors, hospitals (municipal, voluntary/ NGOs), pharmaceutical industries, providers of medical technologies
- Sickness Benefit – for 18 months sickness (after first 6 weeks of sick pay)

Unemployment Insurance

- Unemployment Benefit I – earnings-related, for one year of unemployment (longer for older workers)
- Unemployment Benefit II – means-tested (social assistance for able-bodied persons); unlimited duration; jointly administered by federal Unemployment Insurance and municipalities (since 2005)
- Job creation schemes, vocational training, rehabilitation
- Labour Exchange (Job Centres), career advisory services, case management, loans for self-employment, cooperation with private temporary work agencies
- Labour market monitoring

Accident Insurance

- Industrial injury (including survivors') pensions
- Prevention – regulations, inspectors
- Rehabilitation

Care Insurance

- Lump sum payments for long-term care – graded by need; home and residential care
- Free access for non-waged dependents
- Contractual private and voluntary providers

Need-Based (Means-Tested) Benefits

- Unemployment Benefit II (see above, 'Unemployment Insurance')
- 'Basic benefit' (privileged social assistance for the aged and for the incapacitated)

(*continued*)

(*continued*)

- Social Assistance (SA) – cash benefits and personal social services for all other persons in need, excluding refugees
- Asylum-Seekers' Benefit – reduced social assistance for refugees
- Housing Benefit – help with rent or maintenance of own home
- Legal Aid – cost of lawyer and court
- Students' grants – to secure subsistence; 50 per cent loan

Universal Benefits

- Child Benefit – to all carers of children
- Pension entitlements on grounds of child raising or caring
- Parents' Allowance (since 2007) – earnings-related, €300–1,800 per month, up to 14 months after birth of child
- Day Care Allowance (planned in 2007)

Merit-Based ('Categorical') Benefits

- Provisions for tenured civil servants – old-age pensions, survivors' pensions, subsidy of private health-care cost, special benefits
- War Victims' Benefits (war compensation) – old-age pensions, survivors' pensions

Fiscal Welfare (c. 10 per cent of social budget, 2006)

- Child allowances
- Lower taxation for married couples
- Allowances for savings and for private provision for old age, including occupational pensions

Private Market Benefits

- Sick pay – for first 6 weeks of sickness, earnings-related, paid by employer
- Occupational pensions – limited coverage, soaring since 2001 reform act
- Personal pensions – limited coverage, soaring since 2001 reform act; 'Riester pension' subsidized and regulated by government
- Private health insurance – supplementing or (less widespread) replacing statutory insurance
- Private care insurance – compulsory for non-members of statutory Care Insurance

Social Services

- Under Social Insurance: rehabilitation, nursing, prevention, special treatment (under Health Insurance, Old-Age Pensions Insurance, Accident Insurance)
- Local provision: wide range of services for age groups (children, youth, elderly), families and people with social problems – provided by a mix of municipal authorities (Social Assistance Authority, Job Centres, Youth Welfare Authority, Debt Counselling and other authorities, varying by municipality), regional institutions (Länder), voluntary welfare associations and private providers

General Education

- Pre-school education – poorly developed, set for expansion
- State schools (mostly municipal, under laws of the states) – private schools marginal but expanding
- 7–15/16 years – compulsory primary (7–10) and secondary (11–15/16) education – curriculum varies by *Land*, examinations by school
- 17–19 years (soon 18 years) – optional further secondary education in schools or vocational colleges, leading to final examination (*Abitur*)
- 19+ years – optional higher education at universities or colleges (mostly 3 years bachelor, 2 years master), with means-tested grant (50 per cent loan) for few students; entry requirement: *Abitur*; selection only in some subjects; low fees, spreading since 2007; few part-time students
- Graded structure of secondary education (10–18 years): separate schools for 3 levels of performance (correlated with class origin of pupils) (*Hauptschule*, *Realschule*, *Gymnasium*), only comprehensive schools in some states; some all-day schools (expanding); plus special schools differentiated by type of disability

Vocational Schooling

German 'Dual System' – combining apprenticeship in a private company (2–3? years) with vocational teaching in state schools (1–2 days per week) – attended by 60 per cent of youth leaving secondary schooling at age 15/16

Housing

- 45 per cent of dwellings (34 per cent in East Germany) owner-occupied in 2002, remainder rented
- Dwellings bought for cash price in open market (or from housing association under 'right to buy'), mostly financed by a savings contract with a building society
- Private renting: tenants pay rent to a private landlord according to market price. Rents subsidized by means-tested housing benefit or under social assistance
- Social housing: private landlords or housing associations receive state subsidies to build flats, conditional on charging state-regulated low rents to low-income tenants

Germany – A Conservative Welfare Regime?

In many ways, social policy in Germany reflects the distinctive features of German politics and society (Lessenich, 2003). Politically, Germany is a consensus democracy, distinct from the Anglo-Saxon majoritarian type of democracy. In terms of political economy, Germany is a coordinated market economy, compared to the Anglo-Saxon liberal market economies, as distinguished in the recent varieties of capitalism literature. In terms of social welfare, Esping-Andersen (1990) sees Germany as the epitomy of the conservative welfare regime: achieving a medium degree of decommodification (enabling people to live independently of the market), grading benefits and entitlements by occupation and social status, and upholding a conservative concept of society, emphasizing family, traditional gender roles and intermediate social bodies such as churches, voluntary welfare associations and occupational status groups. He rightly depicts Germany as a middle-ground welfare regime, but the label 'conservative' needs qualification.

First, the German welfare state is more egalitarian and universalist than it looks. Apart from tenured civil servants, Social Insurance coverage has become quasi-universal in all its branches. In old-age pensions, differentiation by occupational groups ceased to exist in 2005. The health system, although formally based on insurance, is strongly egalitarian and near universal – a point obscured by Esping-Andersen's focus on cash benefits.

Second, politically, the German regime is 'centrist' rather than conservative (Schmidt, 2005), shaped by a reformist centre/centre-right party in conjunction with a pragmatic, strong social democratic party (though mostly in opposition). Re-analyzing Esping-Andersen's data, Obinger and Wagschal (1998) found that his conservative type actually falls into two types, a 'centrist European social insurance state' (including Germany) and a type that really meets Esping-Andersen's criteria of conservativism (found in France, Italy and Austria).

Crisis and the Eve of Reform (1995–2000)

Between the mid-1970s and the mid-1990s, the welfare state was under considerable pressure, both economically and politically; there was much talk of crisis, about dismantling the welfare state and, when Chancellor Kohl took office in 1982, calls for a moral change in social policy and society at large. However, the ingrained structure of social security systems survived and even took up the historical challenge of German unification in 1990. But from the mid-1990s crisis had become more real. Several changes heralded transformations of the postwar welfare state.

For a start, political consensus among the major parties and the social partners (the trade unions and the employers' associations), characterizing the postwar period, became brittle. The SDP came to acknowledge that the welfare state not only solves but also creates problems. It has adopted the view that unemployment is partially caused by excessive rates of contributions, raising the price of labour.

Globalization also exerts particular pressures on the competitiveness of the German economy, the world's second biggest export economy. Financing social benefits mostly by contributions rather than taxes makes the German benefit systems particularly vulnerable to the crisis in employment – and to competition by low-wage countries – because half of the contributions are paid by employers as part of labour costs. Similarly, the design of social insurance as pay-as-you-go systems rather than capital funding, in conjunction with high replacement rates, makes the system more vulnerable to the effects of the ageing of the population, especially in the context of one of the world's lowest birth rates.

There are further problems unique to Germany. Since the Second World War, German society had been more homogeneous than other societies, as revealed by data on beliefs and attitudes; the quest for social harmony between social groups was overwhelming. The 1990s, however, have confronted the Germans with a new – or newly perceived – world of social heterogeneity and social cleavage.

First, there is the East/West divide since the 1990 unification. Many support measures for East Germans were financed from social insurance funds (rather than general taxes), thus adding to pressures on social insurance (see the major study by Ritter, 2006). Unemployment in the East is still very high (19.2 per cent in 2006 compared to 10.2 per cent in the West), and economic growth too slow, only slightly above western rates; 'eastern' tax revenues continue to be low; and high transfers from the West will be needed for many years. More than 15 years after unification, there remains divisive resentment between East and West. Some eastern regions are depopulated; racism has spread.

Second, there is a problem of immigration and ethnic conflict. Germany has one of the highest proportions of 'foreigners' in Europe (8.8 per cent in 2005). Politicians have been slow in facing this fact. Between 1988 and 1996, 2.3 million settlers from Eastern Europe and the former Soviet Union and c. 2 million asylum-seekers came to Germany. The poverty rate among 'foreigners' is twice that of native citizens, as is the unemployment rate, 23.6 per cent in 2005; some settlers are becoming marginalized. Some third-generation immigrants are less integrated than their parents and religious fundamentalism has grown, especially among people of Turkish origin, the biggest ethnic minority.

The changing composition of the social budget indicates some new challenges facing the welfare state (Figure 8.3). Health Insurance is a cost factor as can be seen from its growing budget share. The ageing of the population is not fully reflected in Figure 8.3 because its peak lies ahead. All in all, the share of social insurance has grown from below to well above half social spending (including the 'labour market' item largely flowing from Unemployment Insurance). At the same time, Social Assistance and local personal services expenditures have more than doubled, indicating the increase in social risks not covered by the standard systems of social insurance.

Despite the new challenges, there were few signs of a break with the ingrained institutions of the welfare state during the second half of the 1990s. By the time the SDP won the 1998 election, Germany had come to be considered a laggard in adapting to the new exigencies of a globalizing economy. Politicians pointed to the Netherlands, to Denmark, to Britain or the USA as models of reducing unemployment, of deregulating the economy

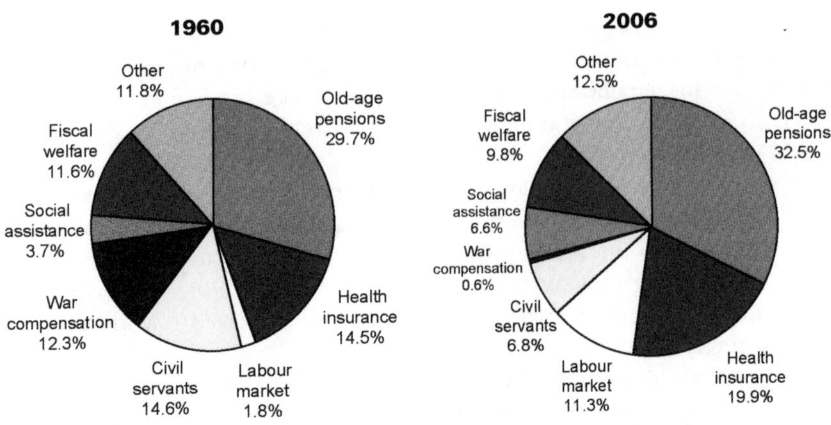

Figure 8.3 The social budget, 1960 and 2006 (excluding education)

Note: Social assistance: including housing benefit, youth welfare and other local personal services. War compensation: covering the war-disabled, war widows and civil compensation cases.
Source: Federal Ministry of Labour and Social Affairs (2007, p.12).

and of successfully restructuring welfare. German unemployment rose, while it fell elsewhere. The German consensus democracy makes it truly difficult to induce changes; political immobility seemed to prevail. Germany is highly fragmented with many 'veto players' (Schmidt, 2005): the Constitutional Court interferes massively with social policy; in the second chamber of the federal parliament, the Bundesrat, where the states are represented, the government party is often in a minority; and states and municipalities have a say in finance, taxation and hospital planning.

However, some reforms took place from within. Existing intermediate institutions like the social insurance agencies and the corporate actors in the health sector (sickness funds and monopolistic doctors' associations) and local governments were mobilized as active policy agents rather than mere administrators, especially in health and SA, but also in old-age pensions. Some new links to private provisions and agencies were forged, especially in the fields of long-term care and social assistance. True to its tradition of gradual adaptation to social change, the 1990s German welfare state was changing but within the framework of old institutions and without the rhetoric of grand reform.

A Centrist Welfare State Confronting Crisis – Between Piecemeal Changes and Paradigm Shifts (2000–8)

After the turn of the millennium German politics eventually began to confront the crisis of the welfare state. Reform debates intensified. However, both politicians and the electorate remained undecided – till the present day

– whether to opt for reasonably consistent neo-liberal or Third Way reforms as carried out in Britain or for preserving the ingrained welfare state with only minor reforms. Vested interests of both clients and providers have counteracted more far-reaching changes in many fields, and politicians have mostly settled on least common denominator solutions. The centrist tendency of the German welfare state persists. Both big parties largely continue to serve the deep-seated expectations of the electorate towards state welfare. The challenge is: can the centrist tradition, which successfully reconciled economic growth and social integration during the golden years of the postwar welfare state, adapt to the current period of welfare state restructuring?

In his second term of office (2002–5) Schröder proclaimed a softly neoliberal reform 'Agenda 2010' with an emphasis on activating labour market reforms building on 1990s municipal reforms. This was a major attack on the social democratic orthodoxy and on trades unions. He managed to get the legislation through Parliament but chose to resign and call for an early election to secure firm support. Unlike Blair, Schröder had failed to generate new public and administrative discourses that would have supported his new policies (Schmidt, 2000, on Schröder's first years). The election brought no clear message: Schröder won a considerable proportion of the vote but lost by a small margin, that is, Angela Merkel's more liberal programme was not really confirmed either. So a Great Coalition was forged in 2005 (by law to last till 2009), which brought Christian Democrats and Social Democrats together under the Christian Democratic Chancellor Merkel. The Coalition reverted to a policy of limited reforms.

Three types of changes characterize the years 2000–8:

- Major departures, that is genuine paradigm shifts, have been achieved in pension policies and labour market policies, but attempts at major health reform failed and critical issues in labour market policies remain untouched.
- Piecemeal reforms continue, especially in family policy, education, immigration and health, with continued emphasis on activating policies, public private mixes, new public management and evaluation in all policy sectors as in many other European countries. So German politics is not totally immobile and incapable of reform but reforms may be too moderate.
- Regarding politics, the labour market reforms enacted in 2005 under Agenda 2010 triggered the most momentous protest movement in German postwar social politics, with the unique outcome of a change in the party system. In 2007, a small protest party fuelled by trades union officers merged with the Socialist Party (the legal successor to the Communist Party, which ruled East Germany 1949–90) to form the party The Left. The Left, headed by a former leader of the SDP, Lafontaine, mustered c. 10 per cent of the electorate in polls in 2007. In East Germany, The Left has a similar share of the voters as the Christian Democrats and the Social Democrats (c. 25–30 per cent each, according to a survey in 2007). Under proportional representation, majorities of

the old ruling parties and coalitions between them become more difficult and the social populism of The Left exerts pressure. The increase in conflict also shows in unprecedented all-out strikes, for example, by hospital doctors in 2006 and by train drivers in 2007.

The landmark *pension* reforms of 2002 and 2005 (enacted in 2001 – the 'Riester reform', named after the minister in charge – and in 2004 respectively) established a multi-pillar paradigm to replace the German mono-pillar paradigm created by the 1957 reform (Schmähl, 2007). This was effectively going back to Bismarck, who conceived of public pensions as just one element in a pension mix. Entitlements to public pensions under the German notional accounts pension formula were lowered, by way of a 'sustainability factor', which reflects among others, population ageing. The age of retirement is to shift from 65 to 67 years. Incapacity pensions had been severely cut as early as 2000. All these reforms were designed to contain non-wage labour costs and prepare the public scheme for the demographic challenges of the future even if two-thirds of funding remains pay-as-you-go.

Under the same Reform Acts, new occupational and private pensions were introduced which are publicly subsidized (by direct subsidies or through tax deductions) and socially regulated by government. Occupational and private provisions for old age had played a much smaller role in Germany than in many other countries but take-up has soared in the wake of the new legislation, nearing 10 million (mostly personal) Riester pensions in 2007 plus new occupational ('Eichel') pensions. For the first time, all three pillars were jointly covered by one act of parliament – a coordinated pension mix – and a joint policy community has emerged. The 2001 Act also introduced a basic benefit, a privileged version of Social Assistance for the elderly and the incapacitated, because public pensions do not provide a minimum pension. The pension reforms indicate a step from the traditional German provider state towards a regulatory state.

By contrast, the reform of the statutory *health* insurance came to nothing. But remarkably it was the first time for a major party in government to call for dismantling a branch of the Bismarckian social insurance. The Christian Democrats advocated switching from earnings-related contributions to a flat 'health premium' under which a shop assistant and a CEO would have to pay the same sum of money into a central fund. The Social Democrats advanced the alternative model of 'citizens insurance' that would universalize the Bismarckian model by extending mandatory membership from workers to all citizens and raising contributions not only from wages but from all kinds of income. Since the two parties are in a coalition government and the two models cannot be reconciled, no structural reform was achieved. Strong vested interests of the medical doctors associations have also barred reforms as before. Health ranks among the big unresolved issues in German social politics during the entire postwar period.

The core of Schröder's Agenda 2010 included the *labour market* reforms enacted in 2002–3 (in force 2003–5), commonly referred to as Hartz reforms, named after the Volkswagen CEO who headed the expert commission (for labour market policy in Germany, see Seeleib-Kaiser and Fleckenstein, 2007). 'Hartz IV', in particular, shifted the emphasis from cash benefits to personal social services to promote passages from welfare to work. But the crucial issue was the merging of Unemployment Assistance for the long-term unemployed, which was earnings-related (though also means-tested), with Social Assistance, which is needs-oriented, means-tested and provides a uniform minimum benefit irrespective of previous earnings (similar to the introduction of Job Seekers' Allowance in Britain nine years earlier, in 1996). This downgrading of Unemployment Assistance signalled social descent to the unemployed. In the face of increasing insecurity in the labour market, this threat resonated well into the middle classes. Since then, 'Hartz IV' has dominated the general social discourse more than any other social policy issue in postwar Germany. Still, the Hartz reforms only refer to ways of accessing the labour market while the labour market as such, especially employment security rules, remains largely unreformed.

The Hartz reforms, together with older issues like unemployment, working poor, child poverty and the situation of third generation immigrants, have also brought the issue of *poverty* to the fore. The renewed interest in poverty shows in discourses on a new 'underclass', in the first official national poverty report (2001, second report 2005), in the ongoing debate on a general minimum wage hitherto unknown in Germany and even in ideas of an unconditional basic income.

The neglect of *education* in the German transfer state was eventually revealed when the OECD-led Programme for International Student Assessment (PISA) shocked the German public in 2001. German schools scored very low and produced more inequality of opportunity regarding class and ethnicity than most other countries. Education has been at the top of the agenda since but to little avail. Federalism acts as a hindrance to reform since education largely falls within the competence of the Länder. New programmes including a day-care allowance for parents of small children (debated in 2007) aim particularly at pre-school education and third-generation immigrants.

Similarly, *family* policy and *gender* relations have also been at the top of the agenda for years. Various changes in taxation, cash benefits, personal social services and legal policy substantially strengthened the position of families, women and children. But these changes were challenged by churchmen invoking the social conservatism characteristic of the German welfare regime.

It remains to be seen if the centrist tradition of political compromise and gradual rather than trenchant reforms can meet the current challenges of welfare state restructuring: if there will be a shift from the transfer state to a social investment state with more emphasis on education and employment, and less on paying for time off employment; if the social insurance paradigm, which implies high non-wage labour cost (employers' contributions), will give way to more financing from general taxes and user premiums (the share of social insurance contributions has actually decreased, from 66 per cent of social spending in 1991 to 59 per cent in 2005); and if the German provider state with its emphasis on service delivery by public agencies will be increasingly replaced by private provision under a new regulatory state, as begun in the areas of long-term care and old-age security.

Over recent years, real and felt insecurity has spread in the population, fuelling the German inclination towards pessimism and calls for state action. The 2007 economic recovery only slightly tempered these tendencies. Even more than before, social policy has moved to the centre stage of politics, liable to be blamed for new insecurities in a globalized world. The 'social' needs to be redefined in an age of transformation. In this situation, Germany is caught between the old political middle ground, which shies away from distinct reform strategies, a growing awareness of the need for change and the new social populists.

References

Abelshauser, W. (1996) 'Erhard oder Bismarck? Die Richtungsentscheidung der deutschen Sozialpolitik am Beispiel reform der Sozialversicherung in den Fünfziger Jahren', in Geschichte und Gesellschaft für Historische Sozialwissenschaft, 22(3), pp. 376–92.

Bäcker, G. *et al.* (2008) *Sozialpolitik und soziale Lage in Deutschland*, 2 vols, VS Verlag für Sozialwissenschaften.

Boeckh, J., Huster, E.-U.and Benz. B. (2006) *Sozialpolitik in Deutschland*, 2nd edn, VS Verlag für Sozialwissenschaften.

Federal Ministry of Labour and Social Affairs (Bundesministerium für Arbeit und Soziales) (2007) *Sozialbudget 2006.*

Lampert, H. and Althammer, J. (2004) *Lehrbuch der Sozialpolitik*, 7th edn, Springer.

Lessenich, S. (2003) *Dynamischer Immobilismus. Kontinuität und Wandel im deutschen Sozialmodell*, Campus.

Ritter, G. A. (2006) *Der Preis der Einheit. Die Wiedervereinigung und die Krise des Sozialstaats*, C. H. Beck.

Schmähl, W. (2007) 'Dismantling an Earnings-Related Social Pension Scheme: Germany's New Pension Policy', *Journal of Social Policy*, 36, pp. 319–40.

Schmidt, M. G. (2005) *Sozialpolitik in Deutschland. Historische Entwicklung und internationaler Vergleich*, 3rd rev. edn, VS Verlag für Sozialwissenschaften.

Schmidt, V. A. (2000) 'Values and discourse in the politics of adjustment', in F. W. Scharpfand V. A. Schmidt (eds) (2000) *Welfare and Work in the Open Economy*, vol. I, Oxford University Press, pp. 229—309.

Seeleib-Kaiser, M. and Fleckenstein, T. (2007) 'German Labour Market Reforms', *Social Policy and Administration*, 41, pp. 427–48.

Thelen, K. (2007) 'Contemporary Challenges to the German Vocational Training System', *Regulation and Governance*, 1, pp. 247–60.

CHAPTER 9

Italy: Still a Pension State?

VALERIA FARGION

Italian Society

Socially and economically, Italy is two countries in one. While northern regions display a dynamic economy, well-integrated into global markets, southern regions still search for a route to economic development, social and political modernization. One critical consequence of this divergence is that southern unemployment rates are nearly 19 per cent whereas north-eastern industrial firms experience labour shortages.

The origins of the north–south divide have a long history. Italian unification in 1861 did little to change the situation and this settlement was little challenged by the fascist regime taking power in 1922, ruling the country until 1944. As a result, throughout the twentieth century, southern regions remained economically and socially backward, more similar to Greece and Portugal than to northern Italy. Postwar governments attempted to redress this territorial imbalance by promoting state-assisted industrialization, setting up huge industrial and petrochemical plants – popularly labelled as 'desert cathedrals' – but the strategy proved a complete failure, ending with most state-owned firms closing during the 1980s. The massive redundancies connected to this downturn further complicated an already quite dramatic situation. Italian southern regions remain socio-economically very distant from European averages.

In addition to this internal division, we can set the Italian case within comparative welfare state typologies. Given the importance of income maintenance programmes (in particular pensions) in Italy, this country appears as a transfer-centred model. Accordingly, Esping-Andersen (1990) classifies Italy as a conservative regime alongside the main continental European countries. On the other hand, there are a number of features differentiating Italy from those countries (e.g. France, Germany) falling into this category. For instance, the Italian welfare state incorporates a national health system granting universal access on the basis of citizenship. This openly clashes with the occupational principles underpinning conservative regimes. Thus, the historical development of the Italian social protection system reflects a complex mix of privileges and inequities not to be found to this extent in continental Europe, notably in relation to:

- overprotection of core labour force sectors and underprotection of the periphery, the unemployed, outsiders and, more recently, 'atypical' (migrant and young flexible) workers;
- generous coverage for certain risks (old age) alongside neglect of others (family needs, unemployment, poverty); and
- misuse and overt abuse of a number of schemes, such as invalidity pensions (where this worked to the advantage of individual beneficiaries willing and able to enter clientelistic exchanges) and health care (where perverse incentives geared the system to the interests of service providers rather than patients).

This configuration largely resulted from a combination of low administrative capacity and weak state legitimization, a largely un-civic political culture, and entrenched distributive politics in the decision-making arena. However, over the 1990s – with the collapse of the so-called First Republic – most of the particularistic mechanisms embedded in the social protection system were severely undermined, and the privileges and inequities mentioned above started to crumble. This process is still underway, the end result appearing unclear.

Italian Welfare Development

The Origins of the Italian Model

The first compulsory social insurance was introduced in 1898, so the Italian welfare state is more than a century old. This programme was very limited, covering industrial injuries for only a small number of workers employed in dangerous plants. Although linked to Bismarck's model of social insurance, Italy proceeded at a much slower pace: insurance for workplace accidents remained the only compulsory programme until 1919. Till then, charitable institutions were the only response to the needs of the poor, apart from the friendly societies set up by the working class, operating almost exclusively in industrialized areas. The power of the Church and the strong Catholic tradition gave rise to a greater number of charities than was common in other European countries. Further, their widespread diffusion made it possible for liberal ruling élites to avoid state financial commitment.

It was only at the end of the First World War that the country experienced a sudden acceleration in social legislation, turning Italy from a laggard into a forerunner. In 1919, a far-reaching insurance programme was introduced, providing coverage not only for old age but for unemployment, a risk that most neighbouring countries started taking into consideration only much later. This contributory benefit scheme was financed through social contributions by employers and employees. Beneficiaries now included agricultural workers – as was normally the case in other European countries.

Social Protection under the Fascist Regime

One of the first measures introduced by Mussolini after the fascist regime took over in 1922 was a repeal of the extension of social insurance benefits to the agricultural sector. However, it would be misleading to downplay fascist intervention in the social field. The regime extended social protection to include certain risks especially relevant for its ideology, such as compulsory insurance for tuberculosis; establishment of family allowances and a single-purpose national agency to protect maternity and childhood; and promotion of occupational health funds by employers' associations to complement corporatist labour agreements. Special privileges were granted to groups crucial to the regime such as judges, journalists, railway or telephone company workers; the extreme fragmentation lamented in postwar Italian welfare state literature was essentially a fascist legacy.

Fascism consolidated the management of different social protection programmes into two major funds. Insurance programmes covering work accidents were merged into a single fund, still responsible for this policy field (INAIL), and in 1935 a major restructuring of the private employees' pension fund was launched, giving birth to what is now the giant of the Italian welfare state, the INPS. Apart from running the pension scheme for private employees and separate schemes for particular groups of workers, the agency was entrusted with responsibility for insurance programmes covering unemployment, maternity, family allowances and tuberculosis in the private sector.

These mergers offered the opportunity to manipulate enormous resources, and added to the fascist strategy of obtaining direct political control over all public agencies. This is particularly relevant in a long-term perspective – the political colonization of social security organizations, which thrived during postwar governments, was a continuation of the fascist practice rather than a deviation inaugurated by Italian Christian Democracy.

Postwar Social Policy

Despite the collapse of the fascist regime, the relegation of the monarchy by popular referendum and the establishment of a Republic, there was no postwar 'revolution' in the Italian welfare state. The coalition government formed by socialists, communists and Christian Democrats initially endorsed the idea of recasting social protection along the lines of the Beveridge Report. As a result, the new republican Constitution reflected a broad conception of social rights. However, no structural reforms were effectively introduced and the shift in 1947 to Cold War confrontation put an end to any such attempts.

The 1948 elections opened a new phase. Christian Democracy gained the absolute majority of the vote in an outright clash against the socialists and the Communist Party. As a result, the former acquired a pivotal position, remaining unchallenged for almost 45 years. Indeed, despite changes in coalition partners, the Christian Democratic Party (DC) was never out of office till the early 1990s, when the whole Italian party system collapsed and DC itself disappeared into two splinter parties.

Throughout this period, the major opposition party was the Communist Party – the largest in Western Europe – which had no hope of gaining office. This situation resulted in both irresponsible government and irresponsible opposition. On the one hand, thriving on permanent incumbency, the DC had the opportunity to expand the public sector and penetrate state administration to a degree unparalleled elsewhere. On the other hand, knowing it would not have to keep its promises, the opposition could easily make unrealistic claims, raising people's expectations.

Demands put forward by left-wing parties – accounting for at least one-third of the electorate – could not be totally ignored. Hence, a sort of trade-off developed between government exclusion and parliamentary inclusion, a process usually referred to as 'negative integration' of the Communist Party with the latter often supporting legislation passed by Parliament. It is on this basis that Italy is likened to the Netherlands, described as a 'consociational' democracy – an attempt to accommodate quite diverse interests and political cultures by extensively developing distributive policies, notably in the field of social protection, while concealing their cost.

The Extension of Social Coverage to the Self-Employed

The centre coalitions running the country from 1948 to the early 1960s focused on economic and industrial development. These years correspond to the Italian 'economic miracle' with massive migrations from the economically deprived regions of the South to northern Italy. The links between the DC and the associations representing the self-employed meant that social policy-making largely ignored industrial workers. Social coverage was substantially increased, but primarily benefiting the self-employed, with a range of privileges granted to small farmers, artisans and shopkeepers rather than to wage-earners.

Separate schemes were progressively set up providing health insurance as well as old-age and invalidity pensions to these groups. But social contributions were set at a much lower level compared to private sector employees, and included a costly 'first generation gift'. As a result, for instance, within just a few years, relevant contributions only covered 10 per cent of the pension benefits going to small farmers and share-croppers. However, since the three pension schemes for the self-employed were consolidated into INPS, other schemes running a surplus helped to balance their deficits, thereby masking the real picture. In the following decades these surpluses disappeared, leading to a need for state financial support.

The financial conditions of pension schemes deteriorated even further due to widespread misuse of disability pensions. By the mid-1970s, the number of people receiving disability pensions reached 5.3 million, greatly outnumbering old-age pensions. Disability benefits were paid after just a five-year contributory requirement, and local commissions had considerable discretionary power in processing relevant applications. As a result, disability pensions became the object of clientelistic exchanges thriving especially in the agricultural sector and in the most impoverished southern areas. Apart from building on patronage ties especially rooted in southern civil society, this kind of outcome was also enhanced by the inadequate coverage offered by unemployment compensation.

Looking more broadly at the distribution of social expenditure among the various income maintenance programmes, at the beginning of the 1950s, pension expenditure represented 45 per cent of total outlays, equal to spending for family allowances. But over the next three decades pension spending increased so that by 1980 it accounted for 80 per cent, while spending on family allowances decreased to about 10 per cent, and sickness, work injuries and unemployment insurance also accounted for 10 per cent (Ferrera, 1984). According to Eurostat data, in 1995 Italy ranked first for pension expenditure among all EU member states, allocating 62 per cent of all expenditure, compared to a European average of 42 per cent, leading to considerable inter-generational inequity in Italian social protection.

The 'Hot Autumn': Social Mobilization and 'Catching Up' by Blue-Collar Workers

Pension reforms introduced in the late 1960s and early 1970s were conceived within a context of mounting pressure exerted by the strikes and street demonstrations of what is popularly labelled the 1969 'hot autumn'. Trades unions were interested in guaranteeing that retired workers maintained a standard of living close to that in the firm and policy-makers were willing to accommodate this so long as it did not entail squeezing alternative allocations and cutting other programmes. As a result, between 1968 and 1975, Parliament approved reforms substantially changing the basis of the pension system, and allowing for an unprecedented improvement in average pension levels.

Within just a few years, old-age protection for private employees became very generous compared to most European countries – with significant financial implications. Policy-makers assumed that industrial expansion experienced during the previous two decades would substantially continue with large enough numbers of workers paying for social contributions, and so postponed the problem to future generations. Tactically this may have seemed a wise move. But, unfortunately, in the following two decades the combined effect of demographic and occupational trends brought about a quite different situation.

Ageing of the population has become a particularly acute problem in Italy, as a result of comparatively higher life expectancy and a sharp drop in fertility rates, the latter placing Italy lowest ranking in Europe. The image of a 'demographic time bomb' is particularly acute for Italy. On the other hand, after the first oil shock in 1973 or earlier, Italian economic development entered a new phase characterized by slow growth and limited job creation. For instance, in 1970, workers contributing to the private employees fund totalled 10.8 million while pension recipients stood at 6.2 million, but by 1990 the figures were 11.3 million and 9.5 million respectively. Under these circumstances there was no way that the pension system could maintain financial viability.

Deviating from the Occupational Model: The Introduction of Universal Health Care

The 1970s pension measures appeared to be in line with the original furrow of the Italian welfare model, even further enhancing differences in treatment among occupational categories. This sharply contrasts with what happened instead in the health sector. In 1978 a National Health Service was established emphasizing universality, equality, uniformity and access. Prior to this, health care was offered by several sickness funds. Coverage varied widely across occupational groups, and regional disparities were superimposed on disparities among social groups. Wealthier northern and central areas were better endowed with hospitals and physicians than were the poorer southern cities and rural areas.

The system came under attack from the late 1960s. However, the consequence here was not rationalization but a radical change. Three factors account for this unusual outcome of Italian social policy-making:

- sickness funds had accumulated enormous debts with respect to hospitals, and state rescue appeared the only possible alternative;
- the creation of the regions in 1970 provided the institutional foundation for the devolution of health responsibilities; and
- the Communist Party considered the establishment of a universal health service as a 'pay-off' for supporting the first 'national solidarity' government.

The passing of the health reforms produced an injection of universal principles into the Italian welfare state, with coverage extended to 3.5 million citizens. There was also a new organizational design with a three-tier system involving central government, the regions and Local Health Units (USL). Although allegedly modelled on the British NHS, the Italian Reform Law attempted to combine central budgeting and planning with local control – a unique and contradictory mix. From the outset, this resulted in widespread central/local conflict. The national government was responsible for raising the money and distributing it to the regions. Pay-roll taxes from employers, employees and the self-employed made up the bulk of funding with general revenues contributing for about 35 per cent of the total. The regions in turn were supposed to allocate resources to Local Health Units. However, the system allowed for decentralized decision-making with respect to levels and delivery of services, in line with left-wing parties' ideals of democratic participation and accountability. As a corollary, lay management committees reflecting the power balance among local parties were responsible for running USLs.

Throughout the 1980s, opinion polls showed Italians expressing increasing discontent with respect to NHS performance and lamenting the poor quality of services provided along with bureaucratic systems that entangled the whole system – causing all sorts of inequities and inefficiencies. Local Management Committees came under the strongest criticism. However, responsibilities were so intermingled that in fact the latter had no discretionary power over a large share of the local budget.

Further, the legislation endorsed a perverse public–private mix. Public hospital doctors were allowed to operate freely in both public and private sectors. Since their pay was unrelated to performance and much lower than earnings from private practice, this arrangement provided a formidable indirect incentive for maintaining public inefficiency. Keeping performance standards low in the public sphere effectively diverted increasing numbers of patients to private facilities that the doctors themselves often owned or where they might work on a part-time basis. Notwithstanding this long list of problems, NHS legislation focused on cost-containment instead of providing guidelines for improving service standards. Given the political context of the 1980s and the powerful interests behind the health system, any attempt to introduce substantial change was politically impossible.

Unemployment: A Mismatch between Needs and Policy Responses

Unemployment policies have always been marginal to the Italian social protection system, and this continued into the 1980s when the jobless total started to soar to double-digit figures. Throughout that decade, passive labour policy expenditure never exceeded 1 per cent of GDP, placing Italy at the bottom of European rankings – where it remains. Such an outcome is less surprising, however, if we consider the labour market regime within which the Italian system of shock absorbers is embedded, for it is based on high levels of labour market regulation.

Until recently, the literature constantly referred to Italy as one of the most rigidly regulated labour markets in the industrialized world. Notably, since the 1960s and especially following the 1970 Workers Code, labour legislation strengthened workers' rights and entitlements at employers' expense, a process progressively leading to a system characterized by wage-setting rigidity, stringent hiring and firing rules, and very limited openings for atypical contracts. Yet, to grasp how the Italian labour market actually works, it is highly misleading to concentrate on rigidity stemming from the regulatory framework. There is a complex mix of decentralized small firms, subject to lesser constraints on employment relationships. One needs also to consider the 'grey' economy and non-dependent labour. In the mid-1990s, workers effectively covered by labour market regulations – namely workers in firms with more than 15 employees plus the public sector – accounted for only about 40 per cent of total employment. The proportion of small firms and self-employment today remains much higher than in most European countries, and more importantly the 'black' economy finds no European equivalent with non-regular work accounting for as much as 22 per cent of total work. In short, in one of the world's most highly regulated labour markets, a large share of the workforce is not covered by such regulation and therefore does not enjoy the employment and social protection attached to it. Not surprisingly, this dual market reiterates the north–south cleavage with the bulk of non-regular work concentrated in the South.

Only minor adjustments were introduced to unemployment benefit throughout the postwar period. The benefit was and remains payable for a maximum of 180 days and its level was upgraded between the late 1980s and early 1990s from a ridiculously low flat rate to 30 per cent of the previous wage. These conditions are largely responsible for spurring on the clientelistic misuse of invalidity pensions mentioned above, a situation that only changed in the mid-1980s when legislative restrictions were eventually introduced to curb the disproportionate growth of these benefits. In sharp contrast, temporary unemployment attracted a good deal of attention. INPS was entrusted with the management of the programme and a specific fund therein was set up for this purpose. During the 1970s and the 1980s, the profile of the fund increased to the point that, in the eyes of the public, the *Cassa Integrazione Guadagni* (Wage Compensation Fund) almost became synonymous for unemployment policies altogether. The measure was extremely generous, offering a replacement rate of 80 per cent of previous earnings and protecting redundant workers from job loss. Eligibility was subject to negotiation between trades unions and employers, and, till 1988, the scheme was entirely state financed.

The programme was supported by both unions and employers because it allowed for a freezing of redundancies while allowing firms to externalize the financial and social costs of industrial restructuring. Highly unionized large firms were obviously in a better position to take advantage of the discretionary procedures involved in the operation of special short-term unemployment compensation. The result was such that this type of benefit entirely lost its temporary nature. Early retirement measures further reinforced the allocative distortion typical of Italian shock absorbers. Along with France, Italy is the country that has most extensively used this measure. During the

1980s, early retirement schemes involved on average 32,000 workers annually, again largely confined to core sectors of the labour force.

The 1990s: The Italian Welfare State in Transition

The 1990s mark a turning point in the development of postwar Italy, often referred to as the transition from First to Second Republic. The collapse of the old party system reflected a deep change in the style and content of policy-making. The change was most clearly visible in macro-economic and financial policies, but could also be seen in social policy reforms where there were open attempts to redress the major distortions of the Italian welfare model.

While most European countries were already striving with fiscal restraint and austerity over the 1980s, Italians public expenditure spiralled out of control. Over the ten-year period from 1980 to 1990, total public expenditure rose from 42 to 53 per cent of GNP, and, although fiscal pressures increased, this failed to cover rising outflows. Thus the gap between public expenditure and revenue rose to twice the European average. In short, distributive games and easy spending dominated the political scene throughout the decade with public debt skyrocketing from 54 to 104 per cent of GNP and the annual budget deficit reaching a 1989 high of 11 per cent. In the 1990s, policy was reversed with Italy's public finances turning at last from a vicious into a virtuous circle. The budgetary gap between revenues and expenditure then narrowed to the point that Italy managed to meet the Maastricht criteria for entering the European Monetary Union – largely unexpected even in the previous year. In 1997 the country reached the required threshold of a 3 per cent annual deficit, and in the next two years consolidated the downward trend even further; in addition inflation was curbed and debt service substantially reduced. These 'radical' achievements, together with the passing of a number of long-needed social policy reforms, were the product of significant political changes.

Exogenous variables played a crucial role here. In particular, the fall of the Berlin wall made it impossible for the DC to uphold its popular image as a bulwark against communism; a 40-year record of corrupt and inefficient state administration combined with an astonishing lack of problem-solving capacity was exposed. The 'clean hands' investigations launched by the judiciary in the early 1990s undermined the legitimacy of the old leadership and many parliamentary members from government parties were charged with corruption and fraudulent behaviour. Thus the core parties of the First Republic, which made up the *Pentapartito* coalition (Christian Democrats, Socialists, Social-Democrats, Republicans and Liberals), almost vanished after the 1994 election. While the old parties were crumbling, two new political actors emerged: the *Lega Nord*, which vociferously campaigned against state centralization, advocating a federal system, and *Forza Italia*, the conservative political movement led by Berlusconi, which won the 1994 elections.

In the midst of such political turmoil, the executive substantially strengthened its position in Parliament, acquiring increasing autonomy in policy-making. The technocratic Cabinets of Amato, Ciampi and Dini thus looked for the support of organized interests in order to counter-balance their political isolation, seeking to pursue their policy objectives through extensive negotiations with trades unions and employers. This resulted in a resurgence of neo-corporatist arrangements. Starting with Prodi's 1996 electoral victory, parties progressively regained a pivotal role. However, the reform trend inaugurated under the technocratic rule of the 1992–5 period actually witnessed a further acceleration during the centre-left governments of 1996–2001 headed by Prodi, D'Alema and Amato. We now provide an overview of such reforms, focusing on pensions, health care, labour market policies and social-care services.

Reforming the Pension System

Over the 1980s, pension expenditure had spiralled totally out of control, although the benefits of these increases were not evenly distributed. Spending levels for the private employees' fund rose by 20 per cent, whereas pension expenditure in the public sector increased by 84 per cent. The pension system therefore increasingly came under attack as being highly inequitable and for granting an intricate maze of privileges, primarily within the public sector – most blatantly 'Baby Pensions', under which civil servants of any age with only 20 years' service were entitled to 'seniority' benefits; in the cases of some female employees this time could even be reduced to 12 years.

There was much Parliamentary debate about pension reform but no legislation was passed until 1992 when the problem was finally approached by a measure raising the retirement age from 60 to 65 for men and from 55 to 60 for women. Three years later the government comprehensively reformed the pension system on the basis of extensive consultation with trades unions and employers. This replaced the old earnings-related formula with a new defined-contribution scheme to be phased in by 2013, with benefit levels linked to life expectancy at retirement age. The standardization of rules for all private employees (and two years later also for public employees) ensured that yield rates would be the same regardless of occupational category. However, the law established an artificial barrier between younger and older workers, openly siding with the latter. This political choice can hardly be considered equitable from an inter-generation point of view; yet, it is not so surprising if one considers it as the result of agreement with trades unions which increasingly comprised elderly and retired workers.

Decentralizing the Health Sector

Throughout the 1990s, Italian governments also introduced major changes in the health sector affecting the public–private mix as well as the centre–local dynamics of the National Health Service. The original 659 Local Health Units were transformed into 199 Local Health Enterprises (ASL) with more operating autonomy, commercial accounting procedures and performance auditing. Moreover, links between ASLs and municipal councils were severed by replacing the old Management Committees with a General Manager appointed by the region (granted a five-year contract). Taking the British experience as a model, but reaching quite different outcomes, a number of elements typical of managed competition were also introduced into the system. Hospitals were allowed to set up independent bodies that could sell their services to ASLs on a tariff basis. However, it was left to the regions to decide how far they wanted to pursue the separation between purchasers (the ASL) and providers (the Hospital Enterprises). As a result, while Lombardy enhanced the formation of autonomous Hospital Enterprises, most other regions opted for an integrated model which kept the majority of hospitals under the jurisdiction of ASLs.

The changes introduced in 1992–3 were complemented by a third reform wave initiated by Health Minister Bindi, culminating in legislative decree no. 229/1999. This legislation for the first time addressed straightforwardly the perverse mix between doctors' private interests and public responsibilities. As mentioned above, doctors had no incentive to increase public sector efficiency: on the contrary they could take advantage of any inefficiency in the public sector to attract patients into the profitable private sphere. The new rules attempted to reverse the situation, combining public health-care improvement with doctors' economic interests: medical personnel were required to work full time for the NHS or opt out of the public system. Doctors opting to work exclusively for the NHS were granted a very substantial salary increase and were allowed to practice privately within public premises, on top of their contractual working hours (so called *intra-moenia* professional activity). On the other hand, doctors opting to maintain – on top of their contractual obligations with the public sector – an independent activity outside the NHS (*extra-moenia*) could do so without being subject to specific regulation by Local Health Authorities but were penalized, both from an economic and a career point of view.

As regards health funding, a new regional tax (IRAP) was established in 1998, levied on all production and professional activities. This replaced compulsory health contributions and was directly collected by the regions. In 2000 a legislative decree on 'fiscal federalism' abolished earmarked state funding which – via the national health fund – complemented the new regional taxes while also allowing for a redistribution of resources in favour of less developed areas.

To summarize, whereas the early 1990s reforms were primarily concerned with cost-containment and efficiency, paving the way for the creation of distinct regional health-care models, centre-left governments in power from 1996–2001 combined increased regional autonomy on the revenue side with a standard-setting role and stringent monitoring by central government. Under centre-left rule, all crucial decisions concerning health care were taken within the institutional context of the State-Regional Board, the national level maintaining substitutive powers in case of non-compliance by regional government.

Reorganizing Labour Market Policies

The provisions adopted from 1991 onwards attempted to set unemployment policies on a new track. The explicit aim of the new law was to end the freezing of employment status for redundant workers with no real possibility of being reintegrated in firms. In order to bring the Wage Compensation Fund (CIG) back to its original temporary purpose, strict limitations were set on both duration and eligibility for benefits. In just five years the number of workers receiving CIG benefits was halved. The 1991 law opened the way to the introduction of workfare principles within Italian social legislation but was unable to trigger a general reorientation of unemployment policies towards the sanctions and obligations typical of 'activation' strategies. In order to extend this type of approach, one first had to reform existing 'social shock absorbers' by providing both adequate unemployment coverage and benefit upgrading. This remains an unfulfilled task. Subsequent centre-left governments proved unable to overcome opposition within their own majority and from the trades unions on the most critical issues.

Very little change has actually been manifest. Thirty-nine municipalities were selected to carry out an experimental minimum-income programme for two years, ending December 2000. On the basis of expert evaluation, the scheme – largely inspired by the French RMI – was supposed to be extended to the whole country and funded by central government. However, governments were unable to fulfil this commitment. Upgrading of the ordinary benefit from 30 to 40 per cent of previous earnings was the only real improvement in unemployment benefits.

In 1997, the Prodi Cabinet also initiated a radical restructuring of the highly bureaucratized and totally inefficient public placement offices (*collocamento*), passing the relevant functions from central to regional government level. The devolution process – completed by 2000 – aimed at bridging the institutional and organizational split between passive and active policies developing as a result of the 1980s measures entrusting the regions (already responsible for vocational training) with employment promotion policies. As in the case of health care, national and regional governments signed a special agreement on the basic functions that new local employment services were to provide throughout the country.

'Discovering' the Personal Social Services

The 1990s represent a turning point also in the area of social care services. According to the Italian Constitution, the regions (established in 1970) were entrusted with legislative power in the field. But for 30 years the Italian Parliament never passed the required guidelines, letting regional governments differentiate their policies to a greater extent than institutionally envisaged. Notably, while southern regions maintained an archaic system mainly providing poor relief and institutional care, northern and central regions stimulated the expansion of a wide range of community services: home helps for the elderly, rehabilitation and training for the handicapped, day-care centres and home nursing for sick and disabled people (Fargion, 1997). The latter were helped by their interaction with a strong system of local government, with municipalities already playing an active role in social services experimentation and innovation. Quite the opposite holds true for southern regions, given the traditional weakness and inefficiency of local government there.

In 1991, Parliament issued regulations on voluntary associations and cooperatives, also legislating on the very sensitive issue of tax concessions to not-for-profit organizations. But the most important step taken by Parliament was the passing in November 2000 of a Reform Law which for the first time provided a comprehensive framework for the management of social care, establishing clear guidelines for regional legislation. The new rules made municipal governments responsible for guaranteeing a well-defined set of social-care services and benefits within their jurisdiction, including home helps, sheltered housing and professional counselling by social workers. Reforms placed the greatest emphasis on the voluntary sector but at the same time clearly stated a public responsibility in the field, and urged local governments to achieve greater transparency in the relationship with private and Third Sector service providers by resorting to vouchers, performance contracts and public regulation of service standards.

This particular law suggests centre-left governments intended progressively to extend the reform process to the whole social protection system, especially to those areas traditionally marginal to the Italian welfare state but increasingly crucial in the light of current social, economic, demographic and family changes. In fact, between 1998 and 2001, the centre-left majority passed a number of other measures aimed at expanding the substantive content of social citizenship, helping transitions in the life cycle. However, trades unions were able to limit the redistribution of resources from overprotected to underprotected risks and categories (as in the case of the government's inability to redesign unemployment benefits by cutting more generous benefits only available for the core workforce in favour of a broader and more equitable system). This explains why, despite the introduction of innovative legislation, social spending distribution did not change very much: at the end of five years of centre-left rule, family, unemployment, housing and public assistance expenditure remained well below European averages, while pension spending remained 20 per cent higher.

The 2000s: From Centre-Left to Centre-Right and Back

Berlusconi and the Trades Unions: From Concertation to Confrontation

Berlusconi's 2001 electoral victory abruptly ended the centre-left government experience, bringing to power the right of centre coalition *Casa delle Libertà*. Natali and Rhodes (2005) commented on Berlusconi's initial programme:

> The government's medium-term economic plan for 2002–2006 set out an ambitious agenda for fiscal reform (including a reduction in personal income tax), labour market de-regulation, increased investment in infrastructure, the reform of the state administration and far-reaching innovations in welfare policy . . . In pensions, the *Casa delle Libertà* proposed an increase in minimum pensions up to a standard Lire 1 million per month (just over 500 euro) alongside tax incentives to encourage supplementary pension schemes, the use of the so-called *TFR-Trattamento di Fine Rapporto* (or severance pay) to finance supplementary pension funds, and the possibility of accumulating income from work with pension benefits after formal retirement. A major new role was foreseen for private institutions through the expansion of supplementary schemes. Increasing employment rates, especially those of older workers (over 50), and reducing recourse to early retirement, became major targets of government policy.

Labour market policies pursued by the Berlusconi Cabinet appear largely in line with its neo-liberal paradigm; but in the case of health policies a gap soon emerged between official commitments and actual policies. During the first year in office the government underscored the value of regional autonomy *per se*, irrespective of the implications for the effective profile of social rights in different parts of the country. In line with the neo-liberal paradigm, this approach was complemented by an option in favour of privatization: strengthened regional autonomy offered more opportunities for the introduction of privatized arrangements. This was crowned by a bill on 'devolution', which envisaged a constitutional amendment granting regional governments exclusive legislative powers with respect to education, health care and the police.

The honeymoon between national and regional governments, however, only lasted for a year. In August 2001, state and regional representatives signed a joint agreement on health funding but problems started when the central government had to fulfil its costly commitments: for almost two years, Ministers kept postponing the identification and subsequent allocation of the VAT share to which individual regions were entitled, although health spending accounts for about 75–80 per cent of total regional outlays. Moreover, while health expenditure kept increasing beyond agreed thresholds, the 2003 national budgetary law barred the possibility for the regions to upgrade the major regional source of health funding – IRAP – or to increase the regional supplement on personal income taxes. The underlying goal of these measures was to prevent overall fiscal pressure from growing, in line with the electoral promise of lowering taxes, but this could hardly be perceived as compatible with the proclaimed ideas of federalism and regional fiscal autonomy. The climate deteriorated to the point that, during early 2004, regional representatives provocatively abstained from participating in the State-Regional Board (Fargion, 2006).

Turning to pensions, one finds a similar discrepancy between initial optimistic promises and actual government policy measures. The government ended up by postponing pension reform until 2004, adopting at that point a milder version of its original plans and leaving the employers' association *Confindustria* quite discontented. The earlier planned reduction in employers' social contributions was eliminated and firms received no compensation for having to give up control over the TFR. Moreover, self-employed contributions were not increased, remaining about half of those paid by employees. The use of severance pay for supplementary funds was no longer automatic (as in the first draft) but subject to individual worker's decisions. This piece of legislation nevertheless represents a turning point in two respects at least: a) it effectively provided the means for establishing a second pillar in the Italian pension system; b) it cut back on seniority benefits – which represented one of the notable anomalies of the Italian welfare state.

This last point requires clarification. Seniority benefits were originally linked only to the number of insurance years (35 and 20 years for the private and the public sector respectively) and were payable before the legal retirement age. During the 1990s, the rules were repeatedly tightened by moving up the age threshold. In 1996–7, to be entitled to a seniority pension, a private sector employee with a 35 years' contribution record had to be at least 52 years old. In 1998 this was increased to 54, and in the following three years it was moved further to 57. The 2004 pension reform fixed an age threshold of 60 years, but to avoid excessive opposition it was postponed to January 2008 (beyond Berlusconi's term of office). This remains one of the most controversial issues not only between the centre-right and centre-left coalitions but also within the latter.

Social Policy Priorities during Prodi's Second Cabinet

Prodi returned to power in May 2006. The new government officially stated one of its first targets was to repeal the provision on the 60 years age threshold. Over the first year and a half of Prodi's second Cabinet, this problem monopolized the entire social policy debate to the detriment of any serious discussion on new social needs related to atypical work, youth unemployment, the frail elderly, social exclusion or child poverty. In short, the divide between old and new social risks surfaced again, as five years earlier, and social policy responses showed a similar bias in favour of the former. Although, according to official estimates, the workers who would suffer from the restrictive rules numbered just over 600,000, the three labour confederations and the refounded Communist Party adamantly supported their claims, ending up securing €10 billion for covering the cost of setting back the age threshold from 60 to 58 years old.

At the same time Ministers for the Family and 'Social Solidarity' have attempted to upgrade family policies. According to Eurostat data, Italian expenditure in this policy area represents 4 per cent of total social spending, compared to an EU 15 average of 8 per cent (and higher levels even in several new member countries). The existing system of child benefits and tax allowances is not only fragmentary – family allowances are only available for low income public and private employees or families below the poverty line with more than three children – but it also produces perverse effects. Experts have pointed out, for instance, that the current tax system favours female inactivity traps in low-income families. However, the introduction of a universal child benefit or a comprehensive reorganization of child benefit and tax allowances is not in sight. The government has allocated €400 million for 2007–9 to create 40,000 new childcare places, increasing coverage to 13.5 per cent, far below the centre-left electoral commitment to guarantee 100,000 new places. The Barcelona target of 33 per cent coverage seems totally out of reach for the near future.

Despite having one of the highest European poverty rates, with as many as 25 per cent of children at risk of poverty, concentrated in large families living in the South, Italy also remains without a national public assistance safety net. The current government has not yet reversed Berlusconi's decision to downgrade the 1998 experimental minimum income programme to an essentially regional and local responsibility: the whole issue remains in political limbo. Frail elderly care is another unresolved problem. In a country that witnesses Europe's highest life expectancy, the number of elderly unable to maintain an independent life is constantly rising and poses major care problems, which the family is increasingly unable to meet. Public social care services are very limited and unevenly distributed. Hiring an immigrant female worker has turned out to be the only solution for many families. According to official estimates there are currently about 900,000 such *badanti*. However, this places heavy financial burdens on families without guaranteeing adequate service quality, and it leaves a growing informal sector characterized by a mix of cheap labour, illegal immigration and very limited social rights.

Conclusion: Still a Pension State

The social policy measures passed by Prodi's second Cabinet confirm that, in spite of changes in political majority, over the last decade no structural change has been introduced in the Italian welfare system to meet new social needs. Neither the centre-right coalition in power between 2001 and 2006 nor the centre-left majority currently in office has continued along the virtuous path inaugurated during the first part of the 1990s. As the title of their book, *Rescued by Europe?*, suggests, Ferrera and Gualmini (2004) argue that external pressure by the EU is crucial for explaining the impressive sequence of social policy reforms characterizing the period 1992–8. The authors adopt a 'learning' perspective, which looks at institutional change as a 'delicate process whereby policy-makers come to adjust the existing institutional status quo in the light of the consequences of past policy and of new information'. In detail, reforms are seen as resulting from a complex learning process greatly stimulated by exogenous variables, and prompted by a sudden change of the actor constellation – following the collapse of the so-called First Republic in 1992.

Within this context, the Maastricht process represents the focusing event that triggered policy change by altering the significance and cost of failure. Especially in the light of subsequent events, it seems we are confronted with a more limited phenomenon, largely dependent on the crucial and unexpected role that the traditionally marginalized European integrationist élite managed to play in the turbulent transitional years. This technocratic minority, coming primarily from the Bank of Italy and its associated Research Institute, was only able to involve wider circles in its modernization project because of the key positions it happened to reach during the 'meltdown' of the old party system, but soon lost its catalyst effect once that fortunate policy window closed. As parties progressively regained power, Italy slipped back to largely ideological and interest-based politics with the negative addition of having a political leadership much older than in any other European country and a party system largely unrepresentative of the younger generations. Given these circumstances, and considering that Italian parties are stubbornly inclined to pursue short-term rather than long-term strategies, we can understand why the social policy reforms of the late 1990s and early 2000s governments did not proceed, hopefully disentangling the inequities of the southern welfare model. This failure paradoxically resulted in adding further generational cleavages to existing social and territorial divisions.

As noted earlier, the logic of the Italian social protection and industrial relations regime emphasized, on the one hand, the distinction between large and small firms, and, on the other hand, the north–south divide. As a result of labour market deregulation measures introduced over the late 1990s, and in the absence of a concurrent reform of social guarantees attached to 'atypical' work, Italy now witnesses a stronger-than-ever generational split cutting across geographical and firm-size differences. On top of the disparities stemming from the entrenched contrast between formal and informal sectors of the economy and between large and medium-to-small firms, a new dividing line is increasingly emerging within the individual enterprise: the adult core-sector labour force enjoying standard, permanent job contracts is confronted daily with growing numbers of young workers with part-time, fixed-term, temporary jobs. These so-called atypical workers only expect much lower social protection levels but, given their precarious position, they are at the same time ready to accept heavier and worse working conditions.

What is the way out? So far, neither centre-left nor centre-right governments have been able to update the old Fordist model. Any serious attempt to redesign the social protection system inevitably entails challenging existing entitlements, and finding the resources to fund adequate protection against poverty and unemployment, as well as housing support, childcare services and family allowances. Given the current distribution of Italian social expenditure and the practical impossibility of further exacerbating fiscal and contributory pressures, pensions appear to be the first candidate of any redistributive effort. For now, this remains wishful thinking, at least until the country and its political leadership manage to come out of this apparently endless political crisis, and start looking ahead instead of backwards.

References

Barbier, J. C. and Fargion, V. (2004) 'Continental Inconsistencies on the Path to Activation: Consequences for Social Citizenship in Italy and France', *European Societies*, 6(4), pp. 437–60.

Brandolini, A. and Saraceno, C. (eds) (2007) *Povertà e Benessere. Una geografia delle disuguaglianze in Italia*, Il Mulino.

Boeri, T. and Perotti, R. (2002) *Meno pensioni, più welfare*, Il Mulino.

Boeri, T. and Tabellini, G. (2007) *Informare per riformare*, www.lavoce.info

Bull, M. and Rhodes, M. (1997) 'Between Crisis and Transition: Italian Politics in the 1990s', *West European Politics*, 20(1), pp. 1–13.

Esping-Andersen, G. (1990) *The Three Worlds of Welfare Capitalism*, Polity Press.

Fargion, V. (1997) *Geografia della cittadinanza sociale in Italia*, Il Mulino.

Fargion, V. (2004) 'Tra Scilla e Cariddi: Le Politiche sociali dei governi di centro-sinistra', *Polis*, 18(3), pp. 383–412.

Fargion, V. (2005) *From the Southern to the Northern Question: Territorial and Social Politics in Italy*, in N. Mc Ewen and L. Moreno (eds), *The Territorial Politics of Welfare*, Routledge, pp. 127–47.

Fargion, V. (2006) 'Changes in the Responsibilities and Financing of the Health System in Italy', *Revue Francaise des Affaires Sociales*, 60(2–3), pp. 285–312.

Ferrera, M. (1984) *Il welfare state in italia. Sviluppo e crisi in prospettiva comparata*, Il Mulino.

Ferrera, M. (1996) 'The "Southern Model" of Welfare in Social Europe', *Journal of European Social Policy*, 6(1), pp. 17–37.

Ferrera, M. and Gualmini, E. (2004) *Rescued by Europe? Social and Labour Market Reforms in Italy from Maastricht to Berlusconi*, Amsterdam University Press.

Maino, F. (2001) *La politica sanitaria*, Il Mulino.
Natali, D. and Rhodes, M. (2005) 'The Berlusconi Pension Reform and the Emerging "Double Cleavage" in Distributive Politics', in J. Newell and C. Guarnieri (eds), *Politica in Italia/Italian Politics*, Istituto Cattaneo- Il Mulino/Berghahn.
Natali, D. (2007) *Vincitori e perdenti. Come cambiano le pensioni in Italia e in Europa*, Il Mulino.
Pizzuti, R. (2007) *Rapporto sullo Stato Sociale 2007. Tra pubblico e privato, tra universalismo e selettività*, UTET Università.
Ranci, C. (1999) *Oltre il Welfare State. Terzo settore, nuove solidarietà e trasformazioni del welfare*, Il Mulino.
Saraceno, C. (2003a) 'La conciliazione di attività familiari e attività lavorative in Italia: paradossi e equilibri imperfetti', *Polis*, 18(2), pp. 199–228.
Saraceno, C. (2003b) 'Changes in Italian Families from the Sixties to the Present', in D. Del Boca and M. Repetto (eds), *Women's Work, the Family and Social Policy. Focus on Italy in a European Perspective*, Peter Lange, pp. 1–32.
Sestito, P. (2002) *Il mercato del lavoro in Italia. Com'è, come sta cambiando*, Laterza.
Trifiletti, R. (1999) 'Southern European Welfare Regimes and the Worsening Position of Women', *Journal of European Social Policy*, 9(4), pp. 63–78.

LIVERPOOL
JOHN MOORES UNIVERSITY
I.M. MARSH LRC
Tel: 0151 231 5216

CHAPTER 10

Russia: State Socialism to Marketized Welfare

NADIA DAVIDOVA AND NICK MANNING

Introduction: Russia or Soviet Union?

The Soviet Union (USSR) was a large and diverse empire, founded in 1917, which not only created a distinct pattern of social policy among the 15 republics that it contained, but imposed this pattern in large part on many other Central European countries. Within this vast area, there was great cultural, linguistic, industrial and natural variation. Even within the USSR, Russians comprised little more than 50 per cent of the population. The 'Eastern Bloc' then separated into 27 separate states, and the USSR itself disappeared in 1991. In this chapter we concentrate mainly on Russia.

Social policy in Russia has been in turmoil since the 1990s. However, there is still considerable continuity from the state socialist era. What was the soviet era about? There have been two dominant views, drawn respectively from either anti-Russian/Cold War or Marxist sympathies. The first was the totalitarian model. This proposed that soviet society was a dictatorship, in which a single party ruled through a non-democratic monopoly of force and centrally planned industrialization. This monolithic structure arose from the personal drive of strong personalities such as Lenin and Stalin, and the military requirements of defending a revolutionary government, first in the 1920s, and then in the Second World War. In the 1980s, however, this model came to be seen as less and less informative of real developments in soviet economic and social development and the model came under strong criticism. Political scientists replaced it with middle-range theories focused on various social actors and institutions, such as interest groups, corporatism, industrialism and a functionalist use of systems theory, all of which tried to identify an alternative dynamic to explain the basic patterns of soviet social change.

The other approach was based on a Marxist-oriented social analysis, traditionally centred on economic development as an integral element in the explanation of political change. In the 1980s this approach, too, acknowledged the apparent autonomy of the political system and began to use ideas such as bureaucratic collectivism, dictatorship over needs, centralized state redistribution and organic labour state, to analyze the way in which political actions appeared to be independent of economic constraints. Neither of these approaches had much to say about social and policy issues, which remained little discussed in commentaries on the USSR. The question arises therefore of how we can characterize the USSR, now Russia, in its approach to social issues and the development of social policy. In Esping-Andersen's (1990) terminology, there has been little analysis of the Russian welfare regime, or regimes, as it emerged over the years. We give a detailed account of how specific policy areas have changed, and conclude with some reflections on whether Russia has now settled into a recognizable social policy regime.

The Post-Transition Welfare State: 1991–9

The Soviet welfare state had been characterized by a universal guarantee of employment, with low, controlled prices and a state system of social and pension provision. At the same time, the role of employers in ensuring the welfare of soviet citizens was significant. When the state socialist system, with its centralized distribution of social guarantees through social consumption funds, collapsed, the Russian state faced the serious matter of choosing a new social paradigm.

Russian economic reforms initially proceeded from the liberal model of efficiency, which sees the social sphere acting as an impediment to development. At the same time it was proposed that existing social policy resources should provide funding for radical reforms. However, some take the view that the economic strategy of the Russian reformers simply did not include any well thought-out social policy.

Policy options were stark. In the short run, a total absence of social support might enable the quickest restructuring of the economy, but it could only be possible with either the use of a Draconian suppression of social unrest (hardly possible in modern Russia), or where the economy was ready for 'take-off' (for example in the Czech Republic, where Klaus has been sympathetic to this idea). The alternative was to take a slower path to economic change, and to target help as sharply as possible in the short term, with the longer-term goal of a Western mix of social insurance and private provision. Russia appears to have opted for the latter, although benefits were still closely tied to enterprises and poorly targeted. However, repeated declarations of social policy reforms, for example in 1993 prior to the new constitution, and in 1997 arising out of the 1996 presidential election campaign ('The Social Reform Programme for 1996–2000') were not being effectively implemented.

In legal and administrative terms, the most significant development was the new constitution proposed and adopted at the end of 1993. Social policy issues were covered in a variety of proposals, but there were also omissions. The constitution has to be read against a background of more detailed social policy proposals issued by Yeltsin in 1993, before the December constitutional referendum. The main policy goal, read partly as an election manifesto, was to proclaim the 'social state'. The constitution, meanwhile, is heavily weighted towards the powers of the President. While Ministers take responsibility for managing various parts of the domestic policy programme, for example in labour, social protection, or health Ministries, presidential decrees continue to take the lead in policy initiatives.

This proclamation of a policy direction towards a 'social state' was followed in 1995–6 by a raft of basic social legislation, immediately on the eve of campaigns for the state parliament and Russian presidential elections. In many ways this took on the populist stamp of the day, adopted out of immediate political interest, frequently in violation of the legislative process. Much of it could not be applied in practice, did not reflect reality and did not take into account specific regional features.

Financial Problems

In particular, none of the proclaimed social goals was possible without adequate financing. The initial solution, to print money or in effect to allow extended credit to central and local government and to enterprises, enabled, through inflation, a rapid and cruel restructuring of incomes. Pensioners and public sector workers, for example, were unable to maintain their incomes, while others were able to advance theirs: both beneficiaries and providers of welfare services suffered.

As in many Western countries, social policy is the most expensive section of public expenditure, and is particularly sensitive to two factors: unemployment rates and pension levels. Both these figures have been the subject of some debate. The official unemployment rate as measured by registration with the Federal Employment Service was about 3 per cent, but labour force surveys (the UN International Labour Organization [ILO] method) indicated that for 1997 it was really nearer 9 per cent with a further 6 per cent on involuntary leave and 5 per cent on short time (Chetvernina, 1997, pp. 227–9). By late January 1999, the ILO recorded a record high, at 12.4 per cent of the economically active population. Although the ILO unemployment rate was much larger than the official figures, it was still lower than many expected. However, with unemployment benefit at around 10 per cent of the average wage, while the average pension was about a third of the average wage, pensions took the lion's share of expenditure. Thus the pension rate drove the social budget.

Up to 1996, the great majority of budget debt occurred in the social sector, resulting in wage arrears for public sector workers and shortages of drugs, books and so on. By 1996, state budget spending on health care, education and other social services constituted only 65 per cent of the 1991 allocations. In fact there have not been forward annual budgets since 1993, since the State Duma has typically taken all year to discuss them, and has merely adopted them retroactively; the approval of budgets would be a minor revolution in the state's social policy, since this would mean that social welfare money would be distributed according to strictly defined rules instead of the personal notions of individual bureaucrats.

A further attempt to reanimate the system of social protection was the splitting of sources of funding, subdivided between four federal extra-budgetary funds and technically outside the state budget: employment, social insurance, pension and medical insurance. Generated since 1991 by a 39 per cent pay-roll tax, in 1994 they amounted to 17 per cent of GDP. The separation of funding not only demarcates liability, but also markedly fragments any unified social policy. Lack of balance in implementing this system, reinforced by economic instability, was leading to financial and organizational incapacity for the state to meet its ambitious social commitments.

The Social Reform Programme for 1996–2000 states quite realistically that in the medium term, a significant rise in the share of social spending in GDP should not be expected. However, periodic suggestions from the Ministry of Labour and Social Development to lower social insurance rates have been voted down by the State Duma despite an argument that raising employees' legal wages would increase total amounts contributed for social welfare purposes. Regular attempts at financial stabilization and budget deficit reduction undertaken by the Russian government had led to a fall in state expenditure of about 10 per cent of GDP, which cut spending on social goals in real terms. Social policy thus remained ineffective, although, as before, social spending represented over half of all consolidated budget expenditures and extra-budgetary funds.

A Permanent Crisis?

The reasons for the crisis in the social sphere lie in labour market processes driving up unemployment, in the growth of long-term wage arrears, in the Pension Fund crisis and in the appearance of deficits on all the extra-budgetary social funds. In 1997–8, strike movements were common in the education and health-care sectors because of systematic non-payment of salaries. It became apparent that social issues could not be resolved simply by increased funding allocations without a change in mechanisms and a reallocation of money expenditure for various purposes.

The end of the 1990s resulted a new turn in Russian policy-making. The government suspended laws for the implementation of which there were no appropriations in the budget. This mainly applied to the social sphere. In relation to social benefits, the Duma resolutely fixed the 'golden rule' that 'laws must be backed up by money', for both off-budget funds as well as for local budgets. At the federal level it was argued that there should be an end to the policy of empty promises by a moratorium on the adoption of new legislative acts establishing such benefits. The new policy direction of the Russian government – abolishing entitlement benefits and gradually replacing them with a limited set of targeted, means-tested benefits – became elevated to the key solution. In addition, responsibility for carrying out some of the functions of social policy (social assistance, education and health care) was being transferred to the local level. The government argued that the most important thing was to bring order to the social benefits system and settle the question of who should get social assistance. The principle on which the traditional Russian system of social transfers had been constructed was based more on demographic categories and characteristics than on the actual level of material security. World Bank experts pointed to the ineffective formal system of social protection. The reason for re-examining the concept is that Russia had more than 150 types of benefits and allowances, given to more than 100 million Russians (two-thirds of the population). Groups with the highest incomes (upper deciles 8–10) received 42 per cent of social benefits expenditure, while those in the lowest incomes (deciles 1–3) only receive 27 per cent (Dmytriev, 1997).

An uncomfortable choice had to be made: either don't pay anyone sufficiently, since there is not enough money for everyone, or drastically reduce the number of recipients. Russian policy-makers and some senior federal officials emphasized that the state should support only the poorest people. According to the opinion of one senior official from the Ministry of Labour and Social Development (the re-organized former Ministry for Social Protection), Russia did not have a social policy; what it had was an attempt to protect all strata of the population without the financial and legislative prerequisites needed to do so.

Above all, enterprise managers no longer had the slightest pretensions to play a leading role in the social sphere as in the soviet past, when enterprises had a significant role in making social provision for their staff: one-third of all the soviet state's social infrastructure belonged to enterprises. In a market economy, oriented towards efficiency, enterprises have found themselves unable to maintain social objectives and with no financial interest in doing so. At the end of the 1990s, 60 per cent of Russian enterprises had actively entered into the process of transferring their social establishments onto the books of local authorities. The reform had two aims: to replace the previous system, in which public access to social goods depended on a person's status at work and particular branch of industry; and to improve the enterprises' financial position, freeing them from social functions atypical for businesses operating in market conditions.

At the beginning of 1998 Yeltsin stated in his Annual Message to the Federal Assembly that Russia needed a new 'upswing strategy', presupposing steady economic growth and economic freedom reinforced by a purposeful state policy. When there is a shortage of budget money, he argued, the only way to improve the social situation is through targeted social assistance. In 1993 he had proclaimed that 'the main goal of reform is to develop Russia as a "social state"', but the priority for reforms for the end of the century seemed far different: tighter financial control, realistic budgets and 'targeted' social policies.

However, the currency crisis and financial default in August 1998 undermined the fragile economic stability developing in 1997, making the implementation of the new social policy package highly problematic. Russia was faced with the complex task of finding a sensible compromise between the demands of economic growth and of social protection. But the 2000 Russian presidential elections automatically shifted the tackling of many social problems into the next century.

In the new socio-economic conditions of the transition economy, the inherited soviet-like system, together with the lack of real reforms, rapidly became both financially unsustainable and incapable of providing key public goods, such as reliable pension payments or poverty relief. To explain the weak capacity of the Yeltsin-era state in formulating and implementing policy, Cook (2005) presents four tentative causes: an exclusive process of policy formulation with international financial institutions' (predominantly the World Bank's) influence; weak elaboration of policies where proposals were often brief, unprofessional, poorly supported by documentation and calculations; lack of administrative and technical capabilities, or the regulatory and legal frameworks, to implement agreed policies; society seen as a constraint rather than as a 'social partner'.

New Millennium: New Social Paradigm?

Objective reasons for the numerous failures of Russian social policy after the beginning of market reforms can be found in financial shortages. More subjective reasons are the holding back of social priorities by Russian politicians. Smirnov *et al.* (2000) argues that

> the social sphere did not represent a political danger, and it has enabled the realization of many economic reforms. The dramatic fall of living standards, development of open and latent unemployment, destruction of the former social schemes in the absence of new ones – in this context a prospect of social explosion did not look unrealistic.

However, an explosion has not taken place, the population has shown rare social tolerance, and in this sense it is necessary to acknowledge the intuition of the authorities. On the other hand, the population has found itself in new market conditions and has had to develop its own ways of survival.

According to an Independent Institute of Social Policy (IISP) survey, social policy in Russia has had two stages. The first stage (from the beginning of the

1990s up to 1996–7) is characterized not by social reforms as such but a primitive reaction to chronic financial deficits. Only from the beginning of 1997 have attitudes to social reforms in Russia gradually changed. Before this time there was an illusion: 'when financial stabilization has been achieved, economic growth will begin by itself, and social problems will be solved'. But by 1997 financial stabilization was achieved, and the problems were still not solved. At the end of the 1990s it became clear that there was an urgent necessity for elaborating a long-term conception of social reforms. A serious demographic situation, undeveloped institutions in the social sphere, failed social processes, especially in the sphere of incomes, and other negative factors appeared to be obstacles for further economic growth. The maintenance of the social sphere as it was practiced previously seemed ineffective, was unpromising and was very expensive. Politicians began to discuss seriously and more pragmatically new labour legislation, pension reform, the existing system of privileges and benefits and other social issues. There was a marked appetite for serious institutional change.

What situation did Putin inherit when he received the presidential reins of government from Yeltsin? The economic reforms of the 1990s had brought significant social costs. Russia had suffered a 50 per cent reduction of GDP, with a corresponding fall in household incomes. At the same time, the former social protection system, which – at least in theory – guaranteed social care to all citizens free of charge, was destroyed without being replaced by anything comparable. This led to a decline in welfare, opportunities and quality of life for a significant part of the population. Its health status, particularly the reproductive health of women, had declined, along with impoverishment, increased income differentiation and social disintegration. Russian society had already paid a high price for the vacuum in social policy existing during the first decade of market reforms, and was waiting for serious efforts to deal with concrete social problems such as poverty, public health, high mortality and chronic unemployment.

The complexity of the situation arose from the stage of development in Russia, which was moving from the soviet system to a desirable long-term model, many parameters of which are still not clear (Gontmakher, 2004). However, the active development of 'human capital' is an indispensable condition for public and economic progress and social well-being. The IMF position, influential for Russian policy-makers, is quite clear: transition countries need to reform their social sectors to promote the welfare of their citizens and spur economic growth (Heller and Keller, 2001). This means building up and redesigning social safety nets and addressing problems in such areas as social insurance, budgetary transfers, health care and education, labour markets and tax administration. It also requires cutting some benefits and privileges. In this sense the formation of a long-term conception of social policy appears to be inevitable.

Since 2000, the context for social policy has experienced major change. First, serious economic growth (first in primary production, then in processing industries) was achieved. Russia had largely overcome the economic crisis caused by the collapse of the Soviet Union. Putin's government was able to announce the next stage of reforms and set out to draft a ten-year plan mapping out a strategy for sweeping change under three headings: modernization of the economy, social policy and restructuring of the power system itself. Among the creators of this plan, the economic and finance ministers in all of Putin's cabinets, had close ties to the former architect of the state privatization programme, a relatively right-leaning liberal politician. 'What we're planning is not a revolution, but it's an attempt to change the existing system of interests. We need to announce that the rules of the game are going to be changed' (quoted in *The St Petersburg Times*, 572, 30 May 2000). If implemented, the plan could double Russia's GDP over the following decade. This became a top priority for the country's authorities, although the economic Minister himself later doubted that this goal could be achieved.

The positive trends in economic development, stable finances and the market allow the government to discuss forming a new model of social security for Russian citizens to underpin their constitutional rights. This model is based on the social insurance principle, including retirement insurance, social insurance and obligatory medical insurance. The President again called in 2005 for a fulfilment of those large-scale strategic tasks the country faced to retain high levels of competitiveness in the world. These tasks were considered as 'system-forming'. 'We need an integral vision of the prospects of Russia's development, with very clear aims and with due account taken of the possibilities to attain them' (RIA-Novosti, July, 2005). Putin added that Russia is unable to solve its strategic tasks 'without the freedom of economic activity and effective social policy'.

The year 2005 was marked by the movement of social problems from the political periphery to the centre of the government's socio-economic programme and politics. The new Federal Law no. 122 came into force, kick-starting the reform of social benefits. The task of poverty reduction came to be seen as equal in importance to the task of doubling GDP. The President proclaimed four high-priority national projects: health, education, affordable and comfortable housing, and development of the agricultural sector. In his 2006 annual message to the federal assembly he announced a large-scale programme to overcome the demographic crisis, particularly the stimulation of birth rates. Thus 2005 could be seen as a crucial year for social policy in which Russia entered a third stage of development since the fall of the USSR.

The economic background seems favourable. Russia's GDP increased by 35 per cent from 2000 to 2005. Official sources reported that over the four years of Putin's government, the Russian population's real incomes have increased by 40 per cent. By 2006, Russia's GDP exceeded the level it was at when the Soviet Union collapsed in 1991. Russia's Stabilization Fund, set up in 2004 to accumulate surplus revenue from high world oil prices, amounted to US$55.7 billion as of March 2006 (Posstat, 2006), exceeding US$71 billion in early 2007 and US$107 billion in early 2008. The Central

Bank reported that Russia's gold and foreign currency reserves stood at US$260 billion as of September 2006, leaving the country with the world's fourth-largest foreign currency reserves after China, Japan and Taiwan.

Putin insisted that 'we must not miss the opportunities now emerging in the Russian economy . . . but we can spend only as much as we earn'. The 2006 budget was the first 'development budget' in several decades, it was officially reported. A 'development budget' implied primarily the implementation of national projects and the development of science-intensive technologies. Under it, spending on education and agriculture increased by more than 30 per cent, on health care by 60 per cent and spending on housing quadrupled. In money terms it meant a social budget increase of US$4 billion (0.5 per cent of GDP).

The President proposed setting up a council to implement these priority national projects that he intended to control personally, and underlined how important it was that legal institutions oversaw the proper use of funds. The Stabilization Fund, where the government accumulated extra funds received from oil exports, had not been set up to solve social issues but to maintain Russia's macro-economic stability. It was created 'to prevent price growth, to keep inflation in check, and to make sure that we can solve social issues in these conditions'. However, in September 2006 the government initiated the creation of a new 'fund for future generations', which could use up to 10 per cent of the Stabilization Fund. The money has been earmarked for education, health-care and social security programmes.

The Putin Years: An Initial Assessment

The relative success in addressing social issues under Putin's administration is due to three critical advantages over Yeltsin's: a more cooperative legislature, a growing economy with rising real incomes and greater state capacity. However, speaking in June 2006, Putin said that high inflation, sectoral monopolization, bureaucracy and corruption are still the main problems holding back Russia's economy. The 'shadow' economy still exceeded 40 per cent of the GDP, and net capital flight from Russia reached US$9 billion in 2005. In a recent study, the Fitch international rating agency said that despite increasing macro-economic stability, the high level of capital flight from Russia reflected a complex business climate and a lack of confidence in state institutions and observance of property rights.

Numerous surveys indicate that a majority of the public believes that the most needy (invalids, orphans, many-children families, pensioners, unemployed, single parents, low-paid workers, students) should receive free or subsidized medical care (in particular), nursery and kindergarten, housing, professional training and municipal transport. There is also a disturbing lack of faith in the future among many sectors of society and most particularly among its poorest sections. The prospect of future reforms has not altered this pessimism.

According to the Constitution, Russia still is a 'social state', but this is no more than a declaration of intentions for an indefinite future. This inconsistency in modern Russian social policy is a result of its conceptualization. The 'social state' is just a special case of the liberal project in Russia. The project is supported by the World Bank and implemented through the state budget. A welfare state aspires for all to enjoy good social standards in pensions, in health services and in education. But a liberal society guarantees only minimal standards and consequently supports only the most vulnerable citizens. Russia has announced that it aspires to good social standards, but the state provides only minimal guarantees for all. There is a basic contradiction: ambitions are large, but resources are inadequate.

The state remains, in spite of everything, the main actor for social policy. There is an even more intensified configuration of power: strong authority of the President, practically a one-party (pro-President) State Duma and the state dependency on local self-governance. The relations of state authorities and business cannot achieve a state of civilized dialogue in any way. The institutions of civil society (such as NGOs, trades unions, employers' associations), because of their general weakness, are not ready to form their own constructive alternatives in the sphere of social policy. These tendencies leave insufficient resources and space for self-organizing communities and citizens, yet on the other hand, state actors propose policy changes that would actually reduce the state's role, eliminate broad subsidies and transfer much responsibility for social provision to individuals and markets.

Economic growth, which has been achieved in Russia since the beginning of century, is not sufficient to reduce social 'deformation'. Privatized markets in housing, education and public health services coexist alongside insufficient basic benefits, low living standards and a deterioration of health. IISP reports that even if the beginning of the new century demonstrates an increasing concern with social problems in Russian society (and not only by the public, but also the government), the conception of 'social policy as such' is still not clear. The borders of social policy resources and responsibility are not outlined, either in a public, political, or academic sense. Two approaches are still mixed up: practically any action in the economic sphere can have social consequences. At the same time there is an urgent need for a transformation of basic institutions in the social sphere, but these transformations in turn will be costly.

Analyzing Different Branches of Welfare

Russia's Demography

Russian authorities acknowledge that the demographic problem is one of the most serious problems Russia has faced. In his annual 2006 address to the nation, Putin reported a recent decline in Russia's population of 700,000 people a year. The United Nations has warned that Russia's population, 142 million in 2006, could fall by as much as a third by 2050. Economic productivity and even state sovereignty could be threatened if this situation does not improve.

The population had been steadily shrinking as death rates greatly exceeded birth rates. There is concern about the country's rapidly ageing population and the problem of alcoholism, both responsible for these alarming trends. Alcoholism particularly is corroding Russian provinces where the economy and infrastructure are poorly developed and there are few jobs. In addition to alcohol abuse, other causes of early deaths include cardiovascular diseases and external factors such as road accidents and crimes.

Tackling Russia's demographic crisis is significantly connected to the country's four priority national projects. Life expectancy for men is, at 58 years, ten years less than for men in China. Officially, the problem could be solved in three ways: cut death rates from unnatural causes; enhance effective migration; and encourage people to have more children (including the increase of child benefits to ameliorate a situation of unhealthy lifestyles and poor living conditions). From 2007 the government has given women at least 250,000 rubles (US$9,200) each as financial tax-free aid following the birth of a second child. The payouts will be revised annually to adjust for inflation, and can only be spent on education, invested in housing, or put to an individual pension account, and only after the child is three years old.

The Pension System

The accumulation of huge pension arrears since the mid-1990s shows that the Russian distributive pension system is in long-term crisis. The burden on working people is growing, especially as, in general, businesses operating in the shadow economy rarely deduct taxes. In addition, the ratio of payers to recipients is gradually falling: in 1991, employed people exceeded pensioners in a ratio of 2.1:1, but by 1997, only by 1.7:1 (BEA, 1998). People over 65 make up 14 per cent of the population at the present time, which means Russia's rate is twice as high as is typical for an industrial society. The prospect of a rapidly ageing Russian population, resulting from marked falls in the birth rate, will aggravate this problem further in the near future.

This kind of social security issue is already a major talking point in many countries. Pensions are highlighted as a crucial problem for a country's financial system. But to achieve political consensus on the reform of pension provision has proved to be extraordinarily difficult in Russia, since pensioners are the most active section of the electorate. Faith (2000) argues that, as in the West, in Eastern Europe and in Russia in particular, most public cash social expenditure went to old-age pension systems based on social insurance (the 'pay-as-you-go' principle):

> Through linear earmarked taxes on wages (levied in most cases on both employers and employees) annual contributions fed current expenditures without any direct links between individual contributions and pensions. However in post-communist countries boundaries between the state budget and social security budget were symbolic and expenditure was not only exposed to day-to-day political decisions but these decisions lacked any public control and transparency.

Discussion of pension reform with an emphasis on the pay-as-you-go component started back in 1995. The government proposed to reform the existing distributive system, gradually introducing elements of compulsorily funded pension financing. The foundation of this reform is a so-called 'mixed model', predicated on implementing three levels of provision envisaging a combination of distributive and accrual principles when securing pensions, as well as an opportunity for citizens to acquire additional optional pensions through non-governmental pension funds. The three parts of the pension system include a basic fixed pension for all senior citizens (roughly at subsistence minimum levels), a state social insurance pension depending on tax contributions and work experience, and supplementary pension insurance through private individual pension accounts.

However, reform was comparatively slow to materialize. Although approved by government, it was postponed because many operational mechanisms were vague and it became effective only from 2002. The government initiated the creation of individual pension accounts and the creation of non-state pension funds. In practice the traditional system was reinforced with two more systems with stronger viability, created due to the pension tax paid by employers to create insurance coverage, and pension savings invested into the stock market. Russia has chosen a compromise model, with changes spread over time, and does not envisage making the funded method of insurance the main component of the pension earned over a working lifetime.

At the moment the average monthly pension is about 26–7 per cent of the average wage, meaning that retirement entails a considerable deterioration in living standards. Under international labour standards, the figure should be 50 per cent. Moreover, the Russian Pension Fund remains a consistent opponent of raising the pensionable age (55 for women and 60 for men) because it would have only a small effect economically and is highly unpopular.

Poverty

From the beginning of the Russian reforms, the issue of poverty was seen as severe, symbolizing the social cost that the population paid in the transition from the Soviet model of welfare to the market. Economic reforms triggered a 50 per cent reduction in Russian GDP, with corresponding falls in the population's incomes. Price liberalization in the early 1990s not only provoked large price rises but also devalued the savings of most of the

Table 10.1 Dynamics of official poverty levels in Russia, 1992–2006

	Distribution across years														
	1992	*1993*	*1994*	*1995*	*1996*	*1997*	*1998*	*1999*	*2000*	*2001*	*2002*	*2003*	*2004*	*2005*	*2006*
Total below poverty line	33.5	31.5	22.4	24.8	22.1	20.8	23.4	29.9	29.0	27.5	24.6	20.3	17.6	15.8	14.3

Source: Russian Federal State Statistics Service (Posstat), www.gks.ru/wps/portal

population – bringing about, in effect, a large-scale redistribution of wealth in Russia.

Over the final decade of the twentieth century, the worst years from the point of view of poverty, were 1992–3 and 1999–2000. In 1992–3, the rise in the number of poor people was the consequence of price liberalization and rampant inflation. In 1999, high poverty rates were the consequence of the 1998 financial crisis and the default on public and private debt.

In recent years, poverty rates have followed a steady downward trend. But despite the relatively satisfactory dynamic of the poverty situation reflected in official statistics, there continue to be substantial variations, from 8 per cent to 70 per cent in some areas in 2004, with real rates higher than official figures. Against the background of Russia's recent dramatic petroleum-led economic growth, an estimated 30 million Russians still live in poverty.

Among the countries of the CIS, Russia also has the most unequal income distribution. The share of the best-off 10 per cent of the 2004 population was 30 per cent of total income, while the share of the poorest 10 per cent was 2 per cent, a wider level of inequality than in other industrial societies. In Russia, the Gini coefficient is closer to that of Third World countries (Manning, 2007). Further growth in inequality may undermine the positive influence of economic growth on the reduction of poverty, as the World Bank (2005) persistently warns. It is in this regard that most serious analysts emphasize that the 2004 goal to reduce poverty sharply was potentially achievable but extremely difficult.

Employment and Wages

One-third of Russian workers receive wages that do not satisfy basic needs (ILO, 1999). The ILO recommended that the government create macroeconomic conditions conducive to a significant increase in real wages. Putin's first step in the employment sphere was to eliminate wages and pensions arrears. Another problem was that the 1971 Labour Code was outdated as the legislative base on which to adjust labour relations. A new Labour Code was adopted late in 2001.

The role of the minimum wage is to fix the minimum level of remuneration for work, preserving workers' dignity. On the other hand, the minimum wage is an instrument of social protection for the most vulnerable workers and a base for social benefits calculation. At the start of the 1991 reforms, the minimum wage was one-and-a-half times the subsistence minimum, but in the course of the transition period this relationship had fundamentally changed (at the end of the 1990s, the gap was five-fold). At the present time, the minimum wage remains well below subsistence levels. According to estimates for 2007, an average Russian needs around 4,000 rubles (US$155) a month to survive. Long debates resulted only in doubling the minimum wage from 1,100 rubles (US$42) to 2,300 rubles (US$89) in September 2007. The government plans to bring minimum monthly pay into line with subsistence levels by 2011.

The Russian labour market has undergone sweeping changes during the period of reform. But the years 2009–11 could be crucial for Russia's economy and its global competitive capacities. The accession of Russia to the World Trade Organization (WTO) may lead not only to the liberalization of trade and attraction of investment, but also to serious implications in the social sphere, in common with every country facing globalization. One major future problem might be the growth of unemployment in the industrial sector. In order to manage the consequences of globalization it is necessary to improve the quality of professional training, one of the goals of current educational reform.

Education and Health Care

Reform of education and health care was inevitable, since they still relied in the 1990s on residual budget funding. But the question then arises as to whether the new system will be a state or a private one. Taking a purely economic approach to health and education will simply put the most important public services beyond the reach of a sizeable section of the population. In the majority of current Western systems, the degree of privatization of these social areas remains small.

This question is high on the Putin Cabinet's priority list. From one side it is acknowledged that post-soviet Russia faced a dramatic deterioration in general physical, mental and social health. Self-reported levels of ill-health in Russia are between 50 per cent and 100 per cent higher than West European averages. Health has proved to be one more price that the Russian nation pays for the policy of reform. From the other side, the country had to utilize its competitive advantages in the field of education to compete within a global market. Public expenditure on health care and education has fallen considerably compared with the communist regime and, as a percentage of GDP, is below levels in Western Europe.

Since 2005 Russia started implementing national projects on health and education, which became the central signposts of current policy reform. In 2005 Russia's Education Minister said that for the first time in the history of modern Russia education expenditure exceeded defence expenditures

(RIA-Novosti, 16 January 2005). Under the country's 2006 budget, spending on education and health care was increased by more than 30 per cent and 60 per cent respectively. Sixty per cent of the population is involved in the sphere of education, and about 80 per cent of Russians up to 35 years of age consider higher education their main goal. The 2002 census indicated that the major positive shift is in higher education (the decade after the 1989 census was marked by a doubling of higher school student enrolment). It is also the first time that the census revealed more women than men with a university education. The President praised these trends, confirming that the state should support its citizens in their desire to improve their level of education.

The modernization of the education system includes two groups of measures: first, to ensure access to quality university education, and, second, to improve the quality of secondary and professional education. In September 2007, the law extending compulsory general education from nine to 11 years came into force. Authorities emphasize that the reform also aims to legalize informal practices in the education process – since some people pay to get enrolled at universities, it might be better to let them pay the money legally. The reform also presupposes that low-income families should have the opportunity of getting high-quality education. The official stance is that the current education system should be flexible. The new concept presupposes that both higher and primary/secondary schools have the right to engage in independent economic activities, including market principles.

The success or failure of Russia's educational policy and the country as a whole depends to a large degree on whether it blends with the world economy. At the conference of European Education Ministers held in Berlin during September 2003 Russia joined the Bologna Convention whose participants aspire to create by 2010 a unified European zone in the sphere of higher education. The main goal of the Bologna process is to promote integration into the EU system of education, an extremely important goal for modern Russia.

Educational reform is moving slowly and with difficulty. According to a working group of the Council on Science, Technologies and Education 'the quality of basic secondary education in Russia is getting worse', and schools lack educational materials, equipment and skilled teachers. A left-oriented coalition called 'Popular Government' claims that state spending on education has dropped and is still falling. They insist on further education spending increases, the development of infrastructure and social guarantees for students and teachers, whose average salary was only 70 per cent of the average national salary. Meanwhile, the marked polarization of the Russian population on the basis of income, is slicing education into layers, with the gradual formation of a hierarchy of 'élite' and 'cheap' educational establishments. Consequently, the chance of receiving specialist or higher education varies dramatically for members of different social groups.

The same situation can be traced in health care. According to the results of the INTAS-funded project 'Health, health policy and poverty in Russia', the poorest strata of the population showing the lowest levels of health find it hardest to obtain access to good-quality health care, since free medical services are being gradually phased out (Davidova, 2007). Experts have described Russian medical services as 'the triumph of paid health care'. State guarantees are covering fewer free services than before, and the Ministry of Trade and Economic Development has suggested amending the Tax Code to stimulate voluntary medical insurance. The new package of social reforms seems to place part of the responsibility for tackling a whole range of social and health problems on the shoulders of the population.

By the end of 2006, the Health and Social Development Ministry also found itself under a cloud over a corruption scandal caused by a nationwide subsidized drug shortage. Junior officials of the compulsory health insurance fund were arrested on suspicion of receiving bribes from pharmaceutical and other companies. Subsequently, more corruption probes were instigated against officials subordinate to the ministry, including the Federal Health and Social Development Agency, the Pension Fund and Social Insurance Fund.

Housing

Housing was a major source of frustration under the soviet system. Waiting lists were very long except for privileged groups such as senior military and party members. From 1991, government reform of housing and municipal services envisaged the transfer of housing either to private ownership, or to municipal control. At the end of 1997 citizens paid, on average, only 38 per cent of the cost of electricity, water, housing services and repairs, the remainder being covered by local budgets. But since the end of the 1990s, utility rates have been gradually rising with the intention that they should be shouldered entirely by Russian citizens, a process almost completed by 2007. Housing privatization began swiftly in the early 1990s; over 70 per cent of Russians were living in their own flats or homes by 2006.

A radical housing programme began in 2002, and its second stage, for 2006–10, has been adjusted to provide affordable and comfortable housing for people. Russia has inherited outdated housing and utility sectors from the Soviet Union and needs to increase construction volumes considerably in order to achieve this ambitious goal. Important elements here are the joint development of regional markets for affordable housing, including housing mortgage facilities, regional infrastructure formation and innovative capacity promotion. The programme's second stage seeks to increase housing construction to up to 80 million square metres a year by 2010, better living conditions for 314,000 families entitled to budget subsidies, more mortgages and a lower number of people on waiting lists for free housing. The construction sector also is problematic: personnel issues need to be addressed and equipment has to be upgraded. The implementation of the national project is the responsibility of the Regional Development Ministry, which means establishing a single vertical technological chain, from government and federal bodies down to municipalities.

While a national priorities list is a major step forward for socio-economic progress, so far the nationwide housing project has created more problems than it has helped solve. According to the Department for Affordable Housing and Mortgages of the Russian Builders' Association (RBA), the start of the housing project coincided with failed public service reforms; this put the construction industry outside government control. This is catastrophic, since the industry is critical to the entire Russian economy. The 'affordable housing' package, passed by the State Duma at the end of 2004, was drafted in a hurry and secretively, without any regard for the opinion of the professional business community. The package was conceptually in line with Russia's main development trends, but it did contain serious errors, which eventually led to a situation where housing supply decreased and prices rocketed. The biggest problem is that there is no balance in how the government plans to bolster supply. Funds are readily funnelled into 'targeted' support for various social groups, fuelling an already high and unmet demand for housing. Unmet demand for housing is estimated to be somewhere between 35 per cent and 50 per cent, impacting on house prices.

Conclusion: Examining the Russian Welfare Model

Esping-Andersen has argued for a new, more realistic welfare model worldwide. A leading issue is that the minimization of poverty and income insecurity is a precondition for an effective social investment strategy (Esping-Andersen, 2002). But Boyko's (2003) analysis of Western images of Russian social policy concluded that the system of social security in the soviet period could not be located within the framework of the well-known typology of Western welfare states in the absence of a market economy. Though the soviet system combined in itself features of universality and corporatism, characteristic to some capitalist models of social welfare (full employment, developed and universal social insurance, advanced system of social protection at the enterprises), this model could be consigned rather to a 'non-welfare state' (Esping-Andersen, 1996). State socialism was a strong and stable system, in which the state was the exclusive employer (Standing, 1999). In post-soviet Russia, the centralization of power and resources is still high, but the withdrawal of guaranteed employment and protected jobs from current policy priorities is notable (Manning, Shkaratan and Tikhonova, 2000). The state retains the role of exclusive distributor of social benefits.

The Russian–Danish project 'Comparative Perspectives on Welfare

Provision and Reforms' (2002) argued that in contrast to the Scandinavian model, Russia is a country with contradictory ideas and structures that are in part historical, which continue to function despite their poor performance. The downfall of the soviet system caused not only serious changes in the legislative and executive institutions of social policy, but also the destabilization of the public situation as a whole. In the period of crisis for the state and its population, the decentralized system appeared to be unable to support social stability in the country or to render real support to citizens facing difficult conditions. The long period of solving social problems using only the 'state beneficence' system, combined with its sudden termination, have left many people feeling vulnerable. People used to receiving state support appear to have difficulty in accepting the social responsibility necessary in the new socio-political and economic circumstances. Nevertheless, researchers concluded that the situation in Russia is not unique. Unexpected transformations from totalitarian to democratic regimes often proceed with difficulty.

In terms of a welfare typology, the new Russian social policy comes nearer to models in which the social provision and services are subsidiary goods subordinate to marked stratification and an increased role for the market. The main problem for current Russian social policy is the great gap between the framework of social policy or 'social projects with special national priorities' and its realization through the existing systems of social insurance, social security, social services and social work. Russia will not increase the volume of social payments at the cost of increasing income tax as is the case, for example, in Scandinavia, despite increasing protests by employees. In this respect the Russian state is much more similar to liberal countries of the combined 'state and market' type. The interaction of these two systems of social welfare maintenance remains tense.

References

BEA (1998) *Survey on Economic Policy in Russia in 1997*, Bureau of Economic Analysis.

Boyko, O. (2003) 'Doubts and Hopes: Western Images of Russian Social Policy', *Universe of Russia [Mir Rossii]*, XII(1).

Chetvernina, T. (1997) 'Forms and Main Features of Hidden Unemployment in Russia', in T. Zaslavskaya (ed.), *Kuda Idet Rossia*, Intertsentr.

Comparative Perspectives on Welfare Provision and Reforms: A Nordic-Russian Workshop, Norwegian University Center (2002) St Petersburg, 24–6 October.

Cook L. J. (2005) *Governance Capabilities and Social Policy Reform in the Russian Federation*, Institute of Legislation and Public Policy, www.ilpp.ru

Davidova, N. (1998) 'Regional Specifics of Russian Mentality', *Social Sciences*, Quarterly Review of Russian Academy of Science, 1, pp. 36–48.

Davidova, N. (2007) 'The Interrelationship of Poverty and Health: The Longitudinal Experience', paper to the international workshop Health, Health Policy and Poverty in Russia, 4–6 May.

Dmytriev, A. (1997) Unpublished Report for Annual International Symposium, Inter-Disciplinary Centre for Social Science, 17–19 January.

Esping-Andersen, G. (1990) *The Three Worlds of Welfare Capitalism*, Polity Press.

Esping-Andersen, G. (ed.) (1996) *Welfare States in Transition: National Adaptations in Global Economies*, Sage.

Esping-Andersen, G. (ed.) (2002) *Why Do We Need a New Welfare State?*, Oxford University Press.

Faith, G. (2000) 'Social Security in a Rapidly Changing Environments: The Case of the Post-communist Transformation', in N. Manning and I. Shaw (eds), *New Risks, New Welfare: Signposts for Social Policy*, Blackwell.

Gontmakher, E. (2004) 'Russian Social Policy as a Sphere of Mutual Responsibility of the State, Business and Civil Society', *SPERO (Social Policy: Expertise, Recommendations, Observations)*, 1.

Heller, P. and Keller, C. (2001) 'Social Sector Reform in Transition Countries', *Finance and Development*, 38(3), September.

ILO (1999) 'Overcoming Adverse Consequences of the Transition Period in the Russian Federation', working paper of International Conference on Social and Labour Issues, October.

ILO (2005) 'Social Protection of the Population: Assessing Social Consequences of the Benefit System Monetization', ILO.

IREX (2006) Survey of Recent Social Policy Studies in Russia, March.

Maleva, T. (2000) 'What Sort of Russia has the New President Inherited? Or Russia's Key Social Problems', briefing paper, Post-Soviet Economies in Transition, Carnegie Moscow Centre, 2(4), April.

Maleva, T. *et al.* (eds) (2007) *Survey of Social Policy in Russia. The Beginning of the 2000s* [*Obzor sotsialnoy politiki v Rossii. Nachalo 2000kh*], Independent Institute of Social Policy –(IISP).

Manning, N. (1998) 'Social Policy, Labour Markets, Unemployment, and Household Strategies in Russia', *International Journal of Manpower*, 19(1–2), pp. 48–67.

Manning, N. (2007) 'Inequality in Russia since 1990', in David Lane (ed.), *The Transformation of State Socialism: System Change, Capitalism, or Something Else?*, Palgrave Macmillan.

Manning N., Shkaratan O. and Tikhonova N. (2000) *Work and Welfare in the New Russia*, Ashgate.

Manning, N. and Tikhonova, N. (eds) (2004) *Poverty and Social Exclusion in the New Russia*, Ashgate.

Ovcharova, L. and Pishnyak, A. (2005) 'Social Benefits: What are the Results of Monetization', *SPERO (Social Policy: Expertise, Recommendations, Observations)*, 3.

Posstat (2006) *Social Position and Living Standards of Russian Population: Collected Statistics*, Russian Federal State Statistics Service.

Rosenberg, D. J. (2000) *Social Policy in Conditions of Federalization of Russia*, Future of Russian Federalism: Political and Ethnic Factors, 25–6 February, Institute for History of Tatarstan Academy of Sciences.

Shlappetokh, V. *et al.* (2006) Interview for *Voice of America*, 13 March, http://www.voanews.com

Smirnov, S. N. *et al.* (2000) 'Social Responsibilities of the State: Shortage or Restructurisation' ['Sotsialnye obyazatelstva gosudarstva: sokrashenie ili restructurizatsiya'], *Universe of Russia [Mir Rossii]*, 1.

Standing G. (1998) 'Societal Impoverishment: The Challenge for Russian Social Policy', *Journal of European Social Policy*, 8(1).

Standing G. (1999) *Global Labour Flexibility: Seeking Distributive Justice*, Macmillan.

World Bank (2005), 'Growth, Poverty and Inequality. Eastern Europe and the Former Soviet Union', WB [www.worldbank.org.ru].

Zubarevich, N. V. (2005) *Regions of Russia: In What Social Space we are Living*, IISP, Pomatur.

CHAPTER 11

Japan: Constructing the 'Welfare Society'

TAKAFUMI KEN UZUHASHI

Overview

Population

Japan is one of the Far East countries sometimes referred to as the Pacific Rim 'Asian Tigers'. The country consists of four principal, relatively small, islands on which 123 million people live; Japan is thus densely populated by most Western standards, a feature also of other Asian Tigers such as South Korea, Singapore and Taiwan. Why they are so densely populated is not clear – although some claim the production of rice as a staple food is a possible cause, as a given amount of rice can feed more people than other grains, rice production being, however, relatively labour-intensive. Whatever the cause, the resulting population density has been a key feature structuring the development of economic and social policy within these countries.

In recent years the issue of population has been attracting more and more attention in Japanese policy planning. This attention is not so much related to the number of the people, however, but rather to the structure of society, that is, the 'problem' of ageing. Japan has seen a much more rapid growth in the proportion of its older people than many other comparative countries, as Table 11.1 demonstrates.

Furthermore Japan will be 'super-aged' by the year 2020, when this proportion (of 65 +) is projected to be 27 per cent. This ageing is also combined with a declining fertility rate. The current fertility rate (2005) in

Table 11.1 Shifting demography of selected countries

Country	*UK*	*US*	*Sweden*	*France*	*Japan*
Move from 7 per cent to 14 per cent population aged 65 and over in years	46	69	82	114	24

Japan is 1.26, far below the replacement level of 2.1. It is obvious that these two trends will have a huge impact on Japanese social policy.

Economic Growth

The other key element structuring policy development in Japan has been rapid economic growth. The scale of growth in the 50 years up to the mid-1970s was quite remarkable – the 'miracle' of the Japanese economy, based especially on the export of popular consumer goods such as cameras, radios, TV sets and cars. GDP per capita in the year 2006 was US$38,000, one of the highest in the world. This rapid economic growth went hand in hand with massive changes in the country's industrial structure. The agricultural and fishery sector, in 1968 employing 21 per cent of the total work force, employed only 5 per cent in 2005 – fewer than in the construction industry. Yet in 2005, 17 per cent were working in the manufacturing industry, 28 per cent in the service industry.

As a result of these changes many people have moved from rural areas to cities, where many large-scale firms were established. In particular, large urban capitals like Tokyo, Osaka, Yokohama, Fukuoka and Kobe have been created. This has also resulted in major changes to family structure, with urban dwellers experiencing different family types from those of their parents in rural districts. There has been a decline in the prevalence of traditional, three-generation, Japanese families, which in tandem with the decline in fertility, discussed above, has resulted in an overall fall in family sizes. The three-generation family type made up 19 per cent of all types in 1966 but declined to 8 per cent in 2005. On the other hand, the nuclear family type and single-unit family are on the rise. The average family size was about five until the mid-1950s, but had been reduced to 2.6 by 2005.

These changes have altered the need for social security, which must now accommodate a modern urban life rather than an agricultural rural life. People in cities no longer expect to rely on traditional family care and support when in need, for example, in the cases of child rearing or caring for older people. Thus the need for state welfare provision has grown steadily. Economic growth, which Japan experienced during the period of urbanization, could afford to fund these welfare costs; and this has resulted in massive changes in social policy over the last 60 years. But the journey to a welfare state has not been a painless one. It took a long time for Japan to create a modern welfare system, and the country is still facing difficulties as a result of both internal and external pressures. This was especially the case after the late 1970s, when the growth rate declined and government budgetary restraints reached crisis levels. As we shall see, this appeared to trigger a watershed for welfare development in Japan; and it is notable that the idea of a Japanese 'welfare society' emerged in this period, supporting the case for welfare retrenchment. We return to these issues later.

A Brief History

Before the Second World War

Japan bade farewell to its feudal economic and political systems and paved the way for the creation of a modern capitalistic nation at the Meiji Restoration in 1867. The government then abandoned past 'close-the-door' policies, seeking to tackle two new goals regarded as essential to avoid the country being colonized by Western powers: the encouragement and development of manufacturing industries and the creation of a strong military.

The period since 1867 is normally divided into two episodes, the first lasting until the end of the Second World War and the second thereafter. These two periods differ in respect of both political systems and economic life and ideas. In short, after 1945, Japan restarted as a democratic nation departing forever from its past militaristic regime. There is not space to explore social policy in the pre-Second World War period in detail here, but two points must be mentioned.

First, social policy developed relatively late. Under the military regime, few social policy measures were enacted in the earlier period. Health services, for example, began to be provided in 1927 on the basis of insurance (Employees Health Insurance, EHI), although this covered only employees in large firms. Pension schemes (Employees' Pension Insurance, EPI), were introduced in 1942, covering similar kinds of workers. And, as with other late-developing capitalistic countries, Japan sought to adopt an insurance basis for provision, aiming to imitate the carrot-and-stick ideas of Bismarckian social insurance.

In Japan, civil servants in central government and armed forces members, with their families, were the first priorities to be covered by the state insurance protection (pension and health) schemes. These were followed later by local civil servants and employees in large firms. However, it was only later, in the post-Second World War period, that other groups of workers and farmers were covered.

Second, the meaning of the term social policy was differentiated. In 1897, early on in comparative terms, the Japanese Social Policy Association was founded, with the aims of social amelioration and reconciliation of classes. The main issue the Association discussed then, however, was Factory Acts. This symbolically shows the importance initially put on the welfare of working people. This too was a feature of social policies in the late-developed nations; and it was only after the end of the Second World War that the idea of citizenship as a focus for policy was introduced.

Even today the concept of social policy in Japanese (*shakai-seisaku*) has a different meaning to that of English. It refers to specific protections for working people as well as more general schemes for citizens, for instance, the Labour Standard Law and industrial relations policy. On the other hand, social security (*shakai-hosyo*), understood as integrating social assistance and social insurance, seems to be similar to the term social policy in English. It embraces not only income maintenance but also schemes for health services and personal social services. Yet housing policy and education are not included in social policy or in social security in Japan.

After the Second World War

From the end of the Second World War to the peace treaty of 1951 Japan was under the joint sovereignty of Allied Forces and the Japanese government. During that time many innovative measures were implemented. These included the establishment of the new Constitution, the reform of farmland and the dismantling of *saibatsu* (financial groups). These measures amounted to a significant degree of democratization.

This second phase is usually divided into three further subperiods, each of them marked by a milestone year.

Arrangement of National Minimum (1945–50s)

During this period, most welfare programmes implemented followed a US model, except for social insurance provision, where the Beveridge Report was reputed to have had a huge influence on policy planning. In 1956, a government White Paper from the Economic Planning Agency declared that Japan was no more a postwar economy. And in the political arena too the year symbolized significant change when the newly amalgamated conservative (Liberal Democratic) party came into power, which it did not cede for the ensuing 39 years.

In more practical terms, this immediate postwar period saw the introduction of new welfare acts and social insurance schemes. There were three welfare acts (one of which was then extended):

- 1946 – the Livelihood Protection Act (the old act – means-tested social assistance)
- 1947 – the Children's Welfare Act
- 1949 – the Disabled Welfare Act
- 1950 – the Livelihood Protection Act (the new act – widening its scope and creating a right of appeal)

A number of insurance schemes were also introduced:

- 1947 – the Unemployment Insurance Act
- 1954 – reform of Employees' Pension Insurance (EPI)
- 1959 – reform of National Health Insurance (NHI), a residual flat-rate scheme managed by local authorities

- 1961 – National Pension Insurance (NPI), also a residual flat-rate scheme managed by local authorities

As a result of these changes, 1961 is referred to in Japan as the year when all of the people were covered by pension and health insurance.

Expansion (1960s–70s)

In the 1960s, the Japanese government policy priority was the promotion of national economic growth, rather than the further development of social policy and social welfare (Campbell, 1992). The prevailing ideology of policy-makers was to increase the size of the cake more rapidly, rather than to share it more fairly. Thus only in the late 1960s and early 1970s, after successful economic growth had been achieved, did any expansion of welfare occur. Major changes included:

- 1963 – the Elderly Welfare Act
- 1966 – the introduction of the Fund of Employees' Pension Insurance
- 1968 – reduction of the health charges borne by insured persons – from 50 per cent of the whole medical bill to 30 per cent (NHI)
- 1972 – the introduction of Children's Allowance – the last-implemented social security provision
- 1973 – reduction of the health charges borne by the insured employee's family – from 50 per cent of the whole medical bill to 30 per cent (EHI)
- 1973 – free medical services for older people aged 70 and over
- 1973 – indexing introduced on a sliding scale system to employees' pensions (EPI)
- 1973 – increases in various insurance benefits (EPI, NPI, the non-contributory Welfare Pension)

As a result of these changes, 1973 is called the first year of welfare in Japan.

Reform and Retrenchment (1980s to date)

In the last two decades of the twentieth century and beyond, however, welfare provision in Japan has been subject to many of the pressures for reform and retrenchment that have been experienced in most other advanced industrial countries. This has led to the introduction of a number of changes aimed at financial tightening, and the growing proportion of older people in the population in the early part of the twenty-first century.

- 1982 – the Elderly Medical Services Act, which abolished free medical services for the elderly aged 70 and over
- 1982 – reformed regulation of the Livelihood Protection Act, which strictly checked fraud

- 1984 – reformed EHI, which introduced a charge to be borne by the insured person of 10 per cent of the whole medical bill
- 1985 – reduction of charge borne by the state, from 80 per cent to 70 per cent, of the running costs of social welfare facilities
- 1986 – reform of NPI and EPI – reduction of benefits, widening its scope through the newly established Basic Pension Scheme
- 1994 – reform of EPI (change of entitlement age from 60 to 65)
- 2004 – reform of NPI and EPI (reduction of benefits and introduction of sliding scale by macro-economic performance)

Based on the changes driven by the pressures of an ageing population, the year 1986 is now referred to as the first year of pension reform.

Outline of Japan's Social Security Programmes

Pensions

Pension schemes, as with health services, are mainly organized on the basis of insurance. All citizens are expected to join the mandatory and contributory insurance schemes to provide for their old age. Until 1985, there were several different kinds of occupational and statutory pension schemes, organized on an industry basis. For instance, workers in private firms, civil servants, self-employed, sailors and national railway workers were expected to join their own independent pension schemes. However, there were a number of problems with such a system. First, there were gaps between, or inequalities within, levels of provision and insurance premia. Second, at times of rapid change in industrial structure, as has been the case in many industries, some insurance schemes faced serious financial problems. For instance, the schemes for sailors and national railway workers were on the verge of bankruptcy in the 1980s.

The 1986 pension reform introduced a new, flat-rate, basic pension scheme, which every insured person of each occupational pension was supposed to join. Since then public pension schemes have been of a two-storied structure. The basic pension is the first floor of protection, and each income-related occupational pension is the second floor – with membership of such secondary provision being mandatory. These reforms also integrated the sailors' pension into EPI and implemented measures for mutual financial cooperation among pension schemes. As a result therefore, the ten occupational schemes existing before 1985 had by 1997 been integrated into one Basic Pension and six occupational schemes.

Since 1986, the wives of male workers (or more accurately the non-working spouses of all workers), who used to be able to join NPI voluntarily, were required to join the basic pension scheme. However, they are entitled to benefits with no additional charges or contributions. Thus the principle of 'one pension for one person' was established as part of the reform process.

Health Services

As a nation, Japan has one of the highest levels of longevity by international standards. Life expectancy in 2006 was 79 for men and 86 for women and there can be little doubt that the development of health insurance schemes, which have improved access to modern medical treatment, have contributed to this phenomenon. Public (mandatory) health insurance is in practice divided into several independent schemes. However, they can be classified broadly into two groups. The first is occupational schemes (EHI and some Mutual Aid Associations, MAA). For these, premia are fixed on an income-related basis. The second is flat-rate residual provision (NHI), administered by local authorities, covering farmers, self-employed and retired people. As a result, when people see a doctor, they pay a charge, and the charge-rate is determined largely as follows (as of 2007):

EHP, MAA, NHI

• Insured person or dependants aged 3–69	30 per cent of health bill
• Dependants under 3	20 per cent of health bill
• Insured person or dependants aged 70 and over	10 per cent of health bill

Social Assistance

Social assistance schemes in Japan are based on the 1950 Livelihood Protection Act. As in most countries, this protection is means-tested. The level of benefits is fairly generous; but the numbers of recipients are relatively small and have actually declined within the last 40 years (Eardley *et al.*, 1996). In 1955, 1.9 million people were recipients but by 1996 this had fallen to 0.9 million. This was only 0.71 per cent of the population. This has risen since 2000 to 1.4 million recipients (1.1 per cent) in 2004, still a much lower proportion than in other advanced countries. There seem to be several reasons for this low, and declining, percentage of recipients of social assistance.

For a start, the legislation stipulates that support and maintenance by applicants' relatives should be regarded as the first port of call in the meeting of basic needs. In line with this, the welfare bureaucracy administering the scheme checks all applications strictly under stringent income and asset tests. Receipt of social assistance benefits is supposed literally to be a measure of last resort. This strict administration provokes a deep sense of stigma among applicants and recipients – and, more generally, among the public at large (Gould, 1993). This is likely to lead to low take-up levels; and, although there is no official governmental survey of these, some critics argue that take-up rates are as little as a quarter of eligible people.

The fall in the number of recipients over the last 40 years is probably largely attributable to rises in the standard of living, and the spread of pension cover. However, in the late 1980s, the fall has been much sharper – from 1.4 in 1985 to 0.9 million in 1990. This may rather be the result of stricter administrative procedures, referred to in official parlance as 'proper or appropriate measures'. By the 1980s the three main categories, by household type, in receipt of assistance benefits were older people, the sick and disabled and lone parents.

Child Allowances and Personal Social Services

Child allowances were the last form of social security provision to be implemented in Japan. The reason for this delay was that, prior to their introduction, there had existed a similar, but non-statutory allowance, paid by private firms to their employees. Even after implementation, these two kinds of allowances could coexist, at least for employees in large-scale enterprises. There are two problems with statutory child allowances, however. The first is that the level of benefit is fairly low. The second is that only families with children under three are entitled to receive it. For this reason the scheme was sometimes referred to as the 'baby and toddler's allowance' (it was extended to children under nine in 2004 and under 12 in 2007).

Personal social services in Japan mainly consist of services for the elderly, the physically and mentally disabled, lone parent mothers, and childcare services. We cannot cover these in detail here, although for discussion of lone parent protection see Bradshaw *et al.* (1996). However, it is important to note that in 1990 the administration of these social welfare services was changed with local authorities (cities, towns and villages as administrative units – about 2,300 in total) becoming responsible for various services to the elderly and the handicapped.

Education and Housing

As we mentioned earlier, education and housing are not generally regarded as part of social policy or social security in Japan. The key features of provision here are shown in the boxes below.

Box 11.1 Education Provision (figures are for 2005)

State Education

6–14 Compulsory elementary (6–11) and compulsory junior high school (12–14), mainly funded by local government, with a long-established national curriculum controlled by Ministry of Education.

15–17 Optional senior high school, subject to entry requirements 97.7 per cent of junior high school graduates go on to this level (including private schools).

18 + Optional higher education, subject to entry requirements, in four-year university or two-year junior college places, funded by central or local government – 47.0 per cent of senior high school graduates go on to this level (including private schools).

Private Education

5–18+ Fee-paying access to private schools, privately funded and controlled, mostly subsidized by state – the proportion of students going to private schools at each level is:

elementary school – 1.0 per cent, junior high school – 6.7 per cent, senior high school – 29.6 per cent, junior college – 92.7 per cent, university – 73.7 per cent.

Pre-school Education

49.3 per cent of 3–5s go to nursery schools, either public (20 per cent) or private (80 per cent), all with a half-day programme controlled by Ministry of Education – called kindergarten in Japan.

31.7 per cent of 3–5s go to full-time day nurseries, either public (54 per cent) or private (46 per cent), controlled by Ministry of Health and Welfare.

Housing Provision

Owner-Occupied 2003 – 61.2 per cent population

Dwelling bought for cash price on open market. Most purchasers borrow a large proportion of the cost as a mortgage from a bank, repaid over 20 or 25 years.

(*continued*)

Public Renting 2003 – 4.7 per cent population

Local authorities are major landlords. Dwellings for low-income residents. Tenants pay monthly rents, which are low compared to the private renting.

Private Renting 2003 – 26.8 per cent population

Tenants pay monthly rent to private landlord, based on the market rate for tenancies. There is no rent subsidy to the low paid and unemployed.

Social Housing 2003 – 2.0 per cent population

Housing associations – private bodies with public regulation and subsidy; no rent subsidy to the low paid and unemployed.

Company House and Official Residence 2003 – 3.2 per cent population

Dwellings for employees and civil servants, provided as part of corporate welfare. Rents are fairly low.

Features of the Japanese Welfare State

The Scale of Social Security

We examine here the level of resources that go into the three main sections of social security, consisting of medical services, pensions and others (see Figure 11.1). The costs of social security in Japan comprised 26 per cent of GDP in the year 2004. This proportion had almost doubled since 1975, but the level is still not high compared to other countries (see Figure 11.2). When comparing the proportions for each section of expenditure, medical services had been at the top of the three until the year 1980; but, since 1981, pension expenditure has been highest – 53.1 per cent in 2004. What is more, viewed from a comparative perspective, the proportion of 'others', which mainly consists of social assistance, child allowance and personal social services, is remarkably small. This low level of provision is certainly one of the distinguishing features of Japanese welfare provision. However, the expansion of elderly care services towards the twenty-first century and Elderly Care Services Insurance Schemes implemented in the year 2000, alongside other factors, are likely to alter the picture to some extent and are expected to boost the proportion of 'others' in the early part of the twenty-first century.

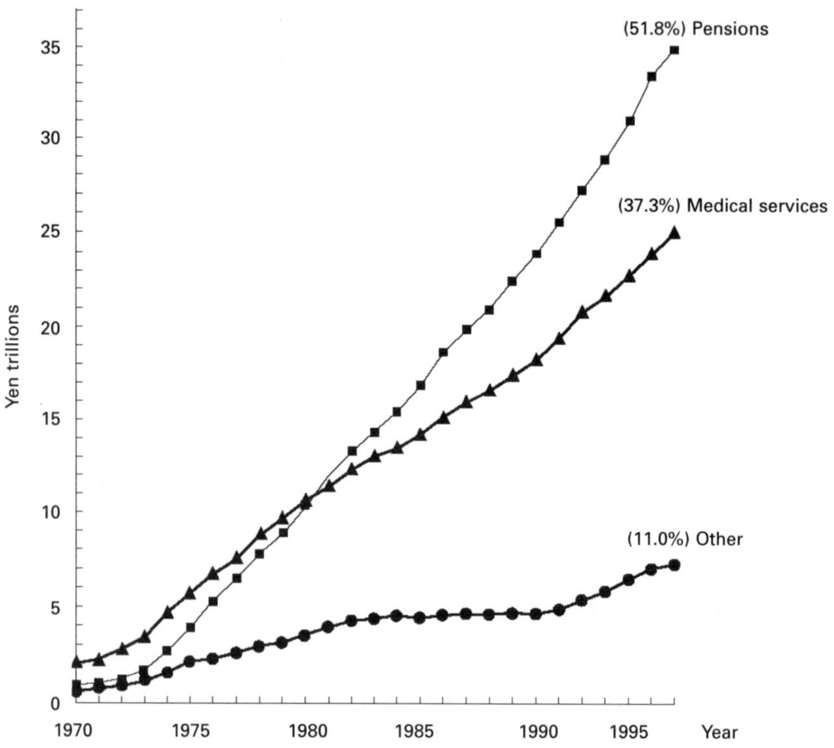

Figure 11.1 Composition of the three main sections of social security
Source: National Institute of Population and Social Security Research, *Shakai Hosho Kyuhu-hi*, 1998.

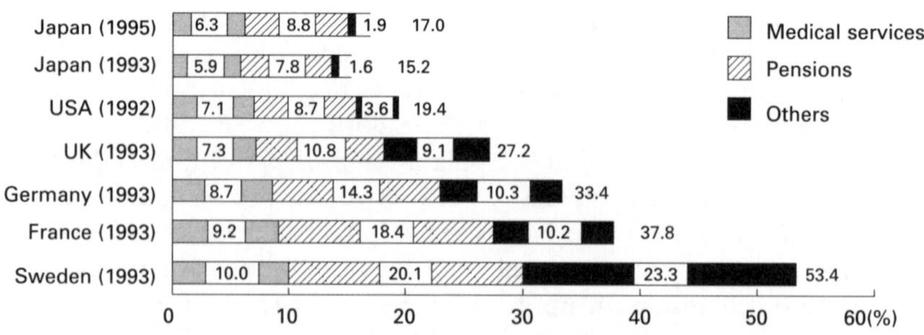

Figure 11.2 Ratio of social security benefits to national income
Source: National Institute of Population and Social Security Research, *Shakai Hosho Kyuhu-hi*, 1997.

Income Distribution and Redistribution

Patterns of equality and inequality in Japan underwent significant change in the latter part of the twentieth century. Table 11.2 shows the income distribution, as expressed by Gini coefficient, and the redistribution effect through tax and social security provision. This table tells us a number of things. First, in the 1960s, during a period of high economic growth, income distribution in Japan became more equal. Second, from 1973–5, during a period of economic turmoil caused by the oil shock, this pattern was reversed for a short while. Third, in the late 1980s, during the so-called 'bubble economy', this trend towards the inequality was accelerated. This last change was mainly the result of changes in asset-based incomes; and even since the bubble 'burst' in the early 1990s, this trend has still been continuing.

Therefore, although the total redistribution effect has been increasing over the last 40 years, income distribution before tax and social security transfers began to move in the opposite direction to a significant extent. In other words, the efforts to redistribute have not been able to offset trends towards greater initial inequality. The result of this is that income equality after transfers in the year 2001 was smaller than that in 1960; and this has led some people to argue that Japan is losing its advantageous position as an egalitarian society.

Of course, cross-national comparisons of income distribution are very difficult to make for a number of well-known reasons. The variability of statistical bases and the different definitions of survey units make direct comparisons difficult. These problems have been resolved to some extent more generously by the establishment of large-scale international data sets such as the Luxembourg Income Study (LIS). Japan was asked to join the LIS project but the Japanese government rejected this proposal for domestic legal reasons.

Table 11.2 Income distribution and redistribution

Year	*Gini coefficient (pre-transfer)*	*Gini coefficient (post-transfer)*	*Net redistributive effect*	*Redistributive effect by tax*	*Redistributive effect by social security*
1961	0.390	0.344	11.8%	–	–
1966	0.375	0.328	12.6	3.7%	8.7%
1971	0.354	0.314	11.4	4.4	5.7
1974	0.375	0.346	7.8	2.9	4.5
1977	0.365	0.338	7.4	3.7	1.2
1980	0.349	0.314	10.0	5.4	5.0
1983	0.398	0.343	13.8	3.8	9.8
1986	0.405	0.338	16.5	4.2	12.0
1989	0.433	0.364	15.9	2.9	12.5
1992	0.439	0.365	17.0	3.2	13.2
1995	0.441	0.361	18.3%	1.7%	15.7%
1998	0.472	0.381	19.2%	1.3%	17.1%
2001	0.498	0.381	23.5%	0.8%	21.4%

Source: Ministry of Health and Welfare, *Survey of Income Redistribution*, each year.

Therefore it is not easy to identify how equal or unequal Japanese income distribution is compared with other countries. At one time the dominant view in Japan was that it was one of the most egalitarian of advanced societies; but, taking recent trends towards inequality and reduced levels of redistribution (Table 11.2), this optimistic view is under revision.

The Japanese Welfare Regime

Although interest in the character of Japan's welfare system has been growing among Westerners, there is still confusion as to the typology of the Japanese welfare state. The reasons for this are two-fold. First, as Japan's data is not included in the LIS, it cannot be proved what 'outcome' social policy in Japan is bringing about in terms of poverty alleviation and income redistribution. Second, scholars in Japan have not attempted to clarify the character of Japan's welfare state using commonly accepted analytical frameworks.

One means of seeking to classify Japanese welfare provision, which has become quite popular (Jones, 1993), is to regard East Asian nations such as Japan as Confucian welfare states. However, this is a somewhat misleading approach: first, because such a general anthropological grasp can not explain the drastic changes of the way of life, and in the way of thinking, which people in Japan have experienced over the last 60 years; second, because even if the mutual care and support provided by family members in three-generation households still remains, it is not influenced by the Confucian ideology in any sense, but rather is peculiar to traditional rural society. Thus, in practice, rapid industrialization has taken over from traditional family welfare. Any attempt to classify the Japanese welfare regime must therefore utilize the methodologies and typologies developed by modern comparative analysis, notably Esping-Andersen (1990), Castles (1985) and Mishra (1990) – the three most influential scholars in this field. Esping-Andersen is the only one of the three to examine Japan. According to his decommodification index (1990, p. 52), Japan is classified as a corporatist regime, though the differences from liberal Great Britain are very narrow.

In terms of the following indices, which are supposed to be key features of the corporatist welfare states such as Germany, France and Italy, Japan can be said to belong to them:

- *stratification* (status-differentiated social insurance schemes, occupational grouping);
- *guiding principles* (hierarchy, authority and direct subordination of the individual to the patriarch or state);
- *preservation* of traditional family structures;
- *ranking* by 'decommodification index';
- *redistributive* impact.

On the other hand, Japan has much in common with liberal welfare state regimes in terms of a strong sense of stigma, modest level of benefits (in particular child benefits) and liberal work ethic. Ragin (1994) therefore places Japan in a sub-type of 'corporativistic countries that lean toward the liberal world'. But this is the only half the story, as discussion of unemployment rates and levels of social security expenditure reveal.

Esping-Andersen refers to the importance of policies to pursue full employment as the crucial character of social-democratic regimes. If this is right, then Japan, where the unemployment rate is very low (3.4 per cent in 1997), might be characterized as a social-democratic, liberal and corporatist welfare regime – obviously a self-contradictory conclusion. And, strictly speaking, even if Japan has enjoyed full employment, this does not necessarily mean that it has a social-democratic regime. Esping-Andersen (1990, p. 28) also emphasizes that full employment is a precondition for social democratic regimes to afford high levels of social security expenditure:

> On the one side, the right to work has equal status to the right of income protection. On the other side, the enormous costs of maintaining a solidaristic, universalistic, and de-commodifying welfare system means that it must minimize social problems and maximize revenue income. This is obviously best done with most people working, and the fewest possible living off social transfers.

While Esping-Andersen points out the 'supplementary' relationship between full employment and high social expenditure as shown above, it is Castles (1985, p. 82), who implies that there can be a 'substitutive' relationship between them:

> real welfare outcomes are not necessarily solely a function of the extent of income maintenance expenditures. They also depend crucially on the level of employment, the level of remuneration accruing from employment and the resulting distribution of primary income from employment.

Therefore, in order to understand Japan's characteristics it is necessary not only to apply the standard, widely accepted, rules but also to develop innovative ways of assessment and categorization.

In this respect, Mishra (1990), with his emphasis on full employment, is helpful. He seems to argue that a policy for full employment basically proceeds alongside a progressive social security policy. But this is not necessarily the case as Figure 11.3 shows, where the horizontal axis is set at 14.5 per cent (the average social security expenditure of seven countries in 1970 and 1989) and the vertical axis is at 3.9 per cent (the average unemployment rates of seven countries in 1970 and 1989).

This shows that in the fourth quadrant, where Sweden remains located and where Austria used to be, we can observe the supplementary relationship – that is, full employment can afford to maintain a high standard of social security expenditure. The first quadrant, where no countries were

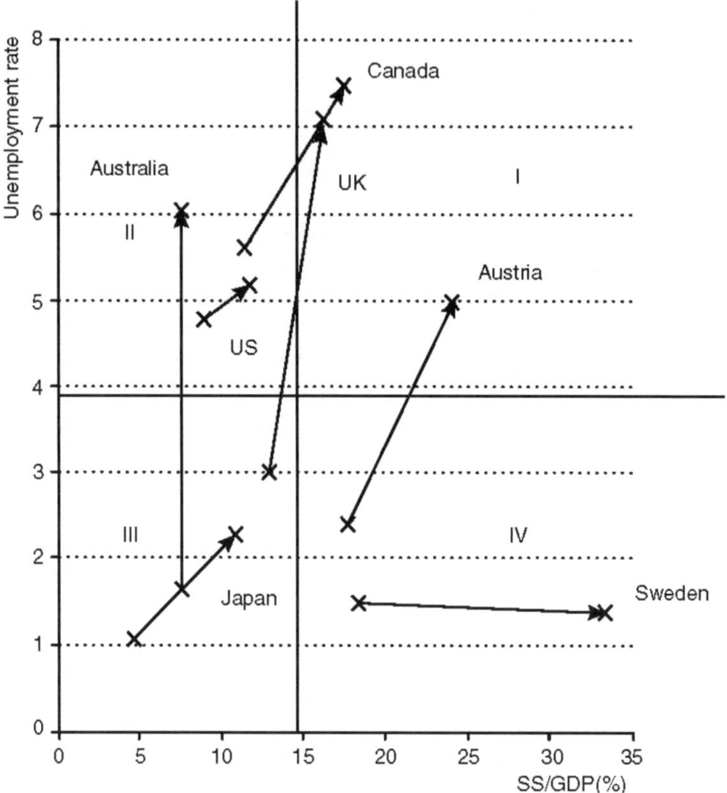

Figure 11.3 The cost of social security, from 1978/80 to 1987/9

Source: International Labour Organization data adapted from *The Cost of Social Security, 11th International Inquiry, 1978–1980* and *The Cost of Social Security, 14th International Inquiry, 1987–1989*.

located in 1970 but Great Britain and Austria were located in 1989, might be regarded as somewhat unstable, because they lack the precondition to compensate the high social security costs by full employment. In the third quadrant, where Great Britain and Australia used to be and Japan still remains, a low unemployment rate and low social expenditure coexist. This suggests that full employment is shouldering the function of social security – that is, that there is indeed a substitutive relationship.

After experiencing a 'crisis' in their welfare states, many countries shifted towards the right-upper quadrant in Figure 11.3 – undergoing a rise in unemployment and an increase in social expenditure. In these conditions, Japan's uniqueness becomes more and more prominent throughout this period. If 'shouldering or substituting the role of social security by full employment', could be regarded as 'workfare', then Japan could be classified as a *workfare* state. However, the workfare by which Japan was characterized primarily till the late 1980s has ceased to function because of the rise of unemployment rate to 5–6 per cent and the retreat of company welfare throughout the 1990s. Even if policy-makers want to make workfare function, it is impossible to do so. The 1990s, the last decade of the twentieth century, is called 'the lost decade' in Japan. Ironically, although various policies, which rest on the idea of workfare, have been implemented across countries, in Japan, workfare was 'retrogressed' in those ten years, contrary to international trends.

The Japanese case contrasts strongly with Sweden where 10 per cent or higher unemployment rates were recorded in the beginning of the 1990s, but improved from 1997, falling to a level of 5 per cent in 1999. In Japan, job creation by large-scale public works is also difficult, partly due to budgetary restraints. In 'the lost decade', serious aggravation of the employment situation was in progress inducing decomposition or polarization of the middle class, and consequently income inequality grew through the 1990s. The conventional Japanese model that rests on full employment, or, to put it in another way, rests on workfare as a substituting mechanism for welfare, is under great pressure as a result of such change (Uzuhashi, 2003).

Welfare Reform and Retrenchment

Financial Deficits

Most of the advanced nations in the OECD faced serious financial (budgetary) deficits in the last quarter of the twentieth century; and Japan was no exception to this. The government tried to improve the budgetary balance several times. For instance, in 1989 Value Added Tax (VAT, called the Consumption Tax in Japan) was introduced and in 1997 its tax rate was raised from 3 per cent to 5 per cent. This did nothing to improve the situation. In 1997, the government enacted a Financial Structure Reform Act with the goal of controlling the ratio of deficits to GDP to within 3 per cent by the year 2003 (from 5.4 per cent in 1997). But the government could not realize this goal.

This financial problem has emerged since the recession following the oil price shocks of the mid-1970s. It is important to notice that this oil price crisis coincided with a period of welfare expansion in Japan – 1973 was the first year of welfare. This has led critics to suggest that the second year never came. This is an exaggeration. But after the late 1970s, the government began tightening controls over social security expenditures, and welfare retrenchment was started.

Welfare Retrenchment

Owing to financial constraints throughout the 1980s and 1990s, every field of Japanese social security underwent thorough reform, and this is still ongoing. Some critics have described this process as 'the complete cut-down of welfare'; but the reality is not so simple, because the motive for reform is two-fold. Facing financial problems is one factor; but at the same time the country is seeking to prepare for the coming ageing of the Japanese population. Measures have been implemented in the field of pensions and health services where the keynote is retrenchment; and in the field of personal social services, new measures for financial funding aiming to widen the scope of beneficiaries, particularly among older people, have been implemented – as represented by the introduction of the Elderly Care Services Insurance Scheme.

A number of objectives and techniques are common across these various reforms:

- *The reduction of financial expenses by central government.* This has occurred in every part of social security schemes, particularly in pensions and medical services. And in some cases, as the other side of these measures, local authorities have been asked to contribute more funding to maintain protection. This can be seen in social assistance benefit, the child-rearing allowance for divorced and unmarried single mothers, and the running costs of welfare facilities such as nursing homes for frail older people.
- *The levelling down of benefits.* This has been most prominent in the pension reforms of 1986. The benefits of Mutual Aid Association (MAA) were reduced to dissolve the inequality between civil servants and employees of the private firms; and the benefits of EPI itself were also reduced sharply to cope with current financial difficulties and to secure future financial stability for the scheme.
- *The raising of user or client charges.* This has been most prominent in the health services, typically shown by the abolition of free medical services for older people aged 70 and over in the year 1982.

Elderly Care Services Insurance Schemes

It is estimated that in the year 1993 there were around 2 million frail older people in Japan needing some intensive care services. This number is projected to rise from 2.8 million in 2000 to 5.2 million in 2025. This is an inevitable consequence of the rapid ageing of the country's population; and it is no exaggeration to say that the issue of how to provide adequate and effective care services to these people has now become of the greatest interest among the public.

Up till now the trend has been for significant numbers of frail older people to be placed in hospitals – often called long-term social hospitalization. This is a product of shortages of welfare facilities, insufficient delivery of home-help support in their residences, and the declining capacity of families to care.

This is neither an effective nor an efficient response. What such people need is not medical treatment but care services; indeed, the cost of the former (medical treatment) is usually more than the latter (care services). However, it is no simple matter to turn to family care for older people. Even with direct aid for helpers, the burden of care is extraordinarily heavy and carers are often exhausted by it. What is more, this form of care has a significant, and damaging, gender dimension, because most of the carers are women, such as wives, daughters or daughters-in-law.

It is within this context the Elderly Care Services Insurance Schemes was implemented in the year of 2000. Its key features are:

1. *Insurer*: local authorities – cities, towns and villages as administrative units.
2. *Insured:* people aged 40 and over (people aged 65 and over are called the first insured, people aged 40–64 are called the second insured).
3. *Fund*: 50 per cent – public fund (central government 25 per cent, prefecture 12.5 per cent, cities, towns and villages 12.5 per cent); 40 per cent – contribution by the insured; 10 per cent – charges borne by the service users.
4. *Services provided*: institutional welfare services and domiciliary welfare services.
5. *Insurance premium*: estimated at about ¥3,000 (about US$28 monthly).

The insured are grouped into two by their age. People aged 65 and over are entitled to care services in circumstances where they are 'frail' (recognized as being in need of care by the organization which is set up by local authorities), regardless of reasons for this need. People aged 40–64 are entitled to similar services, if their frail conditions arise as a result of one of 15 specific diseases. These conditions are classified in five degrees, each of which has a maximum budget. Within this budgetary restriction, the family can choose the kind and amount of the care services. Unlike similar insurance schemes in Europe, cash is not provided to the family.

There have been fierce arguments as to how care services for frail older people should be delivered in Japan. Delivery through the social assistance schemes was considered as an option. This would mean provision financed by the tax revenues, rather than by contributions from insured citizens. In respect of the right of entitlement, however, delivery through the insurance mechanism was thought to be superior to social assistance schemes, because of the stigma attached to assistance discussed above. However, the insurance system is not a panacea. First, there is a concern that people who cannot afford to pay the monthly contribution would be automatically deprived of benefits, as seen in National Health Insurance (NHI) and National Pension insurance (NPI). Second, there is the problem that in some districts people cannot expect to have sufficient quality and quantity of services – what some critics have dubbed 'insurance schemes without delivery of services'. But even with these problems, the implementation of the Elderly Care Services Insurance Schemes means that people enter the welfare market (called the 'silver market' in Japan) with big purchasing power (¥4.8 trillion). This huge demand stimulates the supply of care services in which the private sector comes to play a more and more important role.

Pension Reform

Pension schemes in Japan are facing difficulties arising from the ageing of the population; and, in contrast to the relatively bright future for elderly care services, the outlook here seems more pessimistic. The proportion of the retired older generation to the active working generation, which was 12 per cent in 1970, rose to 30 per cent in 2005 and is projected to reach 50 per cent in 2025. If the pension schemes were run on a fully funded basis, then these demographic changes would not affect the pension finance. This used to be the case in Japan but, during the expansion in the 1970s, provision was changed to a pay-as-you-go base, so that most of the insurance premiums paid by active working people are transferred to pensioners. As early as 1986, the so-called first year of the pension reform, measures were taken to raise the insurance premiums and to cut benefit levels.

In 1997, the Ministry of Health and Welfare (MHW) presented a document called *Plans of Pension Reform: Five Options.* Three out of the five options in this proposed raising insurance premia and cutting benefits. Under these plans, premia would be raised from the current 17 per cent of income (based on a 50:50 contribution from employers and employees) to 26–34 per cent; benefit reductions of 10–40 per cent were proposed. The current expected level for a model married couple, who joined the pension insurance 40 years ago, is ¥230,000 (US$2000) per month – about 62 per cent of the average net income earned by working people. One of the other options then presented was to maintain the current level of benefit with twice the premia as of now; another proposed to replace the public pension (EPI) with private and personal pensions run on a fully funded basis. In such circumstances, many Japanese people, especially those of the younger generations, continue to be worried about the future of public pensions fearing that their own benefits could depreciate to a considerable extent.

Another plausible alternative, which is not referred in the pension reform proposals, is to transfer more tax revenues into insurance finance. This could maintain benefits level and keep premia at current levels. However, it would encounter increasingly strong opposition from the Ministry of Finance, which is now devoted to tackling the financial deficit. Furthermore, tax rises of any kind are unpopular among the public, because there is a sense of distrust regarding tax expenditure. Nevertheless, the future of the pension reform depends on how this balance between taxes, premia and benefits can be resolved.

Future Prospects

Since the late 1970s, and throughout the 1980s, the argument that Japan was developing a new type of 'welfare society' was the basis of official social policy. This had a widespread impact on the implementation of various measures for welfare reform, and was very influential on both policy-makers and academic commentators.

The idea of a Japanese type of welfare society, as formulated in the late 1970s, can be summarized as having three distinct characteristics:

- First, families are ready to give good care services to the older relatives in their homes.
- Second, Japanese companies are providing a high level of corporate welfare to their employees.
- Third, the average savings rate of households is high enough to prepare for longer life expectancy.

Essentially, in Japan, welfare society – rather than a welfare state – has been realized. This is very different from the model in most Western advanced countries, and makes it unnecessary for the state to provide high levels of welfare benefits as in Western welfare states.

Ironically, however, it is now not clear that such a welfare model is seen as appropriate for future policy development. Government policies in the last ten years, from the Gold Plan for the Longevity Society of the MHW to the Elderly Care Insurance Services Schemes, have been based to an increasing extent upon the assumption that the old idea of a welfare society is going bankrupt and changes in government's stance are inevitable.

Nowadays, as noted above, families can no longer afford to give care services to their family members; the scale of the family is getting smaller and more women are becoming engaged in paid work. Corporate firms in the process of downsizing and restructuring have been cutting costs of corporate welfare. And, in addition, the savings rate in Japan is projected to decline with the process of population ageing. These changes will not change the character of Japanese welfare society overnight, of course, but over time the differences between Japan and other advanced nations are likely to get smaller and smaller.

However, by bidding farewell to the welfare society, Japan does not necessarily proceed towards the welfare state. Under the pressure of ageing and tight financial conditions it is difficult even to maintain current levels of expenditure on benefits such as pensions and health services. In other words, with the exception of elderly care services, people cannot expect more from social security in general and will be expected to make full use of their abilities for self-help. The idea of the Japanese welfare society may be out-of-date at the beginning of the twenty-first century; but a set of alternative policies and a new prospect have not yet emerged to replace it.

References

Bradshaw, J. *et al.* (1996) *The Employment of Lone Parents: A Comparison of Policy in 20 Countries*, Family Policy Studies Centre.

Campbell, J. (1992) *How Policies Change: The Japanese Government and the Aging Society*, Princeton University Press.

Castles, F. (1985) *The Working Class and Welfare: Reflection on the Political Development of Welfare State in Australia and New Zealand 1890–1980*, Allen and Unwin.

Eardley, T. *et al.* (1996) *Social Assistance in OECD Countries: Synthesis Report*, Department of Social Security Research Report No.46, HMSO.

Esping-Andersen, G. (1990) *The Three Worlds of Welfare Capitalism*, Polity Press.

Gould, A. (1993) *Capitalist Welfare Systems: A Comparison of Japan, Britain and Sweden*, Longman.

Jones, C. (1993) 'The Pacific Challenge: Confucian Welfare States', in C. Jones (ed.), *New Perspectives on the Welfare State in Europe*, Routledge.

Mishra, R. (1990) *The Welfare State in Capitalist Society: Policies of Retrenchment and Maintenance in Europe, North America and Australia*, University of Toronto Press.

Ragin, A. (1994) 'A Qualitative Comparative Analysis of Pension Systems', in T. Janoski and A. Hicks (eds), *The Comparative Political Economy of the Welfare State*, Oxford University Press.

Uzuhashi, T. (2003) 'Japanese Model of Welfare State: How it was Changed Throughout "the Lost Decade" of the 1990s', in *The Japanese Journal of Social Security Policy* (Web Journal, National Institute of Population and Social Security Research), 2(2).

CHAPTER 12

Korea: Rescaling the Developmental Welfare State?

HUCK-JU KWON

Overview

The welfare state in Korea (also known as South Korea or the Republic of Korea) has evolved over the past 40 years from a bare structure, with a minimal number of programmes, into a fairly comprehensive system. During this time, Korea has acquired distinctive social policy characteristics. One of the important rationales for social policy in the East Asian region was 'welfare developmentalism', which saw social policy as an instrument for economic development. Based on such a policy rationale, Korea's social policy can be summarized as the developmental welfare state (Kwon, 2005). In fact, social policy did indeed prove to be one of the most effective policy instruments during the period of rapid economic growth in Korea (Goodman and White, 1998). There were also downsides to welfare developmentalism. The welfare state protected first the selected group of people who were working at the strategic industries for economic development, leaving vulnerable sections of society outside the system. This resulted in the situation that the welfare state, particularly the pension and health-care systems, reinforced social inequality. This social policy paradigm was allowed to be implemented in practice by the authoritarian politics that spanned from the 1960s to the early 1990s (Kwon, 1999).

Second, the equally important policy dynamic shaping the Korean welfare state was the democratization that took place from the mid-1980s. The dynamic between democratization and the development of the welfare state in Korea has been much more complex than the way in which Marshall once described it, as the development of political and social rights (Marshall, 1964). At times, social policy programmes were introduced or extended to fend off democratization pressures on authoritarian governments, while other programmes were the spoils of democratic political struggles. Korean politics has now successfully shifted to a democratic form; the fragmented social policy programmes such as National Health Insurance were reformed and risk pooling was extended in favour of people who were more risk-prone

(Lee, 1997). This development of the welfare state can be described as a move from a 'selective' to an 'inclusive' welfare state (Kwon, 2005). The culmination of this transition was welfare reform by the Kim Dae-jung government in the wake of the East Asian economic crisis of 1997–8.

The third dimension often identified as a core feature of the Korean welfare state is the notion of Confucian familism, involving 'a strong reliance on the family as the site of social welfare and service delivery' (Goodman and Peng, 1996, p. 193). Social arrangements were based on the assumption of the family as the main provider of care. The traditional image of the family was of a unit composed of three generations, where household work, including homemaking and care-giving, was undertaken by 'housewives'. This ideal-typical family has become a marginal form of family in reality, but the underlying assumption of care responsibility remains based on such a family form. Rapid ageing, and changes in family structure also put strain on the structure of the welfare state in Korea, undermining the traditional rationale of developmentalism and familism. A clear sign of this is that Korea has the lowest fertility rate at 1.13, according to the National Statistics Office in 2007. It can be interpreted as women's response to the Korean welfare regime.

We will first discuss welfare reform after the East Asia economic crisis in 1997–8, a move towards further inclusion incorporating the concept of social rights while maintaining its developmental credentials. Second, we discuss policy issues that emerged after the reform, arguing that it is necessary to 'rescale' the welfare state in order to make it socially inclusive while maintaining its sustainability. Before proceeding, it will be useful to set out the historical development of the Korean welfare state in five stages, explaining the overall structure of social policy programmes.

- **The formation of the developmental welfare state** – The first social welfare programme was Industrial Accident Insurance in 1963, along with a pilot programme for health insurance effected by the military government which took power after a coup d'état in 1961 (Kwon, 1999). It was considered necessary as Korea embarked on an ambitious economic development plan. At the beginning, Industrial Accident Insurance covered people in workplaces of 500 employees or more. In 1962, the government made the existing Civil Service Pension Programme more generous, to mobilize the bureaucracy for economic development.
- **The expansion of the developmental welfare state** – In 1973, the National Pension Programme (NPP) was first considered as an effective measure for increasing domestic savings: capital could be used for industrialization. It was, however, postponed due to the sudden oil price rise and subsequent inflation. In 1977, National Health Insurance (NHI) was introduced for workers in enterprises that employed more than 500: a separate health fund for the civil servants was introduced in 1979.

- **Democratization and the welfare state** – The sudden death of President Park followed by another military man at the helm of power led to a decade-long democratization movement. Political efforts to make the fragmented NHI a universal programme were frustrated by the authoritarian government, but social grievances emerged at the centre of political debates. In the wake of the first democratic election for the presidency in 1987, the government extended NHI to those previously excluded, making it a universal programme. In 1988 the government reintroduced the NPP in the same format as the 1972 proposal. In 1993, the Employment Insurance Programme (EIP) was introduced as Korea prepared to join the OECD.
- **Reform of the developmental welfare state** – In the wake of the East Asian economic crisis, the Kim Dae-jung government strengthened and extended the welfare state in terms of benefits and coverage. The EIP was extended to all workplaces in 1998, although not strictly enforced. The Minimum Living Standard Guarantee was introduced based on the idea of social rights in 2000, replacing the stringently means-tested public assistance programme. In the same year all separated health funds under NHI were integrated, paving the way for a financially and administratively integrated programme. Civil society groups played active roles in strengthening those programmes.
- **Rescaling the developmental welfare state** – Concerned about financial sustainability, the government began to initiate reforms of the NPP, the Civil Service Pension Programme and NHI, while strengthening social service programmes. In 2007, the National Assembly passed the bill that would reduce the level of pensions, while it explored various methods to reduce the cost of NHI. A new programme, Long-Term Care Insurance for the Elderly, was introduced in 2008. Underlying such moves are rapid demographic ageing rates and a very low fertility rate at 1.13.

The Structure of the Korean Welfare State

The Korean welfare state was, by and large, brought into effect by the military government taking power after the 1961 coup d'état (Kwon, 1999). The welfare state comprises four social insurance programmes (health insurance, pension, employment and industrial accident), one social assistance programme (the Minimum Living Standard Guarantee) and three public pensions programmes for special categories of people such as civil servants, private school teachers and military personnel. In the beginning (from 1963), Industrial Accident Insurance covered people in workplaces of 500 employees or more. Since then, the number of the workplaces covered by Industrial Accident Insurance has increased, and at present workplaces with more than one regular employee should join the programme. In 2005, as a result, 44 per cent of employed people came to be covered by Industrial Accident Insurance, the main exclusions being farmers, the self-employed and irregular employees.

National Health Insurance, the second contour of Korea's welfare state, originates from a pilot health insurance programme tried for about ten years from 1965. It became a compulsory programme in 1977, extended to protect workers in large-scale industrial enterprises, public sector workers and private school teachers. By 1987, most employees in industrial sectors had access to health care through NHI, while the self-employed, farmers and others without employers fell outside the scheme, partly because it was difficult to administer actuarial work for them. Another difficulty in including such groups was that they did not have employers to pay half the contributions (Goodman, White and Kwon,1998). NHI was financed by arrangements in which both employers and employees had to pay half. Since the state only provided administrative costs, those without employers could not join in the programme. In 1988/89, the democratically elected government extended NHI to all the population.

Nevertheless, the fragmented structure of NHI gave rise to financial difficulties to health funds for the self-employed and farmers. Under the Kim Dae-jung government (1998–2002), all health funds with NHI were integrated in 2000 despite strong opposition from some trades unions and big businesses (Kwon and Tchoe, 2005). This integration reform settled the long-running debate once and for all, in the process of which the Kim government provided room for civil society groups, such as the Coalition for the Integration of NHI, as one of the important players in health governance. (And this was not just an isolated case, as the tripartite Committee of Employees–Employers–Government, consisting of a range of civil society groups, including associations of trades unions and employers, played a crucial role in the process of economic reform in the wake of the economic crisis.) While in opposition, Kim's Democratic Party maintained a close link with civil society coalitions arguing for this integration. The relationship between government and civil society groups changed in that they are able to make their voice heard in social policy-making. This is a clear contrast to decision-making under the previous regime where civil society groups were excluded.

The third main programme is the National Pension Programme. It was first considered for introduction in the early 1970s, but implementation was postponed due to the oil crisis in 1973, being eventually introduced in 1988. Due to the insurance arrangement, the NPP, like NHI, began with wage-earning employees, and by 1994 it covered 27 per cent of the working population (Kwon, 1999). In 1999, Kim Dae-jung government expanded the programme to the farmers, the self-employed and those with short-term contracts, although they could choose not to join the programme. Currently, the NPP has a huge financial reserve since it has not yet disbursed full pensions because of the requirement for 20-year contributions. In 2007, the

National Assembly passed a government bill, reducing the level of pensions under the NPP. This is discussed below.

Fourth, the EIP, enacted in 1993, was implemented in 1995. Nevertheless, its history goes back to 1963 when the military government of Park Chung Hee first considered its introduction. Instead of unemployment insurance, the government ushered in Industrial Accident Insurance, fearing at that time that unemployment benefits might lead to disincentives to work (Kwon, 1999). In contrast to this policy stance, the introduction of the EIP was a reflection of the government's newly gained confidence after sustained economic development and democratization (Kwon, 2001). As the name of the programme implies, the EIP comprises not only unemployment benefits but also training grants and job security grants. While unemployment benefits are paid to those who lose their jobs, job security grants subsidize employers who retain employees instead of laying them off. Training grants are paid to training institutions, private or public, for training unemployed people, while the unemployed are eligible for allowances during their period of training (Kwon, 2001).

The latest programme is the Minimum Living Standard Guarantee (MLSG), a social assistance programme entirely funded by government (shared by central and local governments), replacing the previous assistance programme, which was very limited in terms of the scope and the level of benefits. The MLSG is based on the concept of social rights so that the poverty line it sets up is higher than that of the previous programme based on the strict means-test. Second, it provides benefits to poor people if their income is below the poverty line, regardless of their age. Under the previous social assistance programme, the poor aged between 18 and 64 were not eligible for benefits and those having family members supposed to help them were also excluded. The MLSG, nevertheless, has a number of work conditionalities: benefit recipients aged between 18 and 64 should participate in training, public work projects or community services.

New social insurance programmes under consideration are long-term care insurance and basic pensions for old age. As we note later, ageing is taking place rapidly in Korea. Among other social expenditure that has risen in relation to the ageing population, health-care costs are the most notable. A bill to introduce long-term care insurance has been passed in the National Assembly, to be introduced in 2008. The basic structure of the programme is social insurance, collecting contributions from citizens and providing care services to elderly needing them because of illness or frailty related to ageing. A bill for basic old-age pensions was also passed in the National Assembly amid the government party's loss of majority. The programme will provide a small amount of cash benefits as basic pensions to those who have not acquired pension entitlements through the NPP.

Table 12.1 shows social expenditure in Korea (in comparison with Taiwan), which has risen steadily for the last four decades but more sharply in the late 1990s. Since the Korean welfare state mainly comprises compulsory

Table 12.1 Social expenditure in Korea and Taiwan (as per cent of GDP)

		1995	*1997*	*1999*	*2001*	*2003*
Korea	Government expenditure	1.3	1.4	2.1	3.3	3.1
	Total expenditure	5.1	7.4	9.8	8.7	
Taiwan	Government expenditure	3.1	3.4	2.9	3.9	3.2
	Total expenditure	2.8		4.0 (in 2000)	4.1 (in 2002)	4.6 (in 2004)

Note: Taiwan's figures are based on GNP.
Government expenditure: expenditure directly spent by the government.
Total expenditure: mandatory expenditure on social insurance by the government, companies and households.
Sources: *Estimation of Net Social Expenditures in Korea on the Basis of the OECD Guideline*, Koh et al. 2003; Taiwan: DGBAS, 2005.

social insurance programmes, government expenditure accounts for less than half of total social expenditure. However, since the Asian economic crisis of 1997–8, government expenditure on social welfare as well as total expenditure has risen sharply, though still below other low-spending OECD countries such as Japan (15.05 per cent in 1998), and the US (14.95 per cent) (Koh, Chang and Lee, 2003). The introduction of the MLSG, expansion of the Employment Insurance Programmes and the increasing cost of NHI accounted for the steady increase of social expenditure in Korea. It will increase further from 2008 as the NPP will provide full pensions for the first time since its introduction. New basic pensions to be given to low-income elderly without other public pensions will contribute to this rise.

Notwithstanding steady expansion, the Korean welfare state has still large gaps in terms of its coverage. For instance, as Table 12.2 shows, the three main social insurance programmes, though allegedly universal, only cover around 60 per cent of wage- and salary-earners. Regarding regular employees, the coverage is close to the level one might expect from 'universal' programmes. In respect to temporary short-term employees, coverage is so low that they cannot be described as 'universal'. The underlying reason for this low coverage is that employers are so eager to save wages and the related costs of the temporary workforce that they are not willing to pay social insurance contributions. The other side of the story is that government is unwilling and somewhat

Table 12.2 Social insurance coverage by employment status (percentage)

	National Pension Programme		*National Health Insurance*		*Employment Insurance Programme*	
	2001	*2007*	*2001*	*2007*	*2001*	*2007*
Wage- and salary-earners	51.8	62.6	54.3	63.9	46.9	55.6
Regular employees	92.7	98.8	94.8	99.3	80.0	83.8
Temporary employees	19.3	33.9	22.2	35.8	20.7	33.3

Note: Wage- and salary-earners comprise regular employees and temporary employees.
Source: Kim, 2001, 2007.

unable to enforce compliance. The present under-coverage of these programmes will imply a future welfare deficit when people need more social protection at times of economic difficulty. With respect to NHI, this is not the case since those who are not enlisted through their workplaces are registered as residence-based members through NHI local offices. The problem of under-coverage will persist without policy intervention since the proportion of temporary employees has steadily increased to more than 50 per cent of all employed persons (National Statistical Office, 2005).

Welfare Reform after the Asian Economic Crisis

Before the economic crisis, Korea had a combination of production and welfare regimes, aimed at economic development, borrowing the terms of Huber and Stephens (2001). The developmental state played a strategic role in the process of industrialization in respect to production (White, 1988; Wade, 1990; Woo-Cumings, 1999). However, it was not just economic policy but also social policy that was institutionalized, in order to play a part in the overall strategy for economic development. Hort and Kuhnle (2000, pp. 167–8) showed that East Asian countries, and Korea in particular, introduced the first social security programmes at lower levels of socio-economic development than in European countries. This suggests that Korea adopted social welfare programmes as policy instruments for economic development. Goodman and White (1998, p. 17) highlighted the characteristics of the East Asian welfare states incorporated in the state developmental strategy: a development ideology that subordinated welfare to economic efficiency, discouraged dependence on the state, promoted private sources of welfare and diverted the financial resources of social insurance to infrastructural investment. The Korean welfare state is an ideal-typical case of the developmental use of social policy.

This preoccupation with economic development led to the welfare state predominantly comprising social insurance programmes for industrial workers, in which people were required to pay contributions prior to entitlement to social benefits. As a result, only selected groups of people had access to social protection, while leaving the vulnerable section of the population outside the system. To avoid a demand for universal entitlement, the state did not provide funding for welfare programmes, but enforced the rules, formal and informal, regulating the payment of contributions for social benefits by companies and their employees. Social insurance programmes were operated by quasi-governmental agencies, working at arms length from the government, not, strictly speaking, part of government.

Because of the system's selectivity, the Korean welfare state had its inevitable downsides. Since social policy programmes covered mainly industrial workers, welfare states tended to reinforce socio-economic inequalities. Kwon (1997) pointed out that the lion's share of redistribution through social policies went to high-income earners, reflecting the fact that wage-earners in large-scale businesses and state sector employees were the first to be covered by social policy programmes. Vulnerable people not only suffered because of their difficult situation but were also stigmatized by being excluded from the welfare state. The authoritarian government maintained a regressive welfare system and suppressed dissenting voices. These characteristics are well summarized by the concept of the 'developmental welfare state', where elite policy-makers set economic growth as the fundamental goal, pursue a coherent strategy to achieve it and use social policy as an instrument for attaining that goal (Gough, 2001).

One may conclude that such a policy regime would lead to extreme social inequality similar to that of Brazil. In Korea, however, this was not the case. Despite limited social policies, the developmental state was able to maintain social inequality at relatively low levels. Cho (2003) argues that the 1949–50 Korean land reforms not only reduced the level of economic inequality but also increased social mobility in that farmers and their children, through education and urban migration, were able to participate in economic development processes in the 1960s and 70s. Given high social mobility, the labour-intensive and export-oriented economic strategy made economic development more broad-based, compared to other late industrializing countries (Kohli, 2004). The developmental state also adopted a number of economic policies aiming to maintain income levels in low income strata.

Such a seemingly magic combination can only be maintained so long as economic growth continues. The economic strategy in the 1970s that gave special treatment to large conglomerates led to deteriorating economic inequality. When Korea was in deep recession in 1979, the political crisis triggered by female workers protesting against low wages and poor working conditions led to the assassination of President Park, showing the vulnerability of Korea's developmental state regime. The succeeding military general, Chun Doo-hwan, pursued a stabilization policy. Due to favourable economic conditions such as the high value of the Japanese yen and low oil prices, the Korean economy was able to bounce back from the middle of the 1980s. The 1980s also witnessed democratization movements that led to the first democratically contested presidential election in 1987, when trades unions were allowed to organize and pursue their economic interests.

In the 1990s, Korea was faced with higher costs and lower productivity increases. Prior to the Asian economic crisis in 1997–8, it was true that the Korean government attempted to carry out reforms towards a high technology- and productivity-based economy to avoid economic deadlock. However, political parties, trades unions and civil society groups strongly opposed them because they feared that it would lead to social disaster, given the inadequacy of social protection. The Asian economic crisis, however, forced Korean society to accept such reforms, and at the same time produced a surprise victory for the centre-left opposition in the presidential election at the end of 1997. The new government established a tripartite committee,

Table 12.3 Unemployment rates in East Asia

	1996	*1997*	*1998*	*1999*	*2000*	*2001*	*2002*	*2003*	*2004*
Japan	3.4	3.4	4.1	4.7	4.7	5	5.4	5.3	na
China	3.0	3.1	3.1	3.1	3.1	3.6	4.0	4.3	4.2
Hong Kong	2.8	2.2	4.7	6.2	4.9	5.1	7.3	7.9	6.8
Korea	2.0	2.6	7.0	6.3	4.1	3.8	3.1	3.4	3.5
Malaysia	2.6	2.4	3.2	3.4	3.1	3.6	3.4	3.6	3.5
Singapore	3.0	2.4	2.5	3.6	3.5	2.8	4.3	4.7	4.0
Thailand	1.1	0.9	3.4	3.0	2.4	2.6	1.8	2.2	2.1
Taiwan	2.6	2.7	2.7	2.9	3.0	4.6	5.2	5.0	4.4

Sources: Asian Development Bank, Asian Development Outlook, 2002, 2005.
Figures for Japan: Japan Statistics Bureau, Japan Statistical Yearbook, 2005, http://www.stat.go.jp/english/data/nenkan/1431-16.htm

able to produce a broad-based social consensus for economic reform while strengthening the welfare state.

Considerable downsides were identified in the Korean developmental welfare state prior to the Asian economic crisis. Social pressure groups, some forming strong advocacy coalitions for a more inclusive social policy, argued for strengthening social protection for the poor and vulnerable people. Nevertheless, their efforts were unsuccessful until the crisis of 1997–8. When this happened, it became clear that the developmental welfare state could not cope with strong social challenges during economic downturns. In particular the developmental welfare state was not able to tackle high unemployment since it was contingent on full employment (see Table 12.3).

Faced with a severe economic crisis, the government quickly implemented social policy reforms to enhance social protection for the vulnerable. This swift response was also related to economic considerations. Before the economic crisis, it was noted by the government that productivity and international competitiveness had deteriorated during the 1990s due to increasing costs including wages, and competition from other East Asian countries such as China and Thailand (Park, 2001). Wage increases were ahead of labour productivity in this period. Structural reforms to overcome the crisis would inevitably create a large number of unemployed. Social policy remained unable to mitigate its effects although the main social policy programmes that had started with workers were expanded beyond large-scale workplaces, and public assistance for the poor was limited, with tight means-tests.

Civil society organizations played an important role in this process. The EIP, consisting of unemployment benefits and training schemes, was extended and strengthened in terms of coverage and benefits, and a new social assistance programme introduced. The advocacy coalitions of civil society organizations pursued the integration of the fragmented NHI, resulting in the new National Health Insurance Corporation, a single national agency for health insurance administration and finance. Through this process, the notion of social rights became an important rationale for the welfare state as well as for economic development.

Despite all these changes, the Korean welfare state maintained the features of the developmental welfare state. First, welfare reform was carried out to meet the policy demands of labour market reform. Second, human capital investment such as training and capacity development was an important rationale, in particular with respect to the Living Standard Guarantee and Employment Insurance Programme. To capture such continuity and change, as argued elsewhere, the Korean developmental welfare state has moved towards an inclusive developmental welfare state (Kwon, 2005).

Rescaling the Developmental Welfare State?

As the Korean welfare state became more inclusive (though not as inclusive as in Western Europe), it is necessary to review the scale of social benefits and address the question of whether the welfare state can be financially sustainable, while the expectation of social protection is commensurate with people's willingness to pay. For example, is it realistic to expect that the public pension programmes will deliver the same replacement rate it promised when only covering a small section of the population? Can NHI cope with all health care demands given demographic ageing and that most health care is provided by private hospitals?

It is true that public expenditure on social protection in Korea is still lower than other OECD countries. The level of expenditure in the future is, however, set to rise sharply, and expected to reach the OECD average in due course (Republic of Korea, 2004). It seems unlikely that the taxpayers' willingness to pay will match this rise. Readiness to pay has remained static since the late 1990s welfare reforms. This leads to the next issue; is there any control mechanism to check increasing social expenditure, and does it work effectively? Can Korean society reach a social consensus on sharing financial responsibility for the welfare state, and who will get which benefits? We also have to question the priority of and balance between social policies and programmes. Is the current composition of the welfare state right for the future? The main programmes of the Korean welfare state are linked to workplaces such as the NPP, NHI, EIP and Industrial Accident Insurance: participations and entitlements are arranged through workplaces. These programmes provide mainly either income support or in-kind services such as health care and training. The Minimum Living Standard Guarantee combines both for low-income households. In contrast, family-oriented social-care programmes for children, the disabled and the elderly are still weak in the Korean welfare state as the family is still regarded as the main site for social care. Will this balance of responsibility between the welfare state and family meet future social demand?

In order to respond to these policy challenges, it will be necessary to rescale the welfare state. The immediate question that arises is how rescaling is different from reforming. Reforming the welfare state implies a restructuring of the welfare state based on a different policy rationale from the previous one. For example, Thatcher's Conservative government tried to 'reform' the welfare state, replacing the principles set by Beveridge and Keynes with the neoliberal paradigm (King, 1999). Pierson (1995), however, sees this reform as an attempt to dismantle the welfare state. This chapter argues that the policy change that has been taking place in Korea is not reforming but rescaling the welfare state since there have not been changes in the principles that Korean society agreed during the late 1990s welfare reforms, particularly the principle that the welfare state should be socially inclusive but economically developmental. This does not mean, however, that social policy stakeholders agree as to the contents and methods of policy changes for rescaling.

A good example of rescaling is recent change in the NPP. Despite the opposition party's initial proposal to change the National Pension Programme into a defined-contribution programme similar to the Central Provident Fund, the National Assembly passed a bill reducing the level of benefits. Although commentators argue that such rescaling would not entirely secure the NPP's long-term sustainability, it would reduce the cost of pensions for the next 30 years. A parallel effort has taken place in respect to the Civil Service Pension Programme (Kwon, 2006). A government-sponsored committee proposed a reduction in the replacement rate of civil service pensions without reforming their main structure.

With respect to the rising costs of NHI, policy stakeholders have not been able to produce a consensus on measures of rescaling. The NHI payment system is based on the principle of fee-for-services, while health-care services are mostly delivered by private hospitals and clinics. Such a system gives physicians and hospitals economic incentives to treat patients more expensively than is necessary. While the scope of health services has been extended and health-care demand has risen, this has led to a sharp increase in health expenditure. While Taiwan, with a similar NHI structure, introduced a global budget system in order to control health-care costs within the public health-care system (Lin *et al.*, 2005), policy stakeholders, government policy-makers and medical professionals are reluctant to open up discussion, mainly due to the lack of trust existing between the parties. During the 2001 health policy reforms, redefining the work of physicians and pharmacists, the government, civil society groups and medical professionals had a serious political confrontation leaving deep political scars.

Demographic ageing will be one of the most important issues facing the Korean welfare state. It will inevitably increase the number of people needing social protection not only in terms of protection against potential risks but also against actual contingencies. It is true that demographic ageing is happening in most OECD countries and many developing countries. What is different in Korea is that the speed and scale of ageing is faster and greater. Table 12.4 shows that the speed of Korean demographic ageing is even faster than in Japan, where social policy has been restructured to meet older people's social need over the last two decades.

Table 12.4 Speed of demographic ageing

	Year reaching the proportion of the elderly			*Time span*	
	7 per cent	*14 per cent*	*20 per cent*	*7–14 per cent*	*14–20 per cent*
Korea	2000	2019	2026	19	7
Japan	1970	1994	2006	24	12
France	1864	1979	2020	115	41
USA	1942	2013	2028	71	15

Source: National Statistical Office, 2005.

At the same time, however, it is worth noting the other side to this story. Korea is witnessing demographic ageing relatively quickly because she enjoyed a converse demographic gift over the last30 years: the increasing proportion of the working population with better productivity rates than the previous generation, a double boost for economic growth. It seems that Korea will enjoy this advantage until around 2020. As Figure 12.1 shows clearly, the payback for this advantage is approaching at the same rate. Unfortunately, however, it is also coming at a time of demographic loss, with decreasing numbers of children.

These demographic trends seem to suggest, first, that future demand from the elderly population for social protection will increase. For example, the number of pensioners will rise sharply, putting huge pressure on the pension fund. Regarding health care, health expenditure will soar as the increasing number of elderly will use health-care services while the quality of medical service they demand will be much higher and more expensive than previously. Increased social services will also be necessary to meet older people's needs.

Second, decreasing numbers of children will not reduce demand for child social services. The record low fertility rate, at 1.13, even lower than that of Japan, is a response, *inter alia*, to the inadequacy of the Korean welfare state

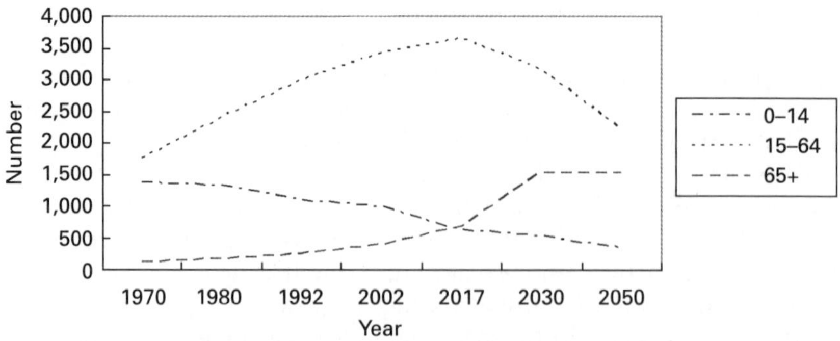

Figure 12.1 Demographic trend in Korea

Source: Data from the National Statistical Office, www.nso.go.kr, on population projection (visited January 2006).

Table 12.5 Distribution of households by numbers of household members in Korea

	One	*Two*	*Three*	*Four*	*Five*	*Six and over*	*Average*
1975	4.2	8.3	12.3	16.1	18.3	40.7	5.0
1985	6.9	12.3	16.5	25.3	19.5	19.5	4.1
1995	12.7	16.9	20.3	31.7	12.9	5.5	3.3
2005	20.0	22.2	20.9	27.0	7.7	2.2	2.9

Source: National Statistical Office, 1975, 1985, 1995, 2005.

with respect to social care for women and children, for example in supporting a young nuclear family to raise their children while older children are still responsible for caring for ageing parents. It has also not been adequate for supporting working parents in balancing out their time between work and family. Of course, there is a range of other social issues underlying low fertility, such as gender equality, social mobility and educational structures, which cannot directly be addressed by the welfare state.

While ageing will increase the demand for social care, the family cannot provide the same level of care that it has done. There are two main reasons for the weakened role of the family in the provision of care. First, the ideal-typical three-generation households, seen as the main site of social care, are not representative of most Korean families. Different family structures are emerging. Table 12.5 shows that the average size of households was five in 1975; that figure came down to 2.9 in 2005. This figure suggests that the typical family is now a nuclear family consisting of parents and one or two children, alongside households comprising single older people and elderly couples. In 2004, older people living in elderly-alone households comprised 22 per cent with elderly-couple only households comprising 39 per cent, while 39 per cent lived with other people.

This growing diversity in family structure does not imply, however, that care is no longer provided by family care-givers such as mothers, wives and daughters. Care-giving is still a family responsibility, but it is done across as well as within households and with a different dynamic from to the past. However, inter-household care-giving is likely to be more time-consuming and demanding from the care-givers' perspective than is intra-household care-giving, in a situation where care-receivers cannot always get support when necessary. In short, changing family structures inevitably lead to demand for state social care provision.

Third, women's labour market participation has increased steadily over the last three decades, reaching about 50 per cent in 2005 (from 39 per cent in 1970), with the male breadwinner and female care-giver model being further undermined. Nevertheless, women are more likely to be employed in a precarious status. Table 12.6 shows that employment status is clearly differentiated by gender. Although both for males and females, irregular employment – meaning being employed under short-term or temporary contract

Table 12.6 Employment status by gender (per cent)

		1990	*1995*	*1997*	*1998*	*2000*	*2005*
Men	Regular	64.5	67.6	64.6	64.7	59.2	62.3
	Irregular	25.5	32.4	35.4	41.9	40.8	37.7
Women	Regular	37.6	42.8	38.4	34.8	31.1	38.2
	Irregular	62.4	57.2	61.6	64.2	66.9	61.8

Source: National Statistical Office, 2006.

without full employment security – has increased, the majority of women are employed in this form as opposed to only a minority of males. It is also more often the case that wage levels in irregular employment are lower than in regular work. Given these conditions, women are likely to carry out both work and family care responsibilities.

One of the main policy responses to ageing and changing family structures is Long-Term Care Insurance, a social insurance programme typical of the Korean welfare state, implemented from 2008. The elderly who need long-term care will get services funded by Long-Term Care Insurance, for which they pay insurance premiums. While care personnel have been trained to meet the new demands of social care, the number of long-term care facilities is estimated to fall far short of predicted demand.

With respect to childcare, the number of facilities has been increasing rapidly over the last decade. In 1995, the number of childcare facilities (private and public) was about 1,900 rising to 27,000 in 2004, with a particularly rapid rise since 2002 (Ministry of Health and Welfare, 2005). In 2004, 24 per cent of children were cared for in childcare institutions.

Policy responses to social care are impressive although the number of facilities remains in short supply. Demographic change is reducing the numbers entering the labour market both in absolute terms, due to decreasing numbers of children, and in terms relative to the elderly population, which the working population has to support. In order to avert labour shortages, it is necessary to allow women to participate in the labour market; this in turn requires social-care programmes for women to move out of the home.

Conclusions

Korea acquired its distinctive characteristics during a period of rapid economic development when the developmental state mobilized economic and social resources for the purpose. During the democratization period, the welfare state was extended to the wider population, but its selective characteristics remained. Welfare reform after the Asian economic crisis changed the complexion of the welfare state in that entitlements to social benefits were set as social rights, while the level and coverage of benefits were strengthened. The developmental welfare state became more inclusive.

Recent policy changes in the welfare state have to be seen from a perspective of rescaling rather than reforming. Policy changes such as in the NPP were based on the same principle that underscored the developmental welfare state. New initiatives on social care are policy responses to ageing and low fertility. The second order objective is to maintain the size of supply to the labour market in the middle of significant demographic shifts through encouraging women's labour market participation and higher fertility; this is indeed quintessentially welfare developmentalism.

It is true that the welfare state in Korea has been extended and strengthened over the last decade. The idea of social rights has been established and coverage became more inclusive. However, it is necessary to see this development from a broader perspective of economic reform taking place at the same time. As we briefly noted, the labour market became more flexible, that is, jobs became more insecure while the quality of employment deteriorated. Welfare benefits were extended in the context of economic changes, which saw companies reducing their own direct welfare costs. In short, the extension of the welfare state has been carried out to facilitate economic changes necessary for a production regime of low cost and high flexibility – the Korean welfare state is still used as an instrument for economic development.

Acknowledgements

I have benefited from discussions with Joseph Wong and Seok Myung Yoon at the Korea–Canada meeting in January 2006. I would also like to thank Si-Yeon Won and Ito Peng for discussions on social care. Some parts of the chapter draw on previous work, and the usual caveats apply.

References

Cho, S. (2003) 'Land Reform and Capitalism in Korea', in C. Yoo (ed.), *The History of the Korean Development Model and its Crisis*, Cobook.

DGBAS (2005) *Statistical Yearbook of the Republic of China*, DGBAS.

Goodman, R. and Peng, I. (1996) 'The East Asian Welfare States: Peripatetic Learning, Adaptive Change, and Nation-Building', in Esping-Andersen, G. (ed.), *Welfare States in Transition: National Adaptations in Global Economies*, Sage.

Goodman, R. and White, G. (1998) 'Welfare Orientalism and the Search for an East Asian Welfare Model', in R. Goodman, G. White and H. J. Kwon (eds), *The East Asian Welfare Model: Welfare Orientalism and the State*, Routledge.

Goodman, R., White, G. and Kwon, H. J. (1998), *op. cit.*

Gough, I. (2001) 'Globalization and Regional Welfare Regimes: The East Asian Case', *Global Social Policy*, 1(2), pp. 163–89.

Hort, S. and Kuhnle, S. (2000) 'The Coming of East and South-East Asian Welfare States', *Journal of European Social Policy*, 10(2), pp. 162–84.

Huber, E. and Stephens, J. (2001) 'Welfare State and Production Regimes in the Era of Retrenchment', in P. Pierson (ed.), *The New Politics of the Welfare State*, Oxford University Press, pp. 107–45.

Kim, Y. (2001) 'The Size of the Temporary Work-force and Their Employment Conditions', Mimeo.

Kim, Y. (2007) 'The Size of the Temporary Work-force and Working Conditions', Mimeo.

King, D. S. (1999) *In the Name of Liberalism: Illiberal Social Policy in the USA and Britain*, Oxford University Press.

Koh, K., Chang, Y. and Lee, N. (2003) *Estimation of Net Social Expenditures in Korea on the Basis of the OECD Guideline*, KIHASA.

Kohli, A. (2004) *State-Directed Development: Political Power and Industrialization in the Global Periphery*, Cambridge University Press.

Republic of Korea (2004) *Medium-Term Plan of Public Finance 2004–2008*, Republic of Korea.

Kwon, H. J. (1997) 'Beyond European Welfare Regimes: Comparative Perspectives on East Asian Welfare Systems', *Journal of Social Policy*, 26(4), pp. 467–84.

Kwon, H. J. (1999) *The Welfare State in Korea: The Politics of Legitimation*, Macmillan.

Kwon, H. J. (2001) 'Globalization, Unemployment and Policy Responses in Korea: Respositioning the State?', *Global Social Policy*, 1(2), pp. 213–34.

Kwon, H. J. (2005) 'Transforming the Developmental Welfare State in East Asia', *Development and Change*, 36(3), pp. 477–97.

Kwon, H. J. (2006) 'Reform of the Civil Service Pension Programme and Policy Issues', *Korean Policy Studies Review*, 15(4), pp. 189–213 (in Korean).

Kwon, H. J. and Tchoe, B. (2005) 'The Political Economy of National Health Insurance in Korea', in M. Kuoivusal and M. Mackintosh (eds), *Commercialization of Health Care*, Palgrave.

Lee, J. C. (1997) 'The Political Economy of Unification and Decentralization in Korea's National Health Insurance', *Social Security Studies*, 12(1), pp. 61–81 (in Korean).

Lin, C.-Y., Chen, D.-y., Liu, I.-C. and Hsiao, N. (2005) 'Political Feasibility Study on the Reform of the Financing Scheme of Taiwan's National Health Insurance Programme', unpublished manuscript.

Marshall, T. H. (ed.) (1964) *Class, Citizenship, and Social Development*, Doubleday.

Ministry of Health and Welfare (2005) *Yearbook of Health and Statistics*, MoHW.

National Statistical Office (2005) *Korea Statistical Yearbook*, NSO.

National Statistical Office (2006) *National Statistical Yearbook*, NSO.

Park, B.-G. (2001) 'Labor Regulation and Economic Change: A View on the Korean Economic Crisis', *Geoforum*, 32(1), pp. 61–75.

Pierson, P. (1995) *Dismantling the Welfare State?: Reagan, Thatcher, and the Politics of Retrenchment*, Cambridge University Press.

Republic of Korea (2004) *Medium-Term Plan of Public Finance 2004–2008*, Republic of Korea.

Wade, R. (1990) *Governing the Market: Economic Theory and the Role of Government in East Asian Industrialization*, Princeton University Press.

White, G. (ed.) (1988) *Developmental States in East Asia*, St Martin's.

Woo-Cumings, M. (ed.) (1999) *The Developmental State*, Cornell University Press.

CHAPTER 13

China: The Art of State and Social Policy Remodelling

KA LIN

Introduction

For the past 50 years, the Chinese social policy discourse has barely been the subject of discussion in international social policy circles. This is in large part due to the dissimilarity of its rationale and approach to that of its counterparts among Western welfare states. In some cases, scholars have identified the Chinese system as a socialist welfare regime (George and Manning, 1980; Deacon, 1983; Dixon and Macarov, 1992). Because China stayed out of the world of welfare capitalism, the possibility of comparing it with other welfare regimes was limited. However, things began to change as China embraced a market approach, thereby establishing a new basis for comparison. Academic interest in Chinese social policy has grown rapidly in recent years due to its prominence as one of the East Asian welfare regimes, a member of the socialist welfare bloc, the largest country in the developing world and the world's third-largest economy. Thus the experience of Chinese social policy development can provide meaningful insights to be used in other social policy contexts.

To study 'Chinese' social policy, it is necessary to trace the history of its development from the beginning of the twentieth century. In the 1920s, China's first set of social policies was issued by the Nationalist regime and included the factory laws (1923, 1929), the regulation of the trades unions (1924) and the rules for administrating charitable rice storehouses (1928). Nevertheless, because the prolonged wars in the first half of the twentieth century caused social disorder and chaos, social policy could not be a major state concern. In 1949, when the Communist Party established its political regime on the mainland, the political map of China was redrawn. A single political legacy, that of the Qing Dynasty, was split into four political regimes: the communist regime in the mainland, the Nationalist regime that fled to Taiwan and the two colonial regimes of Hong Kong and Macao. Due to their dissimilar socio-political contexts, there has been great diversity in the paths taken by these four political regimes in terms of their social policy development. This chapter focuses on mainland 'Chinese' social policies.

Those interested in welfare regimes would enquire as to the nature of the Chinese system and to what model the Chinese system belongs. Although researchers are inclined to consider the typology of regime models presented by Esping-Anderson (1990) as the most useful framework for analyzing features of welfare systems, in fact, this method is not very effective when applied to China. This is because, during the last half-century, the Chinese system of social policy development has passed through three definitive stages, and a separate model of social policy has developed from each stage. The first one was established in the Maoist era, duplicating the soviet model in Russia. It was associated with the ex-socialist model in Europe but contained many collective elements that represented specific elements of the Chinese socio-cultural context. When, during Deng's political regime, economic reforms constructed a 'socialist market' system, the social foundation of the entire society was reconstructed. Consequently, the social policy model was shifted from a socialist command economy model to one of developmental social policy. Again, the systemic changes caused by the growth of market power in the post-Deng era created many 'new' social problems that required the state to introduce redistributive measures.

In order to understand the Chinese system and its policy evolution, the impact of industrialization, urbanization and marketization must all be considered. At the same time, these factors should not be allowed to eclipse the meaning and importance of another set of factors, that is, the state-building process, the state's developmental strategies and its authoritarian context. In China, social policy measures are often used for (conservative) purposes of social control and political mobility. Indeed, its policy development is typically the result of the state's efforts to achieve certain political goals. These factors working together made it possible for China periodically to reconstruct its social policy model. In this chapter, the basic traits of the Chinese system will be illuminated through an examination of each of three evolutionary phases.

The Evolution of the Chinese Social Security System

The Era of Maoist Socialism (1951–77)

In contemporary China, the social security system is a new institutional construct of control and welfare protection implemented by the Communist Party. It has broken away from its previous stage of policy development, as Leung (1994, p. 343) comments: 'Introduced for the first time in Chinese history, the social security programs represented (the state's) unprecedented statutory commitment and intervention in social life.' Borrowing on the experience of the Soviet Union, the establishment of its social security system has served well the state's political and economic needs. The system is underpinned by socialist ideology and makes social insurance its core. The promulgation of the Labour Insurance Regulation of the People's Republic of China in 1951 (amended in 1953) thus became the first landmark of this development. Under this system, social insurance programmes were established for retirement, health care, work injury, sick leave and maternity leave. Benefits from these social insurance programmes were provided not only for insured employees but also to their lineal dependents. Contributions to these programmes came from employer/enterprise, whereas the workers themselves, as the beneficiaries, were not required to pay insurance premiums (Walker, 1991). Through a series of regulations issued between 1950 and 1955, the state also established a social insurance programme for governmental functionaries and civil servants, based on similar principles but financed by different resources, that is, insurance for workers was supported by enterprise/employer contributions, while funding for civil servants came from the state budget (Guo, 1992; Dixon and Macarov, 1992). Although these laws and regulations were later improved, the system's basic structure remained unchanged throughout the period of Cultural Revolution (1966–77).

In addition, the state has consistently used special purposes to formulate its social assistance policies for the poor, as well as to provide for the temporary relief of needy groups. During the 1950s, social assistance was based on the state's need to support those families that lost breadwinners during periods of war; later (especially in the early 1960s), the central task for providing social assistance was to provide relief for the victims of natural disasters. The state also gave preferential treatment to retired soldiers and the dependents of revolutionary martyrs. Even though in later times, when the need to reconstruct the national economy shifted the state's policy-making focus from relieving poverty to providing social insurance, preferential treatment for retired soldiers remained one of four major areas in the work of the Ministry of Civil Affairs. Thus, in the provision of this type of welfare, the concept of particularism can clearly be seen embodied in the Chinese system, in service of the state's nation-building need.

In villages, the state mobilized all peasants to participate in rural cooperatives, and eventually, in the 1950s, integrated them into a powerful commune system that was organized under a three-level administration system: the productive team, bridge and commune. This system served a variety of social, economic and welfare functions (Waller, 1981). With this organizational structure as its basis, a collective welfare system was established that had, as its core, a 'five guarantees' scheme. This scheme, founded in 1956, provided for the basic needs of food, clothing, medical care, housing and funeral expenses for the elders without supporters, the widowed and the totally disabled (Chen, 1994, p. 523). Moreover, a voluntary cooperative medical-care system existed in the agricultural society of the 1960s; by the 1970s, in order to meet the vast health-care needs, a large number of 'barefoot doctors' acted in villages to cope with peasants' health issues.

Despite these efforts made by the state and collectives, the general condition of rural society remained poor; in 1978 (the end of the Maoist era), there were 250 million people living in absolute poverty. The general principles of welfare provision for peasants were self-help, family care and mutual help, while collective assistance and the state's social relief were regarded only as supplemental. Consequently, a system of 'two Chinas' (Davis, 1995, pp. 11–13) was created: urban workers were not only protected with a comprehensive social insurance scheme but also with guaranteed life-time employment, regular salaries, subsidized housing and education for their children. In contrast, for the most part, peasants were excluded from the state's welfare protection and, by necessity, forced to stand only on their own two feet.

Deng-ist Reform and Social Transformation (1978–96)

The Maoist social policy model disappeared after the economic reforms of 1978 onwards. In villages, by having the commune system dismantled and the household responsibility system implemented, the former collective-based welfare system was undermined. In cities, the dissolution of the 'big rice bowl' system, although resulting in the termination of the life-time employment policy, stimulated the growth of the private sector. Thus, in the early 1980s, the state required enterprises in the urban non-state sector to establish their own social insurance fund. Simultaneously, private firms were required to provide commercial insurance for their employees' old-age protection (Chan, Yang and Zhang, 1993, pp. 311–2). In the mid-1980s, urban economy reforms inaugurated a 'job-waiting insurance' in order to enhance a 'rational flow of labourers' between enterprises (MLC, 1990; Leung, 1994; Wong, 1995). By 1993, the state went a step further, setting up an unemployment programme to facilitate the operation of the labour market (Song, 2001).

The social insurance schemes for old-age pensions and for health care were also reformed in the early 1990s. The stimulus for these reforms originally came from financial strains generated by welfare spending: that is, the total expenditure for labour insurance and welfare was 14 per cent of the total labour wages in 1978 but had leapt to 33 per cent by 1991 (NBSC, 1992). Meanwhile, private sector employees were generally excluded from social insurance. In 1991, the state therefore made three major changes to reform old-age pensions (Song, 2001, pp. 32–46). First, employees were required to share the financial burden with the state and their workplace by paying insurance premiums. Second, a new system was established combining social pooling and individual account schemes. Third, the state encouraged enterprises to set up a 'supplemental old-age pension' as a second tier of protection.

Reform was also happening in other social policy areas. The co-payment principle was implemented in medical-care insurance aimed at eliminating waste and improving the effectiveness of the medical system. From the mid-1990s, an experimental programme involving a catastrophic illness insurance scheme and a compulsory savings scheme for individuals' normal doctor visits was tried (Zong, 1997, p. 22). In the early 1990s, the state also reformed its housing policy through commercialization. In the previous system, workers lived in housing provided by their workplaces at miniscule rents. However, this system of public housing deteriorated after enterprise welfare was dismantled. Instead, in 1994, the state set up a compulsory-saving housing fund to help workers purchase commercial houses. The fund was supported by collecting a proportion of employees' monthly salaries so that employees could then access those monies to purchase, build and renovate their houses.

Social policy reform in this period was conducted under the strong political influences of both 'socialization' and privatization. The idea of 'socialization of welfare provision' appeared in the mid-1980s. In its original meaning, it was intended to propel non-public welfare agents into action (see Wong, 1994). However, in its later implementation, various policies were made that supported privatization, but in the name of 'socialization', with the intention of transferring to non-public agents the public responsibilities of housing, health care, education and welfare services. Many critics argued that this meant the state had freed itself from its public welfare obligation, at increased expense to its citizens. For instance, in the fields of health care and education, this transfer resulted in higher user fees but in a lower quality of public services.

In terms of rural social welfare, the economic reform improved the people's living standards; the per capita annual net income of rural households increased from 134 Yuan in 1978 to 1,578 Yuan in 1995 (NBSC, 1996, Table 9-4). The major contributor to this increase was the growth of township enterprises; in terms of social welfare, the state encouraged these enterprises to insure their workers for old-age pensions through a voluntary insurance programme. The Ministry of Civil Affairs promoted this policy first in 1986, then again in 1992. The state also launched its anti-poverty project in the late 1980s, with policy measures including a tax exemption for the self-employed or collective firms, in order to stimulate production in impoverished regions. However, when, as a whole, peasants had no access to the statutory pension scheme, they had to rely on their family members and relatives, with limited support from the collective's welfare.

State Welfare under the 'Socialist Market' (1997–2007)

Between 1997 and 2000, several events occurred heralding the arrival of a new stage of development in Chinese social policy. In 1997, the state established a uniform basic old-age insurance system for enterprise employees combining social pooling and individual accounts schemes. In the same year, the state also instituted a minimum income guarantee for urban households. In 1998, the state introduced a scheme to provide basic medical insurance for urban employees, thereby shifting from enterprises to public agents the finance and benefits of medical-care insurance. This same year, the Ministry of Labour and Social Security was established to administer social security. In 1999, the State Council enacted regulations for unemployment insurance; these regulations effectively standardized and improved the unemployment insurance system. In the following year (2000), a national social security fund was set up under the administration of the National Social Security Fund Executive Council. These events demonstrated that the Chinese government was changing its policy direction and using new approaches to cope with the challenges presented by social security.

Among these policy measures, developments in social insurance programmes (typically old-age pension) should be considered most illustrative. Following the reduction of enterprises in the public sector and the growth of businesses in the private sector, the rate of participation (of the total labour force) in the labour insurance system had shrunk. Accordingly, it became necessary to recruit additional contributors from the private sector. Consequently, focus in the late 1990s was on extending the old-age pension scheme coverage to the private sector; by 2002, this coverage was extended from fully contracted workers to 'flexible' employees. As a result, the number of participants in the basic old-age pension scheme increased from 112 million in 1997 to 174 million in 2005, and in the basic health-care insurance programme from 15 million to 100 million (NBSC, 2006, Tables 23-36 and 23-37). Since this new system of old-age pension is managed and administered by the state, this extension of its coverage meant the state welfare system's power to influence people's living conditions had been increased.

Meanwhile, reform of the ownership structure of enterprises produced a large number of laid-off and unemployed workers in the mid-1990s. In 1997, China had more than 11.5 million laid-off workers (Yao and Li, 1999), with a further 15 million urban jobless people (plus laid-off workers) in the next four years (Wang, 2002, p. 90). This imposed intense pressure on the state to remedy the situation. The government, therefore, developed 'three lines' of social protection for maintaining the livelihood of these workers. First, a basic livelihood allowance was provided to laid-off workers. Second, unemployment insurance benefits were provided, representing an expenditure of 13 billion Yuan in each year between 2003 and 2005 (NBSC, 2006, Table 23-37). Third, in 1999, a nationwide scheme to provide minimum living allowances for urban residents was established. These policies substantially moderated the social risk caused by the rapid impact of economic reforms.

However, policy outcomes in health care and housing were less positive.

On the positive side, health-care insurance in the former system had become a combination of basic medical insurance scheme with individual account programmes added. The disaster insurance scheme established since 1998 had been particularly useful for those not covered by social insurance programmes. In contrast, however, increased costs of medical care and medical examinations undermined the quality of public medical services. Many patients cannot afford the cost of medical care, resulting in fewer hospitalizations and doctor visits. In regard to housing, standards of living for urban Chinese improved in the last decade. For instance, the average living space increased from 13 square metres per person in 1989 to 24 in 2003 (NBSC, 2004, Table 10-1). But the rapid expansion of real estate has also caused housing prices to rise dramatically. For instance, in 1998, the average price of commercial housing nationwide was 1854 Yuan per square metre (Niu and Shang, 2005, p. 15), but rose to 3,199 Yuan by 2006 (*Oriental Morning Post*, 4 September 2006). In many cities (e.g. Beijing, Shanghai, Guangzhou, Nanjing, Hangzhou), the average price of housing in the downtown areas jumped to over 10,000 Yuan (equal to US$1,250) per square metre, a price that is virtually beyond the reach of ordinary people.

In regard to rural social protection, the 'five guarantee' programme is still under operation: at the end of 2003, there were 2.5 million people receiving help from it (IOSC, 2004a). In addition, a voluntary insurance scheme to provide old-age protection for peasants has been developed and, by 2005, there were 54 million farmers participating, with 3 million of them receiving benefits (IOSC, 2006). A new type of rural cooperative medical system was launched in 2003, financed by pooling funds from individual payments, collective support and government subsidies. The state also encouraged local governments to establish a guaranteed minimum income for peasants, using similar principles applied to the urban schemes. In 2005, nearly 6 million rural residents were covered by this programme (Li, 2006). Overall, however, it is difficult for researchers to evaluate villagers' welfare since living standards (in general) have been improved, but, at the same time, little public welfare is provided.

Some Characteristics of Chinese Social Policies

As noted, it is difficult to articulate a discrete Chinese social policy model. Instead, it seems that Chinese social policy has been more of an evolution from one model to another. As a result of this evolutionary process, the Chinese system is characterized by the dominance of social insurance programmes, supplemented by a comprehensive framework of social welfare schemes. These schemes have been introduced at different times, for different motivations, gradually being absorbed into the current system of social welfare. What follows is an outline of the system's policy pattern and its schemes, elaborated though a discussion of the core traits and the basic themes of Chinese social policies. This discussion aims not only to capture the basic features of Chinese social policy models, but also to see the path-dependent effect of this development and the influence of the functional demands created by the growth of market institutions. In order better to understand this system and speculate about future trends, we need to summarize its basic features (see Box below).

Key Features of Welfare Provision

Social Security

Old Age

- Basic old-age pension (social pooling) scheme and individual accounts scheme (retirement age: 60 for male employees, 55 for female cadres and 50 for female workers; 15 years of contribution required for a full pension payment)
- Companies' (voluntary) supplemental pension scheme
- Voluntary old-age insurance scheme for peasants

Unemployment

- Unemployment insurance (maximum benefit: 2 years)
- Livelihood allowance for laid-off workers (maximum benefit: 3 years; this programme was integrated into the unemployment insurance scheme by 2005)
- Various re-employment projects and job-creation schemes, occupational training

Sickness

- Basic social insurance scheme for health care
- Companies' supplemental insurance scheme
- Voluntary insurance scheme for catastrophic illness
- Subsidies for the medical care of civil servants
- Rural cooperative health care

Work injury, maternity leave and child benefit

- Social insurance scheme for work injury (temporary disability benefits, permanent disability benefits, workers' medical benefits, survivor benefits, rehabilitation)
- Social insurance scheme for maternity leave (a childbirth allowance for 90 days)
- Benefits for only-child families

Social assistance, welfare relief and preferential treatment

- 'Five guarantee' system for rural population
- Social assistance for disabled persons, the elders without supporters, and victims of natural disasters
- Minimum income guarantee for urban residents
- Veterans' pensions
- Survivor benefits for the dependants of the revolutionary martyrs

Health-Care Services

- Dominance of the public hospital and other health-care institutions
- Multiple resources for health care: social insurance, voluntary insurance and user fees
- In-patient health care and general primary health care
- Public services such as ambulance services or communal nurse – visits to those elderly with living difficulties

Housing

- 80 per cent of dwellings owner-occupied (in 2006)
- A compulsory saving housing fund scheme for employees to support housing purchasers
- Affordable housing (initiated in 1998 for low-income families)
- The public-rental housing for poor families (established in 77.9 per cent of Chinese cities by 2006)

Education

- Nine years of free compulsory education (in primary and secondary schools)
- Optional for senior high school and university education
- National curriculum and a national system of accreditation
- Dominated by public schools, together with some private schools, with various levels of quality
- Low-interest loan programme for university students

Personal Social Services

- Limited state-administered welfare institutions and various NGO-based welfare institutions
- Family care and the community service network
- Home visits and the state's Starlight Programme to care for elderly without supporters, and those having difficulty with activities of daily living
- Voluntary activities and mutual care among neighbours
- Workplace-organized rehabilitation, nursing and special treatment

An Authoritarian Regime and its Policy Goals

In China, politicians adopt highly conservative social policy measures, regarding social policy as the state-executed instrument of social control. This makes the concepts underpinning European social policies (such as class bargaining, democracy, the left/or the right, and liberal/social-democratic positions – see Higgins, 1981; Korpi, 1989) less effective in the analysis of the Chinese case. Instead, the state's developmental strategy has become the key to policy development. Accordingly, the weakly organized power of both left and right, in a strong authoritarian context, ensures government great autonomy in its policy-making activities. Thus Peng (2003) highlights the role of state bureaucrats in shaping China's policy path, whereas Chen (2003) has stressed authoritarianism as the general context for Chinese social policy-making. This orientation has been reinforced by its socialist legacy, as well as by the notion of a 'developmental state', both of which support an ideal of the 'interventionist state'. These features have significant implications for understanding the Chinese social policy system.

Within this context, the Chinese authoritarian regime often functions in 'crisis management' mode when making social policy. The government often allocates a large sum of its welfare monies to achieve certain policy tasks in accordance with its explicit political needs. For instance, in the late 1990s and early 2000s, the massive number of laid-off workers awoke the state to the risk of social instability. In response, the state set up the 'three lines' of social protection, allocating more than 73 billion Yuan between 1998 and 2003 to laid-off workers, and to re-employment programmes. In 2006, when the state initiated an experimental rural cooperative health-care system, central government allocated 4.7 billion Yuan for its support. Thus, in China, political will is more important than institutional demand for policy development. This brings to the social policy debate an intense focus on social administration issues, typically on fund management of the social insurance scheme, while institutional analysis is relatively weak. This is also the context that makes it possible for the social policy model to change in accordance with the state's political and economic needs as reforms progress.

Also, the interventionist state in China makes the state's developmental strategies the key factor in determining the condition of policy development. As previously mentioned, social policy development in China was initiated by the socialist regime, with the socialist idea of the commonwealth as its guiding principle. In its first stage of development, the regime adopted egalitarian policies, with the assumption that social welfare was a collective responsibility. After economic reforms, the state set as its goal the pursuit of 'GDP-first' development, shifting a socialist social policy model to a productivist one. During this stage, social policy served the needs of economic reform and development. In the post-Deng era, the state's development strategy shifted from one of productivism to one of redistributive social policy, in correspondence to the growth of market institutions. Thus, in each stage of transition, the state's developmental goals and strategies were the keys for system reform and model reconstruction.

A more recent development is 'constructing a harmonious society' as a new developmental goal by government. On 11 October 2006, the ruling party issued a 'Resolution on Major Issues Regarding the Building of a Harmonious Socialist Society', establishing it as the state's developmental goal by 2020. This strategy calls for balancing a set of key relations: harmony between people; harmony between people and nature; and harmony between the economic and social goals of development. It places social justice at the foundation of a harmonious society, with policies targeted at the following issues: narrowing the gap between urban and rural development and between different regions; income (re)distribution; enabling people to lead more affluent lives; establishing a social security system covering both urban and rural residents; improving public service; and fostering a moral atmosphere. With this new orientation, China is modifying its previous productivist and/or developmental social policy strategy, with the intention of building social solidarity and social stability.

The reasons why the state set up this new policy goal are noteworthy: the conflict between economic gains and ecological costs; the need for sustainable development; and income disparities among people at different social levels. For instance, in 2005, the aggregate disposable family income of the richest 10 per cent was eight times higher than that of the poorest 10 per cent, with 60 per cent of the urban residents falling below the average disposable income level (Yang, 2005). Due to these conflicts, policy analysts often highlight the risk of social instability. Some scholars with foreign experience have warned politicians that countries with a per capita GDP between US$1,000 and US$3,000 have a high risk of social instability. China, with a US$1,714 per capita GDP in 2005, is one such country (Li, 2004). Thus it seems necessary for the state to moderate its single-minded economic pursuit by paying more attention to social development. This policy consideration undermines the rationale of marketization, and thus hinders the move in a liberal direction.

Workfare Welfare

In China, welfare benefits are used more to promote production than for individual well-being or citizenship rights. This feature is well demonstrated in the Deng-ist period when a model of productivist social policy was adopted. Yet, even in the Maoist era, there was a strong workfare element embedded in the socialist model: the principle of 'to each according to their work' assumed that increased productivity through everyone's work was the way to a communist society. Later, in the post-Deng era, the idea of productive social policy was promoted in China, moving towards what many other East Asian states called 'productivist welfare regimes' (Holliday, 2000, p. 717; Gough, 2004; Walker and Wang, 2005; Lin, 2007). With these perceptions, China has used social policy as a means to promote the ideas of workfare welfare in numerous ways.

At the institutional level, first of all, Chinese social policy has developed social insurance, a legacy continued till today. Since the system of social insurance benefits is based on the length of one's work period and the amount of one's contribution, this system is, in nature, supportive to the concept of workfare. Additionally, the system of collective welfare that prevailed in the past also reinforced linkages between work and welfare. The enterprise annuity funds were managed and operated in accordance with the market mechanism. Once this system was undermined by economic reforms, a new system, the individual account scheme and voluntary insurance scheme for the old-age pension and health-care insurance, maintained a strong link between work and welfare. Clearly, this structure for social security protection embodies a principle of workfare welfare.

In addition to social insurance, the state has developed policies that support employment services as a way of dealing with unemployment and other poverty-related problems. For example, in the late 1990s, the state required workplaces (and local public agents as well) to establish re-employment centres for laid-off workers. These centres have provided assistance for 24 million laid-off workers registering at re-employment service centres. Local governments also offer skill training, information services and job consultancy through various employment services agents (IOSC, 2004b). The state also encourages labourers to seek employment in both flexible and formal contracted forms. By 2006, most of the unemployed had found jobs with the help of the government-initiated 're-employment project'. Moreover, with the increased number of migrant workers, in 2003, the state formulated the 'National Plan for Training Rural Migrant Workers' and has committed itself to providing occupational training for 60 million rural migrant workers between 2003 and 2010.

With regard to poverty reduction, the guiding idea of the anti-poverty project is to avoid the use of relief funds as a 'blood transfer' to impoverished areas but instead to enhance the mechanism of 'blood production'. Thus, work relief funds are targeted at efforts to strengthen the ability of impoverished areas to become self-supporting, for example, to provide training in advanced practical techniques increasing earned income. The state also provides low-interest loans that are given to promote entrepreneurship, to set up road construction projects and to improve local infrastructure and facilities. Recently, the ideas of an asset-based social policy and the strategy of 'social investment' have been promoted, endorsing the concept of workfare welfare.

Workfare welfare can be achieved not only by active means, but also negatively by creating conditions that compel people to work, such as tightening access and lowering the level of benefits, or even, simply, not providing social security benefits. In China, social security expenditure is low and most rural populations are excluded, having the effect of compelling people to work. For instance, social security expenditure in 1991 and 2004 consumed only around 4–5 per cent of GDP, a very low rate among industrial societies (Yang, 2003, p. 97). Thus, some think that the Chinese model should be considered a residual social policy model (Xu, 2007), as total social welfare spending is very low. Although this view would meet with criticism due to the element of socialistic features that support its social insurance legacy, it does imply the system has to compel people to comply with workfare.

Decommodification and Marketization

In the study of international social policy, the extent of decommodification is critical when analyzing the features of a welfare state model. Like those welfare systems in the socialist welfare bloc, applied to the Soviet Union and many East European states (see Dixon and Macarov, 1992; Deacon, 1983, 2003), the Maoist Chinese system had a high degree of decommodification. Urban workers received social insurance benefits on a non-contributory basis. They enjoyed nearly free medical care as well as housing and education, provided by enterprises and the states. The state's statutory provision for social insurance protected labour rights, and the ideal of a commonwealth was proclaimed (White, 1988; Leung, 1994). Full employment and the standardized eight-grade wage system narrowed the income differentiation between social groups. Collective welfare protection, provided for the majority of the population, reduced the prospect of commodification.

Interestingly, under this model, the general standard income was low, but the degree of commodification was also low. The socialist model of welfare is guaranteed by a set of social policies that lead to 'low wage, high employment, high subsidy and high welfare' (Wang, 2002, p. 74). As a socialist state, it has 'not accepted the idea of the welfare state nor followed the welfare state's practice' (Chen, 2003), but set its policy orientation towards productivism. Hence, social policy is merged with economic policy and employment policy, making this model close to what Titmuss described as the 'industrial achievement model'. In this system, employment-focused social policy does not encourage people to depend on the market system, or to raise the degree of commodification. Instead, a command system economy leaves very little room for the growth of market power. Because of the dominance of public (state and collective) ownerships of enterprises/firms, people have a weak sense of market values, but the norms of compassion, philanthropy, mutual help, altruism and comradeship are accentuated. Thus, the extent of decommodification is important in understanding the Chinese social policies in this model.

However, the degree of decommodification was reduced after the period of economic reforms. Initially, these reforms were mainly intended to improve the economic efficiency of business administration, but they eventually generated a strong market power. The former non-contributory social insurance programmes for urban labourers (supported financially by enterprise contributions: Wang, 2002, p. 5) became contributory, with a personal account scheme added. Trends of commercialization and privatization can also be observed in the policy areas of housing, health care and education. For instance, in rural health care, user charges accounted for 16 per cent of the total medical-care expenditure in 1980, but this rate surged to 87 per cent in 1998 (Zhang, 2004). A Ministry of Health Care report stated that public funds used for health-care expenditure in rural areas had been reduced from 20 per cent (1991) to 10 per cent (2000) of total expenditure (Zhu, 2005).

As counter-measures against a trend of commodification, social policies were used by the state to meet the challenges from enlarged income gaps and unemployment. The establishment of the minimum income guarantee programme opened up a new direction for policy development. In 2005, more than 22 million urban residents received such allowances (Gu, 2005) and by the end of 2003 there were 12.6 million poverty-stricken people in rural China who enjoyed subsistence relief for destitute households. The Chinese government also developed, since 1998, a system of affordable housing and public-rental housing to meet accommodation needs for those low-income families. In 2006, this public-rental housing system was established in 512 cities (78 per cent of total Chinese cities). The state also waived agricultural tax for peasants, and launched a movement to build up a new type of rural society in 2005 (Huang and Wang, 2007). Obviously, these measures had the effect of decommodification.

Despite the implementation of these state policies, their effectiveness against commodification was still too weak to prevent many people from falling into a situation of market dependency. A Blue (discussion) Paper, produced by the Chinese Academy of Social Sciences, states that in 2007, problems including the escalating costs of health care and hospitalization, unemployment, the enlarged income gap are the most pressuring ones. Thus, when the general standard of living is rapidly rising for ordinary people, they complain of the unbearable burden of the 'three mountains' in their life: the financial costs of health care, housing and (child) education. Thus some comment suggests that social policy reforms are intended to set up new rules that demand people pay more. Nevertheless, despite limited state social protection provision, the socialist legacy and the authoritarian model of social policy, block the liberal direction of policy development.

System Integration and Social Inclusion

The Chinese social security system has a low degree of system integration, primarily as a result of the social dualism between urban and rural societies. There are many reasons for this dualism – the lack of capital investment, the low level of technology applied to agricultural production, the state's 'urban-bias policy' under which a large amount of agricultural surplus is transferred into the industrial sector, and because social policy is normally targeted at the urban population (Zhou, 1994; IOCSC, 2001). Social security expenditure for urban residents per capita took 15 per cent of GDP during 1991–2001, but for peasants, it was only 0.2 per cent (Ding, Fu and Cong, 2006). In regard to programme participation levels, most urban residents have participated in at least one social insurance programme, but very few of those living in small towns (13 per cent) and villages (2 per cent) have participated in any of these social insurance schemes (Zhu, 2005). A similar trend can be seen in the use of social security resources: 97 per cent is expended on urban dwellers, while the remaining 3 per cent is spent on the rural population, in spite of the fact that the rural population represents 70 per cent of the total population (Xu, 2007). In education, the allocation of public funds for students in rural primary schools was only 29 per cent of the amount spent on those in urban schools (Xu, 2007). This dualist structure divided Chinese citizens into 'two unequal tiers – the privileged urban and the underprivileged rural' (Fan, 2002:, p. 106).

These varying regional standards of people's livelihoods and welfare also reflect a low degree of system integration. State policy has played a key role in creating these regional variations by implementing policies encouraging the economic growth of the eastern and coast regions, thus widening the gap between China's wealthy coastal regions and the less-developed inner regions. The uneven speed of economic development and large disparities in financial conditions between regions has allowed local governments to set regional standards of welfare benefits in accordance with local conditions, leading to marked regional differences. Thus, those living under the poverty line included 3.7 million people in the eastern region (1.0 per cent of the rural population in this region) and 9.3 million in the middle region (2.8 per cent), but 13.0 million in the western region (5.7 per cent) (NBSC, 2005). This cross-regional disparity in living standards was further enlarged following the period of economic growth. In 1991, the per capita GDP in the eastern region was 1.86 times higher than that in the western region, but this disparity was extended to 2.52 times in 2003 (Zhu, 2004).

This diversity can, in fact, also be observed among urban populations. In China, three systems of social insurance system existed before the system reform, one for each of three different groups in the workforce: state functionaries and civil servants; workers in state-owned enterprises; and workers in collective firms. A collective system of welfare also further increased diversity. Thus, in 1996, a research report authored by the World Bank criticized the Chinese old-age system by characterizing it as a 'fragment' (Song, 2001, p. 43). These systems were integrated after the state-managed social insurance system replaced the former system of 'enterprise welfare' (Leung, 1994; Lin and Kangas, 2006). Nevertheless, since a large number of workers in the private sector remained outside this 'uniform' system of state welfare protection, the issue of 'insiders' and 'outsiders' (i.e. the problem of exclusion from the system), became a major issue. In this regard, 'migrant workers' coming from villages to the cities to earn a living are often used to exemplify problems of exclusion from the system. Due to the rapid speed of urbanization, 80 million rural labourers relocated into cities in the 1990s, a number escalating to 120 million by 2007 (IOCSC, 2002; Lin, 2007).

Because migrant workers stay on the margins of urban and rural worlds, they are used to being excluded from urban and rural social security systems. As the state's statistics bureau revealed, 74 per cent of those peasants working in cities have not participated in any social insurance schemes (Survey Centre, 2006). For this group of workers, the state abolished numerous old regulations, restricting settlement of rural people in cities, and established several principles for handling migration: 'treating fairly, guiding rationally, and improving administration and service' (IOCSC, 2004b). The state has also required local governments to provide services to them that would promote their integration into local communities. In regard to social security, the state advocated their participation in the voluntary old-age pension insurance scheme and for catastrophic illness. It also has required local governments to monitor working conditions, wage standards and working hours of these workers. Furthermore, local government provides them with services to help solve the problems they encounter in everyday life. For instance, in order to protect migrant workers' right to public/compulsory education for their children, the government now requires local public schools to enrol their children. However, to date, services for these workers are still very limited, for example, in the case of child education. Many of their children cannot gain access to urban public schools in cities unless they pay a special fee.

Future Prospects

Social policies are developed by the state to cope with urgent social tasks. To examine future prospects, we need therefore to consider what challenges the state may encounter and in which way the state may respond to them. As Schmidt (1995) observed, 'the degree and formation of state's social intervention are subject to the developmental processes, the degree of prosperity in society, the division of labor and the state's responsibility for the poor'. In the past, China's economic growth contributed to improving the standard of living and to reducing the size of the poor population, and this group of people (defined by the state-established poverty line) was reduced from 260 million in 1978 to 26 million in 2004 (NBSC, 2005). However, in the post-Deng period, successful economic growth has been accompanied by serious problems of unemployment and income inequality; for example, the Gini coefficient rose from 0.26 in 1984 to over 0.5 in 2004 (Zhu, 2006).

Thus, if economic growth benefits only a small part of the population, this growth will be neither sustainable nor healthy. In this regard, the formal policy line of productivism seems inadequate, since the productive model of social policy can be sustained only when the growth of market power does not put at risk the social order. Once this risk becomes real, redistributive measures are demanded. Today, the issues of social justice, social equality, and social solidarity are highlighted in social policy discussion, and the demand for the state to fulfil its welfare obligation more comprehensively raised. Accordingly, in the future, we can expect that redistributive measures will be developed and state welfare will be further extended. As we have observed, the state has set up a new development task in 'building up harmonious society', which supports social policy development in this direction.

Still, the strength of market power has also caused a change in class relations. In recent years, when employment conditions became harsh and private ownership increased its dominance in the national economy, industrial relations worsened. The lawsuits involving labour arbitration for increased wages and improved working conditions escalated, partially due to an increased sense of welfare rights and partially due to the intensified conflicts in industrial relations. In order to protect labourers' interests, the state promoted the idea of tripartism (especially since 2001), encouraging unions to proceed with collective bargaining. The government has also required most employers to sign work contracts with their employees, and to pay legally required insurance fees for them. As reported in 2006 (MOLSS and NBSC, 2006), the Ministry of Labour and Social Security required that 11.3 million employers sign work contracts with their employees and also pay unpaid salaries for 8.42 million workers. In addition, the Ministry demanded that 160,000 enterprises submit their social security contributions to the system. In the near future, we can expect that mediating the relations of different social groups will remain a significant task in social policy activities.

In evaluating the Chinese system, the safety net for people's livelihoods will continue to play a significant role. This safety net consists of family members, relatives, neighbours, volunteers and charitable organizations. This network is significant not only in terms of income security but also, and even more so, in terms of welfare service. Accordingly, the state has to encourage voluntary activities, community services, and to develop family care, mutual support and charity activities. For instance, in recent years, the state began mobilizing rural households to sign a 'family support agreement' among family members, and by the end of 2005, around 13 million such agreements had been signed (IOSC, 2006). In the future, the government will further extend this approach, in order to enhance the role of civil society's agencies in providing welfare.

All in all, in the foreseeable future, the Chinese economy will grow stronger with even stronger dynamics. To serve economic growth, the Chinese government will use social policy to diminish the social risks caused by growing marketization. The system will maintain social insurance schemes as the core of its social policy, while working to enhance system integration. Meanwhile, although the current structure of social security will be retained, the boundaries between welfare sectors will be changed in order to create welfare pluralism. In addition, with the pressure of China's ageing population, the development of social services will become another focus of policy-making.

Acknowledgement

This article is part of the research programme supported by the Ministry of Education in China.

References

Chan, Huo-sheng, Yang, Ying and Zhang, Qing-fen (1993) *The Social Security System in Mainland China* , Wunan Tushu Chuban Youxian Gongsi (in Chinese).

Chen, Liang-jing (*et al.*) (1994) *Encyclopedia of Chinese Social Work*, Zhongguo Shehui Chubanshe (in Chinese).

Chen, She-ying (2003) 'The Context of Social Policy Reform in China: Theorertical, Comparative and Historical Perspectives', in C. J. Finer (ed.), *Social Policy Reform in China*, Ashgate, pp. 23–38.

Davis, D. S. (1995) 'Inequality and Stratification in the Nineties', *China Review*, pp. 1–25, Chinese University of Hong Kong Press.

Deacon, B. (1983) *Social Policy and Socialism: The Struggle for Socialist Relations of Welfare*, Pluto Press.

Deacon, B. (2003) 'The Prospects for Equitable Access to Social Provision in a Globalizing World', in A. Krizsan *et al.* (eds), *Reshaping Globalization: Multilateral Dialogues and New Policy Initiatives*, Central European University Press, pp. 75–93.

Ding, Wenjie, Fu, Xiny and Cong, Feng (2006) 'A Great Trend: How Far Would China Reach at the Stage of "Universal Coverage of Social Security"', *Semi-Monthly*, July (in Chinese).

Dixon, J. and Macarov, D. (eds) (1992) *Social Welfare in Socialist Countries*, Routledge.

Esping-Andersen, G. (1990) *Three Worlds of Welfare Capitalism*, Polity Press.

Fan, C. C. (2002) 'The Elite, the Natives, and the Outsiders: Migration and Labour Market Segmentation in Urban China', *Annals of the Association of American Geographers*, 92(1), pp. 103–24.

George, V. and Manning, N. (1980) *Socialism, Social Welfare and the Soviet Union*, Routlege & Kegan Paul.

Gough, I. (2004) 'East Asia: The Limits of Productivist Regimes', in I. Gough and G. Wood (eds), *Insecurity and Welfare Regimes in Asia, Africa and Latin America: Social Policy in Developmental Contexts*, Cambridge University Press, pp. 169–201.

Gu, R. (2005) 'The Basically Achieved Task of Guaranteeing All Eligible Urban Residents in the Minimal Income Guarantee Programme', *Legal Daily*, 3 January (in Chinese).

Guo, Chong-de (ed.) (1992) *Outline of the Social Security*, Beijing Daxue Chubanshe (in Chinese).

Higgins, J. (1981) *States of Welfare-Comparative Analysis in Social Policy*, Basil Blackwell and Martin Robertson.

Holliday, I. (2000) 'Productivist Welfare Capitalism: Social Policy in East Asia', *Political Study*, 48, pp. 706–23.

Huang, Quanquan and Wang, Yang (2007) '512 Cities Have Established the Public-rental Housing Scheme Nationwide in China by 2006', http://news.xinhuanet.com/house (official website of Xinhua News Agent), accessed 14 February.

IOCSC (2001) 'The Development-Oriented Poverty Reduction Programme for Rural China', http://news.xinhuanet.com (in Chinese).

IOCSC (2002) 'Labour and Social Security in China', http://news.xinhuanet.com/zhengfu/2002-11/18/ (in Chinese).

IOCSC (2004a) 'China's Social Security and Its Policy', http://news.xinhuanet.com/english/2004-09/07/ (in Chinese).

IOCSC (2004b) 'China's Employment Situation and Policies', http://news.xinhuanet.com/english/2004-04/26/ (in Chinese).

IOCSC (2006) 'The Development of China's Undertakings for the Aged', http://news.xinhuanet.com/english/2006-12/12/ (official website of Xinhua News Agent), accessed 12 December (in Chinese).

Korpi, Walter (1989) 'Power, Politics, and State Autonomy in the Development of Social Citizenship: Social Rights During Sickness in Eight OECD Countries Since 1930', *American Sociology Review*, 54(3), pp. 309–32.

Leung, J. C. B. (1994) 'Dismantling the "Iron Race Bowl": Welfare Reforms in the People's Republic of China', *Journal of Social Policy*, 23(3), pp. 341–61.

Li Xiaojia (2004) 'Surmounts the Ridge of Per Capital GDP 1000–3000 USD', *Liberation Daily*, 3 December (in Chinese).

Li Xueju (2006) 'A Review and Comments on the Work in the National Civil Administration', http://www.mca.gov.cn (the official website of Ministry of Civil Affairs) (in Chinese).

Lin, Ka (2007) 'The Sustenance and Loss of a Productivist Social Policy Model in Asia – An Interpretation of the Asian Welfare From a Comparative Perspective', Paper Collection of the International Symposium on Japanese, Chinese and Korean Conference of Social Welfare, Nanjing University, 28 March.

Lin, Ka and Kangas, Olli (2006) 'Social Policymaking and Its Institutional Basis: Transition of the Chinese Social Security System', *International Social Security Review*, 59(2), pp. 61–76.

Lin,Yi (2007) 'Hukou: An Obstacle to Market Economy', http://news.xinhuanet.com/english/ 2007-05/ 21 (in Chinese).

MLC (Ministry of Labour of China) (1990) 'Social Insurance and Worker's Welfare', *China Labour Year Book 1990*, China Labour Press (in Chinese).

MOLSS (Ministry of Labour and Social Security) and NBSC (National Bureau of Statistics of China) (2006) 'Statistical Report on the Development of Labour and Social Security Conditions in China, 2005', http://www.stats.gov.cn (the official website of the State Bureau of Statistics of China) (in Chinese).

NBSC (National Bureau of Statistics of China) (1992, 2004, 2006) *Chinese Yearbook of Statistics*, Chinese Statistical Publisher (in Chinese).

NBSC (1996) 'Annual Per Capita Income and Index of Urban and Rural Households', http://www.stats.gov.cn (in Chinese).

NBSC (2005) 'Report on Monitoring the Condition of Rural Poverty in China 2004', http://www.stats.gov.cn (the official website of the State Bureau of Statistics of China) (in Chinese).

Niu, Li and Shang (eds) (2005) *The Development Report of Chinese Real Estate*, Social Sciences Academic Press (in Chinese).

Peng, B. (2003) 'The Policy Progress in Contemporary China: Mechanisms of Politics and Government', in C. Jones-Finer (ed.), *Social Policy Reform in China: Views from Home and Abroad*, Ashgate.

Schmidt, S. (1995) 'Social Security in Developing Countries: Basic Tenets and Fields of State Intervention', *International Social Work*, 38, pp. 7–26.

Song, Xiaowu (2001) *The Reform of Social Security System in China*, Qinhua University Press (in Chinese).

Survey Centre (the Service Sector of the National Bureau of Statistics of China) (2006) 'Surveys on the Quality of Peasants Livelihoods', http://www.stats.gov.cn, accessed 25 October (in Chinese).

Walker, Alan and Wang, Chack-kie (eds) (2005) *East Asian Welfare Regimes in Transition: From Confucianism to Globalization*, Policy Press.

Walker, Andrew (1991) 'China', in R. Taylor (ed.), *Asia and The Pacific, Vol. 1*, Facts on Files.

Waller, Derek J. (1981) *The Government and Politics of the People's Republic of China*, Hutchinson.

Wang (ed.) (2002) *Restructuring China's Social Security System*, Foreign Languages Press.

White, G. (1988) *Developmental states in East Asia*, New York : St. Martin's Press.

Wong, C. (1995) 'Reforms in Social Welfare System', *China Review*, 13, pp. 1–14.

Wong, L. (1994) 'Privatisation of Social Welfare in Post-Mao China', *Asian Survey*, XXXIV(4), pp. 159–76.

Xu, Daowen (2007) 'The Basic Social Policy Issues in Chinese Reform', *Research on Contemporary China*, 1/2007 (in Chinese).

Yang, Cuiying (2003) *Research on Chinese Rural Social Security*, Chinese Agriculture Press.

Yang, Qian (2005) 'The Income Distance between Chinese Households Over Eight Times', *The First Financial and Economic Daily*, 11 October (in Chinese).

Yao, Chongli and Li, Bin (1999) 'Policies to Cope With the Problems in the Chinese Labour Market', *Contemporary Economic Sciences*, 1 (in Chinese).

Zhang, Xiaobo (2004) 'The Problem of Inequality on Education and Health Care in China', in Yang Yao (ed.), *Transformational China: Examining the Society on Social Justice and Equality*, The Chinese People's University Press, pp. 214–15 (in Chinese).

Zhou, Pei-yan (1994) 'Medical Care Insurance Reform Must Be Implemented', *Xinhua Daily Telegraphy*, 17 February (in Chinese).

Zhu Qingfang (2004) 'Raising the Life Quality and Change in the Consumer Structure', http://www.sociology.cass.cn (official website of Chinese Sociological Association).

Zhu Qingfang (2005) 'Some Urgent Issues to Be Solved for Constructing a Harmonious Society from a View of Social Indication Studies', *Theory And Modernization*, 6 (in Chinese).

Zhu Qingfang (2006) 'Several Questions in the Construction of a Harmonious Society', http://www.sociology.cass.cn (in Chinese).

Zong, Yan (1997) 'Retrospective on 1996 Economic Reform', *Beijing Review*, 40(2), pp. 21–5.

CHAPTER 14

South Africa: Transition Under Pressure

FRANCIE LUND

Introduction

South Africa's political transition from apartheid to democracy in 1994 was accompanied by significant changes in economic and social policies. Social policy was so closely related to the political economy of apartheid that it cannot easily be classified according to any of the conventional welfare regimes. Nevertheless, it has much of interest in the comparative study of welfare systems. The urgency of abandoning the racially discriminatory policies of the former government meant that key elements and stages of the policy process have been telescoped into a short period. During the 1990s, policy formulation, then its translation into legislation, budgetary reallocations, the reorientation of staff, the development of administrative capacity and the adjustment of information and communication systems, all happened rapidly. Tensions always inherent in the policy process were forced to the surface, and have been more visible than they would be in societies where the pace of change is slower. It is possible to see how even in a country so eager to move away from its past, policy changes are constrained by history. As commonly experienced elsewhere, a gap exists between policy acceptance and implementation.

A study of South Africa also forces questions about what is included in the definition of social policy. The country is characterized by pervasive inequality, with extremes of wealth and poverty. A minority of citizens have had access to all the services and technology of very modern societies; the majority have lived without basic services such as water and electricity. There is, thus, a juxtaposition of 'first and third worlds', or development and underdevelopment, within one country. One of the effects of this is that the student can see how the scope of social policy is contingent on assumptions made about what and how basic needs are met. For example, in industrialized countries the provision of water and electricity to households and communities would not normally fall within the scope of social policies regarding health and education. Yet in South Africa, the improvement of health status, through the provision of primary health-care services, will fail unless it is accompanied by a supply of potable water within easy reach of households. Likewise, the impact of improvements to the school system will be diluted if learners are not able to study at home after school because there is no affordable lighting.

We start with a brief history of social policy development during the twentieth century, and then describe present patterns of poverty and inequality, which post-apartheid social policies have had to address. The policy trends in the areas of education, health, social services and income maintenance are presented, with the underlying theme of the shift towards deracializing past policies, and meeting more basic needs. Then four key issues in policy reform are addressed: shifts in resource allocation in social spending, the reform of institutional frameworks, the mixed economy of welfare, and tensions in universal and selective provision. The chapter concludes with a consideration of the main lessons for social policy derived from the period since 1994.

There is a substantive issue about racial naming. Under apartheid all citizens were classified into one of four so-called 'race groups': African, coloured, Indian and white. The term 'black' is commonly used to refer collectively to the three non-white groups, who were disenfranchized. However, Indian and coloured and African people were discriminated against in specifically different ways, and the terms still need to be used.

Phases of Social Policy Development

The foundations of apartheid were laid well before the Nationalist Party came to power in 1948. The seventeenth-century Dutch settlers were followed by the British, and both colonial powers dealt with the indigenous and African immigrant people as inferior races. By the close of the nineteenth century, labour policies had been developed that sowed the seeds for the formal policy of apartheid which was to follow. Gold mines, white-owned farms and the new cities needed workers. The migrant labour policy drew men away from rural areas, while strictly regulating their presence in urban areas. Over the first half of the twentieth century, policies were introduced that stripped Africans, and then coloured and Indian people, of property rights, of free labour mobility and of the right to live where they pleased.

Industrial social legislation developed early in the twentieth century. Compensation for industrial disease and accidents was introduced in 1914, and an unemployment insurance fund in 1937. Benefit levels were racially differentiated, and lower-paid workers and women were disadvantaged. The Cape Town Poverty Survey in the late 1930s modelled itself on Rowntree's surveys of York in England, and showed the extent of poverty, especially among the coloured population. The survey findings were influential in the work of two commissions at that time, which (unsuccessfully) recommended a comprehensive social security scheme. The Gluckman Commission on

Health followed in the 1940s, being years ahead of its time in recommending free health care for all citizens through a system of primary health-care centres. Also in the 1930s and 1940s, state programmes were devised to address the growing number of poor white people through, for example, public works programmes for temporary employment, and nutrition schemes in white schools.

When the Nationalist Party government came to power in 1948, aspects of the citizenship-based aspects of welfare state thinking survived, but for whites only. The underlying model for this provision was a two-generational nuclear family, with a father in formal employment, and a mother doing the reproductive work at home. These Beveridge-like elements were combined with deeply conservative Calvinist religious assumptions about white family life. African, coloured and Indian families were largely expected to take care of themselves, according to their own 'cultural norms and values'.

The 1950s and 1960s saw the consolidation and implementation of apartheid, or separate development, driven by a strong, centralized and authoritarian state. Local authorities had no role in the control or delivery of education, and very little in health or social services. The government created the 'bantustans', mainly undeveloped rural areas that had been traditionally settled by Africans, into which millions of additional Africans were now forcibly displaced and given token forms of 'self-government'.

Across all fields of social policy, patterns of provision emerged that primarily protected white, and later coloured and Indian, interests. The social security system was initially set up to cover white elderly people and white people with disabilities; a bundle of grants and other policy measures provided for the protection of white family life. Gradually, basic state assistance was expanded in scope and coverage, first to urban-based Indian and coloured people, then to African people in rural areas. Finally, all South Africans were covered, though a few of the smaller grants never reached African people in the bantustans (Lund, 2003). Racially differentiated amounts of benefits (the formula in the 1970s was a rands-to-person ratio of 10:5:1 for white: Indian/coloured: African beneficiaries) had been removed by 1993.

Social services developed as a partnership between government and a network of voluntary organizations (Patel, 1992). The state used a combination of subsidies and legislation controlling fund-raising to force all welfare organizations to apply racial discrimination in services. Virtually no attention was paid to the development of the voluntary welfare sector in areas where the poorest people lived. Education policy was deeply inequitable. The wealthy white population had access to free education, though they could opt to pay for élite private schools as well. The Indian population developed a very good network of community-based schools over the first half of the twentieth century; these were broken down by the state, and the state curriculum was imposed. The African population was given 'bantu education', which was based on the idea that African people were naturally inferior, and should only be taught sufficiently to serve the needs of white élites and capitalist industry. A few private schools, mainly religious, provided better-quality education to non-white people. Most of these, as well as mission hospitals, were eventually absorbed by the state.

In similar vein, apartheid housing policy broke up existing neighbourhoods, displacing people either to the bantustans, or to controlled township developments for coloured, Indian and African people far from city centres. The government disallowed or severely restricted private sector involvement in housing for the poor, relaxing this only as late as the mid-1980s. There was a free market in housing for white people and to a lesser extent for Indian and coloured people, with high rates of home ownership as opposed to rented housing.

A series of strikes led by black unions in 1973 marked the beginnings of the breakdown of the old regime. The strikes were followed by the 1976 student uprisings, and the threat of ungovernability coincided with a downturn in the economy and increasing international isolation. By the early 1980s, the government embarked on what has been described as the twin strategies of reform and repression. It started paying attention to the provision of some basic infrastructural development, such as water and electricity in black townships, and addressing racial discrepancies in social spending, while ruthlessly repressing political dissent.

By the end of the 1980s, policy work focusing on the transitional process and on post-democratic reconstruction was underway. Meetings such as the 1990 conference 'Health and Welfare in Transition' in Mocambique were held on social policy issues with the ANC in exile. Within the country, sectoral policy forums were set up, which included a broad range of stakeholders – political parties, the mass democratic movement, professional associations, civic organizations, academics and trades unions, among others. These forums were intended to formulate new policies, and also to stop the then government from unilaterally restructuring social sectors in the interregnum. By the time of the democratic elections in 1994, therefore, significant policy work had been done, and people from opposite sides of the political fence were working together.

Selected Characteristics of South African Society

A few characteristics of South African society demonstrate the kinds of policy challenges that now have to be faced. The population of some 47 million lives in an area about ten times the size of England. The population is relatively young, with half being younger than 20 years old; the proportion of the population aged 65 years and older is around 5 per cent. This age structure carries specific implications for social policy.

South Africa has one of the highest rates of measured inequality in the world. It is classified as an upper middle-income country, but (roughly speaking) in 1993 the poorest 40 per cent of households comprised 50 per cent of the population, and got 11 per cent of overall income, while the richest 10 per cent of households comprised 7 per cent of the population and got 40 per cent of the income (May, Woolard and Klasen, 2000, p. 27).

Unsurprisingly, the patterns of poverty and inequality largely take a racial form. Being born into one of the four classified racial groups determined, and still largely determine, one's life chances and opportunities. Africans constitute 77 per cent of the population, and 60 per cent of Africans are classified as poor. Whites constitute 11 per cent of the population, with only 1 per cent being classified poor. The infant mortality rate in the early 1990s was more than 11 times higher for Africans than for whites. Indicators of human development for white people, and to a lesser extent for Indian people, compare with the best of the upper income countries; those for the African population are as bad as, and often worse than, those for countries with lower wealth levels than South Africa. Steep inequality has emerged within the African population, with the growth of a small very wealthy élite.

The urbanization rate is just over 50 per cent, and millions of poor people live in peri-urban informal settlements where life is hazardous, services are poor and environmental controls are few. However, the rural areas, especially former bantustan areas, continue to experience the highest rates and shares of poverty.

In all countries, social policies regarding income maintenance, social services, education and housing are based, implicitly or explicitly, on some construct of family life. South Africa's social policies have largely assumed the nuclear family form, but in reality extended household structures with members from three and four generations are very common. Also, the forced movement of men has led to the phenomenon of 'double-rootedness': many men have a household in town and a separate one in the rural area. As in other countries, female-headed households in South Africa are poorer and more vulnerable than male-headed households. Women have less access to employment opportunities than men, and when they are employed they are more likely to earn less than men. Yet households headed by younger women, in urban areas, perform better on nearly every important indicator than do households overall. The HIV/AIDS epidemic has led to the recent emergence of child-headed households, most of whose heads in 2005 were between 15 and 17 years old.

South Africa has an exceptionally high unemployment rate, of around 26–30 per cent (Klasen and Woolard, 1999). Unemployment is highest for African people, in rural areas and among women, with African women in rural areas being triply disadvantaged. It also particularly affects young people. In keeping with the rest of the world, there has been a growth in informal work, and in non-standard forms of employment, such as part-time work. Growing numbers of people, therefore, cannot get access to social welfare benefits through their work.

Social Policy Reform: From Racial Ideology to Meeting Basic Needs

The new South African Constitution of 1996 enshrines the idea of national unity, protects both individual rights and cultural diversity and guarantees some socio-economic rights. In its march back to international legitimacy, South Africa signed many international conventions regarding, *inter alia*, human rights, gender equality and the protection of children. These, and the Constitution, mean that South Africa now has a complex mixture of commitments and obligations.

In the early 1990s the ANC as government-in-waiting tabled the Reconstruction and Development Programme (RDP) as the primary mechanism for addressing the apartheid legacy of inequality. It was strongly redistributive in intent, with a central role for government. Policies were to move away from racial and urban biases towards accessible services for the majority of South Africans who are poor and mostly African. Rural areas were especially identified, as well as vulnerable groups, particularly women, children and people with disabilities, and there was a commitment to citizen participation in policy formulation and implementation. The new macro-economic policy – Growth, Employment and Redistribution (GEAR) – was introduced in 1996, a neo-liberal programme emphasizing fiscal austerity, which withdrew in substantial ways from the RDP's commitment to redistribution.

Education

In the post-apartheid era, all people have the right to a basic education, within a framework of a single non-racial school system, with one national curriculum and system of accreditation, rather than the fragmented systems of the past. According to policy, there is compulsory schooling for eight years, with no one excluded on grounds of costs. The 1996 South Africa Schools Act allowed schools to charge fees, but fee exemptions were to be available to poorer students. The very expensive private schools were allowed to continue, now with a more racially mixed student population. More than a decade later, the fee exemption policy is acknowledged to have failed, and in 2007 new attention was given to school (rather than student) fee exemption, and to shifting resources towards poorer schools.

There has been a real increase in the government spending per learner, and racial inequity and the inter-provincial inequity has been addressed (Reschovsky, 2006), though not overcome. The quality of education, especially in formerly African schools, remains extremely poor, despite the substantial government expenditure. There is much larger expenditure on primary and secondary schooling, in line with the commitment to shifting state resource allocation away from tertiary educational institutions. Tertiary fees have risen sharply, making access difficult for those from poorer households. Proportionately more students are now enrolling at the more vocationally oriented technical colleges (many now converted to universities). Some private universities have been established. Early childhood education (ECD) and adult basic education and training both lost ground as priorities in the first post-apartheid decade, but in 2007 ECD received renewed attention.

In most middle- and lower-income countries there is gender inequality in access to all levels of schooling, with lower enrolment and completion rates for girls. South Africa is unusual in having equitable enrolment rates for boys and girls at primary and secondary school levels. However, there are high rates of teenage pregnancy and many girls interrupt their schooling to have a child. Again, unusually, young mothers in South Africa typically return to attempt to complete their secondary schooling.

Health

South Africa has parallel public and private health systems, with the private system including allopathic ('Western'), traditional African and alternative health practices. In the past, public and private services were skewed towards urban areas; the private allopathic health sector accounted for nearly 60 per cent of total health-care spending, yet served only a quarter of the population. Post-apartheid health policy has continued the tax-financed public health system, with an orientation towards free primary health care, delivered through a new district health system. User fees are paid by those who can afford them. Medical aids schemes have to provide a minimum set of health-care benefits, and have had to discontinue the practice of setting up fragmented and separate schemes for the young and healthy. In 2007 the finance minister announced that the introduction of a long-planned national social health insurance scheme, in which all people in formal employment and their dependants would be insured for public hospital treatment, was imminent.

Since 1994, significant progress has been made in vitally important areas, all of which generated controversy before being accepted. The first Health Minister, Nkosazana Zuma, drove the legalization of abortion, stringent controls over the use of and advertising for tobacco, and a generic drugs policy that makes drugs cheaper for the public. The health curriculum has been changed, and newly qualified health personnel are required to do a year of community service in (mostly rural) facilities that have a shortage of staff. Traditional African healers have been integrated in a system of accreditation and licensing, including a professional council.

The most significant health problem is HIV/AIDS. Apartheid laid down conditions favourable to the rapid spread of HIV/AIDS, and South Africa has a very high prevalence rate. The ANC political leadership failed to develop a timely, coherent AIDS policy and this will no doubt be judged its greatest policy failure, across the health, social, political and economic domains. The country has sufficient resources to have addressed this catastrophic epidemic. It has squandered these, and the government has eroded its own national and international legitimacy in incalculable ways.

Social Services

Social services in South Africa have historically been delivered in a partnership between the state and voluntary sector organizations. The usual apartheid pattern prevailed: institutional care and personal social service delivery were skewed towards the white population, and within that towards the elderly white population. During the 1970s and 1980s there was an increase in state subsidization of welfare facilities for the coloured and Indian population as well. There was little support for the development of the voluntary sector in black areas. The welfare White Paper signals a shift away from curative welfare services towards 'developmental social welfare' or social development (the concept was developed by Patel [1992], who drew significantly from James Midgeley's work on social development). The value base of the developmental shift is good in human terms, with its emphasis on independence and self-help.

However, in the face of new demands being made for care of people affected by HIV/AIDS, including hundreds of thousands of orphaned children, it may unintentionally make social services very vulnerable. Studies of welfare and community-based organizations attempting to cope with HIV/AIDS-affected children show that poor communities, worst affected by the epidemic, are prepared to care, but need assistance to do so (Harber, 1998; Akintola, 2004). Social workers in the subsidized voluntary welfare sector continue to do a great deal of time-consuming statutory work for government, for example, in foster care placements and in overseeing offenders on parole. They have little spare capacity to initiate 'developmental' services.

Income Maintenance

South Africa has mixed private and public provision for disability, support in old age and for the protection of child and family life (Van der Berg, 1999; Lund, 2002; Van der Berg and Bredenkamp, 2002). The basic approach is that people should care for themselves where possible, and use government support as a last resort.

People who are formally employed have access to social insurance for retirement provision, occupational disability, maternity benefits and unemployment. Coverage is relatively good for those who have work, and the insurance industry for retirement is a significant pillar of the South African economy. Unemployment insurance is not underpinned by any form of retraining or skills development, and those with no employment record are excluded from access. Large numbers of lower-level workers are unaware of their rights to compensation for injuries at work; an unacceptably large proportion of the compensation payments go to professional fees of lawyers and doctors, rather than to beneficiaries themselves.

An important pillar of the overall social security system is state social assistance, extended to elderly people, people with disabilities and to women and children. Cash benefits are non-contributory (that is, not insurance-based) and means-tested. In 1998 there were about 3 million direct beneficiaries, which by 2007 increased to about 12 million, with most of the increasing numbers being recipients of the new child support grant (CSG) (see Lund, 2008, for an account of this policy reform). The HIV/AIDS epidemic has triggered a crisis of care for children. The CSG is received by the primary care-givers of 8 million children. There are procedures for the formal fostering and adoption of children, with limited financial support for foster parents, but none for adoptive parents. There is a reformed judicial procedure for getting financial support from fathers.

Extensive research points to the role played by income maintenance in general poverty alleviation. The redistributive mechanism in the Old-Age Pension, and to a lesser extent the Disability Grant, lies in the fact that the grant is claimed by individuals but gets pooled as a household resource (Ardington and Lund, 1995; Lund, 2002). This is unlike the case in industrialized countries where the benefit is used largely by individual claimants.

In South Africa, poor elderly and disabled people commonly live in three-generational households, and a disproportionate number of poor young children live in households where elderly pension-receiving people are present (Case and Deaton, 1998). Because much of the pension money goes to the household purse, and because it is delivered deep into rural areas, it has unusual distributive features. It is well targeted towards lower income groups; it is gender sensitive towards women (women draw it earlier and live longer) and towards children. For many older African people who were excluded from formal employment, or were erratically employed, the pension income is the largest and most reliable income they have ever received. Offsetting these positive features are the administrative inefficiencies in the system, which can make access difficult and expensive for elderly and disabled people.

Visitors to South Africa with an interest in social policy and development studies are surprised by the state social assistance system. Those familiar with social security in developing countries, and especially with neighbouring Southern African countries, are amazed at the extent of the system, and many disapprove of the state's taking on so much responsibility. On the other hand, those familiar with, for example, European systems are shocked by how inadequate a safety net it is. If you are poor and young, and have never been in employment, there is no assistance for you at all. If you are in your 50s, have been made redundant, and your unemployment benefits run out after six months, there is nothing to cushion you until, as a woman at 60 and a man at 65, you become eligible for the pension for elderly people.

A Committee of Enquiry into Comprehensive Social Security ('the Taylor Committee') was set up in 2000 to investigate a broad range of social security issues including poverty, health, unemployment and retirement provision, and in particular to explore the gaps between the private and the public pillars in social security. One of its chief recommendations (Department of Social Development, 2002) was a basic income grant for all South Africa's citizens. Though the recommendation has aroused significant national and international support (see for example Standing and Samson, 2003), it has not yet found acceptance from those in key positions of power.

Key Issues

Redistribution

For redistributive policies to have an impact, they clearly have to be accompanied or followed by shifts in resource allocation. Figure 14.1 shows how political changes in the transitional period of 1990/91 to 1996/97 shifted social spending patterns.

The rapid decrease in the defence budget is remarkable, and much of the decrease was diverted to the increase for education. Health received a real increase of 30 per cent in those years, and since then free health care was introduced with only limited additional money. The 130 per cent increase in the

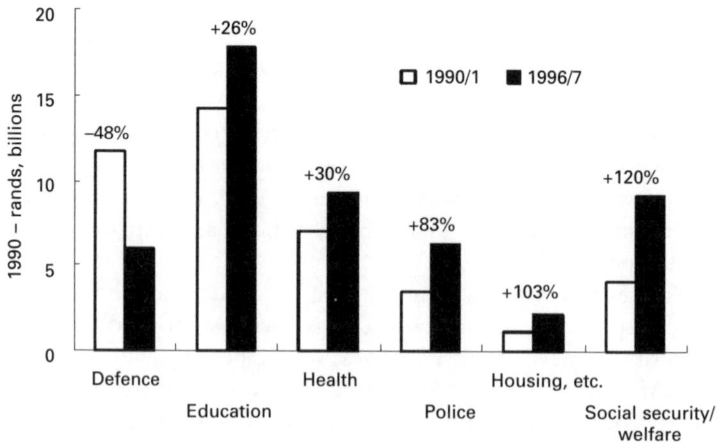

Figure 14.1 Change in general government expenditure on some functions, fiscal years 1990/1 to 1996/7, 1990 rands

Source: Republic of South Africa (1996).

social security and welfare budget was largely driven by the need to overcome the racial disparities in state pensions and grants. That growth then levelled off.

Table 14.1 shows trends in social spending in the period since 1997. All three sectors received increases in the overall amount spent over the whole period. Health and education decreased as a percentage of overall GDP. Social security and welfare spending, on the other hand, increased and this was largely attributable to the implementation of the CSG in 1998, and to increasing applications for the Disability Grant associated with HIV/AIDS. Social security and welfare also grew relative to health. Total public spending was about a quarter of the size of the GDP over that ten-year period.

Table 14.1 Trends in South African public expenditure on health, education, and social security and welfare as percentage of GDP, and all public expenditure as percentage of GDP, 1997/8 to 2007/8

	1997/8	*2002/3*	*2007/8*
Education	R45bn	R62bn	R104.7bn
Education as percentage GDP	6.4	5.2	5.5
Health	R23bn	R31.4bn	R60.3bn
Health as percentage GDP	3.3	2.6	3.1
Social security and welfare	R24bn	R34bn	R89.5bn
Social security and welfare as percentage GDP	3.4	2.8	4.6
H, E, SS and W as percentage GDP	13.1	10.6	13.2
All public expenditure as percentage GDP	27.2	24.3	27.5

Source: Natural Treasury Budget Review, 2001, pp. 202–3; National Treasury Budget Review, 2007, pp. 184–5 and 186–7.

Overall, social spending has held steady, not least because of the remarkable performance of the revenue services in collecting taxes more effectively, and the commitment of the Treasury to allocating some of this additional money to social sectors.

As in all countries, the different sectors compete with each other for a larger share of the expenditure. It is becoming clear in South Africa that attention must be paid to outputs and outcomes as well. The serious problems in education will not all be solved just with more money. Better management of schools is needed; the curriculum needs to be restructured to align it better with the real world of work; more than 90 per cent of the educational budget is locked in to teacher salaries, leaving little over for the building of new schools in rural areas.

Reforming the Institutional Framework

The 1994 government inherited a complex set of racially separated administrations. There were 14 first-tier (central state) departments of health and of education, for example, and 17 for welfare. There was little commitment to public service, no reasonable demographic information on which to base social policies and planning, and outmoded information systems. The new government succeeded in rapidly amalgamating these separate administrations; there are nine provinces, with each provincial department (say, of health or of education) reporting directly to only one national department.

The government committed itself to two goals that were difficult to reconcile: to reduce or contain the size of the civil service, and to make it more racially representative. White bureaucrats were encouraged to leave by offering generous severance packages. Many of the best teachers, black and white, have migrated to the private education sector or to other careers; many social workers have left the voluntary sector for better-paid public sector jobs.

The implications of policy changes on personnel are clearly seen in the health field. The development of district health systems has meant that more staff are needed at lower levels of the professional hierarchy, and at local level and in rural areas – the move that is required is 'downwards and outwards'. Yet professional élites everywhere want to move in the opposite direction – upwards in the status hierarchy and inwards to the urban centres. Many health workers feel ill at ease with aspects of health policy and the effect of AIDS on their working conditions; together with high crime rates, they are pushed into emigrating. Their training has been heavily subsidized by the former and present government, which is thus effectively paying for skills development for other more developed countries. On the other hand, many health professionals from other countries – Ghana, Philippines, Zimbabwe, for example – now come to South Africa. One scheme involves the temporary employment in South Africa of numbers of Cuban doctors. There is an oversupply of doctors in Cuba, and their training in primary health care is appropriate to the new South African health policy. They are placed in rural areas where other doctors will not go, and some do not want to return to Cuba following their contracts (Hammett, 2007), citing especially the much higher South African salaries.

A Mixed Economy of Welfare

It is difficult to characterize South Africa according to any of the conventional welfare regimes put forward by Esping-Anderson to depict industrialized countries, but neither does it easily fit the 'insecurity regimes' used to describe Africa (Gough *et al.*, 2004). Overall, however, there has been a move towards, or entrenchment of, a mixed economy in social provision.

During the liberation struggle, most people assumed that in future the state would play a strong, if not sole, role in social provision. Each sector eyed the bloated defence budget as its own potential future resource base for extending free health, education, social security or housing to all. Some think that the present state commitment to social spending – Table 14.1 shows that spending on health, education and social security and welfare amounted to 13.2 per cent of GDP in 2007/8 – is too great. There are others who agree with an active role for the state, but who question the capacity of government to deliver over the short to middle term, and at least until stronger local government is developed. However, the bantustan policy led to severe underdevelopment of the poorest areas and, at least up until the middle term, the state is the only agency with the resources to address poverty in these areas.

The delivery of state social assistance pensions and grants was largely outsourced to the private sector, which took advantage of the state's lack of capacity to manage or regulate relationships with the private sector, profiting handsomely through delivering state cash transfers to the poorest households. Management of social assistance is now done by the quasi-governmental South African Social Security Agency, but still in association with private firms. The private formal and informal insurance industry is thriving, in the presence of AIDS. Many Africans contribute to more than one funeral scheme, speaking to the deep importance attached to a dignified burial.

An important aspect of the mixed economy of welfare is the care economy. Globally, much of the work of health and welfare is done through the unpaid or low-paid work of (mostly) women. In South Africa, the HIV/AIDS epidemic has placed increasing strains on health and welfare budgets, and on society as a whole. Changes in schooling patterns are visible, as are increasing absentee rates in the workplace. Grandparents and children have to do more of the informal caring work at home. The government has introduced a policy of community care (Hunter, 2005) that is wholly gender-blind, and that will erode many of the gender gains made in the last two decades. The Women's Budget Initiative (Budlender, 1996), a collaborative exercise between government and non-governmental organizations, was used to raise awareness about the hidden work that underpins formal health and welfare services. Greater attention needs to be given to the analysis of changes within the care economy, the costs of time and money borne by (mostly) women, and consequently what policy and resource changes are needed.

Universal and Selective Social Provision

The South African Freedom Charter, formulated in the 1950s, expressed the universal terms in which the struggle for liberation was fought: 'There shall be health, education, land, and security for all'. To attain policy objectives of inclusion of previously excluded groups, there has been a retreat towards more selective provision. Chisholm and Fuller (1996) give an account of the narrowing of policies in education; the introduction of the CSG provides an interesting example of these tensions in the field of income maintenance.

The pattern of income distribution is such that the majority of people (including children) are very poor, and a few people are very rich indeed. This would suggest that the most effective way of reaching poor children would be through a universal grant to all children. This would give the important signal that all children are important. The tax system could then be used to claw back from wealthier households, and wealthier parents and/or care-givers would simply not bother to apply for the Grant. There was some political opposition to a universal grant, and fiscal constraints then forced the administration of a means-test, designed to exclude about 50 per cent of children (Lund, 2008).

Even a sophisticated state would be hard-pressed to devise and administer a means-test that can finely discriminate income and asset levels in households clustered around the 50 per cent level, where the income distribution curve is very flat. Much administrative effort is now being spent on finding ways of keeping some children out, rather than bringing all in (Goldblatt, 2005). This goes against the rhetoric of inclusion that pervades all of the social policies.

Lessons and Future Prospects

What can be learned about social policy in this decade of rapid transition in South Africa? While the racial discrimination of the past is being addressed in many areas, little has yet been achieved in addressing poverty. It is possible, though, to reflect on the policy process and draw out the main lessons learned to date. South Africans have learned how important good censuses and national surveys are for planning, implementation and monitoring. These would be taken for granted in more developed countries, but are quite new in South Africa. A much clearer understanding is now possible of, for example, where the poor are, the economic position of women, the movement of children between households and the effects of spending on social assistance and nutrition and education status.

Those involved in policy-making underestimated three important things. The first concerns time. There was an underestimation of how long it takes to formulate policy, especially when there is a high commitment to public participation, and then to get from policy through legislation to implementation. The parliamentary, legislative and budgetary cycles may as well be set in set in stone, so rigidly are the calendar dates fixed. These procedures are important for orderly governance, but are difficult to reconcile with rapid service delivery, and promoting opportunities for participation in policy-making.

Second, there was an underestimation of the power of the old guard inside the various former administrations to undermine attempts at change. They were familiar with the rules of the bureaucracy, and many have played procedural games with the new politicians and administrators. The new governors by definition could not have had inside knowledge of how the institutions and procedures worked, because they were excluded altogether from governing. In addition, the governing institutions were deeply wired by apartheid characteristics of authoritarianism and lack of accountability to the public. The post-apartheid government took steps to change this mode of governance, but how effective and enduring this commitment will be is an open question.

Third, in health and in social services, there was an underestimation of the 'double hump budget effect', which happens when moving from a curative to a preventive model of provision. Preventive services will, in the longer term, reduce health costs, but until then, one needs to budget for the curative services as well. This must be especially the case in a society such as South Africa, which is highly politically and psychologically traumatized, has one of the world's highest crime rates, high levels of domestic violence and abuse, high incidence of traffic accidents and high rates of disease, which now includes HIV/AIDS. One cannot easily, or in the short term, reduce the demand for curative treatment, care and counselling.

South Africa has learned important lessons about public participation in the policy process. The period since 2000 has also seen widespread popular dissent against the slow pace of delivery in crucial areas such as land reform and housing, and against privatization of services such as water and electricity (Ballard, Habib and Valodia, 2006). There is a greater awareness that asking for participation under conditions of unequal power between stakeholders, for example, between a health specialist and a community health committee, or water engineers and a rural water committee, or the school principal and the new school parent bodies, can disempower, rather than empower, the beneficiaries of services. Participation in local level delivery, however, is critically important so that citizens can practise democracy. Many rural areas are still effectively under the control of the traditional (tribal) authorities (Ntsebeza, 2005), who can easily co-opt the control and benefits of services. Most of them are deeply patriarchal and authoritarian, and limit meaningful women's participation.

It was widely believed that the GEAR macro-economic policy of 1996 would act as a brake on the realization of constitutional commitments in the fields of health, social security, education and housing. In fact, social spending has held relatively steady, as shown, but there has been abject policy failure in the area of HIV/AIDS. There has been extensive infrastructural provision of basic needs of the sort indicated in the introduction to this chapter, yet still far too many under-serviced areas, unaffordable services and lack of consultation. The provision of thousands of housing subsidies for first-time buyers has to be offset against the thousands of farm workers who have been evicted from their homes. And there is general agreement that GEAR's biggest failure has been its failure to create employment on any meaningful scale.

South Africa's post-apartheid re-entry to the international stage has implications for social policy. In the economic realm, the casualization of labour that accompanies globalization, combined with the high formal unemployment rate, means that increasing numbers of people will not get access to formal social protection through their work. There will almost inevitably be a conflict of interests between the organized labour movement in the formal economy, and the new entrants – including migrant workers – to the informal economy, regarding issues of wages and benefits. In the political realm, there will be an issue about citizenship and access to welfare. South Africa is the economic giant of the Southern African Development Community (SADC), capturing three quarters of the total GDP of the nine member countries. Many SADC citizens want to work and trade in South Africa, whose long borders are difficult to patrol. Questions of citizenship, and of access to state social assistance, are forced sharply into focus. This is a very difficult moral issue of social policy, when there is a (dwindling) sense of obligation to compensate SADC countries for their support in the political struggle, but on the other, there is a limit to state resources. In a recent case brought by a Mocambican citizen, the Constitutional Court ruled that people with permanent resident status are entitled to state assistance such as disability grants.

South Africa's political settlement has enabled the building of a tradition of social policy research and writing, which simply could not exist under the oppressive apartheid regime. Academics were isolated from international debates, and there were no reliable surveys on which to base good planning. That has changed, as has the role of academics and other researchers whose priority now is rigorously to monitor and evaluate the impact of the policies in the transitional period, so that future reforms can be built on a reliable base of knowledge.

Key Features of Welfare Provision

Education

State Education and Training

- One national curriculum system of accreditation
- Nine years of compulsory free education; parent contributions allowed
- State nutrition programme delivered through primary schools
- Commitment to Adult Basic Education to address 30 per cent adult illiteracy rate, but few resources allocated
- Policy commitment to early childhood development (pre-school level), but few resources allocated until 2007

Private Primary and Secondary Education

- Fee-paying access to private primary and secondary education

Tertiary Education

- Joint state-subsidized and fee-paying technical, vocational and academic; some private universities

Housing

Private Ownership

- Cash price on open market
- Mortgage from bank or building society, repaid over 20–30 years
- Interest rates around 20 per cent
- In private sector, some housing perks through private firms for senior managers, and through link to provident funds for some union members
- In mining and other industries, extensive hostels for single men, now being converted to family living
- Decreasing numbers of on-farm housing for farm workers
- Decreasing numbers of live-in domestic workers

State Provision

- In civil service, extensive housing subsidies (hence public subsidization of private property ownership)
- R15,000 subsidy for first-time house buyers

Social Security

Social Insurance

- No national insurance
- Contributory insurance-based schemes for unemployment, maternity, incapacity or death caused through the workplace (workers' compensation), retirement provision (pension and provident funds), road accident victims
- Domestic workers recently included in unemployment insurance

Social Assistance

- Income support for elderly people: women at 60, men at 65, non-contributory, means-tested. Additional war-veterans supplement for those who fought in certain wars
- Income support for people with physical and mental disabilities: non-contributory, means-tested, from age 18
- Income support for poor children through child support grant
- Income support for foster parents
- No support for adoptive parents
- Income support to carers of children with severe disability

Social Relief

- Limited disaster relief for victims of floods and fires
- Limited temporary relief (food parcels) to desperately poor

Social Services

State Provision

- Limited state-run institutions for people with drug dependency, and for people with profound mental disability
- Limited direct social work services provided, especially in rural areas where no voluntary sector operates

Formal Voluntary Sector Provision

- State-subsidized
- Undertake statutory services for the state (children's court work, fostering process, probation services etc.)
- Most formal organizations linked to a national council for the field of service such as child and family welfare, aged

Informal Voluntary Provision

- Networks of community-based groups, recently eligible for state subsidy

Private Practice

- Very small body of privately practising social workers and clinical psychologists

Health

State Health

- Tax-based public health system
- Free primary health care through district health services
- Plans for Social Health Insurance, where those who can will pay for service at public hospitals

Private Health

- Parallel private health system; extensive insurance coverage of those in formal employment and with higher incomes
- New legislation re-regulates the fragmented medical aids
- User fees are paid to indigenous traditional healers
- Traditional healers now formally licensed under a health council

References

Akintola, O. (2004) *A Gendered Analysis of the Burden of Care on Family and Volunteer Caregivers in Uganda and South Africa*, Health Economics and HIV/AIDS Research Division, University of KwaZulu-Natal.

Ardington, E. and Lund, F. (1995) 'Pensions and Development: Social Security as Complementary to Programmes of Reconstruction and Development', *Development Southern Africa*, 12(4).

Ballard, R., Habib, A. and Valodia, I. (2006) 'Social Movements in South Africa: Promoting Crisis or Creating Stability?', in V. Padayachee (ed.), *The Development Decade? Economic and Social Change in South Africa, 1994–2004*, HSRC Press.

Budlender, D. (ed.) (1996) *The Women's Budget*, Institute for Democracy in South Africa.

Case, A. and Deaton, A. (1998) 'Large Cash Transfers to the Elderly in South Africa', *The Economic Journal*, 108, pp. 1330–61.

Chisholm, L. and Fuller, B. (1996) 'Remember People's Education? Shifting Alliances, State-Building and South Africa's Narrowing Policy Agenda', *Journal of Education Policy*, 11(6), pp. 693–716.

Department of Social Development (2002) *Transforming the Present, Protecting the Future: Consolidated Report of the Committee of Enquiry into a Comprehensive System of Social Security for South Africa*, Department for Social Development.

Goldblatt, B. (2005) 'Gender and Social Assistance in the First Decade of Democracy: A Case Study of South Africa's Child Support Grant', *Politikon*, 32(2), pp. 239–57.

Gough, I. and Wood, G. with Barrientos, A., Bevan, P., Davis, P. and Room, G. (2004) *Insecurity and Welfare Regimes in Asia, Africa and Latin America*, Cambridge University Press.

Government of South Africa (2001) *National Treasury Report 2001*, Government Printer.

Government of South Africa (2007) *National Treasury Report 2007*, Government Printer.

Hammett, D. (2007) 'Cuban Intervention in South African Health Care Service Provision', *Journal of Southern African Studies*, 33(1), pp. 63–81.

Harber, M. (1998) *Who Wwill Care for the Children? Social Policy Implications for the Care and Welfare of Children Affected by HIV/AIDS in KwaZulu-Natal*, School of Development Studies Research Report No. 17, University of Natal.

Hunter, N. (2005) *An Assessment of How Government's Care Policy is Working in Practice: Findings from KwaZulu-Natal*, School of Development Studies Working Paper No. 42, University of KwaZulu-Natal.

Klasen, S. and Woolard, I. (1999) 'Levels, Trends and Consistency of Employment and Unemployment Figures in South Africa', *Development Southern Africa*, 16(1), pp. 3–35.

Lund, F. (2002) 'Crowding in Care, Security and Micro-Enterprise Formation: Revisiting the Role of the State in Poverty Reduction, and in Development', *Journal of International Development*, 14(6), pp. 1–14.

Lund, F. (2003) 'State Social Benefits in South Africa', *International Social Security Review*, 46(1), pp. 5–25.

Lund, F. (2008) *Changing Social Policy: The Child Support Grant in South Africa*, HSRC Press.

May, J. (ed.) (2000) *Poverty and Inequality in South Africa: Meeting the Challenge*, David Philip/London: Zed.

May, J., Woolard, I. and Klasen, S. (2000) 'The Nature and Measurement of Poverty and Inequality', in J. May, *op. cit.*

Ntsebeza, L. (2005) 'Rural Governance and Citizenship in Post-1994 South Africa', in J. Daniel, R. Southall and J. Lutchman (eds), *State of the Nation: South Africa 2004–2005*, HSRC Press.

Patel, L. (1992) Restructuring Social Welfare: Options for South Africa, Ravan Press. Johannesburg.

Patel, L. (2005) *Social Welfare and Social Development in South Africa*, Oxford University Press.

Republic of South Africa (1996) *Report of the Lund Committee on Child and Family Support*, Government Printer

Reschovsky, A. (2006) 'Financing Schools in the New South Africa', *Comparative Education Review*, 50(1), pp. 21–45.

Standing, G. and Samson, M. (2003) *A Basic Income Grant for South Africa*, University of Cape Town Press.

Van der Berg, S. (1999) 'South African Social Security under Apartheid and Beyond', *Development Southern Africa*, 14(4), pp. 481–503.

Van der Berg, S. and Bredenkamp, C. (2002) 'Devising Social Security Interventions for Maximum Impact', *Social Dynamics*, 8(2), pp. 39–68.

Index

Note: The Index has been constructed to aid cross-referencing and comparison between individual country chapters. As each country chapter deals with most types of basic welfare provision (housing, income maintenance, etc.) and analyses provisions in terms of a common framework (central government, local government, market, state, private, public and voluntary/NGO provision), these themes are not indexed separately here. Individuals named in this index are those whose historical impact has been significant; author references to each chapter are provided at the end of each chapter. General entries such as gender, disability, migration draw together references to that theme whether or not specifically identified as such in the text. Note also that some of the categories present in the first edition are no longer present but that several new categories have been added.